WTO DISCIPLINES ON AGRICULTURAL SUPPORT

Farm support is contentious in international negotiations. This in-depth assessment of the legal compliance and economic evaluation issues raised by the WTO Agreement on Agriculture presents consistent support data and forward-looking projections for eight developed and developing countries (EU, US, Japan, Norway, Brazil, China, India, Philippines), using original estimates where official notifications are not available. Variations over time in notified support in some cases reflect real policy changes; others merely reflect shifts in how countries represent their measures. The stalled Doha negotiations presage significantly tighter constraints for developed countries that provide the highest support, but loopholes will persist. Developing countries face fewer constraints and their trade-distorting farm support can rise. Pressure points and key remaining issues if a Doha agreement is reached are evaluated. Vigilant monitoring for compliance of farm support with WTO commitments will be required to lessen its negative consequences whether or not the Doha Round is concluded.

DAVID ORDEN is Professor and Director of the Global Issues Initiative (GII) of the Institute for Society, Culture and Environment (ISCE) at Virginia Polytechnic Institute and State University. He is also Senior Research Fellow at the International Food Policy Research Institute (IFPRI), specializing in domestic farm policy and international trade.

DAVID BLANDFORD is Professor of Agricultural and Environmental Economics at Pennsylvania State University, where his research focuses on the effectiveness and efficiency of domestic and international policies for agriculture and natural resources.

TIM JOSLING is Senior Fellow at the Freeman Spogli Institute for International Studies at Stanford University. His research focuses on agricultural policy and food policy in industrialized nations, international trade in agricultural and food products, and the process of economic integration.

WTO DISCIPLINES ON AGRICULTURAL SUPPORT

Seeking a Fair Basis for Trade

Edited by

DAVID ORDEN

DAVID BLANDFORD

TIM JOSLING

CAMBRIDGE
UNIVERSITY PRESS

CAMBRIDGE UNIVERSITY PRESS
Cambridge, New York, Melbourne, Madrid, Cape Town,
Singapore, São Paulo, Delhi, Tokyo, Mexico City

Cambridge University Press
The Edinburgh Building, Cambridge CB2 8RU, UK

Published in the United States of America by Cambridge University Press, New York

www.cambridge.org
Information on this title: www.cambridge.org/9781107005440

First published 2011

Printed in the United Kingdom at the University Press, Cambridge

A catalogue record for this publication is available from the British Library

Library of Congress Cataloguing in Publication data
WTO disciplines on agricultural support : seeking a fair basis for trade / [edited by]
David Orden, David Blandford, Tim Josling.
p. cm
ISBN 978-1-107-00544-0 (hardback)
1. Tariff on farm produce. 2. World Trade Organization. 3. Competition, Unfair.
I. Orden, David. II. Blandford, David. III. Josling, Tim (Tim Edward), 1940–
IV. Title: World Trade Organization disciplines on agricultural support.
HF2651.F27A289 2011
382′.63–dc22
2010049733

ISBN 978-1-107-00544-0 Hardback

CONTENTS

FIGURES

TABLES

CONTRIBUTORS

DAVID BLANDFORD is Professor in the Department of Agricultural Economics and Rural Sociology and the School of International Affairs at the Pennsylvania State University. He is visiting professor at the University of Reading and served in 2010 as president of the UK Agricultural Economics Society. Prior to joining Penn State as a department head in 1998 he was as a member of the faculty at Cornell University and head of division at the OECD in Paris. At OECD he led the effort to develop the dynamic global agricultural model that continues to be used in its outlook work. He has authored or co-authored over 100 journal articles and book chapters. Among his books, he is co-editor (with Berkeley Hill) of *Policy Reform and Adjustment in the Agricultural Sectors of Developed Countries* (2006).

LARS BRINK is Expert Advisor at Agriculture and Agri-Food Canada. He has provided advice on domestic support issues to the Canadian government during the Uruguay Round and Doha Round negotiations, in WTO accession negotiations, and related to dispute cases. He contributes regularly to technical meetings on domestic support in Geneva and elsewhere and has advised China's trade officials on domestic support matters for the past decade. In 2008 he served as president of the Canadian Agricultural Economics Society.

FUZHI CHENG is Research Economist at Noble Group, a commodity trading firm specializing in agricultural, industrial and energy products. In this position he is responsible for quantitative analytics and proprietary trading algorisms to assist traders in strategic positioning and hedging. His current research focuses on fundamental analysis, derivative pricing, volatility modeling and portfolio optimization. He was formerly a post-doctoral fellow at Cornell University and is co-editor (with Per Pinstrup-Anderson) of *Case Studies in Food Policy for Developing Countries* (2009).

CAESAR CORORATON is Research Fellow at the Global Issues Initiative, Institute for Society, Culture, and Environment, Virginia Polytechnic Institute and State University. He has been a Research Fellow at the International Food Policy Research Institute (2005–08) and Senior Research Fellow at the Philippines Institute for Development Studies (1993–2005). His research focuses on poverty, trade, and agriculture. He is co-author (with Erwin Corong) of *Philippine Agricultural and Food Policies: Implications on Poverty and Income Distribution* (2009).

IVAR GAASLAND is a Senior Researcher at the Institute for Research in Economics and Business Administration (SNF), a research institute tied to the Norwegian School of Economics and Business Administration (NHH). His research focuses on modeling of agricultural policy, public goods in agriculture and trade policy.

ROBERTO GARCIA is Associate Professor in the Department of Economics and Resource Management at the Norwegian University of Life Sciences. His research focuses on international trade, particularly on agricultural policy and WTO commitments and compliance. He served as a trade advisor to ministries in the Government of Albania during its WTO accession, and continued as a consultant for the country's post-WTO accession compliance efforts and preparation for regional free trade negotiations as part of the EU integration process.

YOSHIHISA GODO is Professor of Economics at Meiji Gakuin University and a part-time lecturer at Waseda University. He is co-author (with Yujiro Hayami) of *Development Economics: From the Poverty to the Wealth of Nations* (2005). His 2006 book *Nihon no Shoku to Nou* (Food and Agriculture in Japan) received the Suntory Prize, one of the most prestigious academic book prizes in Japan. He has served on two advisory boards for the Japanese Prime Minister: the Evaluation Committee for Special Reform Zones (2003–04) and the Council for Regulatory Reform (2002–03).

MUNISAMY GOPINATH is Professor in the Department of Agricultural and Resource Economics and Director of the Graduate Program in Applied Economics at Oregon State University. His research focuses on technical change, economic growth and development, and international trade and investment. He served as an associate editor of the *American Journal of Agricultural Economics* (2004–07) and is co-editor (with Hanho Kim) of *Globalization and the Rural–Urban Divide* (2009).

TIM JOSLING is Senior Fellow at the Freeman Spogli Institute for International Studies and professor emeritus of the Food Research Institute at Stanford University. He is a past president of the UK Agricultural Economics Society, a Fellow of the US Agricultural and Applied Economics Association (AAEA), and a member of the International Food and Agricultural Trade Policy Council (IPC). In the 1970s he developed the concept of the producer subsidy equivalent (PSE) for the FAO, and this was adopted by the OECD as the primary indicator published annually since 1987 of the level of agricultural policy transfers to producers. Among numerous books he has co-authored (with Stefan Tangermann and T. K. Warley) *Agriculture in the GATT: Past, Present and Future* (1996) and (with John Barton, Judith Goldstein, and Richard H. Steinberg) *The Evolution of the Trade Regime: Politics, Law and Economics of the GATT and WTO* (2006).

ANDRÉ MELONI NASSAR is Director General of the Institute for International Trade Negotiations (ICONE) where he served as general manager from 2003 to 2007. From 1999 to 2002, he was a senior researcher at the Economic Research Foundation (FIPE) and associate faculty member at the Agribusiness Studies Program (PENSA), University of São Paulo. His areas of interest are international trade policy and modeling long-run scenarios of supply, demand and trade of agricultural, food and biofuel commodities. He has been the lead agricultural economist or coordinator of ICONE projects sponsored by the World Bank, the William and Flora Hewlett Foundation, the International Centre for Trade and Sustainable Development, and others.

DAVID ORDEN is Professor and Director of the Global Issues Initiative, Institute for Society, Culture and Environment, Virginia Polytechnic Institute and State University, and Senior Research Fellow at the International Food Policy Research Institute. He has been a visiting fellow at the University of New South Wales in Australia, chairman of the International Agricultural Trade Research Consortium, and visiting professor at Stanford University. His previous books include (with Robert Paarlberg and Terry Roe) *Policy Reform in American Agriculture: Analysis and Prognosis* (1999) and (with Tim Josling and Donna Roberts) *Food Regulation and Trade: Toward a Safe and Open Global System* (2004).

ALAN SWINBANK is Emeritus Professor of Agricultural Economics at the University of Reading, UK. His research focuses on the food, farm and bioenergy policies of the European Union and the process of trade liberalization in these products in the WTO. He is co-author (with Carsten Daugbjerg) of *Ideas, Institutions, and Trade: The WTO and the Curious Role of EU Farm Policy in Trade Liberalization* (2009).

DAISUKE TAKAHASHI received his Ph.D. in agricultural science with a major in agricultural economics from the University of Tokyo. In April 2010 he became a post-doctoral research fellow of the Japan Society for the Promotion of Science at the University of Tsukuba.

ERLING VÅRDAL is Professor of Economics at the University of Bergen. He has published within the fields of international macroeconomics and agricultural economics. In agricultural economics his research focuses on public goods in agriculture and trade policy.

PREFACE

Agricultural issues are particularly contentious in international trade negotiations. Many of the problems stem from the trade impacts of domestic support policies designed to maintain and stabilize farm incomes. When the World Trade Organization was launched in 1995, agricultural domestic support was brought under its disciplines. Certain trade-distorting support, evaluated in a specific manner, became subject to limits and all support measures to rules-based scrutiny. The economic objective underlying these legal disciplines was to reduce distortions in world agricultural markets. But the rules left countries with wide discretion over the forms and levels of support they provide to their farmers. Fifteen years later, subsequent negotiations in the Doha Round that have attempted to strengthen the initial rules and tighten the commitments have not resulted in an agreement.

This book examines in depth the many compliance and evaluation issues related to WTO disciplines on domestic support. Part one sets up the analysis. The key analytical questions that arise around disciplining domestic support are laid out in Chapter 1. The second chapter provides the necessary institutional background about the negotiation of the Agreement on Agriculture, its fundamental rules, the implementation experience through the WTO's Committee on Agriculture and dispute settlement cases, and the enhanced but complex proposals on domestic support that emerged in the Doha negotiations.

The second and third parts of the book (Chapters 3–10) present assessments of the domestic support notified to the WTO for compliance verification for eight developed and middle-income developing countries. The authors assess the political economy considerations that have driven domestic policy choices since the Agreement came into effect and estimate supplemental ("shadow") support notifications where countries have lagged in providing information. How each country has claimed to have met its WTO obligations given its policy decisions is examined, and evaluations made of the extent to which some of these claims can be questioned. The relationship between support as notified under the Agreement and an economic interpretation of the implications of that support is a focus of the analysis throughout the book, especially in the crucial area of market price support. Looking forward, projected support through the mid 2010s is evaluated against the existing disciplines and those emerging in the Doha Round. These eight chapters provide a comprehensive assessment for a diverse set of countries of the interface between domestic support policies and the disciplines agreed to in the WTO that has heretofore not been available.

The fourth part of the book is a final chapter that summarizes the country experiences and draws together important lessons about the usefulness of international disciplines on domestic support. The Agreement has proven porous but some convergence of policies among countries has occurred. We conclude that an agreement in line with the Doha draft modalities that emerged by the end of 2008 (and remain the focus of negotiations) would significantly reduce the future scope for trade-distorting domestic support by developed countries that have provided the highest levels of this support. These proposals would be less restrictive for the emerging-market developing countries. This could eventually imply a significantly different pattern in the incidence of global support for agriculture. Many other issues will also remain to be addressed even if a new WTO agreement on agriculture is concluded in the Doha Round. Without a new agreement, agricultural domestic support policies and their effects will certainly continue to be contentious issues in trade relations among countries.

This book originates from a study of domestic support policies and disciplines conducted under the auspices of the International Food Policy Research Institute (IFPRI), Washington, DC. The study was initiated in June 2007 when the Doha negotiators were struggling to find consensus on new rules with incomplete information accessible by governments or publicly available. David Blandford and Tim Josling had been working on an assessment of domestic support and its notification to the WTO for the European Union and the United States. The three editors joined together in September 2007 to develop this book covering eight countries in the context of global agriculture and support policy disciplines.

The study was part of a research and public policy project on Foundation Analysis for Agricultural Trade Reform within IFPRI's Markets, Trade and Institutions Division. Financial support to IFPRI for this project from the Global Development Program of the William and Flora Hewlett Foundation (grants 2007–9399 and 2008–1886) is gratefully acknowledged. Antoine Bouët and David Orden were the IFPRI project leaders and Ann Tutwiler was the project liaison for the Hewlett Foundation. Support of the Division Director, Maximo Torero, and from Klaus von Geber, director of IFPRI's Communication Division, is appreciated. Shirley Raymundo, Marcelle Thomas, Joy Fabela, Tigist Defabachew, and Mary-Jane Banks provided technical and administrative assistance in the book's preparation. We thank Will Martin at the World Bank for his support of the early analysis of the EU and the US by Blandford and Josling that is further developed in two chapters of this book.

We are indebted for reviews of our manuscript to IFPRI's Publication Review Committee, chaired during the study by Ramón Lopéz and Gershon Feder, and to Cambridge University Press. The reviews contributed substantially to the manuscript's development. We thank the anonymous readers in both cases for their suggestions and recommendations.

During the study opportunities arose for the authors to engage in a number of discussions related to the WTO negotiations. Several events were coordinated with the International Centre for Trade and Sustainable Development in Geneva. We thank Ricardo Meléndez-Ortiz, Christophe Bellmann, Jonathan Hepburn and Deborah Vorhies for their facilitation of these activities, and Joanna Hewitt (formerly with the Australian government) and Dimitris Diakosavvas (OECD Secretariat) for facilitating other engagements. Additional venues for presentations included the FAO, German Marshall Fund of the United States, International Food and Agricultural Trade Policy Council, IFPRI, OECD, World Bank, World Trade Institute (Bern), and WTO. At the WTO, we appreciate the participation in a session organized around the study at the 2009 Public Forum of David Walker, chairperson of the Special Session of the Committee on Agriculture, and Valeria Csukasi, chairperson of the Committee on Agriculture. Presentations during the study at professional annual meetings included the Chinese Economic Association in North America, International Agricultural Trade Research Consortium, UK Agricultural Economics Society, and US Agricultural and Applied Economics Association. We thank discussants and audience participants at these presentations and meetings, particularly Carol Goodloe and Anne Effland from the US Department of Agriculture, for many useful observations and comments, as well as those individuals acknowledged by the chapter authors for their contributions.

We are grateful to the authors who prepared the chapters in this volume for their insights, collaboration and cooperation. Completing each chapter, with its support estimates and policy projections, was a challenge the authors undertook with diligence and commitment in the shifting context as the study proceeded of ongoing Doha deliberations, unilateral changes in domestic support policies, and intermittent new notifications by countries to the WTO.

Finally, we particularly express our gratitude to Lars Brink. He provided an invaluable perspective and guidance for the entire book drawing on his extensive and ongoing experience addressing domestic support issues for the Canadian government since early in the Uruguay Round. To turn the phrase we use in the context of the notifications, Lars Brink should be recognized in a shadow role as a fourth editor of the book.

ACRONYMS

General

AMS	Aggregate Measurement of Support
ASCM	Agreement on Subsidies and Countervailing Measures
CTAMS	Current Total Aggregate Measurement of Support
DS: 1–9	domestic support tables
DSB	Dispute Settlement Body
EC	European Communities
EMS	Equivalent Measurement of Support
ERP	external reference price
EU	European Union
FAO	Food and Agriculture Organization of the United Nations
FBTAMS	Final Bound Total Aggregate Measurement of Support
G/AG/N/[country]/[number]	agricultural notifications to the WTO
GATT	General Agreement on Tariffs and Trade
GDP	Gross Domestic Product
IATRC	International Agricultural Trade Research Consortium
IFPRI	International Food Policy Research Institute
IPC	International Food and Agricultural Trade Policy Council
LDC	least-developed country
MPS	market price support
NFIDC	net food-importing developing country
NPR	nominal protection rate
OECD	Organization for Economic Co-operation and Development
OTDS	Overall Trade Distorting Support
PSE	Producer Support Estimate/Producer Subsidy Equivalent

RAM	recently acceded member
SMU	Support Measurement Unit
ST	supporting table
TAMS	Total Aggregate Measurement of Support
TDE	Trade Distortion Equivalent
TRQ	tariff-rate quota
UK	United Kingdom
US	United States
USDA	United States Department of Agriculture
VAT	value-added tax
VOP	value of production
WTO	World Trade Organization

European Union

CAP	Common Agricultural Policy
SAPS	Single Area Payment Scheme
SPS	Single Payment Scheme

United States

ARP	Acreage Reduction Program
ACRE	Average Crop Revenue Election
CBO	Congressional Budget Office
CCP	Countercyclical Payment
CRP	Conservation Reserve Program
FAIR Act	Federal Agriculture Improvement and Reform Act (1996)
FCE Act	Food, Conservation and Energy Act (2008)
FSRI Act	Farm Security and Rural Investment Act (2002)
MILC	Milk Income Loss Contract
MLA	Market Loss Assistance

Japan

ALIC	Agricultural and Livestock Industries Corporation
DPJ	Democratic Party of Japan
EAA	Exclusively Agricultural Area
ICP	Income Compensation Program
JA	Japan Agriculture
LCAPA	Law Concerning the Construction of Agricultural Promotion Areas
LDP	Liberal Democratic Party
MAFF	Ministry of Agriculture, Forestry and Fisheries

MOF	Ministry of Finance
RFISP	Rice Farming Income Stabilization Program

Norway

MAF	Ministry of Agriculture and Food
MGAL	Ministry of Government Administration and Labor
MLSA	Ministry of Labor and Social Affairs
NAA	Norwegian Agricultural Authority
NILF	Norwegian Agricultural Economics Institute
NOK	Norwegian krone
SN	Statistics Norway

Brazil

AGF	Federal Government Acquisitions
BACEN	Brazilian Central Bank
BNDES	National Development Bank
COA	Contract Options Acquisitions
CONAB	National Food Supply Company
EGF	Federal Government Loans
INCRA	National Institute for Colonization and Agrarian Reform
MAPA	Ministry of Agriculture and Livestock
MDA	Ministry of Agrarian Development
PAA	Program of Acquisition of Agricultural Products from Family Farming
PESA	Financial Assets Rehabilitation Program
PGPAF	Marketing Loan Program for Family Farmers
PRONAF	Family Farmers Special Program
SNCR	National System of Rural Credit

India

CACP	Commission on Agricultural Costs and Prices
CCS	Cash Compensation Scheme
FCI	Food Corporation of India
MSP	minimum support price

China

MOA	Ministry of Agriculture
MOF	Ministry of Finance

NBS	National Bureau of Statistics
O&M	operations and maintenance
STE	state trading enterprises

Philippines

AFMA	Agriculture and Fisheries Modernization Act
AFMP	Agriculture and Fisheries Modernization Program
DA	Department of Agriculture
GAA	General Appropriations Act
HRCP	Hybrid Rice Commercialization Program
NFA	National Food Authority
OSEC	Office of the Secretary
PhP	Philippine peso
TRP	Trade Reform Program

PART I

Overview of domestic support issues and WTO rules

1

Introduction

DAVID ORDEN, TIM JOSLING AND DAVID BLANDFORD

One of the more innovative achievements associated with the conclusion of the Uruguay Round of trade negotiations in 1994 was the introduction of a multilateral architecture of rules and commitments disciplining domestic support measures for agriculture. These rules are contained in the Agreement on Agriculture, one of a number of agreements attached to the Marrakesh Treaty that established the World Trade Organization (WTO). As stated in the preamble, to achieve the long-term objective of establishing "a fair and market-oriented agricultural trading system" the WTO members sought "to provide for substantial progressive reductions in agricultural support and protection sustained over an agreed period of time, resulting in correcting and preventing restrictions and distortions in world agricultural markets." The rules and commitments on domestic support are particularly important in this context because of the market-distorting effects of many of the policy measures countries have enacted. In addition, without constraints on domestic support it is hard to envision success in multilateral negotiations to reduce agricultural tariffs, as some countries provide support for their farmers primarily through domestic measures while others rely more heavily on border protection.

Further discussions were initiated in 2000 under a clause of the Agreement on Agriculture that committed the members to continued negotiations on lowering support and protection. When a full new round of trade negotiations – the Doha Round – was launched in 2001, the agricultural negotiations were incorporated into it. Three topics – market access, export competition and domestic support – formed the core of the negotiations on agriculture, as they had in the Uruguay Round. From the start, attention in the new round centered on whether tighter disciplines could be agreed on domestic support, how to achieve balance across the three focal areas (exchanging reductions in domestic support for increased market access through lower tariffs and the reduction or elimination of export subsidies) and what trade-offs were possible between agricultural and non-agricultural components.

As negotiations progressed significant changes occurred in world agricultural markets. International prices that had been depressed in the early years began to increase after 2005. This raised the possibility that a long-term structural shift was taking place toward a tighter balance between global agricultural supply and demand, driven in part by the emergence of new markets for farm-based biofuels. In 2008, this outcome looked increasingly plausible as commodity markets were rocked by sharp price increases, causing anxiety about the supply of food and its affordability for poor consumers in developing countries. Within months a global financial crisis had triggered a deep worldwide recession and commodity prices fell. Despite this, world agricultural prices remained significantly higher through 2010 than when the Doha negotiations began, inducing a positive supply response in global agricultural production and higher farm incomes.

The tightening of food supplies, and especially the market instability of 2008, led many countries to enact short-term measures to stabilize their domestic markets, despite these measures exacerbating the variability of world prices at high cost to others. Calls for new agricultural support initiatives to ensure food security also arose, particularly among developing countries, and there remains uncertainty about the balance between food availability and demand. Agricultural trade potentially plays a constructive role as a complement to domestic production in these circumstances. Trade can alleviate the worst of market volatility and contribute to short-term and long-term global food security. The risks inherent in unilateral responses by countries to price-raising developments in agricultural market were evident in 2008. The relevance of multilateral rules to guide the global agricultural trade system became apparent in an environment of high prices just as it was earlier in the decade when concern focused on the price-depressing effects of agricultural support policies.

Domestic support rules

The rules in the WTO Agreement on Agriculture (hereafter, often the Agreement) divide domestic support measures into four distinct categories. These broadly reflect their potential to distort trade, but also the need to accommodate the negotiating positions of influential countries in the Uruguay Round. The Agreement exempts three categories of measures from any expenditure commitments. First, some measures are agreed to have "no, or at most minimal, trade-distorting effects or effects on production" (WTO 1995). By leaving levels of support in this category (denoted the green box) unconstrained, the Agreement encourages the adoption of policies that fit the criteria for the category.

All other measures are considered to be trade distorting, at least to some extent. Nonetheless, a second category with no expenditure limit is comprised of payments made in conjunction with production-limiting programs, for which the argument was made that the supply constraining aspect limited their trade-distorting effect. Eligibility criteria for this category (the blue box) relate to the fixity of area, yields, livestock numbers, or the amount of production on which payments are made relative to a base level. The blue box emerged as a late compromise in the negotiations that left key support programs at that time in the European Union (EU) and the United States (US) exempt from caps or reduction commitments.

A third exemption, restricted to developing countries, is for investment support generally available to agriculture and for input subsidies generally available to low-income and resource-poor farmers. These subsidies are agreed to be an integral part of development programs. Support through trade-distorting measures of this type in developed countries is subject to constraint. The development program exemption provides a form of special and differential treatment for developing countries, which is one of the fundamental principles built into the WTO framework of rules.

The remaining domestic support measures fall into a less precisely defined residual category (often called the amber box) of interventions and subsidies on output or inputs that are the target of the disciplines. Support under these measures is counted through an Aggregate Measurement of Support (AMS) for each product (product-specific AMS) and a separate total for support that is not specific to particular products (non-product-specific AMS). Among the product-specific measures are production-related direct payments to producers that are not exempt under the green and blue boxes or development programs. Also included in the product-specific AMS is market price support (MPS), calculated "using the gap between a fixed external reference price and the applied administered price multiplied by the quantity of production eligible to receive the applied administered price" (WTO 1995).

The yearly sum of trade-distorting support, the Current Total Aggregate Measurement of Support (Current Total AMS or CTAMS), is subject to a ceiling specified in each country's schedule of commitments. After a phase-in period, this commitment became the Final Bound Total AMS (FBTAMS).[1] However, the Agreement provides for exemptions from the support that is counted in the CTAMS to assess compliance

[1] A country's schedule was established in the Uruguay Round or when the country acceded to the WTO. For ease of exposition, the phase-in Annual Bound Total AMS and FBTAMS commitments will be referred to interchangeably as a commitment, ceiling, limit,

with the FBTAMS limit. These exemptions are under product-specific and non-product-specific *de minimis* allowances. A product-specific AMS is excluded from the calculation of CTAMS if it is below a value corresponding to a specified percentage of the product's nominal value of production. Similarly, the non-product-specific AMS is excluded if it is less than a specified percentage of the total agricultural production value. Developing countries are allowed larger exemptions than developed countries under each of the *de minimis* provisions (up to a threshold of 10 percent of the value of production as opposed to 5 percent for developed countries).

The ceiling commitments for CTAMS were determined by levels of support provided in this category during a base period 1986–88, with a few exceptions for members acceding since the conclusion of the Uruguay Round. Countries that did not include a ceiling commitment on CTAMS in their schedules have an implied zero ceiling and are required under the rules of the Agreement to maintain AMS support within the *de minimis* allowances.

If the international rules on agricultural domestic support are to be effective, compliance must be monitored and enforced. Promulgated rules are subject to differences in interpretation. For these reasons, the Agreement established a Committee on Agriculture and mandated that, among other things, it should serve as a forum for reviewing the implementation of commitments based on notifications submitted by members. The Committee established the process and format for such notifications during its initial meetings in 1995. The WTO members agreed to identify their policy measures, indicate how they were to be classified within the categories in the Agreement, and report levels of MPS and budgetary expenditures or revenue forgone under these measures. The notifications are designed to provide transparency about the domestic support policies of each member. Alleged violations of the rules and commitments can be challenged under the WTO dispute settlement process.

Scope of the book

This book provides a detailed analysis of both compliance and evaluation issues relating to WTO disciplines on domestic support. The submitted

constraint; or cap. When context is clear, either may be called simply the Bound Total AMS. Further commitments that might be made in a Doha agreement will be referred to using similar terms.

and likely future notifications are assessed in depth for a selected group of eight countries. The authors describe the diverse policies that underlie the notifications, illuminate substantial differences in approaches to notifying policy measures and support levels, project support through the mid 2010s, and evaluate those projections with respect to existing and potential WTO commitments.

The analysis focuses on four developed countries (the EU, US, Japan and Norway) and four middle-income developing countries (Brazil, India, China and the Philippines).[2] Among the developed countries, the EU, US and Japan have accounted for nearly 90 percent of the total support (measured in US dollars) subject to ceiling commitments under WTO rules. The EU emerged as a net exporter in the 1980s under its agricultural programs but subsequently modified its policies to reduce price-support incentives to production. The US has traditionally been a low-cost agricultural exporter but increased its subsidies immediately prior to and following its farm program legislation in 2002. Japan is a key agricultural importer with some highly protected sectors, particularly rice. Norway provides an example of an inherently high-cost agricultural producer with high protection and support for domestic products that compete with imports. Japan and Norway are members of the G10 group of countries within the WTO that has sought to retain support and protection for agriculture.

The four developing countries are major agricultural producers and consumers. Brazil, India and China are leading members of the WTO's G20 group of developing countries that has sought tighter disciplines on agricultural support in developed countries. Brazil has successfully challenged agricultural measures of the EU (sugar) and US (cotton) through WTO dispute settlement. Scrutiny of the policies of these emerging-market developing countries, along with those of the developed countries, can facilitate dialogue on a new agriculture agreement and help to minimize future disputes. Brazil is export-dependent in beef, soybeans, cotton

[2] While the WTO refers to its members, within this book we will often refer to them as countries. There were 153 members of the WTO in 2009, one of which is the European Union (EU27 or EU for short), which until November 30, 2009 was known as the European Communities (EC) in WTO documents. The twenty-seven members of the EU are members of the WTO in their own right but in the case of agricultural domestic support the EU applies a single schedule of commitments in place of the schedules of its member states. We shall refer to the EU as a country in this context; when we refer to the EU with fewer than twenty-seven members this is made clear in the text. Switzerland and Liechtenstein apply one common schedule of commitments. Consequently there were 125 schedules of domestic support commitments in the WTO on December 31, 2009.

and sugar. China and India have the world's largest domestic markets for agricultural products. While their volume of trade has been relatively low compared to the size of domestic production, variations in their trade have significant international implications. The Philippines is a populous country for which support for agriculture, particularly rice production, is a key government policy. As a net food importer, the Philippines has played a leading role in the G33 group of countries that are concerned about their continued ability to protect domestic agriculture. Brazil and the Philippines are also members of the Cairns Group, which has argued for more market-oriented rules for agricultural trade.

The framework of WTO rules on domestic support is set out in Chapter 2. It traces the history of the multilateral negotiations on agriculture, provides a comprehensive description of existing rules and commitments on domestic support, describes the review of notifications by the Committee on Agriculture, and discusses those dispute settlement cases in which interpretations of the domestic support rules have been addressed. The new rules and commitments being negotiated in the Doha Round with their tighter and even more complex disciplines are detailed. A global overview of the magnitude of trade-distorting domestic support that developed and developing countries could provide under these rules compared to the continuation of the Agreement frames the country analyses in the chapters that follow. The Doha draft modalities of December 2008 (WTO 2008), though not agreed as final, are shown to reduce significantly the scope for domestic support by developed countries in the disciplined categories; less so for the developing countries.

The notifications of domestic support by the countries covered in depth are analyzed in the following eight chapters. Each chapter provides a concise review of past and anticipated future national policies and the political economy underlying these decisions, with a focus on the measures that governments include in their WTO domestic support notifications. Notifications made since 1995 are presented along with notification information estimated through 2008 for those years for which governments had not submitted notifications to the Committee on Agriculture by June 2010. These "shadow" notifications are based on procedures the authors developed to replicate as closely as possible the most currently available notifications at the time of their assessments by drawing on published data, unpublished documentation and field interviews. The shadow notifications include sufficient commodity and policy coverage to provide estimates of key support components. Shadow information had to be generated for one or more years in all cases because of lags in the notifications. India had only notified its domestic support for 1995–97 and China and the Philippines only through 2004 as late as mid 2010. Relatively long-term shadow notification exercises had to be undertaken in those cases, particularly for India.

In a final chapter we draw together the main conclusions reached from the analysis. We summarize the developments in the forms and levels of support revealed in the country chapters and discuss the changes in support in relation to WTO rules. We provide an assessment of the extent to which the disciplines included in the Agreement have constrained domestic support policies and the extent to which proposed commitments in the Doha Round would serve this function in the future. While it is extremely difficult to change the framework of WTO rules and commitments disciplining agricultural support we offer some suggestions on challenges that will remain to be faced even with successful completion of the Doha Round.

Key issues in the analysis

The analysis presented in the following chapters addresses seven important questions:

1. Do the notifications show that countries have complied with their commitments on domestic support under the Agreement?
2. Do the notifications provide accurate and meaningful measurements of the support provided to farmers by governments?
3. Do the notifications track accurately changes in the nature of agricultural domestic support policies?
4. Have the notifications contributed to greater international transparency on domestic agricultural policies and the support that these provide to producers?
5. Have the disciplines in the Agreement contributed to the reform of agricultural policies and the progressive reduction of trade distortions created by domestic support?
6. Have the disciplines in the Agreement contributed to policy convergence among developed and developing countries and between these groups of countries?
7. Would the proposed disciplines in the Doha negotiations provide stronger constraints on the provision of trade-distorting domestic support and more substantial incentives for policy reform?

Compliance with the Agreement

The notifications are intended to make available, in a standardized format, a systematic categorization of policy measures and to quantify the amount of support they provide. This is designed to create transparency for the purpose of verifying compliance with the commitments under the Agreement. Unfortunately, many countries have been lax in submitting domestic support notifications and delays have often been protracted. The largest agricultural producing and trading countries have sometimes been many years behind in submitting notifications, as shown for the eight countries in our analysis in Table 1.1. This has made it difficult for the Committee on Agriculture to carry out its mandate of providing a forum for reviewing the implementation of commitments.

Delays in notification also made it difficult to analyze the classification of measures by countries and their levels of support during the Doha negotiations. As late as mid 2007, six years into the negotiations, there had been no notifications relating to controversial US farm program legislation introduced in 2002, nor for the EU following policy changes in 2003. Facing possible legal challenge through WTO dispute settlement as to whether it had exceeded its commitment, the US notified its domestic support for 2002 through 2005 in October 2007. Further US notifications for 2006 and 2007, and EU notifications for 2004/05 through 2006/07, were circulated in February 2009 and January–February 2010. Once submitted, the delayed US and EU notifications sharpened the debate on whether support was being notified accurately and how Doha commitments, if applied in the past, would have related to support levels. Without the notifications, it was less clear how policies might be affected by a Doha agreement. Critical information that might have helped to advance the negotiations was missing at key points in the process.

In the country chapters the notifications and shadow notifications are used to examine compliance with domestic support commitments in the Agreement. We show that, in general, countries have stayed within their commitments. However, many issues of interpretation are identified concerning the ways in which policies have been reported by countries. There is evidence of strategic behavior. This is manifest in changes in the way that support relating to some policy measures has been notified or the shifting of measures across categories in order to remain within the commitments imposed by the Agreement without making real changes in the underlying types of measures or levels of support provided.

Table 1.1 *Submission dates of domestic support notifications for 1995–2008*

Year notified	European Union	United States	Japan	Norway	Brazil	India	China	Philippines
	Date of submission (month/day/year)							
1995	4/29/98	6/8/97	6/3/97	9/19/96	2/13/96	5/28/98	—	9/10/97
1996	3/10/99	6/4/98	2/9/99	9/16/97	2/20/98	6/7/02	7/19/01	8/20/98
1997	5/29/00	6/17/99	2/9/00	3/16/99	3/5/99	6/7/02	7/9/01	8/20/98
1998	3/4/01	6/22/01	2/23/01	2/25/00	12/15/00	—	7/9/01	1/12/00
1999	6/11/02	12/23/02	2/5/02	3/5/01	5/2/05	—	1/10/06	8/5/02
2000	3/15/04	3/11/04	5/12/04	2/27/02	5/2/05	—	1/10/06	8/5/02
2001	10/28/04	3/11/04	2/3/05	2/11/03	5/2/05	—	1/10/06	8/5/02
2002	12/4/06	10/4/07	2/3/05	2/15/08	5/2/05	—	3/9/10	11/11/08
2003	12/4/06	10/4/07	2/16/07	2/15/08	5/2/05	—	3/9/10	11/11/08
2004	2/16/09	10/4/07	8/31/07	2/15/08	4/12/07	—	3/9/10	11/11/08
2005	2/16/09	10/4/07	3/11/08	9/3/09	4/29/10	—	—	—
2006	1/6/10	1/13/09	6/25/08	9/3/09	4/29/10	—	—	—
2007	—	1/13/09	—	9/3/09	—	—	—	—
2008	—	—	—	—	—	—	—	—

Notes: General document symbol: G/AG/N/[country]/[number]. In the case of China, which entered the WTO in 2001, the working party document (WT/ACC/CHN/38/Rev.3) provides 1996–98 information. — indicates not notified as of June 2010.
Source: WTO notifications.

A question arises over what are the consequences of a country being in violation of its commitment? A member of the WTO has the legal obligation not to provide certain support, measured in a certain way, in excess of its FBTAMS level. In principle this obligation deters members from providing excessive trade-distorting support. As discussed by Brink in Chapter 2, the WTO rules for dispute settlement come into play when a legal decision is needed on whether the obligation has been violated. No dispute on this issue has yet been concluded so the possible implications of a FBTAMS violation remain uncertain. The infringement of the obligation not to exceed the FBTAMS commitment may constitute, in the WTO, a case of nullification and impairment of the benefits accruing to the complaining member under the Agreement. A common outcome of disputes is that the offending member is required to bring its measures into compliance with its obligation. What the complaining member can expect from a successful case on a violation of the domestic support commitment is the prospect that policy changes required on the part of the offending member will be such that its trade-distorting support is brought below its FBTAMS in future years. The adequacy of those actions could become the subject of further litigation under the dispute settlement rules, as an offending member may seek to change its measures as little as possible while still claiming to meet the requirements of the ruling.

Since the FBTAMS is a yearly commitment, a case of a violation would specifically refer to the year(s) in which the commitment was exceeded. Given the time needed from initiating a case to obtaining a ruling, possibly also involving litigation about implementation, the ruling may be rendered several years after the year of the infraction. This may enable the offending member to claim that it has changed its policies in the meantime such that, under otherwise identical circumstances, there would not have been a violation in the year(s) in question, or alternatively that there is no longer a violation. The new policies might still give rise to alleged violations. Since litigation is costly both for complaining and defending members, there is an incentive for an offending member to ensure that the actions it takes reduce the risk of a new dispute settlement case. However, the amounts of support provided by some members are so large that even marginal changes can dwarf the cost of defending their policies in a dispute, so the power of cost savings in dissuading an FBTAMS violation should not be overstated. The need for continued and timely vigilance on whether countries are meeting their commitments underscores the importance of members having access to up-to-date notifications or, in their absence, to shadow notifications of the kind prepared for this book.

Agricultural domestic support is also subject to discipline under the WTO Agreement on Subsidies and Countervailing Measures (ASCM). One of the functions of the ASCM is to discipline the use of subsidies by allowing a member to seek the withdrawal of another member's subsidy or removal of its adverse effects. The adverse effects include injury to the domestic industry of another member, nullification or impairment of the benefits accruing under an agreement, and serious prejudice to the interests of another member. The subsidies that cause the adverse effects can be those whose support must be counted in CTAMS. Consequently the use of such subsidies faces two kinds of constraints: the collective constraint in the form of the ceiling commitment for CTAMS support on which this book is focused; and those under the rules of ASCM (including possible legal challenge on grounds of adverse effects). This means that the support counted in CTAMS may be provided through measures that do not contravene any ASCM provision but the CTAMS itself may exceed the commitment level. The converse is also possible: a member may be in compliance with its commitment on CTAMS but support is provided through measures that have to be removed or changed because they contravene an ASCM provision.

Accurate and meaningful measurement

While the function of the Agreement is to impose legal requirements on WTO members, its fundamental purpose is to discipline policies that are most likely to lead to distortions in agricultural production and trade and to contribute to a reform process in which the use of trade-distorting policies is reduced. Consequently, it is important to examine the relationship between the ways that support is calculated and notified under the Agreement and an economic interpretation of the implications of that support. To some extent this issue relates to how countries have chosen to notify various policy measures – the category into which these measures have been placed and how the support they provide has been calculated. We examine how countries have notified their payments and transfers under various programs and the extent to which these correspond to an economic interpretation of price or revenue enhancement. One particularly crucial area in which there is a potential dichotomy between a legal and an economic interpretation is that of market price support. The issues involved are sufficiently important to merit an extended introduction.

Economists usually measure market price support provided by government policies as the difference between the domestic price of a product and its corresponding international price. When market price support is measured by this gap it reflects the net effects of domestic price support programs, of border measures – including tariffs, tariff-rate quotas (TRQs) that allow limited imports under lower tariff levels, and export taxes and subsidies – and of non-tariff (technical and other) measures that restrict imports. It would be redundant to add to this measurement a separate calculation of domestic market price support: the latter is subsumed in the former. Redundancy among measures is a reality often faced in the complex arena of farm policy. It reflects the intricate political economy of the determination of agricultural protection and support and the overlapping effects of the policies enacted. The distinctions forged in the Agreement between the three pillars of market access, export competition and domestic support may be necessary in classifying types of policy instruments for legal purposes but do not reflect their interdependence and interrelated effects on markets.

Import tariffs are the most convenient and widely used policy instrument for increasing domestic producer prices. Minimum or floor price guarantees to farmers are also widespread in agriculture. Maintaining an administered price above the world price level requires border protection. The lowering or elimination of an administered price in the absence of a change in border policies often has limited economic implications.

In some cases administered prices rather than border measures are the key policy instrument on which governments focus. In such cases, as evident in chapters that follow for US sugar, widely for the policies of Norway, or for rice in the Philippines, it is the administered price that determines how tariffs and TRQs are applied, rather than border measures determining the levels at which administered prices are set. Moreover, administered prices can be effective in providing price stability to producers in circumstances where tariffs cannot. Administered prices for crops are often aimed at insulating farmers from low market prices when harvests are bountiful. If there is a substantial increase in domestic supply, an importing country, for example, may find that without government intervention the market will only clear at a price below the world price plus tariff. The tariff will not insulate producers from a price decline in this situation, but an administered price, maintained through government purchase and storage of the crop (and possibly subsidized exports), can provide this support.

Measuring market price support as the gap between the price received by domestic producers and a corresponding international price (referred to in the book often as economic market price support) is the approach adopted by the Organisation for Economic Co-operation and Development (OECD) in the Producer Support Estimates (PSEs) prepared annually for its members and several emerging-market economies (OECD 2009). A similar approach was adopted in an ambitious project by the World Bank to assess levels and global trends in agricultural protection and support from the mid 1950s through 2006 (Anderson 2009). However, this is not the approach adopted in calculating the MPS under WTO rules. Some countries were unwilling in the Uruguay Round to bind themselves to domestic support commitments that were dependent on comparing prevailing domestic prices and world prices on an annual basis, since the latter, in particular, can vary due to factors outside policymakers' control. Consequently countries agreed to a less comprehensive measurement in terms of the gap between administered prices, over which they had control, and fixed reference prices, which would not vary with world market conditions or exchange rate fluctuations.

From an economic perspective the WTO's MPS measure suffers from four deficiencies: calculation of MPS only in cases of acknowledged announced applied administered prices under weak rules about what constitutes such a policy instrument; the arbitrary fixity of external reference prices at 1986–88 base-period levels; use of the administered price instead of the prevailing domestic market price to calculate the level of support per unit of output; and ambiguity about the eligible quantity of output from which the MPS is computed. There are only limited circumstances under which these deficiencies are inconsequential. Specifically, if world prices had proven relatively stable around the nominal levels of the 1986–88 base period and administered prices had remained close to prevailing prices in domestic markets, the MPS measured under the Agreement would have been a reasonable proxy for economic market price support, at least for products for which an administered price was acknowledged in notifications and total production was used as the eligible quantity. These conditions have rarely been met and the notified MPS, despite its name, has not been a good indicator of economic market price support.

Instead, as we demonstrate in the country chapters, the MPS in the WTO notifications often does not accurately reflect the effects of government policies on the price signals that determine market outcomes. This creates a significant problem with respect to the economic interpretation of WTO notifications of MPS and, hence, the product-specific AMS and the CTAMS. This limitation of the MPS was recognized during the negotiations, as discussed by Brink in the next chapter, but the empirical consequences of using the particular indicator adopted were unknown. Fourteen years of experience has accumulated from which to assess the magnitude and implications of the problem. As we show across all countries, the MPS component of the AMS calculated according to the Agreement does not provide a time series of the actual price support provided to farmers. The market price support component of the PSE as calculated by the OECD is a better indicator of this support than the WTO's MPS, but it is available for fewer countries and is not the measurement to which the WTO commitments apply. The limitations in interpreting the notified MPS and the implications this has for assessing whether constraints are imposed by the Agreement on trade-distorting domestic support are evaluated throughout the book.

Tracking changes in domestic policies

There have been a number of significant changes in domestic agricultural policies of the countries examined in this book since the creation of the WTO in 1995. It is therefore important to assess the extent to which the approach used in the notifications captures the timing and impact of those changes on the amount of support provided to farmers. In the EU and the US, but also in Brazil and China, as well as the other countries, some major changes in policies have been undertaken.

As a result of a series of policy changes the EU has shifted progressively from supporting the incomes of farmers through the prices they receive to providing direct payments that have been increasingly decoupled from decisions on current production. This process of change was initiated through the MacSharry reforms of 1992–94 and continued through the EU's Agenda 2000, its mid-term review of 2002 and its agricultural policy health check of 2008. In the US, farm support legislation in 1996, 2002 and 2008 eliminated deficiency payments and introduced direct payments largely decoupled from prices and production, but also created new price-linked (countercyclical) payments. The 2008 legislation expanded the menu of price-linked payments by creating a revenue stabilization option for farmers, the Average Crop Revenue Election (ACRE) program. In Brazil, debt rescheduling has emerged as a key support policy. In China, a regime of discrimination against farmers with pricing and tax policies has given way to positive net support, including new direct payments to grain farmers. Japan's new government proposed in 2009 a substantial expansion of direct payments to farmers along lines of those used by the EU and US. These are just some examples of significant changes in agricultural policies; many others have occurred in the countries analyzed.

It is often possible to make a direct link between policy change and subsequent support notifications. The EU provides the best example of notifications that track the gradual replacement of MPS by direct payments over an extended period of time. After the US introduced new farm assistance payments in 1999 in response to falling market prices, after Brazil enacted debt rescheduling in 1995 and 1999, and after China introduced national payments to grain producers in 2004, subsequent notifications reflected the changes in policy and indicate the amount of support provided. In short, the requirement to list and categorize measures has led countries to report new policies in their notifications. Although the categorization of policy measures and notified support levels can sometimes be questioned, shifts in policy measures are clearly visible and a basis is provided for assessing compliance with commitments. Each of the country chapters provides a detailed analysis of these changes and the extent to which they have been captured in the notifications.

Contribution to transparency

Though the Committee on Agriculture designed a uniform template for notifications of domestic support, in practice the approaches taken by countries reflect significant differences, as we demonstrate in our analysis. The categorization of policy measures and measurements of the nominal levels of support are left to each government, though these can be challenged by other countries. We analyze the implications of alternative approaches to categorizing or computing support in a number of cases. Important issues such as the choice of category under which payments are notified and implications of the way in which MPS is calculated are explored. Consideration is given to whether alternative classifications or calculation methods would have generated a notified CTAMS in excess of WTO commitments, effectively making this a binding constraint, and if so what might have been the policy responses.

Trade negotiations are about the future not the past and forward-looking assessments of domestic support notifications through the mid 2010s are presented for each country. Projected notifications are evaluated with respect to the requirements of the Agreement and to the new rules and commitments included in the December 2008 Doha draft modalities. The projections require assumptions about future production levels, world and domestic prices, and national support policies. The authors of the country chapters describe the basis for and uncertainties related to their assessments. Taking appropriate caveats into account, the analysis provides a basis for determining whether WTO domestic support commitments are likely to constrain future policy choices. This is particularly relevant for assessing the potential long-term effects of a new agreement. Yet, the WTO notifications are backward-looking, and thus by default do not provide the explicit, forward-oriented projection information on which to base such assessments.

Contribution to national policy reform

A fundamental question is whether WTO domestic support rules and commitments have created incentives to reduce distortions in production and trade. Whether or not a country is in compliance with WTO obligations is a legal question. However, the process of ensuring compliance has an underlying economic motivation. It is to further this economic objective that WTO rules on domestic support distinguish among categories of measures depending on perceptions of their relative trade-distorting effects, as agreed through a negotiated consensus. When the Agreement was enacted it was hoped that it would serve to guide countries towards the choice of less trade-distorting policies; at a minimum it would constrain the most trade-distorting support from exceeding firm commitments. However, the Agreement contains enough ambiguity and allows sufficient flexibility to raise questions about the extent to which it could act as an effective incentive for reform or a constraint on policy choice. As we demonstrate, the Agreement has provided considerable latitude for countries to adopt diverse support policies and to worry about the impact on various notified categories and their compliance with the WTO rules and commitments only at a later stage.

It is apparent, nonetheless, that consideration of WTO rules has entered increasingly into debates on domestic agricultural policy in many countries. Decision makers are aware of their countries' obligations. The need to comply with WTO commitments has become a factor in national policy deliberations. Although the view is frequently expressed that agricultural policy decisions are made on the basis of domestic criteria, the WTO regime is strong enough that countries have sought to avoid having flagrant violations of their WTO commitments arise through national legislation.

Contribution to international policy convergence

It is difficult to establish whether a clear causal relationship exists between the WTO disciplines on domestic support (and indeed the whole framework of disciplines on domestic agricultural and trade policies in the Agreement and other WTO agreements) and multilateral trends in agricultural policies. We assess the extent to which the WTO disciplines appear to have contributed to international policy convergence. We argue that although the support disciplines seem to have provided some incentives for traditional providers of high levels of agricultural support to reduce these, the picture is a mixed one. The discretion of countries within the rules – to adapt their notifications to existing disciplines without having to make substantive changes in policy – is an enduring weakness of the Agreement. Furthermore, the proposed disciplines in the Doha Round leave scope for significant increases in support by the emerging-market developing economies, creating the possibility for future conflict. The challenge remains to be faced whether a set of multilateral rules will eventually reflect a global consensus about a common end point to which agricultural policies should converge across countries.

Potential contribution of a Doha agreement

The final important question addressed in the book is this: would an agreement along lines of the 2008 Doha draft modalities provide a more effective stimulus for reform than the Agreement has in the past? The rules for domestic support have been a key part of the agricultural component of the Doha Round negotiations. A framework for new rules was agreed in 2004, but subsequent negotiations through 2008 did not produce agreement on the modalities for future commitments. Just before the negotiators failed to reach consensus at the end of 2008, an expanded set of draft modalities that could have provided a blueprint for agreement (WTO 2008) was set out by the chairman of the Special Session of the Committee on Agriculture (the negotiating forum). Domestic support was considered a relatively stable element on which the proposed text had converged, but even in this area several key issues remained unresolved.

Commitments on domestic support would be tightened and extended significantly under the December 2008 draft modalities, as described in Chapter 2 and the country analyses. Ceiling commitments on the CTAMS would be sharply reduced, *de minimis* allowances lowered for a number of countries, and a new limit introduced for total blue box payments. A ceiling would be placed on a new measurement called Overall Trade-Distorting Support (OTDS) comprising the sum of the CTAMS, *de minimis* AMS support and blue box payments. For most developed countries and some developing countries a Base OTDS would be reduced progressively to a Final Bound OTDS commitment. In addition, limits would be imposed on each product-specific AMS and on product-specific blue box payments. These new rules and commitments go much further than the Agreement in constraining the support provided through measures that do not satisfy green box criteria or the exemption under development programs. For the developing countries, some constraints such as the Base OTDS level and product-specific caps would be computed or applied under more lenient parameters than for developed countries.

One perspective on the degree to which the draft Doha disciplines would tighten constraints on domestic support comes from analyzing how past notifications would have related to the new rules and commitments. This question was most relevant during the early years of the negotiations (2001–05) when the broad outlines of possible new disciplines were being hammered out and world market prices were generally expected to remain relatively low. The conclusion for the developed countries is rather striking. For all the years from 1995/96 through 2008/09, the notified CTAMS and OTDS of the EU, as well as blue box payments until 2007/08, would have exceeded the ceiling commitments under a fully phased-in Doha agreement along the lines proposed in 2008. For the US, the notified CTAMS and OTDS would have exceeded final Doha commitments in eight of the fourteen years. For Norway, ceilings on the CTAMS, OTDS and the blue box would have been exceeded in all years. Only for Japan, which took advantage of the rules for calculating MPS to bring its notified support far below its commitment level in 1998, would notified domestic support have remained within the Final Bound Total AMS and Final Bound OTDS commitments under the 2008 Doha draft modalities.

Forward-looking analysis presents a less striking perspective on the extent to which a Doha agreement might constrain levels of domestic support, but it could still have a significant impact on policy deliberations. For the EU, the movement away from MPS that began in 1992 set the notified CTAMS on a downward trajectory that is projected (on the basis of recent policy developments) to continue through the next decade. A Doha agreement phased in by 2016 would reinforce downward pressure on EU support polices. Projections for the US indicate that under relatively strong world prices and the continuation of 2008 support measures, the Doha ceiling commitments on CTAMS and OTDS would not be binding. However, the room for providing additional AMS and blue box support would be relatively small and could dissipate entirely unless the US carefully monitored and adjusted its support policies, which in itself might induce a shift in policy design. For Norway, Doha commitments on domestic support would appear to necessitate policy changes to reduce its CTAMS and blue box payments beyond cuts necessitated by new commitments on market access and export subsidies. And the Doha commitments would preclude the expansion of Japan's support by the magnitude envisaged in government proposals in 2009.

The underlying aim of the Doha draft modalities is to further discipline and reduce trade-distorting support. Taking into account the results summarized here and developed in depth in the chapters that follow, the proposed Doha agreement achieves some progress on the path toward the substantial progressive reductions in agricultural support envisioned in the preamble of the 1994 Agreement on Agriculture. A Doha agreement that tightened and extended commitments in this manner would not end farm subsidies, but it would impose serious constraints on allowable future levels of domestic support from many measures, especially for developed countries that have provided high levels of support in the past.

Meanwhile, the criteria in the Agreement that define eligibility for various categories of measures, together with Bound Total AMS commitments and the *de minimis* allowances, constitute the disciplines to which agricultural domestic support is subject. Noncompliance with the eligibility criteria or support that exceeds the commitments are potentially subject to challenge. Yet, the Agreement has left room for substantial policy discretion. Many issues relating to interpretation and implementation of the Agreement arise in assessing whether or not commitments are being met. The difficulties faced in establishing and enforcing firm rules are apparent from the complexity of the Agreement, delays in notifications, the limited review function performed by the Committee on Agriculture, and arguments raised in several dispute settlement cases. Further progress toward progressive reductions in agricultural support and protection has been thwarted by the impasse through 2008 and beyond in finalizing new, and even more complex, Doha rules.

The overall aim of this book

The problems noted above with respect to timeliness and ambiguities in notifications of domestic support, along with the difficulties faced in reaching a new agreement, suggest that there is a need for external monitoring and evaluation to complement the WTO notification and review process. This is a role that we undertake in this book. External monitoring can provide additional insight into whether countries are complying with their WTO commitments. It can also permit an evaluation of the relationship between the information in the notifications and policy reforms that the Agreement was intended to encourage, as well as an assessment of the economic effects of measures included in the various WTO support categories. Though the issue of compliance is a legal matter, economic analysis sheds light on the underlying objective of conformity – that of the effectiveness of the Agreement in reducing trade distortions associated with agricultural domestic support policies – and whether improved disciplines are needed to achieve this aim. It is our hope that the analysis presented in this book will contribute to the important debate on future policies and to the ongoing challenge of making agricultural support more benign and more consistent with economic liberalism, environmental progress, and the achievement of other public-good policy objectives.

References

Anderson, K. (ed.) 2009. *Distortions to Agricultural Incentives: A Global Perspective 1955–2007.* London: Palgrave Macmillan, and Washington, DC: World Bank.

OECD. 2009. *Agricultural Policies in OECD Countries: Monitoring and Evaluation.* Paris.

WTO. 1995. *Results of the Uruguay Round of Multilateral Trade Negotiations – The Legal Texts.* Geneva.

2008. Revised draft modalities for agriculture. TN/AG/W/4/Rev.4, 6 December.

2

The WTO disciplines on domestic support

LARS BRINK

Proposals in international trade negotiations to constrain the domestic support that governments can provide to agriculture attract substantial interest for several reasons. Domestic support makes a country produce and trade differently from how it would if it fully pursued its comparative advantages. Domestic support can also shift a country's comparative advantage over time and thus change its trade profile. The interest in domestic support in the Doha negotiations was fuelled by the potential to strengthen the provisions of the WTO's Agreement on Agriculture, the awareness of interested parties of those provisions and of the size and nature of support they allow governments at home and abroad to provide, and by the consideration many governments give to enacting suitable farm policies that meet their international obligations. This chapter examines the framework of WTO domestic support disciplines in agriculture in several dimensions. Why are disciplines on domestic support part of the Agreement, which is, after all, an international trade agreement? What is the nature of the constraints and how are they being applied? In particular, how do the constraints limit diverse measures of policy support differently in developed and developing countries? What additional constraints may result from the Doha negotiations? And how might new multilateral domestic support constraints accommodate or influence the future development of policy support to agriculture on a global scale?

History of domestic support discipline in the WTO

In the Uruguay Round negotiations in the GATT (General Agreement on Tariffs and Trade) the sense of "domestic" support was in contrast to

Substantial portions of this chapter were part of the author's 2008 presidential address to the Canadian Agricultural Economics Society and are used with permission (Brink 2009). The views expressed are those of the author alone and not those of Agriculture and Agri-Food Canada. The helpful comments of Kym Anderson, May Chow, Dimitris Diakosavvas, Mike Gifford, Tim Josling, Wilfrid Legg, Will Martin, Alex McCalla, Chung Pa, James Rude, and Steve Verheul are gratefully acknowledged. The input by David Orden merits special grateful mention.

the traditional focus on measures applied at the border to impede import access or facilitate exports. Already thirty years earlier the Haberler Report had outlined three elements of what it called agricultural protection (GATT 1958).[1] Measures that directly discourage imports and measures that directly encourage exports were two of those elements. Measures that "directly encourage home production" were the third element. They maintain "the net reward to the farmer above the level which would correspond to the price at which he can sell his product." This distinction between two categories of border measures and a third category of measures not operating at the border was carried into the architecture of the 1994 Agreement in its three pillars of market access, export competition and domestic support.

The Haberler Report also categorized agricultural protection schemes into two groups based on certain of their other characteristics. One group comprises measures that raise the domestic price received by producers and paid by consumers above the world market price. This, the Report clarified, requires also the use of some form of border measure (import protection or export subsidy) in order to insulate the domestic market from the world market. The other group comprises schemes that allow consumers to pay world market prices but raise producers' revenue "by the payment of some form of subsidy." The Agreement would come to distinguish between two groups of domestic support measures along similar lines, viz., market price support (MPS) and non-exempt direct payments.

By the time the Uruguay Round started in 1986, it had become possible after many years of work to account in one indicator for the support provided through a range of measures. This indicator would include support provided through border measures on imports and exports and support provided through domestic measures, whether by payments to producers or by the maintenance of a gap between the domestic price and the border price. Josling's work on such an indicator was pioneering (FAO 1973, 1975), followed by work at the OECD (1987) and the USDA (1987). Although different in some respects, all three indicators bore the name Producer Subsidy Equivalent (PSE) and were conceptually close by accounting for support provided through a wide range of policy measures operating both domestically and at the border.

[1] Professor Haberler was the chairman of a small panel of experts set up by the contracting parties of the GATT to examine, *inter alia*, international trade trends and their implications, including a "widespread resort to agricultural protection."

Based on the PSE and the related development of relevant data, the United States proposed as early as 1987 that aggregate levels of trade-distorting support be brought to zero over ten years (GATT 1987).[2] The measurement of aggregate support would include both domestic and border policies "that directly or indirectly subsidize agriculture." Market price support would be part of the measurement, whether provided through price policies, variable levies, tariffs, export subsidies, export credits, government support of marketing boards, or other mechanisms. Income support and other support would be part of the measurement whether provided as, *inter alia*, deficiency payments, stabilization payments, acreage payments, subsidized crop insurance, fuel subsidies, or other payments to producers. Some policies (certain payments and aid programs) would be excluded on grounds of being production and trade neutral or having only inconsequentially small effects.

Other methods to aggregate support for a product across many policies included the Support Measurement Unit (SMU) and the Trade Distortion Equivalent (TDE). The SMU suggested by the European Communities (EC) would be based on the PSE but adjusted in three significant ways: to include only policies with a significant incidence on trade, mainly market price support and selected direct payments; to recognize the effect of production quotas explicitly, beyond using only the constrained production volume to measure support; and to use a fixed external reference price for the price gap in order to exclude the effects of changes in world market prices and currency values (GATT 1988b). The TDE suggested by Canada would be based on the PSE but modified to exclude non-distorting policies and to adjust the measured support downwards for less distorting policies (selected payments and MPS associated with certain types of production quotas) (GATT 1988a). Canada explained that the TDE derived from the modified PSE of Tangermann, Josling, and Pearson (1987). The EC, the Canadian and the earlier US proposal all accounted for a smaller policy set than did the OECD PSE. The exclusions tended to be based on the extent to which policies were considered not to distort production and trade. These exclusions foreshadowed what was later called the green box exclusions and even *de minimis*.

[2] The United States referred to the work of the GATT's Committee II, culminating in 1962, which "established the links between national farm programmes and the conditions of international agricultural trade" (Josling, Tangermann, and Warley 1996). The United States also referred to FAO (1985) and to OECD (1987), significantly entitled *National Policies and Agricultural Trade*, which had appeared less than two months before the US proposal.

The 1994 Agreement required separate ceiling commitments on market access, export subsidization and domestic support.[3] The commitment in domestic support was based on what was by then called the Aggregate Measurement of Support (AMS), which continued to include both price support and payment support but no longer explicitly accounted for support provided through measures operating at the border, such as tariffs or export subsidies. The scope of the policy aggregation in the measured aggregate support had thus been reduced to aggregating across many kinds of domestic policies but not border policies. The nature of AMS had shifted from what the United States had proposed in 1987, but the fact that commitments would apply to certain kinds of distorting domestic support started to address the need to account for policies not operating at the border, which the Haberler Report had identified in 1958.

Despite their shared ancestry there are many differences between the Agreement's AMS and the OECD PSE (Diakosavvas 2002).[4] The most important one for economic analysis is that the MPS element of an AMS is calculated from the price gap between an administered domestic price and a fixed external reference price based on the years 1986–88. Although the 1987 US proposal did not say so, its kinship with the PSE implied a reference price that would vary from year to year. However, the EC insisted on fixing the external reference price in order for the reduction to be a predetermined amount, which ignores changes in currency values and world market prices. In contrast, the price gap that matters for economic analysis in a given year is the gap between the domestic price and a reference price representing the opportunity cost, i.e., the actual world market price and the currency value of the year to which the analysis pertains.

The AMS and its use present particular challenges for economic analysis, as the country studies demonstrate in the chapters to follow. This stems partly from the terminology used in the Agreement and perhaps also partly from analysts not always being familiar with the nature of the

[3] A commitment is a legally binding undertaking under the agreements of the WTO, such as the Agreement on Agriculture. The Chairman's text of a draft agreement in July 1990 had similarly identified separate commitments in "internal support", "border protection", and "export competition" (GATT 1990). However, for internal support commitments it envisaged an AMS including "any measure which acts to maintain producer prices at levels above those prevailing in international trade." Although this seemed to include also border measures, the eventual Agreement applied the AMS only to domestic measures.

[4] The OECD has been monitoring the agricultural policies of its membership since 1987 and has been reporting annually the Producer Subsidy Equivalent (PSE), re-labeled as the Producer Support Estimate in 1998 (OECD 2009).

Agreement, its rules and associated scheduled commitments. An AMS is literally a measurement of what the Agreement calls support and not a measurement of distortions. Moreover, this support is measured in ways that deviate not only from how support is measured in the PSE but also from its usual representation in economic analysis. A major reason is that a member's AMSs are used as input in determining whether it has satisfied its legal ceiling commitment on certain support in favor of producers. The legal nature of both the agreed-upon domestic support commitment itself and the Agreement's rules about how to calculate various amounts of support effectively override the use of measurement methods that are more directly based on economics and more amenable for use in economic analysis.

The discipline under the Agreement on Agriculture

Key distinctions in constraining domestic support

The rules and implications of the domestic support provisions of the Agreement have proven to be easily misunderstood. Some misunderstandings seem rooted in overlooking the significance of a few key distinctions in these complex provisions. They include distinctions between measures and support, among measures that are classified in different categories, between applied support and a commitment on support, and between applied support that counts towards the commitment and applied support that does not (Brink 2007). Figure 2.1 shows the important distinctions and interactions of the domestic support provisions in the Agreement. These and other provisions of the Agreement related to domestic support are replicated as Appendix A at the end of the book.

Measures and support are two distinct notions in the Agreement. The domestic support commitment of the Agreement applies under Article 6 to all "domestic support measures in favour of agricultural producers" with some exceptions.[5] A ceiling commitment applies to the yearly sum of some of the amounts of support that certain measures provide. Separating exempt from non-exempt measures is behind the popularly known set of green, blue and amber boxes. Although the Agreement does not identify

[5] Unless otherwise indicated, references to articles and annexes refer to the Agreement (see Appendix A).

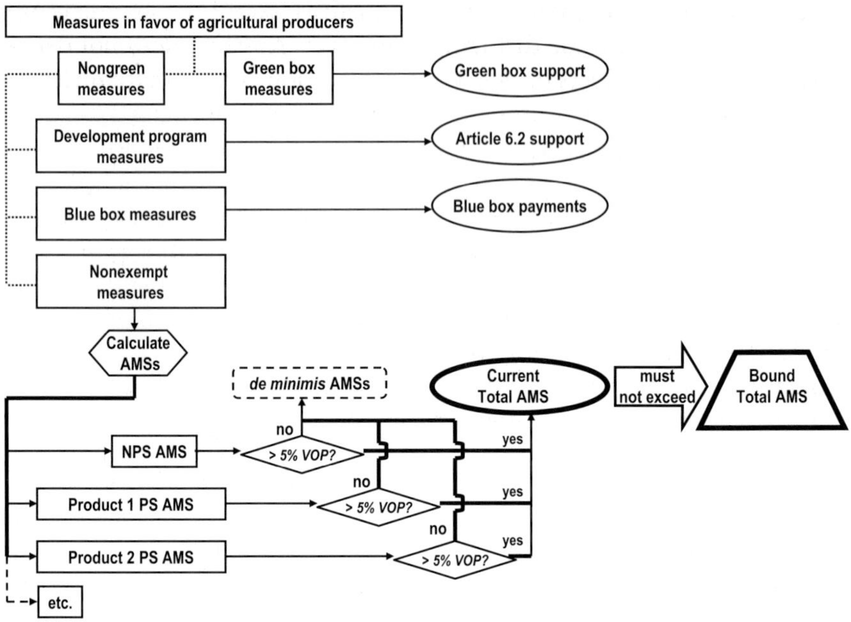

Figure 2.1 Domestic support categories and constraints in the 1994 Agreement on Agriculture
Source: Author's interpretation of the Agreement. The *de minimis* percentages are those of developed countries. AMSs are Aggregate Measurements of Support; NPS is non-product-specific; PS is product-specific; VOP is value of production.

any boxes or colors, it is universally understood that Annex 2 defines the green box and Article 6.5 defines the blue box. The residual subset of measures is less well defined.

Annex 2 requires green box measures to meet "the fundamental requirement that they have no, or at most minimal, trade-distorting effects or effects on production" in order to be exempt from the commitment. Annex 2 also states that the measures shall conform to two basic criteria: the support shall be "provided through a publicly-funded government programme" (which precludes transfers from consumers) and the support "shall not have the effect of providing price support to producers." The text then articulates for twelve types of measures – including nine that involve "direct payments to producers" – the policy-specific criteria and conditions that must be met, together with the basic criteria, for a certain measure to qualify for Annex 2 exemption from the domestic support commitment.

The common shorthand for the measures exempted as green box is that they are not trade distorting. However, Annex 2 does not define "trade-distorting effects or effects on production" nor is there jurisprudence within the WTO on its legal meaning. The policy-specific criteria in Annex 2 leave open the possibility that among the measures meeting these criteria there are some that could have more than a minimal effect on production – in some cases directly and in others by raising agricultural productivity over time. Support through such measures would affect the cost structure of agricultural production, the competitive advantage among countries, and the levels of agricultural output – and thus affect trade. Nonetheless, support through measures that meet the basic and policy-specific criteria of Annex 2 is often said to be non-distorting or only minimally distorting support.

Two kinds of measures are exempt from commitment if they meet certain other criteria or conditions than those of Annex 2. First, trade-distorting measures that meet the criteria in Article 6.5 (blue box payments) are excluded from the commitment. This applies to direct payments under production-limiting programs, and the criteria specified in the Agreement relate to the fixity of area, yields, and livestock heads, and the level of production on which payments are made relative to a base level.

Second, developing countries, but not developed countries, can exempt certain trade-distorting measures if the measures meet the criteria of Article 6.2. No color or box is attached to these measures, but they are often seen as part of a development box relating to special and differential treatment for developing countries.[6] They include investment subsidies that are generally available to agriculture and input subsidies that are generally available to low-income or resource-poor producers, as well as support to encourage diversification from illicit narcotic crops. Developing countries can therefore exempt from commitment certain measures – subsidies on variable inputs – that economic analysis has found to distort production and trade more than market price support, output subsidies, or area payments (OECD 2008).

The Agreement thus identifies three distinct kinds of domestic support measures – green box measures, Article 6.2 measures, and blue box measures – and a non-distinct or residual category of all other measures. The upper left-hand side of Figure 2.1 illustrates this. A measure qualifies for

[6] The Agreement includes a separate Article 15 on the special and differential treatment for developing countries applying to the provisions of the Agreement and to their commitments.

inclusion in a distinct category by meeting that category's criteria. The so-called amber box has no such distinguishing criteria: it consists of the measures that do not qualify for any of the distinct categories.

Another important distinction in the Agreement is between the ceiling commitment on distorting support and the measured applied support that counts towards the ceiling. This distinction has proven particularly difficult to convey in some of the public debate about support levels. A bound tariff and the applied tariff in market access relate to each other in a similar way as the bound ceiling commitment and the measured support in domestic support. However, the measured support that counts towards the commitment is more complicated to express than an applied tariff.

Each member's Schedule of Concessions and Commitments shows the level of the ceiling commitment, called Final Bound Total AMS (FBTAMS).[7] In many cases this level was reached through reductions over several years and each earlier year's bound level also appears in the Schedule without being called final. The FBTAMS commitment consists of a single nominal amount for each year. The year's applied support, measured in certain ways, must not exceed this amount.

The measurement of applied support relies on a number of AMSs. Each AMS is the annual support provided in favor of producers, other than support provided through green box measures (technically the Agreement seems to regard support under Article 6.2 measures and blue box measures as AMS support, although this does not correspond to practice). Separate product-specific AMSs contain the support provided for each product, and a single AMS captures the non-product-specific support provided in favor of agricultural producers in general. The applied support in the AMSs is summed in order to form the year's Current Total AMS (CTAMS). This highlights a crucial distinction: "Aggregate" refers to aggregating support across various policies, such as direct payments, input subsidies, and market price support, and "Total" refers to summing AMSs into a single CTAMS.[8]

[7] The Agreement refers to this as the "Final Bound Commitment Level" (Article 1, see Appendix A). In the section of members' schedules called "Domestic Support: Total AMS Commitments", a column heading refers to "Annual and Final Bound Commitment Levels", where the final entry thus is the Final Bound Total AMS (or FBTAMS) resulting from Uruguay Round implementation or WTO accession. This term is used in the Doha negotiations.

[8] The Agreement defines "Total Aggregate Measurement of Support" and "Total AMS" as a sum of aggregate measurements of support and equivalent measurements of support (Article 1, see Appendix A). It identifies several uses of the term "Total AMS": (a) "Base Total AMS", the support provided in the Uruguay Round base period, (b) "Annual and

CTAMS exempts some AMSs because of the *de minimis* rules: if an AMS is small enough, it need not be included in the calculated sum. To be small enough it can be no more than 5 percent of the product's nominal value of production (VOP) or, for the non-product-specific AMS, the nominal value of total agricultural production. Developing countries use 10 percent (8.5 percent for China). The *de minimis* rules apply to the whole AMS, i.e., an aggregation of support across those measures in effect. The rules do not apply to individual subsidies or support on a measure by measure basis – there is no classification of policies into *de minimis* measures and non-*de minimis* measures.

A *de minimis* allowance can be defined as the amount within which an AMS is excludable from CTAMS. That same amount can also be seen as a *de minimis* threshold, where an AMS switches from *de minimis* status into having to be included in CTAMS. The *de minimis* threshold is different from a commitment. An AMS can increase from zero without any consequence until it reaches the threshold level. When it exceeds that level, the consequence is immediate: the whole AMS (not just the part that exceeds the threshold) is included in CTAMS. There is no obligation to keep an AMS below the threshold if a country has a FBTAMS in its schedule of commitments, in contrast to the legal obligation that CTAMS must not exceed the FBTAMS. Moreover, the *de minimis* threshold is variable because it is a fixed percentage of the nominal VOP, which differs from year to year. If the VOP declines, so does the *de minimis* threshold. If the VOP grows over time, whether through output growth, price increases, inflation or currency depreciation, the *de minimis* threshold also grows. This flexibility is in contrast to the fixity of the nominal value of the FBTAMS commitment.

Many members did not schedule a FBTAMS commitment. Since CTAMS in such cases is constrained to be zero (Article 7), there is no threshold effect: each AMS must simply be kept below the *de minimis* threshold. The absence of a commitment therefore does not preclude

Final Bound Commitment Levels" in the Total AMS section of schedules, i.e., the maximum support permitted to be provided during and after the Uruguay Round implementation period (support limits), and (c) "Current Total AMS", i.e., the level of support actually provided during and after the Uruguay Round implementation period, calculated in a particular way (applied support). To avoid confusion between these uses or with other meanings of "total" we minimize use of the phrase "Total AMS" throughout the book, instead using more explicit expressions to distinguish among FBTAMS (a limit), CTAMS (a measurement of applied support) and other support totals to which we refer at various points.

the provision of support through measures that must be included in an AMS but constrains it to no more than the *de minimis* amount.

An Annex 3 of the Agreement helps to understand what kinds of measures need to be accounted for in an AMS, but Annex 3 is not exhaustive nor is it a definition of the amber box. Annex 3 stipulates that a monetary value of product-specific AMS is to be calculated for each basic agricultural product receiving market price support, non-exempt direct payments, or any other subsidy not exempted from the commitment. Non-product-specific support is to be summed into one AMS in monetary value. Annex 3 gives some basic rules for how to calculate an AMS. "Subsidies" in AMS include budgetary outlays and revenue forgone by governments or their agents. Support at both national and sub-national levels is included in AMS, and specific agricultural levies or fees paid by producers are deducted. Non-exempt direct payments based on factors other than price are measured using budgetary outlays. The measurement of support from other non-exempt measures, including input subsidies, is by government budgetary outlays or by the gap between the price of the subsidized good or service and the market price, multiplied by the quantity of the good or service. The AMS is calculated as close as practicable to the point of first sale of the basic agricultural product. Measures directed at processors are included to the extent that such measures benefit the producers of the basic agricultural product.

Support and subsidies are often interchangeable terms. However, a subsidy has a connotation of a budgetary payment or revenue forgone by government, while support often has a broader meaning. The rules for calculating AMS in Annex 3 require the inclusion of MPS based on a price gap, not on budgetary payments. It is calculated using the gap between a fixed external reference price (based on the years 1986–88) and the applied administered price in a given year, multiplied by the quantity of production eligible to receive the administered price. The term "applied administered price" is not defined in the Agreement. However, including MPS as defined in the AMS is not merely a quibble about words: it demarcates the outer boundaries of the set of support measures that are subject to the Agreement's domestic support discipline. It is also consistent with how some other WTO agreements treat price support: both the GATT and the Agreement on Subsidies and Countervailing Measures (ASCM) make a point of including price support in what they mean by a subsidy (WTO 1995a).

Domestic support notifications and the Committee on Agriculture

The Agreement established a Committee on Agriculture. It is mandated to review the implementation of members' commitments. The review process must be based on the notifications submitted by members and on any requested documentation prepared by the WTO Secretariat to facilitate the process and it provides an opportunity for members to "raise any matter relevant to the implementation" of the commitments. The Agreement is silent on the timing of notification submissions except to say that "any new domestic support measure, or modification of an existing measure, for which exemption from reduction is claimed shall be notified promptly."

The newly-formed Committee on Agriculture adopted notification requirements and formats at its second meeting in 1995 (WTO 1995b). The committee document identifies a need for most members (see below for exceptions) to notify applied domestic support yearly, in addition to the prompt notification of new or modified measures. The yearly notification includes a summary table (called Table DS:1) and tables with supporting material (supporting tables or ST) in a format and numbering system that is common to all members (see Table 2.1). The notification Table DS:1 is a concise statement of the year's CTAMS and the FBTAMS commitment level. The supporting tables (ST DS:1 to 9) give information on the amount of support under each measure, along with calculation methods or data sources. ST DS:1 through ST DS:3 report such information for measures claimed to be exempt from the reduction commitment under Annex 2, Article 6.2 and Article 6.5, respectively. The Committee document lists thirteen categories of green box measures in ST DS:1, adding "other" to the twelve identified in Annex 2.

Calculation of the CTAMS is reported in ST DS:4, which lists and sums the AMSs, including the non-product-specific AMS. The claim for *de minimis* exclusions from the summation into CTAMS is usually made in ST DS:4. Although the substantiation of such a claim requires data on VOP, the notification format does not explicitly require the submission of VOP data. The AMSs listed in ST DS:4 are calculated in ST DS:7 (product-specific AMSs), ST DS:8 (equivalent measurements of support), and ST DS:9 (non-product-specific AMS).[9] ST DS:7 itself draws on ST DS:5 (MPS) and ST DS:6 (certain payments). The required format has column headings for the

[9] The Agreement allows for the use of Equivalent Measurements of Support (EMS) in situations where calculating support with the AMS methodology is impracticable. Annex 4

Table 2.1 *Structure of domestic support notifications*

Table heading	Contents
Table DS:1	Current Total AMS and Final Bound Total AMS Commitment
	Measures exempt from the reduction commitment
Supporting Table DS:1	Green box (Annex 2)
Supporting Table DS:2	Development programs (Article 6.2)
Supporting Table DS:3	Direct payments under production-limiting programs (Article 6.5)
	Current Total AMS
Supporting Table DS:4	Calculation of Current Total AMS
Supporting Table DS:5	Product-specific AMS: Market Price Support
Supporting Table DS:6	Product-specific AMS: Non-exempt direct payments
Supporting Table DS:7	Product-specific AMS: Other product-specific support and total product-specific AMS
Supporting Table DS:8	Product-specific Equivalent Measurement of Support (EMS)
Supporting Table DS:9	Non-product-specific AMS
Table DS:2	New or modified domestic support measures exempt from reduction

Source: WTO (1995b).

reporting period (year), descriptions of the measure, the amount of support, and the levels of price and quantity for measurements based on price gaps.

The Committee on Agriculture document also specifies the intended frequency and timing of notifications, although these guidelines are not legally binding on the member countries. Members with bound commitment levels in domestic support should submit notifications "no later than ninety days following the end of the calendar (or marketing,

specifies the rules for the EMS calculation (see Appendix A). The EU has been the primary member to notify EMS support as part of its CTAMS.

fiscal, etc.) year in question."[10] Members without a FBTAMS commitment should submit "an annual notification", although the Committee can set aside this requirement other than for ST DS:1, 2 and 3. Still more lenient rules apply to least-developed countries (LDCs), which may submit these three supporting tables only once every two years. Further, regarding the new or modified support measures claimed to be exempt under Annex 2, Article 6.2 or Article 6.5 and which the Agreement require to be notified promptly, the Committee specified that they be notified "as far as practicable before such measures are adopted and in any event within thirty days of adoption."

The Committee on Agriculture's notification requirements and formats, including the frequency and timing of notifications, were intended to provide the basis for the Committee's review of members' implementation of commitments, as required by the Agreement. The Committee usually meets four times per year but regular meetings were less frequent for a few years after the launch of the Doha negotiations in 2001.[11] Between 1995 and 2008 the Committee reviewed about 587 original domestic support notifications and more than 100 revisions, corrections, etc. The number would have been larger if more members had adhered to the Committee's notification requirements. This is a cause of concern among members because it makes it impossible for the Committee to carry out its mandate of reviewing members' implementation of commitments. It also complicates or makes impossible the analysis of members' approach to supporting their producers, whether such analysis is desired in the context of the Doha negotiations or in other contexts. Members' concern had by early 2009 reached a level where concrete steps were being discussed in the Committee on how the timeliness of members' submission of notifications might be improved.

The Secretariat's reports on the fifty-three meetings between 1995 and 2008 show that for the domestic support notifications, out of the 2,229 questions members raised, 53 percent concerned green box measures and 47 percent concerned other domestic support issues, such as AMSs. While many questions sought clarification or missing data, others identify issues that could change the CTAMS if the responding member were

[10] An additional thirty days is allowed for submission of a final notification if the initial notification is provisional.

[11] The Agreement specified that negotiations to continue the process of achieving its objectives would be initiated one year before the end of the implementation period (Article 20). These negotiations were integrated into the Doha Round.

to address them as suggested by the questioning member. Often members ask that an exclusion of support from CTAMS be justified by demonstrating conformity with green box criteria or for similar justification of other exclusions. Some notifying members who cannot demonstrate this have then reported the support in question as AMS instead.[12]

The review process in the Committee on Agriculture allows members to raise questions on issues that do not stem from the notifications and exchange information in a more timely setting than if it had to be tied to notifications. The points raised and the underlying arguments in the Committee signal to any member that others are paying attention to whether and how it abides by its commitment and follows the rules of the Agreement. The Committee has no mandate to enforce but only to review the implementation of commitments, which lets some members continue to calculate CTAMS in a particular way in spite of the calculation appearing to others to be inconsistent with the rules of the Agreement.

Dispute settlement involving domestic support

The Committee is not a forum for settling disputes. This is the domain of the Dispute Settlement Body (DSB), which consists of all members of the WTO. It establishes a panel of experts at the request of a complaining member if consultations between the members concerned have failed to resolve the dispute. The panel is essentially an impartial tribunal that hears the arguments of the members involved, which are couched in legal terms with reference to the relevant WTO agreements and which sometimes use economic analysis as supporting evidence. Based on its findings and conclusions and if a rule or commitment has been broken, the panel recommends that the defending member bring its measures into

[12] In its 2005–08 meetings, the Committee on Agriculture reviewed yearly domestic support notifications from six of the eight countries in our analysis, covering altogether twenty-six notified years (submitted by the EU in 2004 and 2006; the US in 2007; Japan in 2005, 2007 and 2008; Norway in 2008; Brazil in 2005 and 2007; and China in 2006). Questions were usually asked at the one or two meetings following the date of the notification. They addressed about 113 different issues and many additional sub-questions were asked in very specific terms. Australia, Canada, the EU, New Zealand and the US raised most of the issues, and the EU and the US were the respondents for most of them, about forty each. More than half of the questions concerned whether certain measures met the relevant criteria of Annex 2. Similar questions were addressed to Brazil whose notification reported use of the development program exemptions. Other questions concerned the measurement of market price support (several countries), EU enlargement, negative AMS (Norway), and the classification of some US support as non-product-specific.

conformity with its obligations. Either side can appeal the panel's recommendations to the Appellate Body based on points of law. The DSB's acceptance of the report of the panel or the Appellate Body makes it a ruling that the defending member must implement as part of its membership obligations.

Considering the high profile of domestic support in the negotiations under both the Uruguay and Doha Rounds and in analysis of the Agreement, surprisingly few disputes about domestic support have been initiated. Prior to 2007 they numbered only two (*Korea – Beef* and *United States – Cotton*) and in neither case was domestic support at the center of the complaint. The fact that most FBTAMS commitments mirrored the high-support 1986–88 base years means that most members' applied support in several years from 1995 onwards has been considerably below their commitment levels, making it more difficult to sustain a claim of FBTAMS violation. The Agreement's "peace clause" (Article 13) precluded through 2003 certain challenges under the ASCM. This may have helped to keep down the number of complaints related to agriculture under the ASCM in the early years of the WTO, but since this clause expired *US – Cotton* has still been the only case of such litigation.

In *Korea – Beef* Australia and the US alleged that Korea's AMS for beef was larger than Korea had calculated, which made its CTAMS exceed the FBTAMS commitment (WTO 2000). The Appellate Body said it was unable to reach a conclusion on this since the panel's work was based on "insufficient factual findings." The panel used a fixed external reference price for 1989–91 instead of 1986–88 as stipulated in Annex 3 to calculate MPS. This may seem to be a technicality but goes to the heart of what the Agreement is: a legally binding instrument and not a blueprint for economic analysis. Nevertheless, *Korea – Beef* did clarify two other domestic support issues. One of these issues relates to the relative strength of the Agreement's different wordings for how to calculate an AMS: "in accordance with" Annex 3 (stronger) and "taking into account" the data and methodology used in establishing the FBTAMS commitment (weaker). The other issue relates to eligible production in calculating a product's market price support under the rules of the Agreement. The quantity that the government has announced is eligible for purchase constitutes the eligible production in this case, even if it then actually purchases only a smaller quantity.

In *US – Cotton* Brazil claimed that the US contravened the ASCM by causing serious prejudice to the interests of Brazil (WTO 2005a). Brazil argued that the Agreement's peace clause did not shelter certain US domestic support programs against such a challenge under the ASCM. The Appellate Body found that this was correct, partly based on the finding that fixed payments under two US programs did not meet the policy-specific green box criteria. Specifically, the criteria under the heading "decoupled income support" do not allow the payment amount to be related to the type of production, a criterion that the US programs could not meet because they prohibited the production of fruits and vegetables on the acreage that determined eligibility for the payments. Support to cotton, when cumulated over several programs and including the fixed payments not qualifying for the green box, was thus found large enough under the rules of the Agreement to disallow the use of the peace clause to shelter against the ASCM challenge in this case. The Appellate Body then found under the ASCM that the effect of numerous price-contingent US subsidies (but not the fixed payments) gave rise to serious prejudice to the interests of Brazil.[13] Subsequent steps in *US – Cotton* have also concerned issues other than the green box compatibility of certain programs. The issues include the implementation of the recommendations of the Appellate Body and the actions that would be permissible under WTO rules. Discussions between the US and Brazil in early 2010 resulted in Brazil agreeing not to impose any of the countermeasures against US trade that had been authorized under dispute settlement rules in exchange for the US agreeing to take several steps. Among these was US funding of technical assistance and capacity building for the benefit of Brazil, perhaps including measures of the kind that many countries report as general services in the green box. The funding would continue until passage of the next US farm support legislation (where cotton programs can be modified) or a mutually agreed solution was reached.

The Appellate Body has reaffirmed in two other disputes that there is a boundary between the domestic support and export subsidy disciplines but that the economic effects of domestic support may spill over to export production. These cases are *Canada – Dairy* (WTO 2001; WTO 2002) and *European Communities – Sugar* (WTO 2004; WTO 2005b; WTO 2005c). A concern was expressed in *Canada – Dairy* that the export subsidy disciplines of the Agreement would be undermined if there was no limit on the exportation of products subsidized under certain domestic schemes. The contrary view was also expressed, namely that it was not for the panel to "collapse" domestic support disciplines into export subsidy disciplines. The Appellate Body believed that if WTO-consistent domestic support

[13] The US fixed and price-contingent payments are described in Chapter 4.

measures were automatically characterized as export subsidies because they produced spill-over economic benefits for export production, the distinction between the domestic support and export subsidy discipline of the Agreement would be eroded. However, the Appellate Body also considered that the distinction between the domestic support and export subsidy disciplines would be eroded if domestic support could be provided without limit for exports. The domestic support provisions of the Agreement along with high levels of tariff protection allow extensive support to producers, compared to the limits imposed through export subsidy disciplines, the Appellate Body explained. It then outlined a technical approach to the export subsidization issue at hand, an approach that it said maintained the export subsidy discipline without erosion while best respecting the integrity of the two disciplines. Giving further attention to the distinction between domestic support and export subsidy disciplines, the Appellate Body later explained that subsidies may be granted in both domestic and export markets, provided that the disciplines imposed by the Agreement on the levels of subsidization are respected. In other words, a particular scheme may provide both domestic support and export subsidies, in which case both the domestic support commitment and the export subsidization commitments need to be complied with.

In *EC – Sugar* the parties expressed concern about any redrawing of the boundary between domestic support and export subsidies or they invoked the Appellate Body's view, stated earlier in *Canada – Dairy*, of the distinction between domestic support and export subsidy disciplines. The Appellate Body considered that its interpretation concerning export subsidization in *EC – Sugar* did not erode the boundary between domestic support and export subsidies recognized under the Agreement. Its interpretation, it said, respects the boundary between the two and operates to ensure that countries provide domestic support and export subsidies in conformity with their obligations. In arbitration this interpretation was expressed as domestic support being the source of the export subsidy that was found to exist in *EC – Sugar*.

In 2007 two cases were initiated where possible FBTAMS violations are central to the dispute (WTO 2007a, 2007b). Following consultations with the US, Canada and Brazil each requested that a panel on US domestic support be established and the DSB established a single panel for the two cases. The background of what has come to be known as the Total AMS (TAMS) case included the complainants' continued frustration over the large amounts of support provided to producers of a fairly small number of crops in the US. Canada argued, for example, that not only was this support large, but the delivery mechanisms were such that production incentives were distorted. The importance placed on domestic support rules and commitments in Doha was also part of the background.

Canada and Brazil contend that the US violated its FBTAMS commitment in almost every year between 1999 and 2005. They argue that the US improperly excludes some support from CTAMS as green box support, such as its fixed payments (earlier found to be non-green in *US – Cotton*) and payments under a large number of programs related to disasters or emergencies, whose conformity with the green box criteria is being tested for the first time in the TAMS case. Canada and Brazil also contend that the US improperly counts some support as part of non-product-specific AMS instead of product-specific AMSs, fails to report some support, and under-reports other support. When the CTAMS is calculated properly, they contend, the US exceeded its FBTAMS commitment by billions of dollars in the years in question (see Chapter 4). The 2008 US farm support legislation replaced some of the measures named in the case with the same measures under new legal authority, eliminated some measures and introduced new ones. While some observers argue that this has reduced the extent of the change in US policy that would flow directly even from an outcome of the case favorable to Canada and Brazil, a clarification of some issues in policy classification and measurement would materialize regardless of the outcome. The intensity of pursuing the case may be linked to developments on domestic support in the Doha negotiations.

The Doha negotiations on domestic support

The Doha negotiations on agriculture follow the three-pillar architecture of the Agreement. By early 2008 the Doha draft modalities provided a blueprint for many of the rules and commitments that members might agree to in the negotiations. Although the draft modalities on domestic support were then modified several times, the modifications were relatively minor and with a few exceptions domestic support was considered a stable element in the version of draft modalities that was reached at the end of 2008 (WTO 2008). These provisions are replicated as Appendix B of this book.

Key distinctions in constraining domestic support under a Doha agreement

The draft modalities propose fundamental changes to the Agreement. They include new ceiling commitments on Overall Trade-Distorting

Domestic Support (OTDS) and on the sum of blue box payments; reductions in FBTAMS commitments and *de minimis* percentages; new limits on product-specific AMSs and on product-specific blue box payments; new rules to govern certain tradeoffs between the limits on product-specific AMS and blue box support; and modification of some green box criteria. In general developing countries would take smaller reductions than developed countries or none at all. Many of the new provisions would not apply to LDCs (thirty-two members in 2008) or to certain other members, according to a large flora of exempting provisions in the draft modalities. Most reductions would be implemented over a number of years, such as five or eight, depending on conditions similar to those determining the size of the reduction. Figure 2.2 shows the structure of the domestic support provisions of the December 2008 draft modalities, also summarized in Table 2.2.

The new ceiling commitment on OTDS would apply for developed and many developing countries to all non-green-box support except support under Article 6.2. This commitment would derive from a Base OTDS established for each member other than least-developed countries and some other developing countries. Base OTDS would take into account both the nominal values of the member's FBTAMS commitment and the size of its agriculture sector as measured by agricultural VOP. The Base OTDS is the sum of the Final Bound Total AMS commitment under the Agreement, 10 percent of the total value of agricultural production (developing countries use 20 percent instead of 10 percent), and either blue box payments during a specified base period or an additional 5 percent of the total value of agricultural production.[14] Twenty-one members would reduce their OTDS commitment from the Base OTDS level, with developing countries making two-thirds of the reductions made by the majority of developed countries.

Under the draft modalities, eighteen of the thirty-one members with FBTAMS commitments would reduce this commitment to a varying extent. The large domestic support commitments of the EU, the US and Japan motivated the idea of harmonizing (tiered) reductions. This concept was initially associated with Canada's delegation (Brink 2001) and is represented in the draft modalities. Harmonization means that the

[14] The 10 percent of historical total VOP in agriculture (developed countries) is sometimes thought, although the draft modalities do not say so, to represent the sum of all product-specific and non-product-specific *de minimis* allowances in a historical period, i.e., 5 plus 5 percent of historical VOP. Once the Base OTDS is established, the origin of the various elements used to establish it no longer matters.

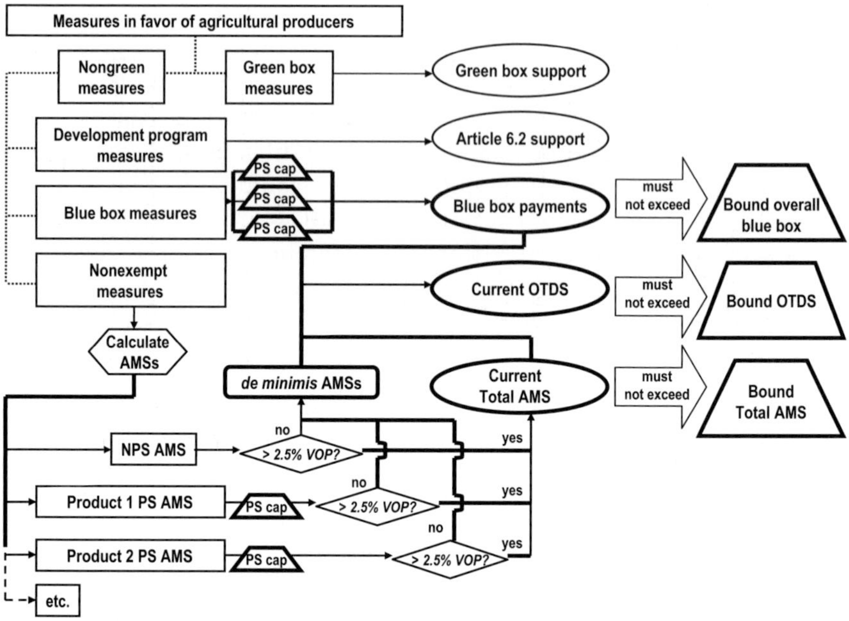

Figure 2.2 Domestic support categories and constraints in the 2008 Doha draft modalities
Source: Author's interpretation of WTO (2008). The *de minimis* percentages are those applying to most developed countries. *De minimis* percentages of 5 percent or 4.2 percent would apply to other developed countries and 10 percent, 8.5 percent or 6.7 percent would apply to developing countries, all based on countries qualifying for inclusion in particular groups. AMSs are Aggregate Measurements of Support; NPS is non-product-specific; PS is product-specific; VOP is value of production.

members with the largest base amounts in the form of Base OTDS and FBTAMS would see the largest percentage reductions. In the Doha draft modalities the size of the reduction would be given by placing a member in one of three tiers according to the size of its base. Some members whose bases are large relative to the size of their agriculture would reduce by more than what would follow strictly from being placed in a particular tier. A fourth tier would provide developing countries with special and differential treatment. The harmonizing nature of the Doha reductions would apply mainly to the developed countries with the largest Base OTDS and FBTAMS. Many developing countries, including those with a very large Base OTDS, would not reduce it at all, even though their Base

Table 2.2 *Summary of the December 2008 Doha domestic support draft modalities*

Establish and reduce OTDS commitment	Base Overall Trade-Distorting Domestic Support (OTDS) is sum of existing FBTAMS commitment and usually 15 percent of value of 1995–2000 agricultural production for developed countries (25 percent and choice of 1995–2004 for developing countries). Many developed countries reduce by 80 percent; 70 percent; 55 percent, if Base OTDS greater than US$60 billion; US$10–60 billion; less than US$10 billion (larger reduction for developed countries in middle tier if Base OTDS exceeds 40 percent of value of production). Some developing countries reduce by 37 percent. Some developed and most developing countries do not reduce, depending on absence of FBTAMS commitment, recent accession or other factors. Differentiation among developing countries regarding need to schedule OTDS commitments.
Reduce FBTAMS commitment	Existing FBTAMS commitment to be reduced. Many developed countries reduce by 70 percent; 60 percent; 45 percent, if existing commitment greater than US$40 billion; US$15–40 billion; less than US$15 billion (developed countries in middle and bottom tier reduce by more if existing commitment exceeds 40 percent of value of production). Some developing countries reduce by 30 percent; most developing countries do not reduce.
Introduce limits on product-specific AMSs	Set limits on AMSs for individual products. Developed countries set limits at product's average 1995–2000 AMS support (1995–2004 product-by-product proportions for US only). Certain provisions for new products. Special formula for cotton. Three more flexible options for developing countries.
Redefine and limit Article 6.5 support (blue box)	Blue box to include also direct payments that do not require production under similar criteria as under production-limiting programs. Total blue box payments limited to 2.5 percent of value of 1995–2000 agricultural production (5 percent and choice of 1995–2004 for developing countries). Special rule for developed country with blue box payments as very large share of 1995–2000 trade-distorting support.
Introduce limits on product-specific blue box payments	Set limits on blue box payments for individual products at product's average 1995–2000 blue box support (special rules for the US only). Flexibility under certain conditions and facility to increase limits on product-specific blue box payment if appropriate reduction in limit on product-specific AMS. Greater flexibility for developing countries.

Table 2.2 (*cont.*)

Reduce *de minimis* percentages	Most developed countries reduce *de minimis* percentage by 50 percent. Some developing countries with FBTAMS commitment reduce by 33 percent. Other developed and developing countries reduce less or do not reduce.	
Modify criteria in Annex 2 (green box)	Base period to be defined, fixed and unchanging for structural adjustment (investment) and regional assistance programs; defined and fixed base period for decoupled income support also to be unchanging. Such base periods to be notified. For developing countries only: General Services to mention certain policies and services related to rural development, such as infrastructure services, drought management and flood control, nutritional security, and issuance of property titles; make criteria less stringent for disaster and insurance programs; accommodate some price policies in the green box with no need to count market price support as AMS support.	
Staging of implementation	Developed countries: OTDS: cut by 33 percent (25 percent for some) on first day, then five annual cuts. FBTAMS: cut by 25 percent on first day (7.5 percent for some), then five annual cuts. *De minimis* percentage: full cut on first day.	Developing countries: OTDS: cut by 20 percent on first day, then eight annual cuts. FBTAMS: cut by 3.3 percent on first day, then eight annual cuts. *De minimis* percentage: full cut by third year.
	All: Limit on blue box total, product-specific AMSs, product-specific blue box payments: mostly in full on first day.	

Source: Author's summary of WTO (2008).

OTDS is large not only because VOP is large but also because the percentage applied to determine it is larger than for the developed countries.

The new ceiling commitment on a member's total of all blue box payments would equal a given percentage of VOP in a historical base period. Developed countries' commitments would generally equal 2.5 percent of the average total value of agricultural production in 1995–2000 (special parameters would be used for members whose support in 1995–2000 included an exceptionally large share of blue box payments). Developing countries would generally use 5 percent and either 1995–2000 or 1995–2004. The Agreement's criteria for excluding blue box payments from the CTAMS (Article 6.5) would be expanded so that certain direct payments that "do not require production" qualify for exemption if they also meet criteria relating to various fixed bases. This broadening of the definition, which was introduced by the US, would accommodate in a redefined blue box its countercyclical payments first legislated in 2002 (USTR 2005).

Under the Doha draft modalities most developed countries would immediately reduce the *de minimis* percentage by 50 percent, from 5 to 2.5 percent. Developing countries with FBTAMS commitments would reduce by two-thirds of the developed country reduction, i.e., from 10 to 6.7 percent. Twenty-one out of 125 members would reduce their *de minimis* percentage to a varying extent under these rules. Developing countries that did not schedule a FBTAMS commitment would not reduce their *de minimis* percentage. A member's *de minimis* allowances would continue to be calculated by applying the *de minimis* percentage to the relevant product-specific or non-product-specific VOP.

The draft modalities would introduce new limits on product-specific AMSs, generally set for developed countries in relation to their applied AMS support in 1995–2000 but with many special rules applying.[15] Developing countries would set their limits on product-specific AMSs in accordance with a variety of rules designed to provide considerable flexibility to those members that did not have large product-specific AMSs in a base period. The draft modalities would also establish new limits on product-specific blue box payments. They would generally be set in relation to past blue box payments but, recognizing that very few members have made such payments in the past, a number of rules allow for the establishment of limits on product-specific blue payments in many other ways. These rules tend to allow more flexibility for developing countries. Certain flexibility is also provided in the special rules applying to the US.

[15] Although not mentioned in the draft modalities, it is understood that product-specific limits would also apply to any future EMSs.

The introduction of product-specific limits mirrors some of the ideas considered in the Uruguay Round negotiations about the measurement and use of AMSs to constrain trade-distorting domestic support on a product-by-product basis. The introduction of an OTDS commitment and a blue box commitment also represent the Uruguay Round ideas of constraining all domestic support other than support under measures that meet certain criteria.

While the draft modalities would generally tighten members' constraints on trade-distorting domestic support, some such support, in particular Article 6.2 support in developing countries (development programs), remains untouched by constraints. Moreover, a plethora of special exemptions or flexibilities would apply to many subsets of members, whether developing or not, such as recently-acceded members, very recently-acceded members, members with or without a FBTAMS commitment, and net food-importing developing countries. Several special rules apply to the US only. Table 2.3 shows the forty conditions affecting members' treatment for OTDS, FBTAMS, blue box and *de minimis*, not counting the many special treatments in product-specific limits. The prevalence of special cases erodes to some extent the ability of the generally strengthened provisions in the draft modalities to effectively constrain future trade-distorting domestic support for a wide range of countries, as subsequent chapters demonstrate in depth.

The Doha draft modalities would make several changes to the Annex 2 criteria for green box measures. For developing countries the non-exhaustive list of general services in the green box would be extended to also mention policies and services related to farmer settlement, land reform programs, rural development and rural livelihood security; among them infrastructure services, drought management and flood control, and nutrition security programs. In addition, developing countries would not need to account for MPS in the AMS when they procure public stocks at subsidized prices in certain situations from low-income or resource-poor producers. This would effectively include some MPS measures in the green box. For all members the draft modalities would introduce more explicit rules to govern any updating of the base period that determines direct payments under decoupled income support, structural adjustment assistance (investment) and regional assistance programs. This tightens the qualifications for including these measures in the green box. The draft modalities would also introduce minor changes to recognize that different programs providing relief from natural disasters operate differently, such as natural disaster payments, crop insurance, and payments for the destruction of animals or crops to prevent certain pests and diseases.

Table 2.3 *Subsets of members identified in the Doha draft modalities on domestic support*

For OTDS commitments	For FBTAMS commitments	For *de minimis* thresholds	For overall blue box commitments
Developed countries (18)			
		General (9)	General (8)
			Special (1)
Tier 1 (1)	Tier 1 (1)		
Tier 2 with additional effort (1)	Tier 2 with additional effort (1)		
Tier 2 (1)	Tier 2 (1)		
	Tier 3 with additional effort (3)		
Tier 3 (6)	Tier 3 (3)		
			RAM (9)
RAM with FBTAMS commitment (2)	RAM with FBTAMS commitment (2)	RAM with FBTAMS commitment (2)	
SLIRAMET (5)	SLIRAMET (1)	SLIRAMET (5)	
VRAM (2)	VRAM (2)	VRAM (2)	
	Without FBTAMS commitment (4)		
Developing countries (107)			
			General (106)
			Special (1)
With FBTAMS commitment (10)		With FBTAMS commitment (10)	
	With FBTAMS commitment > $100 million (7)		
	With FBTAMS commitment < $100 million (3)		
NFIDC (4)	NFIDC (4)	NFIDC (4)	
		SLIRAMET (1)	
VRAM (2)	VRAM (2)	VRAM (2)	
Without FBTAMS commitment (91)	Without FBTAMS commitment (91)	Without FBTAMS commitment (90)	

Table 2.3 (*cont.*)

For OTDS commitments	For FBTAMS commitments	For *de minimis* thresholds	For overall blue box commitments
		Support to subsistence and resource-poor farmers (assumed 0)	

Notes: RAM indicates Recently-Acceded Members; SLIRAMET, Small Low Income Recently-Acceded Members with Economies in Transition; VRAM, Very Recently-Acceded Members; NFIDC, Net Food-Importing Developing Countries. Figures in parentheses indicate the number of members in each subset.
Source: Subsets and number of members based on author's interpretation of WTO (2008).

The draft modalities would replace the Agreement's provisions about reviewing the implementation of commitments with a new article designed to enhance the Committee's role in reviewing and monitoring the implementation of the rules and commitments (see Annex M in our Appendix B). This article would also address the notification obligations and formats associated with the new commitments under the draft modalities. Members would need to provide more information in a more timely way on domestic support, under binding rules that would be part of the new agreement itself and not just in the form of hortatory language in a decision of the Committee on Agriculture. The draft modalities pay particular attention to the information to be provided on measures claimed to meet the criteria of the green box. Members would review the effectiveness of the monitoring and surveillance mechanisms, although this would be possible no earlier than three years after the beginning of the new agreement.

Future entitlements to distorting support

Combining the parameters of the Doha draft modalities on domestic support from December 2008 (WTO 2008) with certain data and assumptions makes it possible to estimate each member's future commitments and allowances under a Doha agreement based on these modalities (Brink 2009). For this global overview assessment, Bound OTDS commitments, FBTAMS commitments, overall blue box commitments, and *de minimis* allowances in US dollars were calculated from each member's scheduled Final Bound Total AMS commitment, past blue box payments, past total value of production, and yearly exchange rates. Data were mostly from a series of WTO papers (TN/AG/S/*), notifications to the Committee on Agriculture, and material referred to in acceding members' schedules. A variety of other sources were drawn upon as needed.

Establishing Base OTDS and calculating *de minimis* allowances requires VOP data. VOP from the above sources for a small number of members was complemented with estimates from national sources, the OECD PSE database, or extrapolation. VOP was to the extent possible expressed in the member's currency or in the currency it uses in notifications. A proxy for VOP in the form of value added in agriculture in current US dollars was used for many smaller developing countries (World Bank 2007).[16] This underestimation of VOP by value added leads to an underestimation of Base OTDS and *de minimis* allowances for the developing countries as a group. The *de minimis* allowances were calculated from nominal VOP for 2001–03, which was the most complete data at the time of the analysis, and converted to dollars at average 2001–03 exchange rates. The elements needed to establish a Base OTDS were expressed in the currency of the member's VOP (sometimes different from that of its FBTAMS commitment) and added to form the Base OTDS in dollars, converted as needed at 2006 exchange rates. The reduced OTDS commitments under the draft modalities were calculated in the currency of the member's VOP. The new reduced Final Bound Total AMS commitments were calculated in the currency of the commitment (sometimes different from the local currency or the currency the member uses in notifications). The resulting nominal amounts, when not already in dollars, were converted to dollars using 2006 exchange rates.

The results for most of the individual members are summed and shown as totals or world shares in Table 2.4 for two groups of members: the eighteen developed country and 107 developing country members. The parameters of the draft modalities differ considerably between these groups and dividing into these two groups follows the practice in the negotiations, although it does not reflect the heterogeneity among the developing countries. The analysis does not consider any product-specific limits and does not estimate future applied support – these issues are addressed for selected countries in the chapters that follow.

[16] Throughout the book dollars ($) refers to US dollars (US$) unless otherwise noted.

Table 2.4 *World sums and shares of developed and developing countries for key elements of domestic support disciplines*

	Pre-Doha		Doha	
	Value	World share	Value	World share
	Billion US dollars	%	*Billion US dollars*	%
Final Bound Total AMS			*Limits after reductions*	
All developed countries	155	91	51	82
All developing countries	15	9	11	18
World	170	100	62	100
Blue box			*New limits*	
All developed countries	Not applicable		20	35
All developing countries	Not applicable		36	65
World	Not applicable		56	100
De minimis allowances			*Allowances after reductions*	
All developed countries	66	32	34	21
All developing countries	142	68	131	79
World	208	100	165	100
Overall Trade-Distorting Support (OTDS)	*Base OTDS*		*New limits after reductions*	
All developed countries	274	61	60	27
All developing countries	176	39	165	73
World	450	100	225	100

Notes: There are no blue box limits in the Agreement on Agriculture. World refers to all WTO members.
Source: Author's calculations (Brink 2009).

The world sum of FBTAMS commitments under the Agreement is \$170 billion. Developed countries have the overwhelming share of this sum, amounting to \$155 billion. As discussed by Brink (2009) and further developed in Chapter 3, the twenty-seven-country European Union (EU27) by itself accounts for more than half of the world sum. Because developed countries have most of the FBTAMS commitments and most developing countries have none, developed countries continue to account for a predominant world share of 82 percent even after the seemingly large percentage reductions of the Doha draft modalities. However, after reducing the FBTAMS commitments to their new levels, the developed countries' sum declines to about \$51 billion in a world sum of \$62 billion.

There are no ceilings on blue box payments in the Agreement. The new ceilings established on blue box payments under the draft modalities would sum to \$56 billion for the world, of which developed countries would be entitled to \$20 billion and developing countries \$36 billion.

The *de minimis* allowances under the Agreement sum to \$208 billion for the world, based on the above assumptions. Developed countries' allowances sum to \$66 billion and those of developing countries sum to \$142 billion. Applying the draft modalities reductions in *de minimis* percentages would generate a world sum of \$165 billion, consisting of \$34 billion for developed countries and \$131 billion for developing countries (still based on 2001–03 values of production). Overall, the *de minimis* percentage under Doha would be four times larger for most developing than for developed countries. China's VOP surpasses that of any other member, including the EU27 and the US (see Chapters 3, 4, 9 and 11). In combination with its unchanged 8.5 *de minimis* percentage, China's *de minimis* allowances account for more than one-third of the developing country total under either the Agreement or Doha draft modalities. By comparison, the *de minimis* allowances of the EU27 and US combined fall by nearly one-half (to around \$25 billion, see Brink (2009) and Chapters 3 and 4) under a future 2.5 *de minimis* percentage. The share of China's *de minimis* allowances in the world total, which is about the same as for the EU27 and US together under the Agreement, increases under the Doha modalities to a share that is double that of the EU27 and US together.

Because *de minimis* allowances continue to be calculated from nominal annual VOP, they are larger than shown in Table 2.4 at the higher prices prevailing for most commodities since 2006. VOP and hence the *de minimis* allowances are expected to continue to grow over time for most members. This would increase the contrast between the sums of the *de minimis* allowances of developed and developing countries. Faster growth of agricultural VOP in developing countries would further increase this contrast. To illustrate, suppose the annual growth rate of nominal value of agricultural production is one percentage point among developed countries but two percentage points among developing countries. From 2002 to 2023 the VOP in developed countries would grow by 23 percent and in developing countries by 52 percent, and the *de minimis* allowances in developed and developing countries would increase correspondingly.

The Base OTDSs sum to $450 billion for the world: $274 billion in developed countries and $176 billion in developing countries. The reductions in the draft modalities generate a world sum of OTDS commitments of $225 billion, i.e., a cut by half. Developed countries would be entitled to $60 billion of OTDS support and developing countries to $165 billion. The Doha OTDS limits would make it impossible for most members to increase the sum of blue box payments and AMS support (Current Total AMS and *de minimis* AMSs) to the level it could reach under the Agreement (assuming blue box payments would not exceed historical levels). It would be impossible to reverse the EU policy reforms, and no developed country would be able to raise support as far as in the past in case of a large price decline. The constraint on most developing countries' OTDS support would equal the Base OTDS, without any reduction. Most developing countries have in the past provided little non-green-box support. As subsequent chapters demonstrate for four large middle-income countries, there is scope for relatively large increases from these low past levels in the OTDS and AMS support that developing countries would be able to provide within their limits, as well as through continuation of the Article 6.2 exemption for development programs.

The sum of FBTAMS commitments, blue box limits and *de minimis* allowances for developed countries equals $105 billion under implementation of the Doha draft modalities, compared to OTDS commitments summing to $60 billion. For developing countries the sum of the component constraints is $178 billion, compared to OTDS commitments summing to $165 billion. The draft modalities indicate that for members with Bound OTDS commitments, a lower OTDS commitment overrides the sum of the constraints on the components of applied OTDS support (blue box support, *de minimis* AMS support, and AMS support that counts in CTAMS). When the OTDS commitment is lower than the sum of the constraints on the components, the amount of support provided in one or more of the components has to be less than would be allowed within the component-specific constraint itself.[17] The OTDS commitment would thus constrain many members' future applied OTDS support more tightly than would the sum of the component constraints, particularly so for developed countries but less for developing countries.[18] In many cases the caps on product-specific AMSs and blue box payments would add further effective constraints on the applied support that counts towards the various simultaneous ceilings.

The FBTAMS and OTDS commitments are constant in nominal currency units (such as dollars or national currency) while the *de minimis* allowances increase as nominal VOP increases. Over time the *de minimis* allowances will therefore account for a growing share of most members' entitlements to provide AMS support, although product-specific caps will to some extent limit the generality of this phenomenon. The OTDS commitment is relatively larger for developing countries in general than for developed countries, as a result of the larger percentage of VOP used to establish the Base OTDS and the smaller or absence of reductions from base. Still, the OTDS commitment eventually would bind the effective use of growing nominal *de minimis* allowances by developing countries under a Doha agreement. The developing countries except China remain entitled to support agriculture without any constraint through the not-very-specific criteria of Article 6.2 for development programs, and some may choose to do so if they were constrained by FBTAMS or OTDS commitments.

Summary and conclusions

The difficulties in agricultural trade that the Haberler group was set up to address were to some extent tackled with the introduction of domestic

[17] This rule does not apply to the *de minimis* allowances of recently acceded members. In addition, the OTDS constraint is not as binding as it appears relative to the component constraints for members with a FBTAMS commitment because of the practical impossibility of fully using at the same time all *de minimis* allowances and the FBTAMS commitment (Brink 2006). The sum of all applied *de minimis* AMSs (whether product-specific or non-product-specific) and CTAMS will always in practice be smaller than the sum of all *de minimis* allowances and the FBTAMS commitment. The reason is that there is no *de minimis* AMS for a product for which the AMS is large enough (exceeds the *de minimis* threshold) to be counted in CTAMS. That product's theoretical *de minimis* allowance can thus not be used. The same reasoning applies to the non-product-specific AMS.

[18] Underestimation of the *de minimis* allowances makes little difference for the shares among groups of countries. It does matter, however, when adding the allowances to the draft Doha blue box limits and FBTAMS commitments so this sum of constraints on the components can be compared to the OTDS commitment. It also matters when the allowances are used as the starting point for the above projections to 2023.

support constraints in the WTO's Agreement on Agriculture. Some kinds of distorting support in both developed and developing countries escaped constraints, and the measurement of support through an AMS deviated from other ways of measuring support. The size and nature of the domestic support that WTO member countries provide were made more transparent by the requirement to submit notifications to the Committee on Agriculture. The yearly amounts of support classified by given criteria have to be notified, as does the introduction or modification of measures that are claimed as exempt from the ceiling commitment on CTAMS. Member countries review the notifications in the Committee on Agriculture several times per year. Between 1995 and 2008 the Committee reviewed around 700 domestic support notifications and revisions. They gave rise to more than 2,200 questions in the Committee, divided about equally between questions on annual support and questions on measures claimed as exempt from commitments. However, many member countries' record of adhering to the notification due dates is patchy at best and very poor in some instances.

Doha would introduce more constraints than presently in the Agreement, including a limit on OTDS, a limit on overall blue box payments, and individual limits on product-specific AMSs and on product-specific blue box payments. Many existing commitments and thresholds would be reduced. While Doha would significantly constrain the future distorting support of several members compared to past amounts, special provisions for numerous other members would erode its effectiveness in containing other large amounts of distorting support. Such special provisions would apply to recently-acceded members, very recently-acceded members, certain other recently-acceded members, net food-importing developing countries, and developing countries generally, as well as through special provisions seemingly designed for individual members, whether developed or developing countries.

With few exceptions members have in the past been far below their FBTAMS commitment, including in the eight countries discussed in subsequent chapters. Under a Doha agreement based on the December 2008 draft modalities, several constraints would apply simultaneously to overlapping measurements of distorting support. Most members face only small or no reductions in such constraints, so they would be allowed to provide almost the same amounts and kinds of distorting support as they could have provided in the past. Still, some developed countries in particular who have been close to their FBTAMS commitment or who take significant reductions from the base amounts of the new constraints would not be allowed the same amounts of the same kind of support as they provided or could have provided in the past.

Developing countries as a group and also some developed country members would have considerable room for maneuver between the amounts of distorting support they have provided in the past and what they would be allowed to provide under future constraints. Most developing countries have been unable to provide much or any distorting domestic support in the past, but some developing countries have demonstrated growing ability and willingness to provide such support (Anderson 2009). As the economies of developing countries grow over time, and especially if they grow rapidly, many developing countries will soon approach the same levels of economic wellbeing where the developed countries saw fit in the past to deliver significant support to farmers, often by distorting measures. Some developing countries might choose to use this future capacity to increase domestic support within the rules and commitments governing the use of domestic support and border measures.

The total amounts of distorting domestic support that developing countries could provide within their commitments would remain large with a Doha agreement. Developing countries as a group would be entitled to provide almost three-quarters of the world total of distorting domestic support below the ceilings on OTDS and developed countries as a group slightly more than one-quarter. On some kinds of distorting domestic support developing countries other than China would continue to face no constraint on certain investment and input subsidies. All countries would also be entitled to provide unlimited amounts of support under measures that meet the criteria of the green box, which would encompass a larger set of measures for developing countries than for developed countries.

If some developing countries use their future economic capacity to significantly increase various forms of distorting domestic support to agriculture, some interesting implications could follow. In the past the large amounts of distorting domestic support in some developed countries have generated concerns both in other developed countries and in developing countries. Imagine a world where most developed countries' distorting domestic support was considerably more constrained, and some developing countries had become the large providers of such support. Might low-support developing countries then direct their concerns about policy-driven distortions to the high-support developing countries? Might developed countries, most of which would be constrained to be relatively low-support countries, join the low-support developing countries in voicing their shared concern over the trade distortions caused by large amounts of distorting domestic support in some developing countries? These and related questions – along with more traditional concerns about high levels of support by developed countries – lead to the detailed investigations presented in subsequent chapters for eight selected countries of the size and nature of their past and possible future support under the WTO rules.

References

Anderson, K. (ed.) 2009. *Distortions to Agricultural Incentives: A Global Perspective 1955–2007.* London: Palgrave Macmillan, and Washington, DC: World Bank.

Brink, L. 2001. Establishing domestic support commitments through a harmonization formula. Working Paper 01–2, International Agricultural Trade Research Consortium (IATRC), October. www.iatrcweb.org/publications/working.htm (accessed August 12, 2008).

2006. WTO constraints on US and EU domestic support in agriculture: The October 2005 proposals. *The Estey Centre Journal of International Law and Trade Policy* 7(1): 96–115.

2007. Classifying, measuring and analyzing WTO domestic support in agriculture: Some conceptual distinctions. Working Paper 07–02, International Agricultural Trade Research Consortium (IATRC), April. www.iatrcweb.org/publications/working.htm (accessed August 12, 2008).

2009. WTO Constraints on domestic support in agriculture: Past and future. *Canadian Journal of Agricultural Economics* 57(1): 1–21. DOI: 10.1111/j.1744-7976.2008.01135.x.

Diakosavvas, D. 2002. How to measure the level of agricultural support: Comparison of the methodologies applied by OECD and WTO. In *Agricultural Policies in China after WTO Accession*. Paris: OECD.

FAO (Food and Agriculture Organization of the United Nations). 1973. Agricultural protection: Domestic policy and international trade. Conference, C 73/LIM/9. Rome.

1975. Agricultural protection and stabilization policies: A framework of measurement in the context of agricultural adjustment. Conference, C 75/LIM/2. Rome.

1985. International agricultural adjustment. Fifth progress report. Conference, C 85/21. Rome.

GATT (General Agreement on Tariffs and Trade). 1958. Trends in international trade – A report by a panel of experts. October.

1987. United States proposal for negotiations on agriculture. MTN.GNG/NG5/W/14, 7 July.

1988a. The Trade Distortion Equivalent (TDE): An aggregate indicator of adverse trade effects of measures of support and protection for agriculture. MTN.GNG/NG5/W/46, 23 February.

1988b. Short-term measures (other than immediate measures) in the framework of the measures proposed by the European Communities. MTN.GNG/NG5/W/62, 10 June.

1990. Framework agreement on agriculture reform program – Draft text by the chairman. MTN.GNG/NG5/W/170, 11 July.

Josling, T. E., S. Tangermann, and T. K. Warley. 1996. *Agriculture in the GATT.* New York: St. Martin's Press, Inc.

OECD. 1987. *National Policies and Agricultural Trade.* Paris.

2008. *Agricultural Policy Design and Implementation – A Synthesis.* Paris.

2009. *Agricultural Policies in OECD Countries: Monitoring and Evaluation.* Paris.

Tangermann, S., T. E. Josling, and S. Pearson. 1987. Multilateral negotiations on farm-support levels. *The World Economy* 10(3): 265–281.

USDA (US Department of Agriculture). 1987. Government intervention in agriculture: Measurement, evaluation, and implications for trade negotiations. Foreign Agricultural Economic Report No. 229, Economic Research Service, April.

USTR (US Trade Representative). 2005. Implications of US WTO proposal on trade-distorting domestic support. Doha Development Agenda Policy Brief, October.

World Bank. 2007. World Development Indicators. http://ddp-ext.worldbank.org/ext/DDPQQ/member.do?method=getMembers&userid=1&queryId=6 (accessed May 9, 2008).

WTO. 1995a. *The Results of the Uruguay Round of Multilateral Trade Negotiations – The Legal Texts.* Geneva.

1995b. Notification requirements and formats. G/AG/2, Committee on Agriculture, 30 June.

2000. Korea – Measures affecting imports of fresh, chilled and frozen beef. Report of the Appellate Body, WT/DS161/AB/R and WT/DS169/AB/R, 11 December.

2001. Canada – Measures affecting the importation of milk and the exportation of dairy products. Report of the Appellate Body, WT/DS103/AB/RW, 3 December.

2002. Canada – Measures affecting the importation of milk and the exportation of dairy products. Report of the Appellate Body, WT/DS103/AB/RW2, 20 December.

2004. European Communities – Export subsidies on sugar. Report of the Panel, WT/DS265/R, 15 October.

2005a. United States – Subsidies on upland cotton. Report of the Appellate Body, WT/DS267/AB/R, 3 March.

2005b. European Communities – Export subsidies on sugar. Report of the Appellate Body, WT/DS265/AB/R, 28 April.

2005c. European Communities – Export subsidies on sugar. Award of the Arbitrator, WT/DS265/33, 28 October.

2007a. United States – Subsidies and other domestic support for corn and other agricultural products. Request for Consultations by Canada, WT/DS357/1, 11 January.

2007b. United States – Domestic support and export credit guarantees for agricultural products. Request for Consultations by Brazil, WT/DS365/1, 17 July.

2008. Revised draft modalities for agriculture. TN/AG/W/4/Rev.4, 6 December.

PART II

Developed countries: have high levels of support come down?

3

European Union

TIM JOSLING AND ALAN SWINBANK

Notifications of the level of domestic support by the EU to the WTO since 1995 reflect a substantial shift in the nature of domestic farm policy over that period. These policy changes have reduced the amount of support given by instruments that are most likely to distort trade. Though domestic support notifications are only one component of a full evaluation of the impact of policy changes on trade patterns, they are intended to indicate the extent to which such changes have moved countries along the path toward policies that have less impact on other countries. They monitor compliance with rules and commitments that were introduced to provide disciplines for certain types of domestic policies that were deemed to be particularly disruptive of trade. Other parallel disciplines that apply to tariffs (elimination of non-tariff barriers and binding tariff levels) and export subsidies (binding and reducing both expenditures and quantities of exports benefiting) have also impacted the levels of support and protection of EU agriculture.

The EU has in recent years expanded its membership to twenty-seven countries, in the process changing the nature of the agricultural sector. It has substantially reformed its Common Agricultural Policy (CAP), moving from price support for the major commodities to a comprehensive system of payments to farmers that are less related to present production. In addition, the EU has been the respondent in several challenges in the WTO that involve agricultural products.[1] The Doha Round trade negotiations would, if concluded, add further constraints on the CAP.

The authors would like to thank David Orden, Lars Brink and David Blandford for helpful comments on earlier versions of this chapter, as well as the participants in the IFPRI Workshop at which the results were originally discussed. We would also like to acknowledge useful conversations with staff of the European Commission and of the OECD without in any way burdening them with any responsibility for the material presented.

[1] No WTO case has challenged the EU's compliance with its domestic support obligations, though as noted in Chapter 2 the findings in the *Canada – Dairy, EC – Sugar, Korea – Beef* and *US – Cotton* cases have implications for domestic support.

The changes in both the composition of the EU and the nature of the farm policies provide a challenge for anyone attempting to anticipate future notifications, as major policy changes are introduced over time and unevenly across the EU membership. The apparent precision in allocating support to the various boxes whose criteria are contained in the Agreement on Agriculture dissipates when faced with staggered implementation of policies by twenty-seven member states. This adds importance to the careful calculation of the level of domestic support, but also introduces an element of uncertainty. The shadow notifications and their projection into the future described below must be interpreted with this caution in mind.

We begin with a description of the policy context of the domestic support notifications, including the successive reforms of the CAP. The notifications themselves are then discussed in some detail showing the link between the WTO categories of domestic support and the changes in policy. In looking at notification compliance with the Agreement, the question of the interpretation of the level of market price support is raised and some other notification issues, including the impact of alternative notification decisions, are addressed. The potential impact of a Doha Round agreement is explored in the following section. This entails projecting the notifications forward, based on current policy and market trends, and noting the places where the new constraints might impinge on policy choices. A summary and conclusions section rounds out the chapter.

Domestic support in the EU

The level of farm support in the EU has historically been high relative to that of many other countries (Anderson 2009, Swinnen 2009). The high level of that support has been criticized by trading partners, as has the nature of the support measures used. The CAP was introduced forty-five years ago, when agriculture in the original six member states was still recovering from the devastation of the Second World War. Countries agreed on the need to offer secure markets within the EU through protection against imports and the purchase of surplus products for disposal abroad. Import protection was given by means of a levy that varied inversely with world prices (a variable levy) so that imports would enter the domestic market at a predetermined threshold price. On the export side, a subsidy (known as an export refund or restitution) was paid that covered the difference between domestic intervention prices (at which supplies were purchased off the domestic market) and the world price.[2] Thus domestic prices were supported by flexible border instruments at a level that reflected political decisions by the (agricultural) Council of Ministers.

With such a controlled market, the need for internal subsidies was minimal. Domestic (taxpayer-funded) subsidies were the exception rather than the rule, being limited to products of mainly regional importance such as durum wheat and olive oil, to livestock grants paid to hill farmers, and to the crushers of EU-grown oilseeds. The oilseeds subsidy was a contentious scheme that provoked a trade dispute with the United States.

A succession of reforms in the past twenty years has changed the nature of the CAP and the policy environment in which EU agriculture exists (Josling 2009). In 1992 a significant change (the MacSharry reforms) was initiated that introduced direct payments in compensation for price cuts in cereals and beef, and the support arrangements for oilseeds were revised. These cereal and oilseed payments, based on the area grown, represented the first major change in the measures used by the EU to support its farm sector since the 1960s.[3] The reforms reduced the reliance on intervention and the subsidization of exports in the cereals market by cutting the domestic support price. The reduction of cereal prices and the consequent decline in the need for export subsidies allowed the EU to agree to restrictions on export subsidies in the GATT Uruguay Round, as embedded in the Agreement and the EU schedule.

Domestic subsidies were also constrained in the Agreement, in particular those that were deemed to be most trade distorting. The extent to which the new direct payments, related to past output and tied to quantitative restraints, should be disciplined was a major topic for negotiation at the Blair House meeting of November 1992, at which the EU and the US agreed on the main parameters of the final Agreement. The device of the blue box was introduced at that time as a way of placing the MacSharry compensation payments (and the US deficiency payments) in a category separate from the most trade-distorting subsidies as measured by the AMSs and commonly called the amber box.[4] The blue box payments were

[2] Both the threshold price and the intervention price were linked to a target price that was intended to give an acceptable level of farm income. The system described here operated for cereals; other crops and livestock products had regimes of a broadly similar nature.

[3] The MacSharry reforms also increased, and extended, the range of headage payments for beef farmers, and brought those for sheep and goats into a comparable framework.

[4] The term amber box is used inconsistently by commentators, sometimes including and sometimes excluding the *de minimis* amounts that are not counted in the CTAMS. Throughout, we use amber box to indicate the sum of all AMS support: CTAMS plus the

not subject to reductions, though they could only be made on limited acreage or livestock headage. Thus the blue box became the way in which the reformed CAP became consistent with the Agreement's constraints.

The mix of policies in the EU changed relatively little from 1995 to 2000, as the reforms in the cereal and oilseed sectors were being assimilated. But budget pressures and the prospect of ten new members from eastern and central Europe led the EU to consider further reforms. These were incorporated in a decision known as the Agenda 2000 reforms that were agreed in 1999. These reforms had a noticeable impact on the EU domestic support notifications, maintaining the direction of the 1992 reforms but pushing somewhat further. The Agenda 2000 reforms consolidated payments for cereals and oilseeds into a single payment to eligible farmers. Intervention prices were reduced by 29 percent for cereals (including a more substantial cut for rice) and, from 2005, they were to be lowered by 15 percent for butter and for skim milk powder, reducing the gap between these administered prices and the fixed reference prices.[5] Changes in the beef regime also modified the notifications somewhat: to the existing subsidies for suckler cows and the special beef premium were added a slaughter premium and some supplementary payments. These were notified as blue box payments, as they were limited to base levels of livestock numbers.

Even more significant in their impact on the EU's domestic support notification have been the reforms enacted since that time. Notably among the policy changes are the 2003 Fischler reforms, the changes in the regime for the Mediterranean crops in 2004, the reform of the sugar policy in 2005, and the reform of the fresh and processed fruit and vegetable policies in 2007 (Swinnen 2008). A change in the wine policy took place in 2008 and the impact of that reform is also reflected in our projected notifications for the years beyond 2009. The introduction of the Single Payment Scheme (SPS) with its Single Farm Payment, the key ingredient of the 2003 reform, further separated payments from current production. In the CAP Health Check, agreed in 2008, a further decoupling of SPS payments was undertaken. The 2004/05 notification of domestic support included some of these decoupled payments under the Fischler reforms, those that

product-specific and non-product-specific AMSs that fall below the *de minimis* threshold, as Brink refers to it in Chapter 2.

[5] The Agenda 2000 package also agreed on a new dairy premium from 2005, to compensate dairy farmers for the scheduled reductions in butter and skim milk powder intervention prices. In G/AG/N/EEC/17 the EU said it intended declaring these payments in the blue box.

were made in 2004, but the main impact appeared in the notifications for 2005/06 and 2006/07, by which time most of the policy changes had been implemented. Some residual impacts of this reform are expected to show up in the subsequent years, as indicated by the shadow notifications and projections reported in this chapter.

Notifications of domestic support 1995/96–2008/09

The first notification of domestic support by the EU, in 1995/96, coincided with the final years of the implementation of the MacSharry reforms.[6] Direct payments (the area payments on cereals and oilseeds, and the headage payments on beef and sheep) were placed in the blue box, as they were associated with limits on production.[7] As a result, the original notifications, from the 1995/96 marketing year, included a large CTAMS component (50 billion euro) and smaller but sizable blue box (21 billion euro) and green box (19 billion euro) payments.[8]

When the EU notified its level of domestic support in February 2010, it covered support up to the 2006/07 marketing year. Extending these notifications for an additional two years (shadow notifications) required a replication of the most recent notification using where possible publically available statistics and the calculation of the elements in the shadow domestic support notifications using updated information.[9]

Table 3.1 shows the notifications from 1995/96 to 2006/07, together with the shadow notifications calculated through 2008/09. The twelve notifications from 1995/96 to 2006/07 show a marked reduction in price supports compensated by an increase in direct payments. The CTAMS fell from around 50 billion euro in 1995/96 to 27 billion euro in 2006/07, a 46 percent decline. Blue box payments rose over the period, from 21 billion

[6] The compensation payments were introduced progressively in the marketing years 1993/94–1995/96.

[7] No estimate exists of what would have been the AMS notifications before 1995, had they been required. But it is likely that, in the eight years between the 1986–88 base and 1994/95, trade-distorting support (as measured by the CTAMS) fell from about 80 billion to 50 billion euro. The MacSharry payments cushioned this by means of the 21 billion euro compensation payments placed in the blue box. Green box eligible policy support probably rose modestly over the same period.

[8] The relevant notification went through a number of revisions and corrections. The figures used here take into account all these modifications through February 2010.

[9] Details of the construction of the shadow notifications are given in Josling and Swinbank (2008) but the data reported there has been updated. The EU's notification for 2007/08 (G/AG/N/EED/68) appeared as the manuscript went to press and could only partly be taken into account. It shows many of the potential notification changes discussed in this chapter.

Table 3.1 *Summary of EU domestic support notifications and shadow notifications, 1995/96–2008/09*

	Notifications[a]						
	1995/96	1996/97	1997/98	1998/99	1999/2000	2000/01	2001/02
Type of support *Billion euro*							
Green box	18.8	22.1	18.2	19.2	21.9	21.8	20.7
Blue box	20.8	21.5	20.4	20.5	19.8	22.2	23.7
Current Total AMS	50.2	51.2	50.3	46.9	48.2	43.9	39.4
of which, MPS and EMS	46.6	47.6	47.0	43.6	44.7	40.4	36.1
Total *de minimis*	0.8	0.8	0.5	0.4	0.4	0.5	0.8
Product-specific	—	—	—	0.1	0.1	—	0.2
Non-product-specific	0.8	0.7	0.5	0.3	0.3	0.5	0.6
Total support	90.6	95.6	89.4	87.0	90.3	88.5	84.5
Share of total support %							
Green box	21	23	20	22	24	25	24
Blue box	23	23	23	24	22	25	28
Current Total AMS	55	54	56	54	53	50	47
De minimis	1	1	1	—	—	1	1
Total	100	100	100	100	100	100	100
Value of production (billion euro)	207.4	219.7	217.8	213.5	233.7	243.4	246.4
Bound Total AMS (billion euro)	78.7	76.4	74.1	71.8	69.5	67.2	67.2
CTAMS as share of binding (%)	64	67	68	65	69	65	59

Notes: Small differences in totals are due to rounding. — indicates zero.

[a] The EU notified for the EU15 for years up to 2002/03, the EU25 for the years 2003/04–2005/06 and the EU27 for 2006/07. The shadow notifications are for the EU27. In January 2011, based on the reforms it had undertaken for fruits and vegetables, the EU notified about 8 billion euros less EMS price support in its CTAMS for 2007/08 than included in our shadow notification.

Sources: EC notifications to WTO and authors' calculations.

					Shadow notifications[a]	
2002/03	2003/04	2004/05	2005/06	2006/07	2007/08	2008/09
20.4	22.1	24.4	40.3	56.5	56.0	56.6
24.7	24.8	27.2	13.4	5.7	4.9	4.7
28.6	30.9	31.2	28.4	26.6	24.7	22.1
25.3	27.6	28.1	25.6	25.3	23.6	21.4
1.9	2.0	2.0	1.3	1.9	1.6	1.7
0.9	0.9	1.0	0.2	0.4	0.3	0.3
0.9	1.1	1.1	1.1	1.4	1.2	1.3
75.6	79.7	84.9	83.4	90.7	86.3	85.1
27	28	29	49	64	66	67
33	32	33	16	6	5	5
38	39	37	34	29	28	26
2	2	2	2	2	2	2
100	100	100	100	100	100	100
243.0	267.4	278.7	271.6	294.0	306.5	298.6
67.2	67.2	67.2	67.2	72.2	72.2	72.2
43	46	46	42	37	34	31

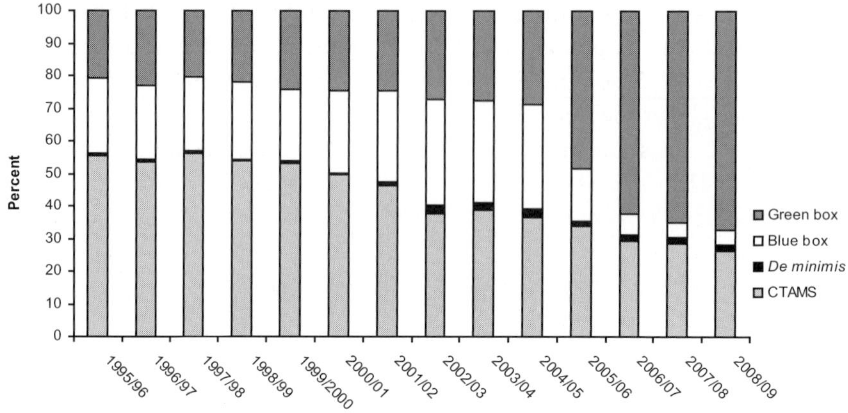

Figure 3.1 EU domestic support notifications and shadow notifications
Sources: EC notifications to WTO and authors' calculations.

to 27 billion euro in 2004/05 but fell sharply to 5.7 billion by 2006/07. Green box payments rose from 19 billion in 1995/96 to 24 billion euro in 2004/05 and to 57 billion euro by 2006/07, suggesting that about 38 billion euro in less trade-distorting payments (green box) has replaced 38 billion euro of more trade-disruptive support (blue and amber boxes). Table 3.1 also shows a shadow notification estimate for the CTAMS of 22.1 billion euro in 2008/09, assuming continuing the trend in the notifications. The blue box estimated notifications for the last two years shows a decline (discussed more fully below) to about 5 billion euro. Anticipated notification of the green box suggests that this has remained at about 57 billion euro as most of the shift in support payments to the green box has already taken place. Total domestic support, including CTAMS, *de minimis*, blue box, and green box has declined somewhat from around 90 billion euro in the period after the Uruguay Round to around 85 billion in 2008/09.[10]

The trends in the various categories of support are clear from Figure 3.1 and the lower half of Table 3.1, which indicate the share of notified support reported in each category. The share of the green box in that total support has increased from 21 percent to 67 percent over the period. The switch from blue box to green box has been accelerating in recent years, with the blue box support falling from 23 percent in 1995/96

[10] The total domestic support calculated here is not to be confused with the OTDS, the indicator under discussion in the Doha negotiations, which excludes green box support.

to just over five percent of total support in 2008/09. Current Total AMS still accounts for 26 percent of EU total support, but this is down from 55 percent in 1995/96. The EU's d*e minimis* AMS support has been very small throughout the period.

Tables 3.2–3.5 show more detail of the EU's domestic support notifications, extended to bring them up to date through 2008/09. The green box category (Table 3.2) contains a mix of programs, ostensibly not triggered by price or output. Over time the most significant components of the green box have been investment aids and general services (including program administration).[11] Environmental and regional aids have expanded, reflecting changing emphases in farm spending. However, the most significant change in the green box is the emergence in the notifications starting in 2005/06 of decoupled income support SPS as a major category of spending. The amount notified was nearly 15 billion euro in 2005/06 and about 31 billion euro in 2006/07. Along with about 2.3 billion euro for the Single Area Payment Scheme (SAPS) that operates in most of the new member countries, this is now the most significant share of the domestic support provided by the EU.

The blue box payments are shown in Table 3.3. The EU notifies the payments that go to crop and livestock producers under schemes where eligibility is limited by hectarage of crops or by headage of livestock. The major items have been the crop and oilseed payments based on land under cultivation at the time of the MacSharry reforms. These payments were originally intended as temporary compensation for the reduction in cereal prices toward world market levels: in practice they have become entitlements converted into the SPS. Premia for beef production made up a large proportion of the livestock blue box payments, again reflecting price adjustments in the MacSharry reform process. The reduction in the blue box payments in 2005/06 and 2006/07 mirrors the growth of decoupled payments (the SPS and SAPS) notified in the green box as described above; the European Commission considers that these direct payments that have successively been incorporated into a total farm package are much less related to the production of particular commodities than the previous compensation payments. Although the EU policy change of 2003 did break to a considerable extent the link with production, some vestiges of production-related payments have still survived. The blue box is not entirely empty.

[11] The EU's domestic food aid is a small fraction of green box spending, in contrast to the US (see Chapter 4). Anton (2009) provides a more detailed account of the EU's green box notifications.

Table 3.2 *Composition of EU green box notifications and shadow notifications, 1995/96–2008/09*

	Notifications					
	1995/96	1996/97	1997/98	1998/99	1999/2000	2000/01
	Million euro					
General services	5,007	6,472	5,523	5,018	5,277	4,743
Public stockholding	—	—	—	19	20	19
Domestic food aid	289	400	295	276	278	270
Decoupled income support (total)	245	221	215	129	958	493
Single Payment Scheme (SPS)	245	221	215	129	958	493
Single Area Payment Scheme (SAPS)	—	—	—	—	—	—
Income insurance	—	—	—	—	—	5
Crop insurance/ disaster relief	329	376	328	183	366	391
Producer retirement	210	948	620	709	793	663
Resource retirement	1,026	1,528	332	428	122	88
Investment aids	6,603	4,972	4,897	5,401	5,745	6,210
Environmental payments	2,783	4,224	3,687	4,965	5,459	5,725
Regional assistance	2,289	2,990	2,271	2,041	2,900	3,239
Total	18,779	22,130	18,167	19,168	21,918	21,847

Note: — indicates zero.
Sources: EC notifications to WTO and authors' calculations.

						Shadow notifications	
2001/02	2002/03	2003/04	2004/05	2005/06	2006/07	2007/08	2008/09
5,636	5,229	5,016	5,717	5,671	6,801	5,687	5,778
18	24	55	32	60	37	42	45
243	278	307	313	328	752	399	419
166	2	9	—	16,671	32,952	33,495	33,692
166	2	9	—	14,734	30,672	31,179	31,361
—	—	—	—	1,937	2,280	2,317	2,331
11	—	9	—	8	13	6	7
399	811	706	406	399	1,157	696	673
802	849	814	800	772	676	782	769
92	110	123	221	112	362	186	201
5,355	5,265	6,822	6,691	7,305	4,534	6,123	6,295
5,519	5,010	5,234	5,420	5,558	5,491	5,343	5,409
2,420	2,826	2,980	3,133	3,397	3,755	3,218	3,297
20,661	20,404	22,074	24,391	40,280	56,530	55,974	56,585

Table 3.3 *Composition of EU blue box notifications and shadow notifications, 1995/96–2008/09*

	Notifications					
	1995/96	1996/97	1997/98	1998/99	1999/2000	2000/01
Crop payments (fixed area and yields)	*Million euro*					
Maize	973	1,223	1,213	1,182	1,159	1,486
Other cereals	8,639	10,001	9,555	9,372	8,842	10,019
Oilseeds	2,381	2,439	2,369	2,264	1,318	1,984
Pulses	523	525	618	647	524	450
Flaxseeds	72	97	129	166	307	113
Set-aside compensation	2,112	1,828	1,251	1,272	1,848	1,527
Durum supplements	948	1,081	1,016	993	1,006	1,074
Voluntary set-aside	—	—	—	—	—	—
Silage	—	—	—	—	—	59
Rice	—	—	41	81	124	113
Seeds	—	—	—	—	—	—
Hops	—	—	—	—	—	—
Grain legumes	—	—	—	—	—	—
Other crops	—	—	—	—	—	—
Single Payment Scheme (SPS)	—	—	—	—	—	—
Total	15,648	17,193	16,191	15,978	15,128	16,825
Livestock payments (fixed number of head)						
Suckler cow premium	2,446	2,043	1,695	1,669	1,628	1,777
Special beef and veal premium	1,407	1,239	1,341	1,297	1,299	1,530
Slaughter premium	—	—	—	—	—	494
Beef supplemental payments	—	—	—	—	—	148
Deseasonalization premium	23	40	45	24	3	—
Ewe and goat premium	1,321	1,007	1,171	1,536	1,734	1,449
Dairy payments	—	—	—	—	—	—
Total	5,197	4,328	4,252	4,526	4,664	5,398
Total	20,846	21,521	20,443	20,504	19,792	22,223

Notes: — indicates zero.

[a] Totals for 2005/06–2007/08 include miscellaneous payments not shown of 129, 162 and 81 million euro respectively.

Sources: EC notifications to WTO and authors' calculations.

						Shadow notifications	
2001/02	2002/03	2003/04	2004/05	2005/06	2006/07	2007/08	2008/09
1,614	1,580	1,198	—	—	—	—	—
10,718	10,184	10,802	—	—	—	—	—
1,846	1,200	1,361	—	—	—	—	—
515	474	507	—	—	—	—	—
91	54	70	—	—	—	—	—
1,893	1,616	1,843	—	—	—	—	—
1,242	912	1,113	1,110	501	138	138	138
38	58	70	—	—	—	—	—
75	74	110	—	—	—	—	—
113	118	—	427	261	174	174	174
—	—	—	109	46	22	22	22
—	—	—	13	3	3	3	3
—	—	—	71	59	—	—	—
—	—	—	70	138	698	1,213	1,213
—	—	—	15,774	7,256	1,851	1,480	1,480
18,144	16,268	17,074	17,573	8,264	2,886	3,030	3,030
1,959	2,226	2,092	2,228	1,320	1,246	1,246	1,246
1,748	1,946	1,929	2,122	826	120	60	—
1,025	1,719	1,727	1,620	517	245	122	—
295	484	489	486	—	—	—	—
—	—	—	—	—	—	—	—
554	2,085	1,471	1,837	942	398	398	398
—	—	—	1,370	1,454	641	—	—
5,582	8,459	7,708	9,663	5,182[a]	2,811[a]	1,907[a]	1,644
23,726	24,727	24,782	27,237	13,445	5,697	4,937	4,674

Table 3.4 *Composition of EU Current Total AMS notifications and shadow notifications, 1995/96–2008/09*

	Notifications					
	1995/96	1996/97	1997/98	1998/99	1999/2000	2000/01
	Million euro					
Market Price Support	33,957	35,074	35,085	34,486	34,139	31,049
Beef	13,962	13,787	13,525	13,375	13,089	11,190
White sugar	5,971	5,896	5,867	5,811	5,758	5,809
Butter	4,210	4,210	4,210	4,210	4,444	4,444
Common wheat	2,593	2,963	2,861	3,091	2,923	2,271
Barley	2,247	2,683	2,703	2,686	2,541	2,195
Skimmed milk powder	1,806	1,660	1,516	1,508	1,371	1,508
Wine	1,706	1,937	1,937	1,828	2,052	807
Olive oil	1,380	1,873	2,268	1,798	2,070	2,070
Maize	786	936	1,045	952	1,003	707
Rice	507	540	511	438	393	393
Other products[b]	495	526	580	617	547	464
EMS	12,603	12,557	11,865	9,073	10,565	9,331
Apples	2,517	2,101	1,953	1,918	2,192	2,249
Tomatoes	4,690	4,880	4,531	2,105	2,518	2,655
Pears	742	595	612	551	603	629
Cucumbers	656	435	611	589	575	539
Other products[c]	2,291	2,608	2,221	2,083	2,625	2,452
Non-exempt direct payments	3,621	3,532	3,395	3,388	3,452	3,529
Tobacco	1,040	1,005	870	910	985	964
Cotton	800	773	809	715	624	795
Other products[d]	1,780	1,754	1,716	1,763	1,844	1,770
Current Total AMS	50,181	51,163	50,346	46,947	48,157	43,909

Notes: — indicates zero.

[a] In a step we did not want to prejudge in the estimation, the EU notification for 2007/08 (in January 2011) eliminated the EMS price support for apples, tomatoes, pears, cucumbers and almost all other products. Therefore our shadow notification value exceeds the notified CTAMS.

[b] Other products include rye, triticale, sorghum, oats and pigmeat.

						Shadow notifications[a]	
2001/02	2002/03	2003/04	2004/05	2005/06	2006/07	2007/08	2008/09
27,986	17,979	19,526	19,645	16,095	15,791	14,486	13,189
9,709	—	—	—	—	—	—	—
5,732	5,604	5,610	6,969	6,674	6,767	5,209	4,734
4,444	4,444	5,012	4,084	4,077	3,581	3,568	3,228
1,237	1,395	1,455	1,842	1,707	1,741	1,839	1,891
1,640	1,633	1,860	2,081	1,800	1,910	2,061	1,901
1,371	1,645	1,602	1,216	996	908	961	954
892	—	—	—	960	875	875	—
2,676	2,123	2,649	2,556	—	—	—	—
380	379	391	500	478	521	568	194
397	406	421	19	—	—	—	—
403	352	527	379	363	363	279	286
8,155	7,361	8,063	8,475	9,476	9,476	9,066	8,237
2,060	2,119	2,625	2,769	2,614	2,652	2,625	2,625
1,944	1,972	1,888	1,643	1,866	2,149	2,041	2,095
543	596	584	659	637	638	584	584
535	593	781	748	720	797	781	781
2,181	2,082	2,184	2,655	2,678	2,365	2,159	2,151
3,250	3,258	3,302	3,095	2,856	1,365	1,127	691
952	950	924	917	811	416	416	416
575	731	769	725	740	—	—	—
1,724	1,577	1,608	1,452	1,305	949	711	275
39,391	28,598	30,891	31,214	28,427	26,632	24,680	22,117

[c] Other products include peaches, table grapes, oranges, artichokes, lemons, and other fresh fruits and vegetables.

[d] Other products include bananas, tomatoes and other fruits and vegetables for processing, and durum wheat supplements.

Sources: EC notifications to WTO and authors' calculations.

Table 3.5 De minimis *exemptions from CTAMS in EU notifications and shadow notifications, 1995/96–2008/09*

	Notifications					
	1995/96	1996/97	1997/98	1998/99	1999/2000	2000/01
	Million euro					
Sum of AMS support (amber box)	51,006	51,925	50,833	47,358	48,550	44,454
Total *de minimis*	825	762	488	411	394	545
Product-specific	49	34	2	63	103	8
Non-product-specific	777	728	486	348	291	538
	5% of total value of production (million euro)					
Non-product-specific threshold	10,370	10,985	10,890	10,675	11,685	12,168

Sources: EC notifications to WTO and authors' calculations.

The Current Total AMS (Table 3.4) includes three main categories of support. The first and principal component is market price support (MPS) for products for which an administered price is applied. The MPS is calculated by multiplying the difference between the administered price and a fixed reference price by the quantity of eligible production. An Equivalent Measurement of Support (EMS) is calculated for those products (mainly fruits and vegetables) where the domestic market is supported but no reference price has been established (due usually to the seasonality of the product) and so where the calculation of MPS is not practicable. A third component is the non-exempt direct payments that do not fall under either the green or blue boxes.[12]

The MPS has been steadily reduced as the various reforms have taken effect. From a peak of 35 billion euro in 1997/98 MPS had fallen to 16 billion euro by 2006/07 and is calculated to have been down to 13 billion by

[12] Producer levies are subtracted from product-specific support, as has been the case for sugar in the EU. This is explicitly allowed under the Agreement and is separate from the question of negative MPS calculations described below.

						Shadow notifications	
2001/02	2002/03	2003/04	2004/05	2005/06	2006/07	2007/08	2008/09
40,155	30,459	32,844	33,257	29,680	28,485	26,245	23,769
764	1,861	1,954	2,043	1,252	1,852	1,565	1,652
190	923	901	956	193	445	332	332
574	938	1,052	1,087	1,059	1,407	1,233	1,320
12,321	12,148	13,369	13,935	13,580	14,701	15,323	14,932

2008/09. The EMS has also fallen though less steeply through 2006/07, as many fresh fruits and vegetables were still protected by price support schemes. Non-exempt direct payments have fallen since 2004/05, as reforms of individual commodities have converted such payments into contributions to the SPS and SAPS budgets. These payments were made per unit of production or per hectare and cover such products as dried fodder, tobacco, bananas and fruits and vegetables for processing. By the time that the reform of each of these commodity programs has been completed the direct payments category within CTAMS will essentially be empty: the shadow notifications estimate a sum of 0.7 billion euro in this category by 2008/09.

The treatment of negative amounts for the MPS and EMS when administered prices are below the reference prices is worthy of note. For durum wheat in all years and for oats in some years, the resulting negative AMS is zeroed-out in the CTAMS calculation. Thus the EU excludes negative AMSs from the definition of CTAMS, an interpretation that is clear and consistent but not always followed by other countries. However, in the case of potatoes for processing to starch, the negative EMS is allowed to offset positive non-exempt direct payments in calculating the product's support. Thus the negative amount does play a role in offsetting positive support for the product from other instruments. Still, also in this case any resulting negative net support is zeroed-out when calculating CTAMS.[13]

Table 3.5 shows the effect of the *de minimis* exemptions in reducing the notified CTAMS. Product-specific *de minimis* was a small component of the EU's AMS notification until 2001/02, when for three years it approached 1 billion euro. The EU indicates in its notification when it claims *de minimis* exemption for product-specific support. It has also notified as non-product-specific support an amount ranging from 291 million euro in 1999/2000 to an estimated 1.3 billion euro in 2008/09. The relatively small amount of support notified as non-product-specific AMS has always been far less than the 5 percent of total value of production allowed as a *de minimis* amount.[14] The table shows the total of all support that is excluded from the CTAMS on these grounds. It is of note that where the product-specific AMS is negative and therefore zeroed out, no claim of *de minimis* is made. These negative amounts are therefore not accounted for in the table as *de minimis* exemptions. In some years the positive non-exempt direct payment for potatoes for processing to starch was large enough to offset the negative EMS for that product: in those years the EU did claim *de minimis* exemption. There have been no cases for that product where the positive support alone would have exceeded the *de minimis* threshold. Only in such cases would the treatment of negative support components become of significance.

For the EU, the level of world prices has had rather little influence on the notified level of domestic support. The base period for determining the Bound Total AMS commitment (1986–88) was a time of low world prices. The low prices were reflected in the level of reference prices that were used to calculate the AMS and EMS for products with price support. As a consequence, base period market price support was relatively high. By 1995, the first year of implementation of the Agreement, the situation on world markets had changed. One might have expected a significant drop in support levels. But the higher world prices were not reflected in the EU's notifications because of the WTO-mandated use of a fixed external reference price when computing levels of MPS. The calculation of the MPS component of AMS (and EMS) from world prices of more than twenty years ago

[13] This differs from using the negative AMS or EMS resulting from negative price support (when administered prices are lower than the reference price for the commodity) as an offset against positive AMSs in other commodities, resulting from price support or other instruments. The EU has not made use of such a questionable tactic.

[14] The two items identified as constituting the non-product-specific AMS are insurance subsidies and interest rate concessions.

illustrates the weakness of these measures as a meaningful reflection of the actual level of support given by administered prices.

Consistency with WTO limits

Under the Agreement, the Bound Total AMS was to be reduced from the 1986–88 Base Total AMS, by 20 percent over the period until the year 2000. The EU (at that time the EU12) declared a Base Total AMS of 73.53 billion euro, which with a 20 percent reduction would have given a bound level in 2000 equal to 58.82 billion euro. However, a credit of 2.38 billion was negotiated as an adjustment for policy changes, and this led to a Final Bound Total AMS (FBTAMS) of 61.20 billion euro being agreed to (see Supporting Table 9a in the EU's base data for 1986–88 in G/AG/AGST/EEC). Enlargement to the EU15 necessitated some further changes. A Bound Total AMS of 78.7 billion euro was calculated as the EU15 limit in the first year of implementation, based on the support levels of the three new members. The revised FBTAMS was fixed at 67.2 billion euro for the EU15. Enlargement to twenty five in 2004 and to twenty seven in 2007 has led to further discussions about the appropriate ceiling commitment for the EU. From 2003/04 to 2004/05 the notifications have been for the EU25, as indicated in a footnote in the EU's submission, even though enlargement took place in the middle of the 2003/04 marketing year.[15] The accession of Romania and Bulgaria in 2007 was reflected in the notification for 2006/07, and the shadow notifications reported in this chapter reflect this change.[16] The EU claimed a FBTAMS for the twenty-seven members of 72.2 billion euro.

The EU has never had any difficulty staying within its scheduled limits, in part because of the high Base Total AMS it recorded and in part as a result of the steady progress of reform, moving away from price support toward direct payments. Figure 3.2 shows the CTAMS in relation to the scheduled limit. In the 2006/07 notification, the CTAMS stood at 26.6 billion euro, and our shadow notification for 2008/09 shows the level

[15] On p. 18 of G/AG/N/EEC/53, the following footnote appears: "This notification covers support to the European Union after enlargement on 1 May 2004. Price gap calculations are performed on EU25 production levels for a twelve-month period and include direct payments to twenty-five member states." It is not clear why the EU chose to make an EU25 declaration for 2003/04, given that accession took place on May 1, 2004.

[16] The corresponding footnote in G/AG/N/EEC/64, notifying the 2006/07 domestic support amounts, indicates that it "covers the EU27 for the full twelve-month period 2006/07" though the accession date was January 1, 2007.

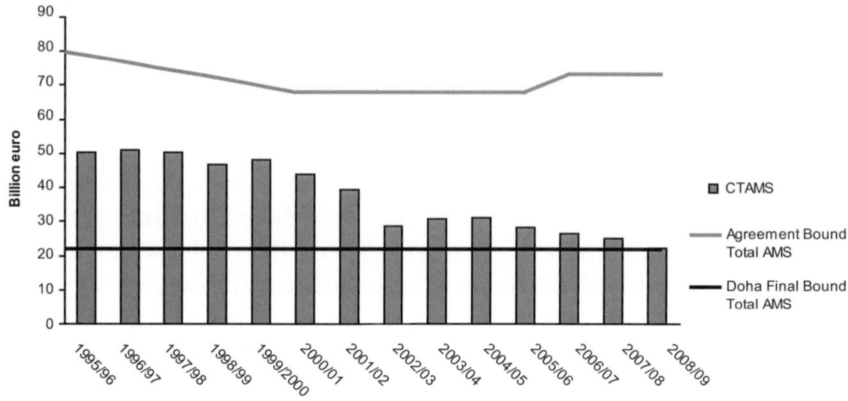

Figure 3.2 EU notifications of CTAMS compared with commitments agreed in the Uruguay Round and proposed in the Doha Round

at 22.1 billion euro without taking the 2007/08 reduction in notified EMS into account. Projected notifications below incorporate the shift and indicate that the level of AMS support may drop marginally further after 2009/10. The situation gives the EU considerable scope for additional support under its commitment or for reductions as part of a Doha agreement. The suggested limit under negotiation in the Doha Round (discussed below) is 21.7 billion euro. Thus, the Doha commitment would have constrained past EU domestic support but the cut required to meet the potential Doha Final Bound Total AMS commitment has already happened.

Policy interpretation of the notifications

The level of domestic support is only one aspect of the degree to which EU agriculture is accorded favorable treatment. Tariffs on agricultural products are generally higher than for non-agricultural goods, and often higher than for many other developed countries for the same product. In addition, export subsidies help to keep up prices of products produced in surplus to domestic requirements. Domestic support (particularly through direct payments) has become more important to maintenance of farm income as tariff levels have declined and export subsidies have been cut back. But to see the implication of this shift, one needs to consider the significance of the particular measurement of support that is notified to the WTO and compare this with other measurements that can and have been used to monitor support to the farm sector.

The EU has changed its policy quite radically since the WTO came into existence, and the path of the notifications of trade-distorting support has been sharply downward. But the linkage between the two is not clear-cut. The amount of MPS notified to the WTO is based on applied administered prices, eligible quantities, and fixed reference prices. As discussed in Chapters 1 and 2, these calculations should not be interpreted as estimates of the level of protection of domestic producers in any one year.

One question that suggests itself in the case of the EU is whether the CTAMS moves broadly in tune with policy reform and liberalization. Does a shift in the AMS for a product (specifically, the MPS component of it that corresponds most closely to the move towards less price support) have any value as a monitoring device? One lesson is that the notified AMS can overstate the impact of policy change. This can arise, for example, as a result of changes in the design of price support policy. The abolition of an applied administered price, even though import protection is still in place, removes the product from the MPS calculation and perhaps even from the CTAMS. The EU's 2003 decision to remove intervention for rye resulted in an elimination of the notified AMS for rye, and one can expect a similar result in the 2009/10 notification for the subsequent decision to eliminate intervention for maize.

Not only is the product-specific AMS incomplete as a measurement of support, the method of calculating the AMS can lead to paradoxical results. For example, buoyant prices for butter and skim milk powder in the late 2000s, pushing above EU support prices, probably encouraged switching of raw milk supplies into these utilizations. This will have increased the EU's current AMS on these products by increasing the eligible quantity, even as price support became redundant of market signals as prices rose. This is because, for milk, the EU declares AMS support based almost exclusively on butter and skim milk powder production, rather than on overall EU milk production, presumably because these were the only dairy products for which intervention prices were set. In other circumstances, however, the benefit of the support of all dairy products does, of course, find its way back to dairy farmers in the price that they receive for milk when market prices are low, regardless of only butter and skim milk powder production entering the AMS.

Most basically, the more plausible indicator of the price advantage given by policy to domestic producers is the MPS calculated by the OECD and reported as one element in the Producer Support Estimate (PSE). The

OECD indicator uses annual, market-based farm-level producer prices, total production levels and year-by-year reference prices generally based on world prices to calculate MPS.[17] To further explore the linkage between the WTO notifications and the development of EU agricultural policy it is instructive to compare the way in which the notified MPS indicator reflects major changes in commodity programs and border protection, as reflected in the OECD measurement.

To make this comparison the MPS as calculated by OECD with annual producer prices, total quantities and annual reference prices were substituted in place of the WTO notified applied administered prices, eligible quantities and fixed reference prices. For two reasons, one would expect the OECD MPS under this calculation to be generally greater than the WTO notification: the producer price includes the impact of border measures and the production can be more than that eligible for support. Only where the OECD's year-to-year reference price is above the fixed reference price would one expect to see the OECD-based indicator below that notified to the WTO.

Figure 3.3 shows the aggregation for those eight commodities that are included in the WTO notifications of MPS and are also recorded in the OECD PSE database from which its MPS is calculated. The eight commodities account for nearly 60 percent of the EU's notified MPS in 1995/96, dropping to about 40 percent in our shadow notifications.[18] For the first part of the period the WTO MPS is considerably above the OECD MPS, especially in 1996 when world agricultural commodity prices were high. The EU notification of MPS shifts sharply from overstating the protection as measured by OECD in the first six years, to understating in the second six years until rising world prices and policy reforms for sugar close the gap for 2006 and 2007.

The cause of the over or understatement in the aggregate support numbers can be assessed by disaggregating the difference into its three

[17] The PSE also differs in other important ways from the WTO domestic support categories. The indicators differ in coverage: the WTO notification covers in principle all of agriculture, whereas the PSE is calculated on the basis of the most significant products and then aggregated up on the assumption that excluded products are afforded the same protection. See OECD (2009) for a discussion of the calculation of PSEs.

[18] The comparisons are for common wheat, durum wheat, barley, maize, oats, rice, sugar and beef. To make the comparisons as compatible as possible the prices were adjusted when necessary to ensure that they were at the same level of product processing as the notified MPS (e.g., processed sugar in both measurements not the farmgate value of sugar beets utilized by OECD).

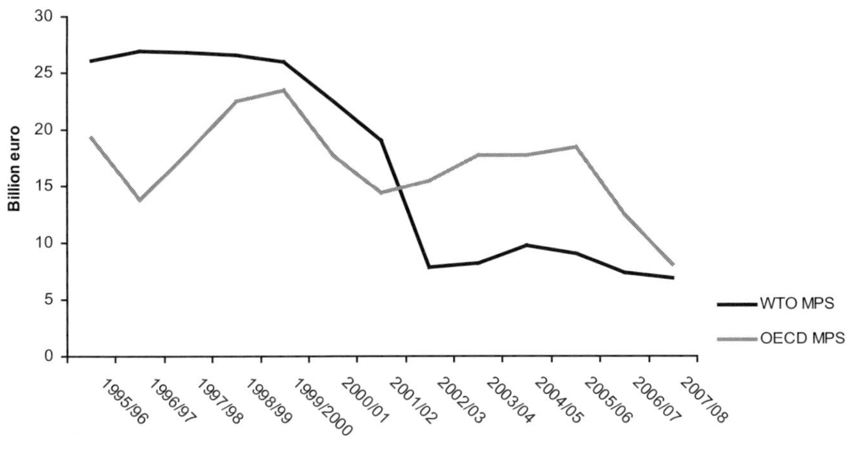

Figure 3.3 EU market price support from notifications and OECD
Source: Authors' calculations based on WTO notifications and OECD statistics.

components: the quantity difference, the reference price difference and the domestic price difference. The use of eligible quantities rather than total production appears to understate protection for the eight commodities in the comparison by only a modest amount. The fixed reference price used in the WTO notification of domestic support, perhaps surprisingly, overstates protection in the EU. The overstatement picks up the fact that the reference prices as used in the WTO calculation (based on the 1986–88 average) have been somewhat lower than the corresponding annual international prices, showing a larger price gap from which to calculate the MPS. But the major discrepancy between the two indicators arises from the use of the administered price rather than the producer price. Surprisingly, use of the administered price often overstates the MPS in the EU, and the discrepancy is significantly greater in the first half of the time period. It is apparent that the relationship between the administered price and the producer price is a key element in understanding the linkage between changes in notified MPS and the economic price support provided through domestic policy and border protection.

The aggregate numbers reflect the underlying commodity calculations. For common wheat the administered price (the intervention price) is above the producer price for the first part of the period, reflecting the fact that the intervention price was not totally effective as a floor price. But continued CAP reform cuts the intervention price and for a time it is lower than the producer price. The use of eligible quantity in the WTO MPS does not cause any divergence, as the whole of wheat production is notified as eligible for intervention. However, the fixed reference price, set at 1986–88 levels, was considerably lower than the annual reference prices, accounting for the main part of the overstatement of MPS in the WTO notifications compared to OECD's measure. Similar situations are noticeable in the cases of durum wheat and barley, though in the case of oats the (common cereals) intervention price is lower than the producer price over much of the period, and for maize the producer price stays well above the intervention price, supported by border measures.

A change in the administered price for rice in 2003/04 (a halving of the intervention price) shows up in the WTO MPS but the producer price drops by much less. The explanation is in the maintenance of border protection that keeps the market price above administered price levels. In this case, the fixed reference price understated the world market price over the period until 2003, while the WTO MPS in the last five years has matched the annual indication of the level of protection for this product. Sugar accounts for about 20 percent of the notified MPS shown in Figure 3.3 and somewhat exceeds the OECD MPS in most years. After 2005, the WTO and OECD MPS for sugar fell markedly as administered and producer prices came down, but the OECD measure fell further as world prices also strengthened.

For beef, the reform of 2000 shows up clearly as a drop in the intervention price: the policy change was to introduce a true (low) safety net and avoid the problem of having to buy up beef into intervention when demand was in any case weak. The impact on the WTO MPS is dramatic: as the intervention price falls below the fixed reference price the price support for beef turns negative. The producer price does not drop at that time, and indeed increases after the reform. In the case of sheepmeat (not included in the comparison shown in Figure 3.3) the EU ceased to notify an administered price from 1998 as a reflection of the decision not to intervene in that market.

This comparison of the WTO MPS with an alternative indicator that takes into account the producer price and the annual level of world prices demonstrates the care needed to evaluate the domestic support notifications. They do pick up changes in policy prices. But they do not reflect the change in the market price, which is more relevant for looking at the trade impact of EU policies. Nor do they keep up with trends in world market price conditions. Some readjustment of the method of calculating of this measure may soon be in order.

Alternative notifications

So far the discussion has mostly assumed that there is no ambiguity with respect to the allocation of the elements of domestic support into the categories (boxes) of the Agreement. Such ambiguity does exist, and can be potentially important in the context of domestic and trade policy. By estimating alternative notifications, it is possible to see the range of ambiguity that exists and hence the scope for governments to claim compliance with WTO constraints on dubious grounds. Such alternative notifications are also useful to illustrate possible results of WTO panel recommendations or the outcome of negotiations.

The main issue that has been raised with respect to the reform of the CAP and the EU's WTO notifications has revolved around the direct payments, and more specifically the incorporation of these into a single farm payment under the SPS. The payments per hectare that were introduced in the MacSharry reforms were notified as blue box because they were limited to historic hectarage eligibilities and based on regional yields. In addition, they were not linked to prices. But the SPS introduced in the Fischler reforms of 2003 was in part intended to move subsidies into the green box, to avoid the constraints imposed on the blue box (by its definition) and the CTAMS (by the ceiling commitment). So the question arises whether the placement of the SPS expenditure in the green box is likely to be controversial.

Several commentators have addressed this issue. McMahon (2007), Swinbank (2008) and Swinbank and Tranter (2005) raise questions about the extent to which the payments under the SPS are compatible with the green box. They point out that the reforms to the fruit and vegetables regime, making land on which fruit and vegetables are grown eligible for SPS payments, has overcome the problem the United States encountered in the WTO upland cotton case.[19] But as annual payments are still made to farmers on the basis of the land at their disposal, and cross-compliance

[19] In that case, the WTO panel concluded that cotton (and other program crop) payments were not compatible with the green box as they were not completely divorced from production, as land could not move to fruits and vegetables (see Chapters 2 and 4 for further discussion).

Table 3.6 *Impact of different assumptions about SPS and SAPS direct payments for EU 2008/09 notification*

Notification category of SPS and SAPS direct payments	Shadow notification for 2008/09		
	CTAMS	Blue box	Green box
	Billion euro		
All in the green box	22.1	3.2	58.1
All in the blue box	22.1	38.4	22.9
All as non-product-specific AMS	58.6	3.2	22.9

Source: Authors' calculations.

applies, the authors raise the question of whether the SPS does fully meet the criteria of paragraph 6 for the green box.[20]

Table 3.6 shows the range of possible notifications under different decisions with respect to the appropriate categorization of the EU's SPS and SAPS direct payments using our 2008/09 notification. With these payments (shown in Tables 3.2 and 3.3) placed completely in the green box, that box would be expected to have reached over 58 billion euro in 2008/09. If, however, all such payments had to be notified as blue box, that box would exceed 38 billion euro. If the direct payments were to be considered as neither green nor blue box compatible (an unlikely event), then the CTAMS would rise to around 58 billion euro, depending on the payments being all product-specific or all non-product-specific AMS.

Given the EU's commitment under the Agreement, the impact of different notification assumptions is not great. The constraint of 72.2 billion euro for the CTAMS is not approached, and neither the blue nor green boxes are limited.[21] However, the situation would be drastically changed if the Doha Round were to be completed. In all cases except where the direct payments are notified in the green box (where no limit exists), the

[20] Moreover, they suggest that the EU's contention that the SPS is a decoupled payment would not be enhanced in any dispute settlement case by statements from senior members of the EU's policy community suggesting they do affect production (See, for example, Agra Europe's report on the European Parliament's opposition to a 20 percent voluntary rate of modulation, because of fear of distortion of competition between the member states; March 9, 2007: EP/1–2).

[21] Inclusion in the blue box of new or modified subsidies, however, could be challenged, but these subsidies could be transferred to AMS without violating the CTAMS limit.

WTO constraints under a fully phased in Doha agreement would be violated by the support we estimate for the year 2008/09. Indeed, the level of SPS and SAPS direct payments alone would exhaust the limit for OTDS, discussed below, leaving all other support to be eliminated or changed to green box compatible payments.

For a number of years the EU has encouraged the use of biomass for renewable energy production, and of biofuel (liquid or gas) in transport. In 2009 it determined new targets: that across the EU 20 percent of all energy supplies should come from renewable resources by 2020, and that by the same date, in each member state, 10 percent of transport fuel should be derived from renewables (in practice this will largely be biofuel).[22] Member states can grant investment subsidies for on-farm investments in bioenergy under the so-called Second Pillar of the CAP (anaerobic digesters, establishment grants for planting *Miscanthus*, etc.) and these, we believe, are notified to the WTO as green box payments. The Fischler reforms of 2003 introduced an area payment on energy crops, although this was abolished by the Health Check in 2008. This subsidy has been reported in the blue box.

The main schemes to encourage the up-take of biomass for energy purposes, however, are not reported by the EU as agricultural subsidies. The member states devise their own schemes to achieve the EU mandates. In the United Kingdom, for example, electricity suppliers must source a specified proportion of their supplies from renewable sources or pay a penalty (the "buy-out" price), creating a financial incentive (borne by the consumer) to generate electricity from renewable sources. For road transport, a lower road-fuel tax applies on biofuels in the UK, and in addition a Renewable Transport Fuel Obligation applies. Thus both users and taxpayers are supporting the uptake of biofuel. Swinbank (2009), whilst broadly of the view that these schemes are *not* notifiable under the Agreement, concluded that if the EU's biofuel support had to be declared as amber box support then it could account for about 16 percent of the EU's ceiling on CTAMS. Clearly, if new Doha constraints were to apply, and the EU had to declare its support for biofuels, this could be a serious challenge.

[22] Directive 2009/28/EC of the European Parliament and of the Council of 23 April 2009 on the promotion of the use of energy from renewable sources and amending and subsequently repealing Directives 2001/77/EC and 2003/30/EC, *Official Journal of the European Union*, L140, 5 June 2009. Debate has continued about the levels of biofuel mandates since that time.

Doha and projected domestic support notifications, 2009/10–2015/16

In addressing the question of the significance of a Doha agreement that further restrains domestic support it is necessary to supplement the shadow notifications by projecting these notifications into the future. Such projections require that one make assumptions about policy decisions over the next half decade. In addition, one has to make assumptions about the membership of the EU in the future, and about its budget decisions. Production levels for the calculation of the market price support component of the AMS (and EMS) also need to be projected.[23] Projections of support can then be calculated and compared to the EU commitment under the existing Agreement and under the possible constraints of a Doha agreement.

With respect to policy assumptions, one might expect a reasonably stable trajectory in the CAP for the next few years. Discussions of policy change are already under way in the context of the next financial perspective, to be agreed by 2013. The Health Check initiated by the European Commission (2007) and agreed by the EU Ministers introduced a further movement toward decoupling in the interim. Though political events could still hamper reform, financial restraints are likely to be the main driver of future policy. The shadow notifications discussed above for the period up to 2008/09 already indicate the substantial shift of support into the green box as member countries moved fully toward decoupled payments. The assumption has been made that future policy developments involve a continuation of these expenditures.

On the issue of enlargement, Croatia and Macedonia, together with Iceland, could conceivably join in a few years if they are deemed to have adequate internal infrastructure to administer the EU policies and are deemed strong enough to participate in the single market.[24] Adjustments to the Bound Total AMS and the support levels of the EU would be small as a result of the accession of these three countries. Of much more potential significance is the possibility of Turkish membership. Turkey is a large country with a substantial agricultural sector. The adjustments to the WTO notification of domestic support would be of significance, but there would undoubtedly have to be some significant policy adaptations

[23] Although prices in world agricultural commodity markets and global macroeconomic conditions (particularly as they affect exchange rates) are also relevant to the policy environment, as indicated earlier the use of fixed reference prices effectively insulates the EU's AMS from these factors.

[24] Other parts of the former Yugoslavia are less likely to be considered for accession within the six-year time frame used here.

and a possibly lengthy transition period. Given the political sensitivity of Turkish membership, we have chosen to make the assumption that it will not happen in the period up to 2016.

In the absence of a Doha agreement the present domestic support limit will continue to apply to the EU. As the CTAMS is not projected to rise, there should be no risk of the limit being breached. However, the Doha negotiations include in the December 2008 draft modalities a number of changes to the Agreement that would have an impact on the constraints on EU policy from WTO obligations. In order to examine the impact of these changes on future notifications, we assume that new WTO support commitments are implemented over the period 2010/11–2014/15, so that all new reductions and bindings apply fully by the notification year 2015/16.

The EU would fall into the first tier of countries in terms of cuts from the Base OTDS and Final Bound Total AMS being proposed in Doha (see Table 2.2). The implications for the EU commitments and allowances of these and other Doha proposals in the December 2008 draft modalities are summarized in Table 3.7.[25] The Base OTDS, from which reductions would be measured, would be 110.3 billion euro for the EU15. Thus the level for the Final Bound OTDS would be 22.1 billion euro given the 80 percent reduction under consideration at that time. The Final Bound Total AMS would be reduced by 70 percent from the pre-Doha level of 67.2 billion euro to 20.1 billion euro; a blue box limit of 5.6 billion euro would be introduced; and the *de minimis* allowances would be reduced to 2.5 percent of the production values. Limits on OTDS and CTAMS would be phased in, while the blue box and *de minimis* constraints would apply immediately. In addition to the constraints on OTDS, CTAMS and overall blue box support, the draft modalities also propose restrictions on product-specific AMS and blue box amounts. The draft suggests caps on product-specific AMS support at the 1995–2000 levels.[26]

The enlargement of the EU, from fifteen countries when the Agreement came into effect in 1995 to twenty-seven countries in 2007, poses some unique problems for the interpretation of EU domestic support notifications and the projection of notifications under a possible Doha agreement. The main consequence of enlargement for domestic support constraints

[25] For a discussion of the impact of the mid-year 2008 Doha draft modalities on market access and export competition, as well as the levels of allowable EU domestic support, see Jean, Josling and Laborde (2008). Bureau and Gohin (2009) provide an assessment of the effects of the EU's domestic support and border policies internally and on world markets.

[26] Some flexibility is included in those cases where the AMS for a product has recently been higher than in the base period.

Table 3.7 *OTDS, CTAMS and blue box support limits and the* de minimis *allowance for the EU under the Doha draft modalities*

	EU15		EU 27	
	Million euro			
Final Bound Total AMS		67,159		72,244
Value of Production (average 1995–2000)	222,577		259,269	
10 percent value of production		22,258		25,927
5 percent value of production	11,129		12,963	
Blue box (as it is in excess of 5 percent value of production)[a]		20,888		20,888
Base OTDS		110,305		119,059
Final Bound OTDS (after 80 percent reduction)		22,061		23,812
Final Bound Total AMS (after 70 percent reduction)		20,148		21,673
FBTAMS as share of value of production (1995–2000)[b]		21.8%		18.7%
Blue box limit				
2.5 percent value of production (average 1995–2000)		5,564		6,482
Blue box relative to trade-distorting support (average 1995–2000)[c]		30.1%		30.1%
De minimis				
50 percent immediate reduction		2.5%		2.5%

Notes: See Table 2.2 and Appendix B regarding all notes.

[a] Paragraph 1(c) condition: picks up blue box when above 5 percent of production value.

[b] Tests for application of paragraph 14: less than 40 percent so additional effort does not apply.

[c] Tests for paragraph 39: less than 40 percent so special rule for blue box limit does not apply nor phased reduction allowed.

Source: Authors' calculations based on WTO (2008).

involves the nature of the aggregation of the WTO limits. Most of the twelve new members that have joined the EU since 1995 have themselves notified support under the Agreement.[27] The EU chose to add the FBTAMS

[27] The ten new members that joined the EU in May 2004 were the Czech Republic, Estonia, Cyprus, Latvia, Lithuania, Hungary, Malta, Poland, Slovenia, and Slovakia. Romania and

limits of the new members to the EU15 limit of 67.2 billion euro to report its new limit of 72.2 billion euro to the WTO Committee on Agriculture for 2006/07 (G/AG/R/53). This represented an increase of 4.9 billion euro. Butault and Bureau (2006) estimate that these countries had domestic support expenditures in 2001 of about 1.5 billion euro. If there is no conclusion to the Doha negotiations, it seems unlikely that other countries will find it worthwhile to examine and challenge the change in the WTO commitment of the EU as a result of enlargement: the EU Current Total AMS for the EU27 is still likely to be well below the ceiling used for the EU15. But the change in the FBTAMS due to enlargement would seem to add to the flexibility of the EU in meeting any more stringent obligations that might come from a Doha agreement. The impact will also depend on how the Base OTDS for the EU27 is calculated. The base calculations for the EU27 are also shown in Table 3.7, implying a Final Bound OTDS of 23.8 billion euro and a Final Bound Total AMS of 21.7 billion euro. Table 3.8 shows the phase-in of these limits for the EU27. However it should be noted that the determination of the precise reduction commitments for an EU that includes twelve countries that did not fall into the top tier of domestic support levels in the base period (and in some cases were not even WTO members) requires a political rather than a statistical decision.

Table 3.9 shows the projected levels of EU27 support under the various categories for the period to 2015/16. The decoupled income payments and other expenditures under the green box are assumed to stay at the 2008/09 level which could prove an underestimate. Trade-distorting support, taking into account the elimination of EMS price support in the EU's 2007/08 notification, is likely to decrease slightly further as the transition arrangements for certain commodity programs continue. The projections suggest that the OTDS will fall somewhat from the estimated level of 19 billion euro for 2009/10 to 17 billion euro in the year 2015/16. The CTAMS is likely to decline modestly as some administered prices are changed, including the elimination of intervention for minor cereals. No changes in the blue box subsidies are envisaged; these continue to reflect the low levels of support associated with production limiting programs that resulted from the reforms of 2003 and the Health Check. No change in the amounts of the *de minimis* support is foreseen.

Bulgaria joined in 2007. Of these twelve new members, four countries (Estonia, Lithuania, Malta, and Romania) had FBTAMS ceilings at zero (Butault and Bureau, 2006). Poland, Hungary, and the Czech Republic had significant FBTAMS ceilings. Hungary was able to modify its own FBTAMS ceiling to account for inflation before that amount was added to the EU limit.

Table 3.8 *Phased reductions of limits on OTDS and CTAMS for the EU27 under the Doha draft modalities*

	Immediate	Year 1	Year 2	Year 3	Year 4	Year 5 (Final)
Reduction commitments	*Cumulative proportions of the base to be cut*					
Base OTDS[a]	0.33	0.42	0.52	0.61	0.71	0.80
Final Bound Total AMS[b]	0.25	0.34	0.43	0.52	0.61	0.70
Scheduled limits[c]	*Million euro*					
Bound OTDS	79,373	68,260	57,148	46,036	34,924	23,812
Final Bound Total AMS	54,183	47,681	41,179	34,677	28,175	21,673

[a] Initial reduction of one-third, with remainder phased-in in five equal steps (Table 2.2 and Appendix B, paragraph 5).
[b] Initial reduction of 25 percent, with remainder phased-in in five equal steps (Table 2.2 and Appendix B, paragraph 15).
[c] Limit applies after reduction at end of year in corresponding column is made.
Source: Authors' interpretation based on WTO (2008).

Table 3.9 *Projected levels of EU27 domestic support, 2009/10–2015/16*

	2009/10	2010/11	2011/12	2012/13	2013/14	2014/15	2015/16
	Billion euro						
Green box	56.8	56.8	56.7	56.6	56.7	56.7	56.7
OTDS	19.4	17.2	17.3	17.0	17.1	17.2	17.2
Blue box	4.7	4.7	4.7	4.7	4.7	4.7	4.7
Current Total AMS	13.1	10.9	11.0	10.7	10.8	10.9	10.9
Total *de minimis*	1.6	1.6	1.6	1.6	1.6	1.6	1.6
Total support	76.2	74.0	74.0	73.6	73.8	73.9	73.9

Note: Projections include an adjustment for the decline in notified EMS price support for 2007/08.
Source: Authors' calculations.

From our shadow notifications and projections and assessment of the EU's Doha commitments the OTDS limit would appear to have been binding in 2015/16 without the decline in EMS support notified for 2007/08 in January 2011. Following that decline, the projected level of support is around 7 billion euro below the OTDS limit. A Doha commitment would reinforce the downward movement the EU has undertaken in reducing notified CTAMS as CAP reforms have been implemented, but would not constrain the EU beyond decisions taken in advance of an agreement. There is even more flexibility available for CTAMS by the year 2015/16. With EMS eliminted, the projected CTAMS is about 11 billion euro below the Doha commitment level of 21.7 billion euro. This again leaves room under the potential Doha commitment for some re-expansion of trade-distorting support. But the EU shows no inclination to revert to past forms of price support nor to expand its subsidies provided through non-exempt direct payments that would be notified in CTAMS. The year 2013 is the start of a new budgetary cycle in the EU, at which time the funding for the CAP could well be trimmed for internal reasons.

The main pressure from the Doha rules might be on the elements of AMS support where product-specific caps could prove constraining for some commodities. Given our projections, natural variations in the level of eligible production for products where MPS continues to be calculated could well lead to product-specific AMS limits being violated in some years. Some reduction of MPS would seem to be required. Obviously, an update of the fixed reference prices could lower the MPS, but changes in reference prices were not envisaged in the Agreement and have not been under discussion in the Doha Round. Administered prices could be lowered, though the effect of this may depend on the parallel reductions in tariffs. Reductions in the product-specific MPS (and hence the AMS) can also be made in a relatively easy way by limiting the production eligible for support buying.

Although the aggregate blue box limit does not appear binding on projected EU expenditures, blue box limits at a product-specific level are likely to have some impact. Though the total blue box spending may be decreasing as payments move to the green box, those for individual products cannot increase to make use of that slack. So the product-specific limit could become binding in some cases, though the overall binding is unlikely to be relevant as a policy constraint. As blue box payments are tied to fixed yield, areas, and head of livestock, the restriction implies no possibility of any rebasing of such payments.

Taken together, these results should be interpreted as an indication that, while the EU has largely moved its support measures in a direction consistent with the constraints that would be introduced by the Doha draft modalities, a Doha agreement would have at least some additional effects on EU policy. In order to stay within the new limits, the EU has to ensure that direct payments can continue to be notified as green box without being challenged by other countries. Notified MPS support and blue box payments will have to be kept essentially at or below their present levels in order to meet the product-specific limits implied by the Doha draft modalities. However, the control of the level of domestic support is within the hands of the EU: unlike the situation in the US (see the following chapter) relatively little of the support provided to farmers in the EU is subject to increases if market prices fall.

Summary and conclusions

The EU has provided the highest absolute level of trade-distorting domestic support among WTO members to its agricultural sector. As a result, both the current policy environment and the possible changes under further reforms are of widespread interest. The Agreement was negotiated to bring restraints on policies such as the EU's CAP and can in part be judged by whether these restraints have been effective. The process of monitoring domestic support should reflect the policy changes that have come about as a result of the adoption of the Agreement. EU notifications were available through the marketing year 2006/07, and the evaluation of policy change can be based on these notifications. The extension of these notifications through 2008/09 is undertaken in this chapter to continue to trace the trends in policy from earlier in the decade.

The level of all of the support notified for agriculture in the EU has been reduced by 2008/09 from around 91 billion euro in the mid 1990s, and the composition of this support and its classification under the Agreement has changed rapidly with domestic policy reform. The progress of that reform shows up clearly in the notifications. The CTAMS, particularly its MPS component, has declined over the years as price support levels have come down. The shift toward direct payments shows up clearly, particularly for the marketing years 2004/05 and 2006/07 when the SPS was introduced and stabilized. The initial SPS payments under the 2003 reform of the CAP were notified in the blue box, but subsequently were shifted increasingly to the green box. The later SPS payments are not tied to the production of particular commodities, nor do they vary with commodity prices; they are therefore *prima facie* eligible for the green box, and therefore unrestricted. These payments amounted to about 31 billion euro in 2006/07. Shifting to payments that meet the criteria of the blue box and green box has freed up the CAP from immediate restraint on CTAMS by the domestic support provisions of the Agreement. Our shadow notifications, and subsequent EU notifications bring the story further up-to-date. The switch in support away from the most trade-distorting categories towards those deemed to be non- or minimally-distorting is reflected in these notifications. Projections beyond 2008/09 show a continuation of the pattern though 2015/16 as most of the major sectors have been reformed and as payments have been progressively decoupled from production and prices. In large part the shift in the composition of support has reflected real policy changes rather than simply the manipulation of policy instruments to take advantage of the method of calculation. The caveat we have shown is that the decline in notified MPS and CTAMS since 1994/95 overstates the decline in economic price support for commodities with administered prices.

The conclusion of the Doha Round would have the effect of locking in the reforms that have occurred through international disciplines. Under the proposed regime in the December 2008 draft modalities, if implementation started in 2010/11, the limits on OTDS and CTAMS by 2015/16 leave the EU without the flexibility to provide the amounts of trade-distorting support that the CAP provided in the past. The EU would have to maintain the shift of support to the green box. Given the pressures to limit spending under the new budget decisions after 2013 some further budget reductions are possible. In addition, one might expect some degree of shifting of expenditures on aspects of farm and rural policy back to the member states. Though this in itself does not reduce the domestic support, the end result could be increased spending on such initiatives as rural infrastructure and non-farm employment generation that fall outside the Agreement on Agriculture. Whether these developments will be delayed if the Doha Round is abandoned is debatable. But the conclusion of Doha would certainly mark a decisive point in the long story of the development of international rules to constrain domestic farm policies in the EU.

References

Anderson, K. (ed.) 2009. *Distortions to Agricultural Incentives: A Global Perspective 1955–2007.* London: Palgrave Macmillan, and Washington, DC: World Bank.

Anton, J. 2009. An Analysis of EU, US and Japanese green box spending. In *Agricultural Subsidies in the WTO Green Box: Ensuring Coherence with Sustainable Development Goals,* ed. R Meléndez-Ortiz, C. Bellman, and J. Hepburn. Cambridge University Press.

Bureau, J. C., and A. Gohin. 2009. Farm support policies in the European Union: An appraisal of their non-distortionary effects. In *Non-distorting Farm Support to Enhance Global Food Production,* ed. A. Elbehri and A. Sarris. Rome: FAO.

Butault, J. P., and J. C. Bureau. 2006. WTO constraints and the CAP: Domestic support in EU 25 agriculture. IIIS Discussion Paper 17, Trinity College, Dublin.

European Commission. 2007. Implementation of the CAP reform in the Member States. http://ec.europa.eu/agriculture/markets/sfp/index_en.htm#capinfosheets (accessed March 23, 2008).

Jean, S., T. Josling, and D. Laborde. 2008. Implications for the European Union. ICTSD/IPC/IFPRI Project on Draft Agricultural Modalities. Paper presented at a seminar in Geneva, March 12.

Josling, T. 2009. EU15 and EFTA. In *Distortions to Agricultural Incentives: A Global Perspective 1955–2007,* ed. K. Anderson. London: Palgrave Macmillan, and Washington, DC: World Bank.

Josling, T., and A. Swinbank. 2008. European Union: Shadow WTO agricultural domestic support notifications. IFPRI Discussion Paper 809.

McMahon, J. A. 2007. Trade policy reform through litigation. *EuroChoices* 6(2): 42–47.

OECD. 2009. *Agricultural Policies in OECD Countries: Monitoring and Evaluation.* Paris.

Swinbank, A., 2008. Potential WTO challenges to the CAP. *Canadian Journal of Agricultural Economics* 56(4): 445–456.

Swinbank, A., and R. Tranter. 2005. Decoupling EU farm support: Does the new single payment scheme fit within the green box? *The Estey Centre Journal of International Law and Trade Policy* 6(1): 47–61.

2009. EU Support for biofuels and bioenergy, environmental sustainability criteria, and trade policy. Issue Paper 17, ICTSD Program on Agricultural Trade and Sustainable Development.

Swinnen, J. F. M. (ed.) 2008. *The Perfect Storm: The Political Economy of the Fischler Reforms of the Common Agricultural Policy.* Brussels: Centre for European Policy Studies.

Swinnen, J. F. M. 2009. The growth of agricultural protection in Europe in the 19th and 20th centuries. *The World Economy* 32(11): 1499–1537.

WTO. 1994. *Results of the Uruguay Round of Multilateral Trade Negotiations: The Legal Texts.* Geneva.

2008. Revised draft modalities for agriculture. TN/AG/W/4/Rev.4, 6 December.

4

United States

DAVID BLANDFORD AND DAVID ORDEN

Domestic support for agriculture by the United States has proven to be contentious in the World Trade Organization and a center of attention in the Doha negotiations. The United States signaled its willingness to accept tighter disciplines on domestic support but insisted on a harmonization of support levels, in effect reducing allowable domestic support in the EU by a greater amount. The US position has also been to require significantly increased market access in other countries, including the emerging markets. In addition to the tension over the level of US domestic support in the Doha Round, several challenges under the WTO dispute settlement process have raised questions about whether the United States is correctly notifying its support to the WTO. Even without a Doha Round outcome, US domestic farm programs will be the subject of international scrutiny.

The first part of this chapter provides a brief review of the political economy of US farm policies, including a synopsis of the Food, Conservation, and Energy (FCE) Act of 2008. The following section discusses US domestic support notifications from 1995–2008. We then assess compliance with the Agreement, including an examination of subsidies that arguably are misclassified, underreported, or omitted from the notifications. The following section provides projections of US support through 2016. These projections are compared to existing support commitments and those proposed in the December 2008 Doha draft modalities. The final section of the chapter provides a summary and conclusions, including a discussion of options for future US policy under tighter WTO constraints.

Helpful comments and suggestions are acknowledged from Anne Effland, David Laborde, Will Martin, Larry Saunders, Randy Schnepf, Bob Young, Ed Young, and Carl Zulauf. Tim Josling was instrumental in the development of the Blandford–Josling WTO simulator used to evaluate projected US subsidies under potential Doha constraints. We thank, in particular, Lars Brink for many constructive comments.

Domestic support in the US

Agriculture in the United States today scarcely resembles the troubled sector of the Depression-era 1930s that led to the introduction of farm support programs. Structural change has created a trimodal farm sector. At one end of the spectrum are highly efficient commercial farms producing the bulk of the nation's food and fiber. At the other end are small farms that account for most of the enumerated units but only a small share of total output. In the middle are a group of farmers caught up in the dynamics of agricultural modernization.[1]

As an exporter of primary agricultural products, the US has maintained a relatively open market. Tariffs on agricultural imports are generally low (with a few exceptions, notably dairy products and sugar) and have been stable, with limited cuts to meet WTO commitments (Blandford, Laborde, and Martin 2008). However, the situation has been more fluid in the domestic support arena due to substantial changes in policy measures since the Agreement on Agriculture came into effect. Annual acreage set-aside to limit supplies, a cornerstone of farm programs since the 1950s, was abandoned in 1996 and was not resurrected during a subsequent period of low commodity prices. Deficiency payments, providing support from the federal government budget and tied to prices and the production of specific crops, were replaced in 1996 by fixed direct payments, decoupled from any direct link to market conditions and current production decisions. Public stockholding and export subsidies to dispose of surpluses have almost disappeared; binding production quotas for peanuts and the entire tobacco price support program have been eliminated with compensatory (buyout) payments being made to producers.

There has also been some reversion in the last decade to subsidies tied to prices or production. Deficiency payments linked to market prices (but less closely than before to planted acreage) were reintroduced in 2002. Biofuel mandates and subsidies have emerged as an influential aspect of US policy in light of the terrorist attacks of September 11, 2001, higher oil prices, and growing environmental concerns about climate change. With agriculture's new battle cry of "food, fiber and fuel" the demand-augmenting and price-stimulating effects of biofuel policies have added a new twist to the debate about the impact of US subsidies on world markets. When grain prices rose rapidly in 2008, concerns not voiced since

[1] The transformation of American agriculture in the twentieth century and the evolution of US farm policy are well described by Gardner (2002 and 2009).

the 1970s were raised against a policy of long-term, subsidized idling of millions of acres of farmland for supply control and environmental purposes under the Conservation Reserve Program (CRP). Biofuel subsidies and mandates subsequently have come under increased scrutiny in terms of their effects on world food prices.

Throughout these various policy changes, the ability of the powerful US farm lobby to command support in the political arena has been evident. Under the FCE Act of 2008, farmers retain a stream of fixed direct payments until 2012 despite back-to-back years of record net farm income in 2007 and 2008. The more trade-distorting price support and countercyclical income support programs were also extended. In addition, the 2008 legislation included an Average Crop Revenue Election (ACRE) revenue-guarantee program under which payments could be substantial in an era of volatile prices. Agriculture also has strengthened its ability to influence agricultural prices through energy policy. The farm sector remains well positioned to receive support in the event of a wide range of contingencies.

US farm policy since the Agreement

Policy measures in the US have evolved over time with direct government payments emerging in the 1980s as a key instrument to compensate farmers for lower support prices. Reforms adopted in the 1996 Federal Agriculture Improvement and Reform (FAIR) Act included a decoupling of payments on eligible base acres from market prices and crop planting decisions, an end to annual acreage reduction (set-aside) programs (ARPs), and the capping of price-support loan rates at low levels.[2] One key factor that drove the FAIR Act reforms was a sharp rise in commodity prices in late 1995 (Orden, Paarlberg, and Roe 1999). As market prices rose above the target prices that triggered payments under the 1990 farm bill, decoupling from prices became a plausible option. In contrast, the Agreement on Agriculture had a minimal impact on the mix of policies

[2] The term "base acreage" refers to the acreage on which payment eligibility is determined; "deficiency payments" refer to subsidies provided on a fixed amount of base-acre output when market prices are below a legislated "target price," and "loan rates" refer to price guarantees for all output of eligible commodities. The 1985 and 1990 farm bills provided limited flexibility for farmers to reallocate part of their base acreage among crops without losing payment eligibility, but deficiency payments were suspended on that acreage if alternative crops were grown. Loan-rate price guarantees can be secured in several ways, resulting in several corresponding loan-rate program benefits, as shown in Table 4.3.

adopted in 1996. Meeting the US commitments under the Agreement required few policy changes and no reductions in the level of support beyond that already undertaken in the 1985 and 1990 farm bills. The main change in the FAIR Act, as Josling, Tangermann, and Warley (1996) observe, was from one non-limited category of farm support to another – from deficiency payments notified in the blue box to fixed direct payments notified in the green box.

In 1995 both short-term and structural factors were viewed as evidence that agricultural prices would remain high throughout the decade. When this scenario proved erroneous and prices fell, calls arose for the virtual rewriting of farm policy to restore the traditional safety net. Supplemental crop market loss assistance (MLA) payments and various disaster relief payments were enacted between 1998 and 2001 and this led the farm lobby to seek a new farm bill a year before the FAIR Act was scheduled to expire.

The Farm Security and Rural Investment (FSRI) Act, signed into law in May 2002, continued fixed direct payments and extended these to soybeans and other oilseeds. The crop market-loss payments that had been appropriated annually were converted into mandatory countercyclical payments (CCPs) tied to market prices. In addition, price-supporting commodity loan rates were raised slightly and several new price supports were added. Thus, the new legislation provided both substantial new support guarantees and familiar policy measures for farm constituents. Nearly $50 billion of new funding was made available for commodity support. However, farmers retained planting flexibility: fixed direct payments and countercyclical payments were based on past production and did not require farmers to grow specific crops.[3]

The conservation and environmental programs included in the FSRI Act highlight another aspect of policy flexibility. The authority for the CRP increased from 36.4 million acres to 39.2 million acres. However, most of the new environmental expenditure went on measures to assist livestock producers and for conservation practices on land that remained in production. Long-term land idling has historically been enacted as a supply control and conservation measure during times of low prices (the 1930s, the 1960s, and again in 1985) and has been allowed to expire when market demand strengthened (during World War II and in the 1970s).

[3] The decoupling of support from production decisions was partly undermined by a one-time option to update the acreage bases determining the direct payments and the base acreage and fixed yield levels determining the countercyclical payments.

Expenditures on the CRP and other environmental payments are notified in the green box, as discussed below. Competitors in world markets typically do not complain about the reduction in US production caused by the CRP. The program has occasionally been criticized by importers for unnecessarily restricting output and keeping world prices higher than otherwise, but this was not an issue with the low prices that prevailed in 2002.

The 2008 FCE Act

As new farm legislation made its way through Congress in 2007, the strategy of farm groups was to protect the structure and funding of the commodity programs, while seeking to build a broader coalition for a congressional voting majority (Orden, Blandford, and Josling 2010). By then, commodity prices had strengthened and were projected to remain sufficiently high to reduce sharply expenditure on price-linked payments during the period covered by the new legislation.

The five-year FCE Act that became law in June 2008 distributes expected mandatory expenditures for the fiscal years 2008–12 in a broadly similar way to that anticipated under an extension of the preceding legislation. An increase in total expected outlays of $5 billion and marginal shifts in spending among categories reflected the effort to attract a broad coalition of political support from proponents of nutrition, conservation, and energy programs and a host of other constituencies.

Projected spending of $41.6 billion on commodity programs for 2008–12 was primarily composed of fixed direct payments that were successfully defended from reductions by traditional recipients of support. Commodity support expenditures were $59.3 billion during the previous five fiscal years and, when the FSRI Act was being written, had been projected to rise to as much as $78 billion (Chite 2007). Hence, although farmers retained their support programs, they did not avoid a squeeze-down of payments under the higher market prices anticipated in the FCE Act. Authority for enrolment of land in the CRP was reduced to 32 million acres, but expenditure authority for other conservation programs increased. Projected total conservation spending reached almost 60 percent of projected commodity support, compared to just one-quarter during the previous five years. In this sense, in the event that high prices were realized, a substantial relative shift would occur towards conservation and the environment in farm program outlays. But farmers remained well-protected if prices proved lower than projected – through retention, and even a marginal strengthening, of the loan-rate and countercyclical tiers of commodity support. The FCE Act also offered new demand-augmenting support for fruits and vegetables, but in the face of opposition from growers did not authorize their production on base acres.[4] It extended dairy support through a Milk Income Loss Contract (MILC) program. New payments to processors of domestic or imported cotton replaced the "Step 2" payments to processors of domestic cotton that had been ruled to be in violation of WTO rules in the *United States – Cotton* case (WTO 2005).

Throughout the debate on the FCE Act most farm groups remained wary of changes to existing programs, despite record prices for farm products in the first half of 2008. Nor was there much budgetary incentive to change policy measures. Relatively high prices and hence low anticipated expenditures on price support were built into the baseline budget projection used by Congress in framing the new legislation (CBO 2007). There was no repeat of the opportunity presented in 1995–96 to reallocate overestimated projected expenditures for price-dependent payments to fixed payments (Orden, Paarlberg, and Roe 1999). New measures could deliver higher spending in the FCE Act only if their fiscal cost was approved by the Congress, while preserving existing loan rate and countercyclical programs under low projected expenditures came at little political cost to the farm lobby.

With high commodity prices, the fixed direct payments came under scrutiny in the farm policy debate. While the WTO rules encourage decoupling as a way to provide non-distorting support, the US fixed direct payments made up a large share of anticipated support expenditures under the FCE Act. Proponents of other initiatives saw a reduction in these payments as a way to fund their priorities. The payments were retained only after rancorous argument, particularly on the issue of income eligibility limits for recipients, which were tightened modestly in the final Act.

Expenditures on traditional within-year crop and revenue insurance programs, which are subsidized by the government, had expanded in

[4] Domestic producers of fruits and vegetables were concerned about expanded supplies and lower prices and objected to having to compete with farmers that receive payments on base acres. The WTO, without considering any price effects, concluded in the *United States – Cotton* case that the restrictions on planting fruits and vegetables made the US direct fixed payments inconsistent with the green box criterion that decoupled income support payments not related to production. The FCE Act only includes a small pilot program to allow the production of certain fruits and vegetables (for processing) on base acreage (60,000 acres in seven Midwestern states) with any acreage planted being ineligible for support payments during that year.

the early 2000s. Despite cost-reducing measures in the FCE Act, subsidies were projected to rise because higher commodity prices increase the nominal value of losses from adverse events. Congress had also appropriated disaster relief payments for agriculture in many years. The FCE Act authorized mandatory funding of nearly $4 billion over five years for five disaster relief programs. This was a step towards avoiding a squeeze-down of support by ensuring at least some availability of funds for disaster relief without the need for annual congressional appropriations.

The sharp rise in prices in 2008 also shifted the policy focus towards a new instrument that is capable of providing support even if prices remain relatively high. The FCE Act adopted an optional revenue-guarantee program, the Average Crop Revenue Election (ACRE) program, whose payments are likely to be notified as product-specific trade-distorting support in the WTO. Starting with the 2009 crop, farmers electing ACRE for the duration of the FCE Act incur a 20 percent cut in direct payments and a 30 percent cut in the applicable loan rates for all covered crops. In exchange, if crop revenue for a state (calculated as yield per planted acre times a national price) is below a guaranteed level (based on a moving average of past prices and crop yields) participating producers can benefit. If they incur a loss of revenue for that crop on their farm, producers are provided payments of up to 25 percent of the revenue guarantee. Once the initial per-acre guarantee is established, it cannot vary by more than 10 percent from the previous year's guarantee, moderating any sharp downturn in revenue. Although ACRE payments decline once market-derived revenue stabilizes, compared to traditional programs ACRE raises the price level at which subsidy payments will occur during a transitional period of falling prices. Its proponents acknowledged that ACRE provided an opportunity to avoid a squeeze-down of subsidy payments as a result of high prices. Nevertheless, with the penalty incurred from reduced direct payments and lower loan rates, only 10–20 percent of the acreage of the three largest eligible crops (corn, soybeans and wheat) was enrolled in the program in 2009.

One other change in the 2008 FCE Act proved to affect the US domestic support notifications to the WTO. The United States modified the way that its dairy support program is defined in the FCE Act. This change in definition resulted in a reduced quantity of milk being notified as eligible for market price support (MPS) by the US for 2008 (in September 2010), and hence a reduction in the support subject to its commitment, lessening the constraint on other forms of trade-distorting support.

Table 4.1 *Summary of US domestic support notifications and shadow notification, 1995–2008*

	Notifications						
	1995	1996	1997	1998	1999	2000	2001
Type of support	*Billion dollars*						
Green box	46.0	51.8	51.3	49.8	49.7	50.1	50.7
Blue box	7.0	—	—	—	—	—	—
Current Total AMS	6.2	5.9	6.2	10.4	16.9	16.8	14.5
of which, MPS	6.2	5.9	5.8	5.8	5.9	5.8	5.8
Total *de minimis*	1.6	1.1	0.8	4.7	7.4	7.3	7.1
Product-specific	0.1	—	0.2	0.2	—	0.1	0.2
Non-product-specific	1.5	1.1	0.6	4.6	7.4	7.3	6.8
Total support	60.9	58.8	58.3	65.0	74.0	74.2	72.2
Share of total support	%						
Green box	76	88	88	77	67	67	70
Blue box	12	—	—	—	—	—	—
CTAMS	10	10	11	16	23	23	20
Total *de minimis*	3	2	1	7	10	10	10
Total	100	100	100	100	100	100	100
Value of production (billion dollars)	190.1	205.7	203.9	190.9	184.7	189.5	198.5
Bound Total AMS (billion dollars)	23.1	22.3	21.5	20.7	19.9	19.1	19.1
CTAMS as share of binding (%)	27	26	29	50	85	88	76

Notes: Small differences in totals are due to rounding. — indicates zero.
Sources: US notifications to WTO and authors' calculations.

						Shadow notification
2002	2003	2004	2005	2006	2007	2008
58.3	64.1	67.4	72.3	76.0	76.2	99.6
—	—	—	—	—	—	—
9.6	7.0	11.6	12.9	7.7	6.3	7.1
5.8	5.8	5.8	5.9	6.2	6.2	6.1
6.7	7.8	6.5	6.0	3.6	2.2	4.2
1.6	0.4	0.7	0.1	0.2	0.1	0.1
5.1	7.4	5.8	5.9	3.4	2.0	4.1
74.6	78.8	85.5	91.3	87.4	84.6	110.8
78	81	79	79	87	90	90
—	—	—	—	—	—	—
13	9	14	14	9	7	6
9	10	8	7	4	3	4
100	100	100	100	100	100	100
194.6	216.5	235.7	236.0	246.4	307.0	335.3
19.1	19.1	19.1	19.1	19.1	19.1	19.1
50	36	61	68	41	33	37

Taken together, the measures adopted in the 2008 FCE Act prove the continued strength of the farm lobby. The slight increases in loan rates and the introduction of ACRE in the FCE Act strengthen policy measures coupled to production. The support price increases are likely to be innocuous so long as market prices remain above loan rates, while ACRE opens a new avenue for support.[5] Arguments will be made to extend these trade-distorting safety net programs. With a strong farm lobby continuing to influence US domestic support policies the rules of the WTO could play an important role in influencing future policy decisions.

Notifications of domestic support, 1995–2008

As of the beginning of 2010, the United States had made notifications of domestic support to the WTO for the thirteen years from 1995 to 2007.[6] The notification for green box support is on a federal fiscal year basis (October–September). The product-specific tables for AMS support are on a marketing-year basis. The non-product-specific AMS data relate to both marketing years and fiscal years.[7] As a result, the aggregations used in calculating the notified AMS support include data for a mixture of years.

Table 4.1 provides a summary of US notified support in each year and Figure 4.1 shows the percentage composition of support.[8] Estimates (a shadow notification) are provided for 2008.[9] Total notified support rose

[5] Sugar is an exception because the sugar loan rate is typically above world market prices. The loan rate for raw cane sugar is increased in the FCE Act from $0.18 per pound to $0.1875 in 2012. The Secretary of Agriculture is required to set domestic marketing allotments at no less that 85 percent of estimated quantities for domestic human consumption and to purchase sugar to produce biofuels if necessary to avoid forfeitures of sugar under the loan rate price-support program, thus insulating domestic producers from price pressure due to increased imports.

[6] The notifications are available online in the G/AG/N series of documents (e.g., G/AG/N/USA/66 for the notification for 2006 and 2007).

[7] The periodicity of the estimated data on non-product-specific support is unclear in some cases. It is possible that some of the source data relate to calendar years.

[8] The US notification for 2004 contains an error for the market price support (MPS) calculation for sugar. This was notified as $1,219.8 million, but the correct value is $1,186.0 million, which is used in all the relevant tables and figures in this chapter for numerical consistency.

[9] The principal source of information is the Commodity Estimates Yearbook of the Commodity Credit Corporation for FY2010 – Mid-Session Review July 2009 (USDA 2009a). As discussed below, changes in the way that the dairy support program is defined in the FCE Act affected the eventual US notification of MPS for 2008. Such a change was not incorporated at the time of our estimate of CTAMS, which therefore overstates the notified dairy support.

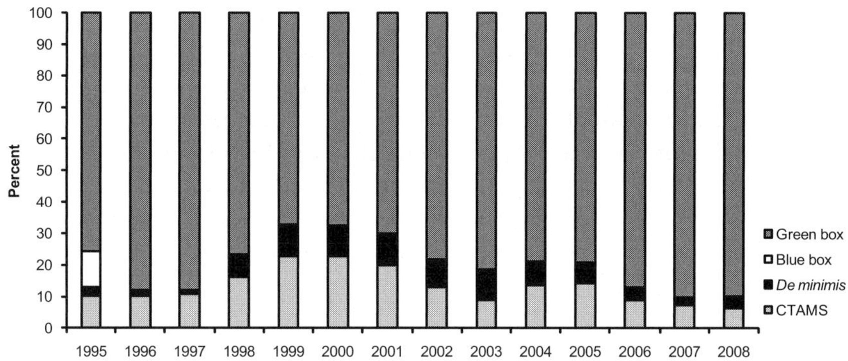

Figure 4.1 US domestic support notifications and shadow notification
Sources: US notifications to WTO and authors' calculations.

from around $60 billion in the mid 1990s to an estimated $111 billion. The largest category is the green box and both CTAMS and non-product-specific AMS support notified as *de minimis* are significant components of total support in some years. Table 4.2–Table 4.5 provide more detail about the components of each category.

Green box support

The green box has expanded from $46 billion in 1995 to an estimated $100 billion in 2008, when it accounted for 90 percent of total notified US support. Table 4.2 shows the components of green box expenditures. Domestic food aid is the most rapidly growing category, accounting for over 75 percent of the green box total in 2008. The main food aid program provides low-income families with benefits that can be used to purchase essentially any grocery item, hence this demand-augmenting program does not favor domestic over foreign producers. Excluding the food aid programs, green box support rose from $8.5 billion in 1995 to $24.7 billion in 2008. In terms of payments to farmers, decoupled income support has been the most important component in the green box. Decoupled income support is composed mostly of fixed direct payments initiated in the 1996 FAIR Act, but also includes peanut and tobacco buyout payments since 2002 and 2004, respectively. Disaster relief and environmental payments have also been important in the green box. Together these three categories totaled almost $13 billion in 2008.

Table 4.2 *Composition of US green box notifications and shadow notification, 1995–2008*

	Notifications					
	1995	1996	1997	1998	1999	2000
	Billion dollars					
General services	6.4	6.6	6.8	7.2	7.7	8.6
Public stockholding	—	—	—	—	—	—
Domestic food aid	37.5	37.8	36.0	33.5	33.1	32.4
Decoupled income support[a]	—	5.2	6.3	5.7	5.5	5.1
Income insurance	—	—	—	—	—	—
Crop insurance/ disaster relief	0.1	0.2	0.2	1.4	1.6	2.1
Producer retirement	—	—	—	—	—	—
Resource retirement	1.7	1.7	1.7	1.7	1.4	1.5
Investment aids	0.1	0.1	0.1	0.1	0.1	0.1
Environmental payments	0.2	0.3	0.3	0.3	0.3	0.3
Regional assistance	—	—	—	—	—	—
Total	46.0	51.8	51.3	49.8	49.7	50.1

Notes: — indicates zero.

[a] Subtracting peanut and tobacco buyout payments, fixed direct payments were $5.3 billion in 2003–04, and $5.2 billion in 2005–08.

Sources: Notifications to WTO and authors' calculations.

							Shadow notification
2001	2002	2003	2004	2005	2006	2007	2008
9.2	10.3	10.9	11.2	11.3	10.8	10.7	10.8
—	—	—	—	—	—	—	—
33.9	38.0	42.4	45.9	50.7	54.2	54.4	75.9
4.1	5.3	6.5	5.3	6.2	6.1	6.1	6.1
—	—	—	—	—	—	—	—
1.4	2.1	1.7	2.0	0.7	1.1	0.9	2.3
—	—	—	—	—	—	—	—
1.6	—	—	—	—	—	—	—
0.1	0.1	0.1	0.1	0.1	0.1	0.1	0.1
0.3	2.5	2.5	3.0	3.4	3.7	3.8	4.4
—	—	—	—	—	—	—	—
50.7	58.3	64.1	67.4	72.3	76.0	76.2	99.6

Table 4.3 *Composition of US Current Total AMS notifications and shadow notification, 1995–2008*

	Notifications					
	1995	1996	1997	1998	1999	2000
	Million dollars					
Market Price Support	6,213	5,919	5,816	5,776	5,921	
Dairy	4,693	4,674	4,455	4,332	4,437	
Sugar	1,108	937	1,045	1,093	1,180	1,133
Peanuts	412	308	315	350	303	330
Other support[a]	—	-22	423	4,616	10,942	
By crop						
Corn	—	—	—	1,534	2,554	2,787
Cotton	—	—	466	935	2,353	1,050
Dairy	-38	17	—	228	223	693
Rice	—	—	—	—	435	624
Soybeans	—	—	—	1,275	2,856	3,614
Tobacco	—	—	—	—	924	519
Wheat	—	—	—	516	974	848
Other[b]	38	-38	-44	129	622	867
By type of measure						
Loan deficiency payments	—	—	3	2,708	6,062	6,192
Marketing loan gains/ payments	—	—	26	1,072	1,830	813
Certificate exchange gains	—	—	—	6	175	619
Commodity loan forfeiture	—	—	—	6	642	20
Cotton user marketing	—	—	416	280	446	237
Milk income loss contracts	—	—	—	—	—	—
Oilseed payments	—	—	—	—	458	921
Emergency payments[c]	—		—	208	683	1,473
Other support[d]	-53	-22	-23	337	567	498
Miscellaneous payments[e]	53	—	—	—	79	231
Current Total AMS	6,213	5,898	6,238	10,392	16,862	

Notes: — indicates zero.

[a] Sum of non-exempt direct payments from notifications supporting table DS:6 and total other support from DS:7.

[b] Other products listed in Table 4.4.

[c] Market loss payments and various disaster assistance from notifications supporting table DS:6.

[d] Total other support from notifications supporting table DS:7 (includes storage payments, commodity loan interest subsidies, bioenergy program payments).

[e] Trade adjustment assistance and other miscellaneous payments.

Sources: US notifications to WTO and authors' calculations.

							Shadow notification
2001	2002	2003	2004	2005	2006	2007	2008
5,826	5,771	5,758	5,832	5,908	6,154	6,238	6,134
4,483	4,509	4,515	4,646	4,794	4,882	5,011	5,007
1,032	1,262	1,242	1,186	1,114	1,272	1,227	1,127
311	—	—	—	—	—	—	—
8,656	3,867	1,193	5,763	7,035	1,588	22	921
1,326	—	—	3,059	4,490	—	—	—
2,810	1,187	435	2,238	1,621	1,365	—	—
—	1,795	222	16	361	162	5	905
763	712	503	131	133	—	—	—
3,623	—	—	—	—	—	—	—
—	—	—	—	—	—	—	—
—	—	—	—	—	—	—	—
135	172	33	318	431	61	16	16
5,400	508	320	3,333	4,750	157	7	4
604	167	87	321	243	8	—	—
1,974	316	306	1,450	1,171	967	—	—
17	658	—	7	4	—	—	—
182	—	—	—	—	—	—	—
—	1,795	221	9	352	157	—	900
—	—	—	—	—	—	—	—
—	110	1	40	90	6	5	5
430	289	257	586	410	293	9	12
49	23	—	17	15	—	—	—
14,482	9,637	6,950	11,595	12,943	7,742	6,260	7,056

Table 4.4 *US CTAMS notifications and shadow notification by product, 1995–2008*

	Notifications					
	1995	1996	1997	1998	1999	2000
	Million dollars					
Apples					99	175
Apricots						2
Avocados						
Barley				84	40	70
Beef, cattle, sheep						
Beef and veal						
Blueberries, wild						
Cattle and calves						
Chickpeas						
Corn				1,534	2,554	2,787
Cotton			466	935	2,353	1,050
Cranberries					20	
Dairy	4,655	4,691	4,456	4,560	4,660	5,070
Dry peas						
Grapes						
Hogs and pigs						
Honey						29
Lentils						
Livestock						
Lychee						
Minor oil seeds						
Canola				8	39	82
Crambe					1	2
Flaxseed				2	11	25
Mustard seed	<0.5	<0.5	<0.5	<0.5	1	<0.5
Rapeseed	<0.5	<0.5	<0.5		<0.5	<0.5
Safflower	<0.5	<0.5	<0.5	<0.5		3
Sesame						<0.5
Sunflower					143	161
Mohair	15				2	2
Oats				20	31	45
Olives						
Onions						
Orchards/vineyards						

							Shadow notification
2001	2002	2003	2004	2005	2006	2007	2008
			83	46			
		<0.5	<0.5	<0.5			
1,326			3,059	4,490			
2,810	1,187	435	2,238	1,621	1,365		
4,483	6,305	4,737	4,663	5,155	5,044	5,017	5,913
		14	32	37	30		
	2			11	14		
23				14			
<0.5	<0.5		<0.5				
12							
<0.5							
	2						
55							
	5	4	3	2	1	1	

Table 4.4 (*cont.*)

	Notifications					
	1995	1996	1997	1998	1999	2000
	Million dollars					
Peaches						
Peanuts	415	299	306	340	349	438
Pears						
Pecan trees						
Potatoes						
Rice					435	624
Rye						
Sheep and lamb						
Sorghum				63	154	85
Soybeans				1,275	2,856	3,614
Sugar	1,091	908	1,011	1,055	1,207	1,177
Tobacco					924	519
Tomatoes						
Wheat				516	974	848
Wool	38				9	33
Current Total AMS	6,213	5,898	6,238	10,392	16,862	16,843
Sum of product-specific AMS[a]	6,311	5,937	6,475	10,550	16,891	16,906

Notes: No value either means no notified support or AMS below the *de minimis* threshold for that year. The 2004 MPS for sugar was incorrectly notified as $1,219.8 million; this table uses the correct value of $1,186.0 million; other support in the sugar AMS for 2004 is $62 million.

[a] Includes *de minimis*.

Sources: US notifications to WTO and authors' calculations.

							Shadow notification
2001	2002	2003	2004	2005	2006	2007	2008
305	66			89			
763	712	503	131	133			
22	23						
			130	140			
3,623							
1,061	1,328	1,250	1,248	1,199	1,280	1,236	1,139
	8	7	7	7	7	7	4
14,482	9,637	6,950	11,595	12,943	7,742	6,260	7,056
14,706	11,227	7,386	12,275	13,061	7,913	6,497	7,155

Table 4.5 De minimis *exemptions from CTAMS in US notifications and shadow notification, 1995–2008*

	Notifications					
	1995	1996	1997	1998	1999	2000
	Million dollars					
Sum of AMS support (amber box)	7,696	7,052	7,042	15,134	24,297	24,184
Total *de minimis*	1,483	1,155	804	4,742	7,435	7,341
Product-specific	97	40	236	158	29	63
Non-product-specific	1,386	1,115	567	4,584	7,406	7,278
	%					
De minimis as a share of CTAMS	24	20	13	46	44	44
De minimis as a share of summed AMS support	19	16	11	31	31	30
Major components of non-product-specific *de minimis*				*Million dollars*		
Irrigation projects	380	380	349	349	316	316
Crop and revenue insurance	913	636	119	747	1,514	1,396
Market loss and countercyclical payments	—	—	—	2,811	5,468	5,463
	5% of total value of production (million dollars)					
Non-product-specific threshold	9,506	10,285	10,194	9,544	9,237	9,476

Note: — indicates zero.
Sources: US notifications to WTO and authors' calculations.

							Shadow notification
2001	2002	2003	2004	2005	2006	2007	2008
21,535	16,328	10,187	18,087	18,923	11,343	8,520	11,231
7,052	6,690	3,237	6,491	5,980	3,601	2,260	4,176
224	1,590	436	714	118	171	237	99
6,828	5,101	2,801	5,778	5,862	3,430	2,023	4,077
49	69	47	56	46	47	36	59
33	41	32	36	32	32	27	37
300	300	300	269	269	240	240	240
1,770	2,889	1,862	1,123	756	1,613	801	2,880
4,640	1,804	544	4,288	4,749	1,488	893	864
9,925	9,729	10,824	11,784	11,800	12,321	15,352	16,765

Current Total AMS

Table 4.1 shows that AMS – including the CTAMS plus product-specific and non-product-specific AMSs notified as *de minimis* – can vary substantially from year to year depending on prices and production.[10] In periods when prices are low, such as 1999–2000, support increases markedly in comparison to periods such as 1996–97 when prices of farm products were relatively high.

The notified US CTAMS is composed entirely of product-specific support. Table 4.3 shows the MPS component by major commodity, as well as payments by major commodity and by type of policy measure. The MPS component is based on administered prices (loan rates) that exceed the fixed reference price levels in the US schedule under the Agreement. MPS amounts to roughly $6 billion in most years, with the largest proportion of this (an average of 80 percent over the period) attributed to the dairy program. The MPS for peanuts was eliminated as a result of the buyout of production quotas in the 2002 FSRI Act.

While most of the support for dairy and sugar is provided through MPS, support in CTAMS for most other products is through non-exempt direct payments and other forms of support.[11] The three crops that have benefited most are corn, cotton and soybeans with 28, 26 and 20 percent, respectively, of total payments for 1995–2008. Almost 75 percent of total non-exempt payments and other forms of support were made up of loan deficiency payments (50 percent), certificate exchange gains, and marketing loan gains, which collectively constitute the three principal mechanisms providing price support to US farmers without the government having to take ownership of the products.

The dairy and sugar MPS have consistently accounted for significant shares of the CTAMS. Table 4.3 also demonstrates the influence of market prices on US WTO notifications. When crop prices have been low subsidies included in CTAMS have increased for the major field crops and their share of support has been important. Cotton, which has been particularly

[10] Blue box support is not important for the United States because the deficiency payments for major crops included in this category were eliminated in 1996 by the FAIR Act. The blue box payments shown in Table 4.1 for 1995 were distributed among crops as follows: barley, $151 million; corn, $3,009 million; cotton, $901 million; oats, $12 million; rice, $511 million; sorghum $320 million; and wheat, $2,127 million.

[11] The notable exceptions for dairy are $673 million through a market loss payment in 2000; $1,795 million under MILC payments in 2002; and an estimated $900 million of MILC payments in 2008.

contentious in the WTO negotiations, has accounted for as much as 19 percent of the US CTAMS (in the years 2001 and 2004).

When prices are high, price-linked subsidies decline and this reduces notified support. With high commodity prices, the CTAMS averaged $7 billion in 2006–08. The modest increase from 2007 to 2008 is almost entirely due to higher support for dairy due to lower milk prices and higher payments under the MILC program.[12] Despite some weakening of prices in late 2008, support for crops was not estimated to have increased significantly. The product-specific AMS for almost all products is estimated to be below *de minimis* thresholds in 2007 and 2008. This is in sharp contrast to the situation just a few years earlier, when the notified CTAMS was in the $11–13 billion range (2004–05) and the *de minimis* threshold was exceeded for most of the major crops.

Table 4.4 provides more detailed information on the product composition of the notified CTAMS. If a notification was provided for any product during the period 1995–2007 it is included in the table but any AMS below the *de minimis* threshold is not shown. Product-specific *de minimis* has generally not been a major factor in reducing the US notified CTAMS. One notable exception was an emergency payment to livestock farmers of $1.1 billion in 2002 which was excluded from the CTAMS because of *de minimis* and accounted for most of the increase in product-specific *de minimis* in that year (Table 4.1). The *de minimis* exclusion has also reduced significantly the number of years for which AMS support has been included in CTAMS for a wide range of products. For example, a positive AMS applied to barley in every year with the exception of 2007, but after the application of *de minimis* a barley AMS was included in the CTAMS in only five of the fourteen years.

Table 4.4 reveals that notifications have been made in various years under different headings for related products. For example, notifications have been provided for individual orchard and vineyard crops as well as for an aggregate of those crops; the same applies to livestock. The impact of this on the CTAMS is unclear. For example, it is possible that part of the support notified for livestock in 2002 as *de minimis* would have been counted in the CTAMS if it had been apportioned to individual livestock categories. This is not to imply that the notification was deliberately intended to achieve that effect, but when appropriate data are not

[12] Compared to our shadow estimate the changed definition of the dairy support program in the FCE Act resulted in a reduction of $2.1 billion in the CTAMS due to lower notified MPS. With higher payments than projected for cotton, the final notified CTAMS for 2008 was $6.3 billion.

available the mixing of overlapping product categories in the notifications complicates the issue of identifying accurately the amount of support provided for individual products. This could prove contentious under a Doha agreement with product-specific AMS caps.

Comparison of MPS measurements

Comparisons of the MPS as notified to the WTO to that calculated using the approach adopted by the OECD are shown for dairy (milk) and sugar for 1995–2007 in Figures 4.2 and 4.3. A key difference in the OECD approach is that annual domestic prices (rather than an administered price) are compared to annual international reference prices (rather than a fixed 1986–88 reference price). The pattern of differences between the two measurements is similar for both commodities. The WTO MPS is quite stable in each case and is substantially below the OECD measure in most years. The eligible quantities in the WTO measure are almost identical to total milk and sugar production, so the difference between the two arises from differences in the prices used. The WTO MPS understates the actual protection provided annually to domestic producers by border measures (tariffs, TRQs and for dairy some export subsidies) and domestic supply management (for sugar in some years), reflected in annual domestic prices. In addition to capturing this protection, the OECD MPS reflects changes in the level of protection due to changes in world market prices.

Most of the difference between the WTO and OECD MPS for milk arises from fluctuations in domestic producer prices in comparison to the administered price. The administered price for milk declined from $243 per metric ton in the 1986–88 base period to around $218 per metric ton in 1999. By contrast the producer price was $274 per metric ton in the base period and has increased with annual fluctuations to $403 per metric ton in 2007. Fluctuations in world prices also affect the comparison between the two MPS measurements. The fixed reference price used in calculating the WTO MPS is $160 per metric ton, similar to the corresponding OECD average reference price of $176 per metric ton for 1986–88. By 1995 the OECD annual reference price had risen to $210 per ton and reached $313 per ton in 2007, twice the level of the fixed reference price used in the WTO calculation. Thus, even though the two measures converge during 2005–06, the OECD MPS is based on higher domestic and international prices than those in the WTO MPS. The administered and fixed reference prices used in calculating the WTO MPS in this case only coincidentally reflect the actual price support provided to US dairy farmers.

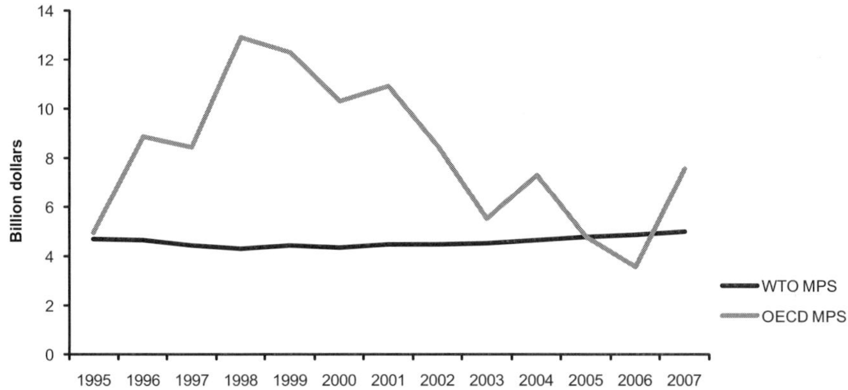

Figure 4.2 US market price support for dairy from notifications and OECD
Source: Authors' calculations based on WTO notifications and OECD statistics.

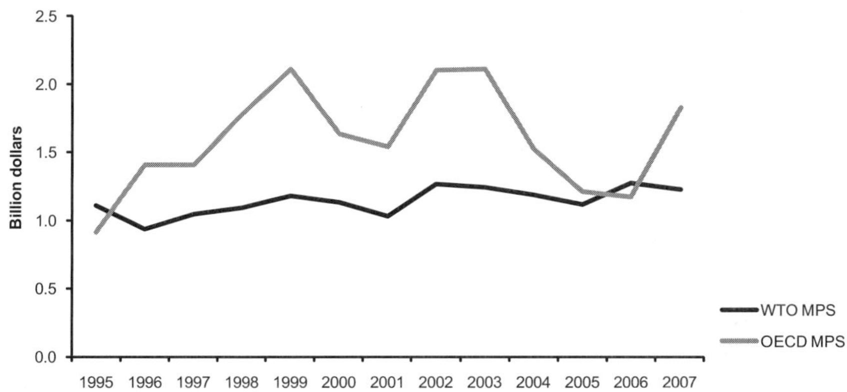

Figure 4.3 US market price support for sugar from notifications and OECD
Source: Authors' calculations based on WTO notifications and OECD statistics.

For sugar, the OECD MPS also exceeds the WTO MPS in most years due primarily to domestic producer prices in excess of the administered price. The latter has been virtually constant (at $396.8 per metric ton, except for $374.8 during 1996–2001 when a penalty under the 1996 FAIR Act was in effect). Producer prices ranged from $47 (2000) to $142 (1996) per metric ton higher.[13] For sugar, the fixed reference price is $231 per metric

[13] Producer prices as reported in the OECD PSE database are below the administered price, ranging from $296 per ton in the 1986–88 base period to $315 per ton in 2007. The WTO

ton for the WTO MPS, while OECD's average international price for the 1986–88 period was $202 per metric ton. By the time the Agreement came into effect in 1995 the international price was $329. It fell as low as $177 in 1999, stayed at or below the fixed reference price through 2004, but was $375 by 2006. For sugar, use of the fixed reference price kept the notified WTO MPS lower than would have been the case with an annual reference price when world prices were low.

On the basis of these results, it might be tempting to dismiss administered prices as playing an insignificant role in US farm policy. Particularly for sugar, this would be a serious error. Sugar imports under a TRQ are carefully managed on a month-by-month basis to keep supply aligned with domestic demand. The management of quantities through the sugar import regime (and sometimes domestic supply control) has been used to keep prices at the processor level above the support level, as reflected in the MPS comparison. Although the government procures very little sugar, the administered price is the policy fulcrum for quantitative management. The industry is keenly aware of the critical policy role played by the administered price. It is defended as the basis for operating the sugar program and border measures in such a way as to avoid sugar being accumulated by the government instead of being sold commercially.

Non-product-specific AMS support

The United States has excluded non-product-specific AMS support from its notified CTAMS under the *de minimis* provision in all years. The *de minimis* exclusion has been extremely important. Table 4.1 shows that *de minimis* support as a whole has accounted for up to 10 percent of total notified support. The total of AMS *de minimis* exemptions was equivalent to roughly 45 percent of the notified CTAMS on average, and almost reached 70 percent in 2002 (Table 4.5). Most of this is non-product-specific support, which has exceeded $4 billion in eight years. However, because of the large total value of US agricultural production (averaging around $220 billion between 1995 and 2008), non-product-specific support would have had to have been at least $1.8 billion greater than the maximum notified amount in order to breach the 5 percent *de minimis* threshold (this calculation relates to the 1999 notification). On average,

administered price and reference price refer to raw cane sugar after mill processing, whereas OECD converts its prices to a farmgate level by multiplying by 0.6 to adjust for processing costs. The producer prices given herein and the OECD MPS in Figure 4.3 are recalibrated to the raw sugar level for comparison to the WTO MPS.

the non-product-specific AMS has been \$7 billion below the *de minimis* threshold, and it declined to a relatively low level of \$2 billion in 2007.

Several important forms of support are included in the non-product-specific AMS. Crop MLA payments from 1998 to 2001 and countercyclical payments initiated in 2002 alone exceeded \$4 billion in five years, most recently in 2005. Crop and revenue insurance subsidies have been another important component, exceeding \$1.5 billion in six years. Lesser payments include irrigation subsidies and payments under various emergency assistance and other programs.

The variability in key components of the non-product-specific AMS is also apparent in Table 4.5, and again this relates to price movements. Support increased sharply in the late 1990s as Congress responded to declining prices by authorizing crop MLA payments. These were paid to farmers in proportion to their total eligibility for direct payments and required no specific planting decisions; on this basis they were notified as non-product-specific AMS.[14] The countercyclical payments introduced in the 2002 FSRI Act are directly linked to market prices of specific crops but are based on fixed levels of past output. Again, they have been notified as non-product-specific AMS because the payments are not dependent on annual decisions to plant specific crops. The introduction of these price-responsive forms of support has contributed to an increase in the non-product-specific AMS and has also made it more variable. Since 1998, when MLA payments were first introduced, such support has varied between \$0.5 and \$5.5 billion. Recently, with prices for major crops relatively high in 2007 and 2008, countercyclical payments have been relatively low, at around \$0.9 billion. The non-product-specific AMS is estimated to have increased to \$4 billion in 2008, due to larger payments under crop and revenue insurance programs resulting from higher prices and hence higher premium subsidies. The non-product-specific AMS estimated for 2008 was equivalent to 58 percent of the notified CTAMS, thus accounting for over one-third of the non-green box support provided to US farmers in that year.

Consistency of US support with WTO commitments

The sole quantitative commitment on domestic support under the Agreement is the Bound Total AMS. For the United States, this was reduced from \$23.1 billion in 1995 to \$19.1 billion in 2000 (Table 4.1).

[14] Market loss assistance payments provided for some commodities (e.g., dairy) were notified as product-specific AMS, as noted above.

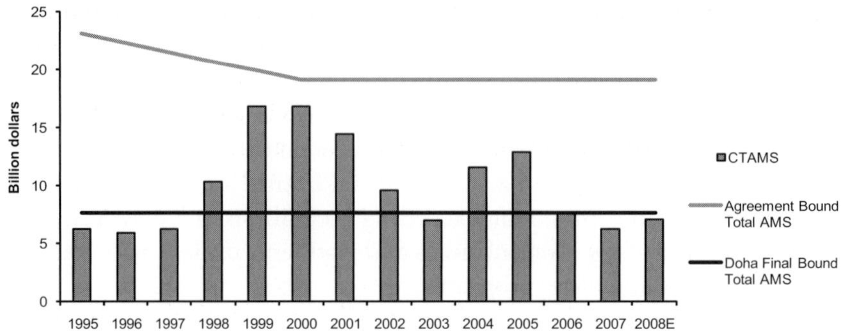

Figure 4.4 US notifications of CTAMS compared with commitments agreed in the Uruguay Round and proposed in the Doha Round

Given the non-product-specific *de minimis* exemption, despite substantial fluctuations in the notified CTAMS the United States has not exceeded its Bound Total AMS under the Agreement (Figure 4.4). However, a significant reduction is being proposed in the Doha negotiations – from $19.1 billion to $7.6 billion. The US notified CTAMS has exceeded the lower figure in eight of the fourteen years from 1995 to 2008. Even with relatively high crop prices in 2007–08, the CTAMS, while comfortably within the binding under the Agreement, is very close to the proposed binding under Doha if there is no change in the method of notifying dairy support. The issues involved in meeting proposed new commitments on support are clearly of major importance for the United States and are examined in more detail below.

Even without a new WTO agreement on agriculture, an important issue for the United States is the notification status of some of its programs in light of the *US – Cotton* case (WTO 2005) and further challenges to its support payments by Brazil and Canada in the Total Aggregate Measurement of Support (TAMS) case (WTO 2007a, 2007b). For the three years with the highest notified CTAMS (1999–2001) US AMS support would have exceeded the Bound Total AMS commitment without the *de minimis* exemption for non-product-specific support, as shown in Table 4.5. The addition of just the MLA payments from the non-product-specific *de minimis* would raise the CTAMS above the ceiling commitment in those years.

The cotton case ruling casts doubt on whether US fixed direct payments, which are currently notified as green box support, qualify for that category because production of some crops (particularly fruits and vegetables) was precluded on the program base acres for which payments are made. Table 4.6 presents two alternative summations of the notified US CTAMS with the inclusion of the fixed direct payments. The United States would have violated its Bound Total AMS in a number of years in each case. If the direct payments were notified as non-product-specific AMS (following the approach used by the United States for countercyclical payments) the Bound Total AMS would have been reached or exceeded in five of the fourteen years (1998–2002). In those years, the non-product-specific AMS would have exceeded the *de minimis* threshold and been counted in the CTAMS. Alternatively, if crop MLA and countercyclical payments, as well as fixed direct payments, were counted as product-specific AMS, as some analysts argue, the United States would also have exceeded its commitment in five of the fourteen years (1999–2001 and 2004–05). For these years the sum of the product-specific AMS in the CTAMS is sufficiently high to exceed the Bound Total AMS.

Other alternative subsidy measurement

Beyond the traditional price and income support programs (direct payments, countercyclical payments, and loan-rate program benefits), a number of questions arise on how subsidies are being captured in the US notifications. Here we discuss briefly five categories that may be misclassified, underreported, or omitted from the US notifications. This may become important if support commitments are tightened in a Doha agreement.

Disaster payments

The US notifies various types of disaster payments in the green box, as product-specific support, and as non-product-specific support. The Canadian request for establishment of a panel in the TAMS case listed forty-eight separate disaster programs over the period 1999–2005 (WTO 2007b). Crop insurance and disaster relief payments notified in the green box range from a low of $100 million in 1995 to a high of $2.3 billion in 2008 (Table 4.2). Important questions are whether all disaster programs have been included in the US notifications, whether those notified in the green box satisfied the relevant criteria, and whether annual support through these programs has been measured correctly. Some disaster relief programs could be judged to provide product-specific payments that do not qualify for the green box. Inconsistency with specific green box

Table 4.6 *Alternative summations of US AMS support and fixed direct payments, 1995–2008*

	1995	1996	1997	1998	1999	2000	2001	2002	2003	2004	2005	2006	2007	2008
Fixed direct payments included in non-product-specific AMS														
Hypothetical CTAMS (Billion dollars)[a]	6.2	5.9	6.2	20.6	29.7	29.2	25.4	20.0	7.0	11.6	12.9	7.7	6.3	7.1
As share of ceiling (%)	27	26	29	100	149	153	133	105	36	61	68	41	33	37
Market loss assistance, countercyclical and fixed direct payments included in product-specific AMS														
Hypothetical CTAMS (Billion dollars)[b]	6.2	11.1	12.5	18.9	27.8	27.4	23.2	16.7	12.8	21.1	22.9	14.4	12.3	13.1
As share of ceiling (%)	27	50	58	91	140	143	122	88	67	111	120	75	65	69

[a] Fixed direct payments are only added to the CTAMS and count against the ceiling if their inclusion in the non-product-specific AMS causes it to exceed the *de minimis* threshold. Fixed direct payments exclude buyout payments for peanuts and tobacco that are included in notified green box decoupled income support.

[b] Peanut and tobacco buyout payments not included as product-specific support.

Sources: US notifications to WTO and authors' calculations.

criteria regarding the reference period against which a loss is measured, and the amount of the loss that triggered payments, would be among the reasons for such judgments (see Appendix A for the criteria specified in the Agreement).

Federal tax exemptions for agriculture

US domestic support notifications do not include revenue forgone due to special tax exemptions for agriculture. In its request for a TAMS panel, Brazil identified diesel fuel and gasoline tax exemptions, tax exemptions for agricultural vehicles, and income tax concessions as subsidies that might need to be notified (WTO 2007a). Among the income tax concessions are special capital gains treatment for unharvested crops (notified by the United States as a subsidy under the Agreement on Subsidies and Countervailing Measures (ASCM)), preferential cash accounting rules for farm operations, and preferential availability of income averaging over time. The OECD includes the income tax concession as a payment based on overall farming income and energy subsidies as a payment based on input use in its PSEs. US income tax concessions are reported to have increased from $554 million in 1995 to $1,250 million in 2008, and were as high as $2,456 million in 2003. Energy subsidies, defined as the "value of Federal and State exemptions or reductions in excise and sales taxes on diesel fuel for farmers relative to the standard rate taxes on fuels", are simply reported by the OECD as a constant $2,385 million from 1986 through 2008.

Crop and revenue insurance costs

US notifications for crop and revenue insurance report net indemnities (indemnities minus premiums paid by producers) as non-product-specific support. There are additional expenditures on crop and revenue insurance programs arising from the payment of delivery costs to private insurance agents. The latter are not reported in the notifications, but they have been substantial, averaging about $900 million per year from 1995 through 2008, whereas net indemnities averaged $1,100 million. One can argue that the reimbursements excluded from the notifications are made to companies on behalf of the policyholders (producers of the insured crops), and should therefore be notified as non-product-specific support.

Irrigation and electric power

The US reports interest on the debt for irrigation project construction in its non-product-specific AMS, arguing that "irrigators repay the premium but not the interest." The subsidy has been reported as declining from $380 million in 1995 to $240 million by 2006 (Table 4.5). Arguably, this interest subsidy could be considered part of expenditures "directed to the provision or construction of capital works" and exempt from the AMS calculations under the green box criteria of Annex 2 of the Agreement. Not having claimed that exclusion, the United States might, but does not, include subsidies to agricultural irrigators that arise from lower repayment of capital costs based on assessed "ability to pay" programs. Under these programs a reduced capital cost is charged to farmers and a higher cost is paid by hydroelectric power authorities (again, it might be argued that these subsidies should be in the green box). No notification is made for irrigation subsidies related to maintenance and operating costs (which irrigators apparently pay), nor for the benefits from water charges to farmers that are below those for other users (which is a common practice). No allowance is provided for preferential charges for electricity used by agriculture, either to move water from its source to farmland or for on-farm use of electricity. The extent of subsidies for irrigation and electricity and how these are notified are issues for other countries (see Chapters 8 and 9, India and China). A more systematic and consistent approach to the measurement and notification of these subsidies would be useful in the WTO.

Ethanol

The issue of how ethanol subsidies are notified has become germane. Most important is the forgone revenue from the federal ethanol tax credit to fuel blenders and additional state tax provisions. These tax credits could collectively total $7–8 billion or more on corn-based ethanol alone by 2022. If these amounts were to be counted in the AMS, its nominal level would be substantially higher.

The United States has notified the federal ethanol tax credit to the WTO as an industrial subsidy under the ASCM. However, ethanol is included in the set of products defined as agricultural under the WTO agreements, so the tax revenue forgone could also be appropriately notified under the AMS, with ethanol considered the relevant product. At issue would be the extent to which the tax credit is judged to be a "measure directed at processors" and thus subject to inclusion in the AMS (under Annex 3, paragraph 7 of the Agreement) "to the extent that such measures benefit producers of the basic agricultural product." If ethanol is indeed a "basic" agricultural product, the issue would center on the extent to which the blenders' tax credit is passed through to producers of ethanol.

If ethanol were not to be considered a basic agricultural product, the tax credit to blenders could still be an instrument of domestic support. To the extent that an ethanol tax credit increases corn prices, it might be judged to be a measure directed at processors that affects the price of corn as a basic agricultural product. This would correspond to the way the United States formerly notified Step 2 payments to processors of domestic cotton as part of the cotton product-specific AMS before these payments were eliminated as a result of the *US – Cotton* case.

The use of mandates in conjunction with tax credits raises the issue of whether such a policy is judged a "measure" that could be included among "all … domestic support measures in favour of agricultural producers" and thus subject to discipline under the Agreement on Agriculture (Article 6 and Annex 3). As shown by de Gorter and Just (2009), when a mandate is not binding, the tax credit adds substantially to the level of production of ethanol, its price, and the price and output of corn. In contrast, when a mandate is binding, the effects of the tax credit on producers are minimal. In the latter case, it is the binding mandate that influences ethanol and corn production and prices and, one can argue, should be subject to the AMS discipline.

The CTAMS would be composed of a curious mix of policies if ethanol subsidies were included. A common metaphor for US policy has been that it has one foot on the gas pedal and one foot on the brake in terms of production. The "on the gas" part has been the focus of attention regarding the US AMS; that is, what is the value of subsidies that stimulate production? The "on the brake" part has been programs that idle land: these have been notified in the green box for long-term conservation land idling and the blue box for short-term acreage set-asides. With ethanol mandates and subsidies, the new metaphor for agricultural policy would be that it has its feet on two accelerators. But these policy approaches have different effects on world prices, and thus on the interests of various trade partners and constituents within these countries. The traditional accelerator of supply expansion drives world prices down. The new accelerator of demand augmentation, through ethanol policy, drives world prices up. Commodity market events since 2006 have demonstrated the potency of the latter type of policies.

Projected US notifications and WTO constraints

In order to examine the impact of the existing disciplines for agricultural domestic support and of the new disciplines proposed in the Doha negotiations, projections of support under major categories in the US notifications were derived through 2016 using program parameters from the 2008 FCE Act. The projections are based on the domestic support simulator developed by Blandford and Josling (2007). Data for future production and prices are derived primarily from the February 2009 USDA baseline (USDA 2009b). Peanut price projections were derived from the March 2009 CBO budget baseline (Hull, Langley, and Hitz 2009). That is also the source for expenditures under conservation programs and crop and revenue insurance. Overall, the commodity prices used in the projections are relatively high due to a range of factors, including domestic demand for biofuels, and strong overseas demand for US commodities due to income growth, dietary change, and an anticipated weak dollar.

In projecting the CTAMS, two key assumptions are made about future US notifications. The first relates to the notification of the MPS for dairy. As noted earlier, the FCE Act introduced a definitional change in US dairy policy. Prior to the Act the US dairy support program was defined with respect to a support price for milk. That structure was reflected in US notifications because the MPS calculation was applied to total milk production. The FCE Act redefines the program in terms of support for three dairy products: butter, cheddar cheese, and non-fat dry milk. Support prices for these products are set to be consistent with the previous support price for milk ($9.90 per hundredweight). However, as a result of this change the United States eventually notified MPS for dairy for 2008 on the basis of the production of the three products concerned, rather than the total volume of milk. It is clear that the United States will continue to exercise this option in notified dairy support in the future. As noted above the redesign of the dairy support program led to reduction of $ 2.1 billion for 2008 compared to notifying MPS for all milk production that year. In the projections, MPS is assumed to be notified using the new procedure and assuming no subsequent changes to dairy price support policy through 2016 that further reduce the notified MPS.

A second key assumption concerns the ACRE program. This program has the potential to generate large support payments during periods of relatively high prices. Despite an initial modest sign-up rate for the largest-acreage eligible crops in 2009, it is likely that ACRE or similar programs will remain part of US farm policy in the coming years. For this reason, understanding the performance characteristics of this new program versus traditional programs is important. In the projections it is assumed that all acreage is enrolled in the traditional programs. However, the implications of the ACRE program for future notifications are also discussed.

Under the Agreement

Table 4.7 summarizes projected notifications in the various boxes through 2016 under the Agreement. Green box support is projected to increase steadily from $100 billion in 2009 to $118 billion in 2016. This is primarily due to increased expenditures on domestic food assistance programs, with expenditures on conservation programs also projected to increase from $4 billion in 2009 to over $6 billion in 2016. On the basis of these projections, green box support would make up roughly 90 percent of the US total support by 2016, a similar percentage to that in 2008.

The US CTAMS has varied substantially from year-to-year, but the relatively high commodity prices foreseen by USDA and other analysts imply that projected support expenditures for major crops are extremely modest. The notified product-specific AMS for most major products other than dairy and sugar would qualify for *de minimis*. On the basis of these projections, the CTAMS would stay far below the US Bound Total AMS of $19.1 billion. The projected CTAMS would amount to $4.5–$5.0 billion, composed almost entirely of market price support for dairy and sugar.

Over the period 1995–2008 *de minimis* non-product-specific support has been an important component in the US notifications. With the relatively high commodity prices assumed through 2016, there are only modest countercyclical payments for cotton and peanuts. In contrast, crop and revenue insurance subsidies are expected to be high, averaging about $4.7 billion per year due to the higher prices.[15] The projected non-product-specific support in 2016 is $5 billion, including countercyclical payments. This easily falls under *de minimis*. With a projected value of production around $265 billion, there is room for more than $8 billion of additional non-product-specific support without crossing the *de minimis* threshold.

The difference between the notified CTAMS and the Bound Total AMS would be $14.1 billion in 2016, shown in Figure 4.5 as the "Available CTAMS." Domestic commodity programs could provide that much additional notified CTAMS and the United States would still meet its WTO commitment. As long as non-product-specific support was kept under the *de minimis* threshold, additional support in the CTAMS and non-product-specific AMS categories combined could

[15] These estimates of crop and revenue insurance subsidies exclude adjustments estimated by CBO to average $168 million over 2008–11 (due to reduced program costs) and $3,189 million in 2012 (due primarily to delay of some payments to lower the projected five-year cost of the FCE Act).

Table 4.7 *Projected levels of US domestic support under the Agreement, 2009–16*

	2009	2010	2011	2012	2013	2014	2015	2016
	Billion dollars							
Green box	99.7	102.2	104.8	107.6	110.0	112.4	114.8	117.5
Blue box	—	—	—	—	—	—	—	—
CTAMS	4.6	4.6	4.7	4.8	4.9	4.9	5.0	5.0
Total *de minimis*	6.9	6.1	5.6	5.5	5.5	5.6	5.7	5.1
Product-specific	0.2	0.1	0.1	0.1	0.1	0.1	0.1	0.1
Non-product-specific	6.6	6.0	5.5	5.3	5.4	5.5	5.6	5.0
Total support	111.2	113.0	115.2	117.8	120.4	123.0	125.5	127.7

Note: — indicates zero.
Source: Authors' estimates.

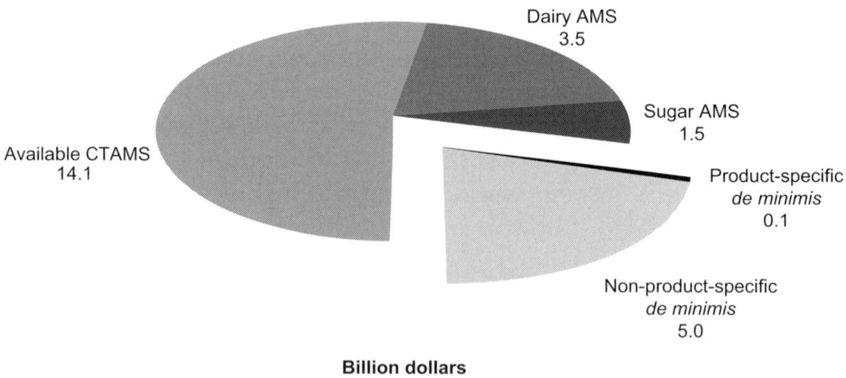

Figure 4.5 Projected composition of US AMS support in 2016 and available CTAMS under the Agreement
Source: Authors' estimates.

be over $22 billion in 2016 without violating US obligations under the Agreement. Additional product-specific support could be provided up to *de minimis* thresholds. The 2008 FCE Act paid little regard to the implications of any future WTO commitments and does not address issues that have been raised by WTO dispute settlement rulings, in particular the consistency of US fixed direct payments with Annex 2 of the Agreement. However, with projected high commodity prices, the fixed direct payments could easily fit within the Bound Total AMS in the future, whether counted as product-specific or non-product-specific support. Likewise, were a judgment made that ethanol blender tax credits (not incorporated into these projections) should be notified in the product-specific AMS category, they could also be included without violating the US limit.

This picture of essentially no constraint on US support under the Agreement could change if prices are not as strong as foreseen by USDA. Nevertheless, prices would have to fall substantially from recent and projected levels to trigger large payments with the loan rates and target prices specified in the 2008 FCE Act.

Under the Doha draft modalities

The United States falls into the second tier of the draft modalities for Base OTDS and Final Bound Total AMS reductions (see Table 2.2). The draft modalities are complicated for the United States, involving several provisions that are either unique or of particular relevance to its situation (WTO 2008). Of note are:

1. the expansion of the blue box criteria to include payments based on 85 percent or less of a fixed and unchanging base level of production – this implies that US countercyclical payments (but not ACRE payments) would be eligible for inclusion in the blue box, rather than being notified as AMS support;
2. a proportionately lower AMS limit for cotton than for other products, with an accelerated reduction schedule;[16]

[16] The United States had not offered a counter-proposal on the special cotton provisions, but it was widely anticipated that they would require further negotiation. When the negotiations broke down in December 2008, the cotton provisions were left unaddressed, so the US position remained undeclared. The special treatment of cotton support also applies to the EU and other cotton producers (see Appendix B).

Table 4.8 *OTDS, CTAMS, blue box and cotton support limits and the* de minimis *allowance for the US under the Doha draft modalities*

	Million dollars
Final Bound Total AMS	19,103.3
Value of production (average 1995–2000)	194,139.3
15 percent value of production	29,120.9
Base OTDS	48,224.2
Final Bound OTDS (after 70 percent reduction)	14,467.3
Final Bound Total AMS (after 60 percent reduction)	7,641.3
FBTAMS as a share of value of production (1995–2000)[a]	5.4%
Blue box limit (2.5 percent value of production 1995–2000)	4,853.5
De minimis	
50 percent immediate reduction	2.5%
Cotton special provisions	
Base AMS for cotton (million dollars)	800.5
Cotton AMS reduction (assuming 60 percent FBTAMS reduction)[b]	82.2%

[a] Tests for less than 40 percent, so additional effort does not apply (Table 2.2 and Appendix B, paragraph 14).
[b] Application of the cotton AMS reduction formula (Appendix B, paragraphs 54 and 55).
Source: Authors' calculations based on WTO (2008).

3. a special provision for the US calculation of other product-specific AMS limits; and
4. a special provision for the calculation of product-specific blue box limits, with a more stringent cap proposed for cotton.

Some of the principal implications of the proposed Doha draft modalities for the United States are summarized in Tables 4.8 and 4.9. The US Base OTDS from which reductions are to be made is $48.2 billion, comprised of the Final Bound Total AMS of $19.1 billion plus 15 percent of the US total agricultural value of production, which averaged $194.1 billion during 1995–2000. With the proposed 70 percent reduction, the final binding for the OTDS is just under $14.5 billion at the end of the proposed five-year implementation period.[17] The 60 percent reduction in the Final Bound Total AMS would

[17] During the December 2008 negotiations a further reduction to $14 billion was discussed.

Table 4.9 *Phased reductions of limits on OTDS, CTAMS and cotton AMS for the US under the Doha draft modalities*

	Immediate	Year 1	Year 2	Year 3	Year 4	Year 5 (Final)
Reduction commitments	*Cumulative proportions of the base to be cut*					
Base OTDS[a]	0.33	0.40	0.48	0.55	0.63	0.70
Final Bound Total AMS[b]	0.25	0.32	0.39	0.46	0.53	0.60
Cotton AMS[c]	0.25	0.25	0.82	0.82	0.82	0.82
Scheduled limits[d]	*Million dollars*					
Bound OTDS	32,310	28,742	25,173	21,604	18,036	14,467
Final Bound Total AMS	14,327	12,990	11,653	10,316	8,978	7,641
Cotton AMS	600	600	142	142	142	142

[a] Initial reduction of one-third, with remainder phased-in in five equal steps (Table 2.2 and Appendix B, paragraph 5).
[b] Initial reduction of 25 percent, with remainder phased-in in five equal steps (Table 2.2 and Appendix B, paragraph 15).
[c] Two-year phase-in period, with higher total reduction percentage than other products (Appendix B, paragraphs 54–56).
[d] Limit applies after reduction at end of year in corresponding column is made.
Source: Authors' interpretation based on WTO (2008).

reduce this cap to $7.64 billion. Total blue blue box payments would be limited to a maximum of $4.85 billion and the product-specific and non-product-specific *de minimis* thresholds lowered immediately to 2.5 percent of production values. The AMS limit for cotton would be reduced by 82.2 percent from a base value calculated as $800 million to $143 million. The cotton limits would have an accelerated phased-in period (20 months) compared to the five-year implementation for the phase-in of reduction commitments for Bound OTDS and Bound Total AMS.

Though the Doha bindings would not come into force for a number of years, it is instructive to examine whether the final proposed commitments would have been binding on past policies as notified. This question was particularly relevant through the early years of the Doha Round WTO negotiations (2001–05) when the broad outlines of possible commitments were being hammered out.[18] In this context, a comparison of the Final Bound OTDS of $14.5 billion to the sum of CTAMS, total *de minimis* and blue box support (Table 4.1) shows that past notified US support would not have been in compliance in the years 1995, 1998–2002 and 2004–05. The CTAMS would have exceeded the Final Bound Total AMS of $7.6 billion in 1998–2002 and 2004–06. The non-product-specific AMS would have exceeded 2.5 percent of the value of production from 1999–2002 and consequently would have been added to the CTAMS in those years. Product-specific cotton support exceeded the proposed limit under the Doha draft modalities every year with the exception of 1995 and 1996 and blue box expenditures in 1995 also exceeded the proposed Doha limit. The implication is that the constraints discussed in the Doha Round would have required policy changes if they had been applied in the past.

Table 4.10 contains calculations for the product-specific AMS limits under the Doha draft modalities for the forty-seven product categories for which an AMS was notified for at least one year since 1995. The sum of product-specific limits is just over $15 billion, almost double the proposed Final Bound Total AMS. Thus, the United States would not be able to provide the full amount of support allowed for each specific commodity while respecting its aggregate commitment.

The implications of the Doha bindings for the US vary by product. Only two of the forty-seven product categories for which an AMS was notified would have a zero AMS binding. These are avocados, for which a small amount of trade-adjustment assistance payments was notified in 2005 and the commodity aggregate beef, cattle and sheep for which a modest amount of assistance under a grant program was notified in 2006. Both of these fall outside the 1995–2004 base period for determining US product-specific caps under the Doha draft modalities, although assistance to beef, cattle and sheep producers could be provided under other categories included in Table 4.10. That is, if the methodology specified in the modalities is applied strictly, some products appear to be eligible for multiple caps (for example, those products notified separately and under aggregates such as livestock and orchards and vineyards).

Two of the products, dairy (with the calculations still based on total milk production) and sugar, would be subject to a special three-year phase-in for the reduction specified in the draft modalities, since their average AMS in the two notifications prior to the December 2008 draft

[18] Sumner (2005) provided an insightful early analysis at that time.

Table 4.10 *Product-specific US AMS bindings under the Doha draft modalities*

	Applicable modalities[a]	Base AMS	Year 1	Year 2	Year 3	Notified AMS 2007
		Million dollars				
Apples	25	76.6	76.6	76.6	76.6	—
Apricots	25	1.8	1.8	1.8	1.8	—
Avocados		—	—	—	—	—
Barley	23	27.4	27.4	27.4	27.4	—
Beef, cattle and sheep		—	—	—	—	—
Beef and veal	25	1,254.8	1,254.8	1,254.8	1,254.8	—
Blueberries, wild	25	1.8	1.8	1.8	1.8	—
Cattle and calves	25	1,255.4	1,255.4	1,255.4	1,255.4	—
Chickpeas	24	0.2	0.2	0.2	0.2	—
Corn	23	1,106.4	1,106.4	1,106.4	1,106.4	—
Cotton[b]	23	1,136.1	600.4	142.5	142.5	—
Cranberries	25	10.7	10.7	10.7	10.7	—
Dairy[c]	23,26	5,030.3	4,947.2	4,864.0	4,780.9	5,016.5
Dry peas	24	34.8	34.8	34.8	34.8	—
Grapes	25	131.2	131.2	131.2	131.2	—
Hogs and pigs	25	512.8	512.8	512.8	512.8	—
Honey	23	2.9	2.9	2.9	2.9	—
Lentils	24	6.1	6.1	6.1	6.1	—
Livestock	25	1,255.4	1,255.4	1,255.4	1,255.4	—
Lychee	25	0.2	0.2	0.2	0.2	—

Table 4.10 (*cont.*)

	Applicable modalities[a]	Base AMS	Year 1	Year 2	Year 3	Notified AMS 2007
		Million dollars				
Minor oil seeds						
Canola	23	15.1	15.1	15.1	15.1	—
Crambe	24	<0.1	<0.1	<0.1	<0.1	—
Flaxseed	24	<0.1	<0.1	<0.1	<0.1	—
Mustard seed	23	0.1	0.1	0.1	0.1	—
Rapeseed	23	<0.1	<0.1	<0.1	<0.1	—
Safflower	23	0.5	0.5	0.5	0.5	—
Sesame	23	<0.1	<0.1	<0.1	<0.1	—
Sunflower	23	35.5	35.5	35.5	35.5	—
Mohair	23	3.1	3.1	3.1	3.1	0.8
Oats	23	9.4	9.4	9.4	9.4	—
Olives	25	2.9	2.9	2.9	2.9	—
Onions	25	35.1	35.1	35.1	35.1	—
Orchards and vineyards	25	798.2	798.2	798.2	798.2	—
Peaches	25	22.0	22.0	22.0	22.0	—
Peanuts	23	249.2	249.2	249.2	249.2	—
Pears	25	14.0	14.0	14.0	14.0	—
Pecan trees	25	11.7	11.7	11.7	11.7	—
Potatoes	25	133.4	133.4	133.4	133.4	—
Rice	23	313.7	313.7	313.7	313.7	—
Rye	25	1.4	1.4	1.4	1.4	—

Sheep and lamb	24	7.0	7.0	7.0	7.0	—
Sorghum	23	42.6	42.6	42.6	42.6	—
Soybeans	23	1,123.7	1,123.7	1,123.7	1,123.7	—
Sugar	23,26	1,257.8	1,213.9	1,169.9	1,126.0	1,235.8
Tobacco	23	142.9	142.9	142.9	142.9	—
Tomatoes	25	86.2	86.2	86.2	86.2	—
Wheat	23	231.4	231.4	231.4	231.4	—
Wool	23	10.1	10.1	10.1	10.1	6.7
Total for all products		16,392.3	15,729.5	15,144.5	15,017.4	6,259.9

Notes: — indicates zero.

[a] See Appendix B for applicable paragraphs.

[b] The effective binding shown for cotton is that implied by the special reduction provisions, but the base value is not adjusted for those provisions.

[c] Dairy binding calculated on the basis of total milk production as notified for 2006 and 2007.

Source: Authors' calculations based on US notifications.

modalities (2006 and 2007) was more than 130 percent of their base levels). The cotton binding would be superseded by additional provisions. In the absence of these provisions the cotton AMS binding would be reduced from a base value of $1.5 billion to a bound value of $1.1 billion over a period of three years. The additional provisions result in a reduction from just over $800 million to a bound value of $143 million over a period of twenty months, as shown in Table 4.9.

Overall, the application of the rules specified in the modalities appears to leave a considerable amount of space for policy flexibility by providing product-specific AMS limits for virtually all important and minor US agricultural commodities, even if the actual notified support for some of these has been small in the past. But it may be difficult to keep within some of the product-specific caps if prices were to fall. The cap on corn at $1.1 billion, compared with a notified AMS well in excess of this value when prices have been low (see Table 4.4), is particularly noteworthy in this respect. A comparison of the data in Table 4.4 on the notifications for 1995–2008 to the product-specific AMS limits in Table 4.10 reveals that no less than 115 of the 153 notified AMS values included in CTAMS (75 percent) would have exceeded the proposed Doha limits (even without any trade-off to the blue box, discussed below). This includes all the notified AMS values for barley, corn, oats, soybeans and wheat. It suggests again that the proposed product-specific AMS limits could be extremely important.

Table 4.11 contains information on product-specific blue box bindings included in the draft modalities. The US limits are based on the maximum potential expenditure on countercyclical payments under the 2002 FSRI Act. The draft modalities include a special provision for the US, allowing base values of product-specific blue box support of either 110 percent or 120 percent of the amounts derived from applying proportionately legislated maximum permissible expenditure under the 2002 FSRI Act to 2.5 percent of average value of production for 1995–2000. Using the lower of the two proposed parameters (110 percent), the product-specific blue box caps would permit support through countercyclical payments equivalent to roughly 61 percent of the legislated maximum. The higher figure (120 percent) yields 66 percent of the maximum. As indicated in Table 4.7, maximum permitted payments within the overall blue box limit would be $4.8 billion. This implies that it would only be possible to exploit the full allowance provided by the individual blue box caps under the lower (110 percent) binding, as shown in Table 4.11.

The draft modalities indicate that countries can elect to increase the blue box binding for individual products by reducing that product's corresponding AMS binding. This is done on a dollar-for-dollar basis, except

Table 4.11 *Product-specific US blue box bindings and the trade-off with product-specific AMS bindings under the Doha draft modalities*

	Base AMS binding[a]	Blue binding 110%	Blue binding 120%	Legislated maximum CCP	AMS binding if blue is increased to maximum[b]
	Million dollars				
Barley	27.4	32.0	34.9	46.7	12.7
Corn	1,106.4	2,359.8	2,574.3	3,224.2	242.0
Cotton[c]	800.5	336.3	366.9	1,376.5	—
Oats	9.4	5.3	5.8	8.7	6.0
Peanuts	249.2	149.5	163.1	200.9	197.8
Rice	313.7	234.9	256.3	323.1	225.5
Sorghum	42.6	106.8	116.5	147.4	2.0
Soybeans	1,123.7	400.4	436.8	550.3	973.8
Wheat	231.4	1,041.1	1,135.7	1,421.5	—
Total	3,904.4	4,666.1	5090.3[d]	7,299.3	1,659.9

Notes: — indicates zero.

[a] It is assumed that the applicable figures for the calculation are the bindings that result after the application of any reduction provisions. This column matches the final product-specific bindings in Table 4.10, with the exception of cotton which is subject to a special provision for its base-period value (see Appendix B, paragraph 55).

[b] For cotton and wheat where insufficient product-specific AMS entitlement exists to reach the legislated maximum CCP, the full AMS entitlement is applied to the blue box.

[c] In the case of cotton, a $1 increase in the blue box entitlement requires a $2 reduction in the AMS; this is applied to the figure in column 1. Cotton blue box bindings are reduced substantially by the paragraph 56 condition.

[d] Total exceeds permitted blue box maximum of $4,853.5 million. Increases in blue box limits only apply if initially scheduled; any subsequent changes would require reductions elsewhere, such that the initial overall blue box limit is not exceeded (Appendix B, paragraph 45).

Source: Authors' calculations based on WTO notifications and WTO (2008).

for cotton where the rate is one dollar of expanded blue box binding for each two dollars given up from the AMS. Table 4.11 analyzes the effect of this provision for the case of the 110 percent initial blue box binding. As shown in the last column, box-shifting from the product-specific AMS to the product-specific blue box could achieve the legislated maxima for all CCP commodities individually except for cotton and wheat (this is without considering any additional constraints imposed by the overall blue box limit). For those commodities the AMS binding is too low to be able to achieve the legislated CCP maximum. In addition, the sum of the individual product bindings would exceed the overall blue box limit. Hence any choice to increase individual bindings to the legislated maximum, which would have to be declared in the initial scheduling of commitments, would imply trade-offs in order to satisfy the overall blue box constraint.

Future compliance with Doha

With buoyant agricultural prices in 2007–08 the prospect of a new era of higher prices has been widely discussed. Price projections are subject to uncertainty, but a shift to higher levels certainly has implications for the tightness of domestic support commitments.

To assess the implications of a Doha agreement in line with the December 2008 draft modalities, the following assumptions were made:

1. The first year for implementation of a new agreement is 2011 with complete implementation by 2015;
2. The Final Bound OTDS, Final Bound Total AMS, blue box and cotton AMS commitments and the *de minimis* threshold and phase-in periods are those shown in Table 4.8 and 4.9;
3. The parameters of US support programs are those of the 2008 FCE Act. Market price support for dairy is assumed to be notified on the basis of the three processed products rather than total milk production. However, possible ACRE revenue-guarantee payments are not included in the basic calculations;
4. The final product-specific AMS bindings included in Table 4.10 are imposed;
5. The 110 percent product-specific blue box bindings (second column in Table 4.11) are applied; and
6. No allowance is made for the transfer of product-specific AMS to product-specific blue box.

Table 4.12 *Projected levels of US domestic support under the Doha draft modalities, 2010–16*

	2010	2011	2012	2013	2014	2015	2016
	Billion dollars						
Green box	102.2	104.8	107.6	110.0	112.4	114.8	117.5
OTDS	10.7	10.3	10.3	10.4	10.6	10.7	10.2
Blue box	—	0.5	0.5	0.4	0.3	0.3	0.2
Current Total AMS	4.6	4.7	4.8	4.9	4.9	5.0	5.0
Total *de minimis*	6.1	5.1	5.0	5.1	5.3	5.4	4.9
Product-specific	0.1	0.1	0.1	0.1	0.1	0.1	0.1
Non-product-specific	6.0	5.0	4.9	5.0	5.2	5.3	4.8
Total support	113.0	115.2	117.8	120.5	123.0	125.5	127.7

Note: — indicates zero.
Source: Authors' estimates.

Table 4.12 summarizes the projected notifications by category. The only change from Table 4.7 is the emergence of a modest amount of blue box payments by switching countercyclical payments from the non-product-specific AMS, and a corresponding reduction in the amount of *de minimis* support under the latter. Figure 4.6 shows how the reductions in the US commitments for the OTDS, the CTAMS, and the overall blue box relate to projected notifications. The reduction in the OTDS ceiling does not become binding even by the end of the implementation period, but the leeway in the commitment, resulting from the limit being higher than projected notifications, is substantially reduced. These projections suggest that in the first year of implementation of a Doha agreement, there would be a roughly $18 billion cushion between the applied OTDS and the bound level. By 2016 this would have declined to around $4.3 billion. The reduction in the Bound Total AMS is also significant, with a decrease in the CTAMS support cushion from over $8 billion in 2011 to less than $3 billion by 2016. Projected blue box payments remain far below the ceiling – the overall blue box limit does not have a constraining effect on the projections since high prices mean that countercyclical payments are low. The analysis also shows that non-product-specific AMS stays below the *de minimis* threshold, but the margin is reduced to roughly $1 billion.

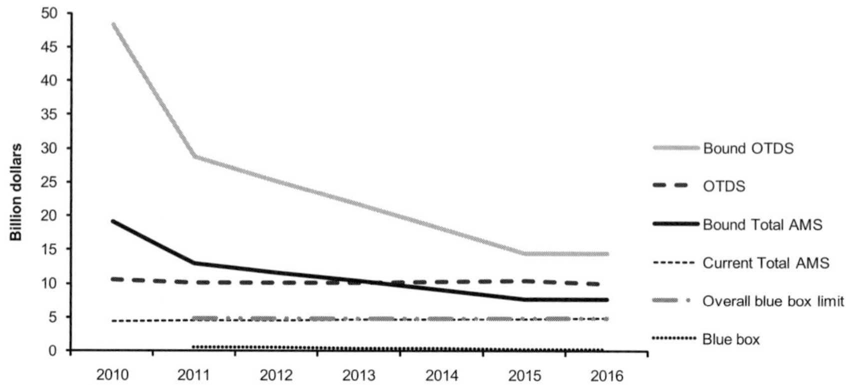

Figure 4.6 Projections and proposed Doha commitments for US OTDS, CTAMS and overall blue box support
Source: Authors' estimates.

AMS support, even within *de minimis* allowances, may also face a limit imposed by the room left within the OTDS binding after accounting for CTAMS and blue box payments.

We also analyzed the implications of the product-specific AMS and product-specific blue box bindings for some of the most important commodities: barley, corn, cotton, dairy (based on total milk production), peanuts, rice, sorghum, soybeans, sugar, and wheat. Our projections suggest that the AMS binding would become operative for dairy and sugar from the first year of the implementation period and throughout. There is a gradual increase in the amount by which the product-specific AMS binding for these commodities is exceeded (Figure 4.7) from around $200 million in 2011 to $400 million for sugar and to $600 million for dairy by 2016. The AMS for sugar is increased by higher sugar administered prices (loan rates) in the FCE Act and by a projected expansion in sugar production. The higher AMS for dairy is attributable to expanding milk production. Our projections also imply that the blue box binding for cotton would be exceeded in the initial years of a new agreement, but higher projected cotton prices eliminate this problem from 2014 onwards.[19]

[19] Earlier projections based on lower cotton prices suggested that both the product-specific blue box and AMS commitments could be binding for cotton (see Blandford, Laborde, and Martin 2008). The potentially binding product-specific dairy limit seems to provide one incentive for the redefinition of dairy support in 2008.

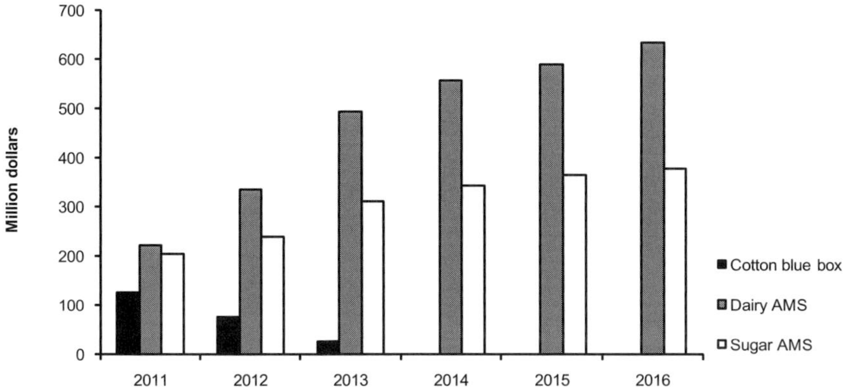

Figure 4.7 Amounts by which proposed US product-specific Doha commitments are projected to be exceeded
Source: Authors' estimates.

In summary, the new Doha commitments would certainly be more stringent than those of the Agreement. They might constrain US farm programs in terms of choice of measures or subsidy levels. Strengthened disciplines would reduce the leeway the US would have for providing trade-distorting support but still provide limited flexibility if prices remain relatively high. The net outcome projected for 2016 is illustrated in Figure 4.8, which shows projected CTAMS, blue box and product-specific and non-product-specific *de minimis* support compared to the potential limit of almost $14.5 billion under a Doha constraint on the OTDS. The difference between the OTDS limit and the sum of projected support is shown as the "Available OTDS." Projected blue box payments (counter-cyclical payments) are only $0.2 billion, well under the modalities cap of $4.8 billion. The CTAMS (dairy and sugar MPS) is projected at $5.0 billion, compared to the proposed cap of $7.6 billion. Product-specific *de minimis* support is negligible and non-product-specific *de minimis* support is projected at $4.8 billion. These projections and caps leave room for various additional OTDS support of $4.3 billion. The latitude for additional support is therefore limited, unless the United States further reduces the notified AMS for dairy and sugar.[20]

[20] The inclusion of a provision in the 2008 FCE Act to divert government purchases of sugar to the production of ethanol opens up the interesting possibility that the sugar program (or some part of it) could be defined as a bioenergy program. This might also be used to

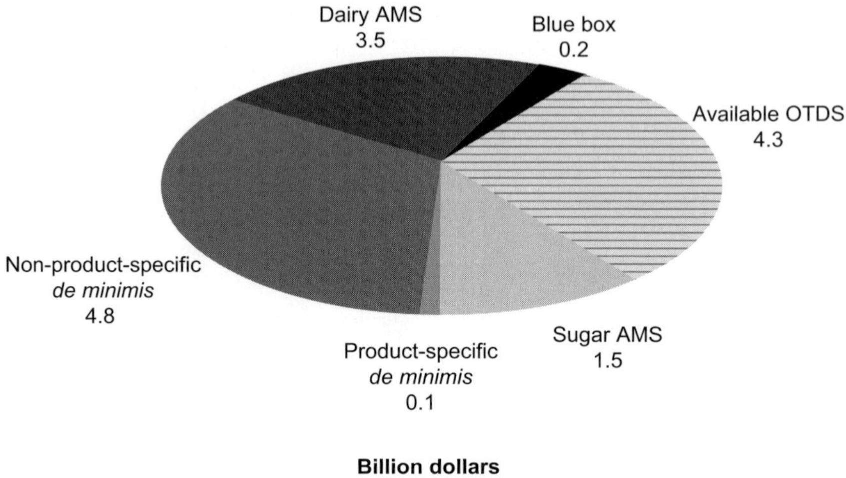

Figure 4.8 Projected composition of US OTDS in 2016 and available OTDS under proposed Doha commitments
Source: Authors' estimates.

Uncertainty due to the ACRE program

Thus far the implications of the new ACRE state revenue-guarantee program have not been considered in the projections of US support. Significant enrollment in the ACRE program and payments triggered by revenue variability could affect compliance with US commitments under the Agreement. The program makes payments when revenue for a crop in a state falls below a moving average of past levels. Payments can be triggered by a decline in the US price, state yields, or a combination of the two. USDA price and yield projections reflect recent trends and exhibit limited variability, so ACRE payments are not triggered using those numbers. However, actual prices and yields inevitably prove more variable than projections. No ceiling exists on guaranteed revenue and ACRE can provide assistance when revenue declines but prices remain above marketing loan and countercyclical support prices. Because ACRE payments are linked to both current prices and production, it is likely that they will be classified as product-specific AMS support.

relieve any pressure on sugar protection that arises from changes in market access (tariffs and tariff-rate quotas) under a new WTO agreement.

The potential magnitude of ACRE payments for corn, soybeans and wheat was examined by Zulauf and Orden (2010). As a counterfactual historical analysis, they assumed for illustration that all the acreage for these crops was enrolled in an ACRE program during 1996–2008 instead of the actual US support programs during that period. They estimated the annual payments that would have been made under ACRE given the changes in annual prices and state yields and acreage that occurred each year.

With ACRE in operation during 1996–2008, there would have been no countercyclical payments. With loan rates reduced by 30 percent in the ACRE program, there also would have been no loan-rate-related payments. Total ACRE revenue guarantee payments would have been only $14.7 billion, in part because in some years higher yields offset lower prices sufficiently such that payments would not have occurred, while the traditional price support programs made payments. The relatively low ACRE payments for 1996–2008 would not have caused the CTAMS to exceed the US commitment under the Agreement in any year. Peak estimated annual ACRE payment for the three crops was $5.2 billion in the 1998 crop year, compared to $3.3 billion in AMS notified for these commodities. Since the 1998 CTAMS was only $10.4 billion the increase due to ACRE would not have violated the US commitment.

In a forward-looking analysis, the potential ACRE payments for the years 2009–12 were estimated given the higher prices for corn, soybeans, and wheat projected by USDA in January 2009 for these crop years. For each year, the analysis considered cases where the percentage changes in prices, yields and acreage compared to USDA's projections matched the percentage changes that took place in one year between 1996 and 2006 (providing eleven such cases of changes). The sum in any crop year of the highest projected ACRE payments to corn, soybeans, and wheat over the sets of applied changes was $14.2 billion, again assuming all acreage is enrolled in the program. Thus, it seems possible that with the higher price levels prevailing since 2007 the United States could exceed its Bound Total AMS of $19.1 billion if market conditions change sufficiently from year-to-year to trigger significant ACRE payments. In contrast, none of the cases of changes in price, yield and acreage triggered countercyclical or loan-rate-related payments for any year when it was assumed that all acreage of corn, soybeans and wheat remained in the traditional support programs during 2009–12.

The possibility of large ACRE payments under some of the cases analyzed poses additional challenges for the United States in meeting potential Doha commitments. The proposed product-specific AMS caps are among the relevant constraints. For corn and soybeans, estimated payments for each crop year exceeded the Doha product-specific caps in three and four of the eleven cases of changes, respectively. For wheat, projected payments exceeded the Doha product-specific cap for seven of the eleven cases for the 2009 and 2010 crop years and for six cases for the 2011 and 2012 crop years. The actual participation rate in ACRE, in addition to future fluctuations in prices and output, will affect the likelihood that ACRE payments would pose a challenge for meeting future Doha commitments. For example, if the share of base acres enrolled in the ACRE program in 2009 (roughly 10–20 percent) remained the same through the mid 2010s, AMS support would likely remain below the Doha product-specific caps. Sign-up rates are high enough that the ACRE program or some variant of it will probably remain part of future US farm support policy. A Doha agreement would make it difficult to design such a program both to stay within the US commitments and attract substantial participation. Thus a Doha agreement could shape future US policy.

Summary and implications for US agricultural policy

This chapter has examined past and proposed US domestic support in the light of existing and potential WTO constraints. In the first section we provided a brief review of US farm policies since the Agreement on Agriculture came into effect, including a synopsis of the Food, Conservation, and Energy Act of 2008. Our review highlights the shifting alignment of US support policies: initially a response to relatively high prices when the 1996 farm bill was enacted with the first US fixed direct payments, then the impact of relatively low prices when policies were reconsidered in the 2002 FSRI Act and price-linked countercyclical payments were re-institutionalized. In 2008, market prices were again strong, but with the exception of the potentially significant ACRE program there was little change in basic support policies. This meant that US price-linked subsidies were projected to fall sharply under the 2008 FCE Act, compared with levels early in the 2000s, with higher subsidies projected for crop and revenue insurance. We also highlighted acreage-idling under the CRP and increased spending on other environmental programs, which are measures in the green box and subject to its rules.

The second section provided an assessment of US domestic support notifications to the WTO from 1995–2007 and a shadow notification estimate for 2008. Green box expenditures for domestic nutrition programs dominate the total dollar value of support notified by the United States. The main notified components for agriculture include fixed direct payments, disaster assistance, and environmental payments in the green box; market price support for dairy and sugar and substantial price-linked expenditures (loan program payments) in the product-specific AMS; and non-product-specific AMS support qualifying for the *de minimis* exemption (crop MLA payments, countercyclical payments, and crop and revenue insurance subsidies). The AMS price-linked payments have varied from a low of near zero (1996, 2007 and 2008) to a high of $9.7 billion in 1999, while crop MLA payments and countercyclical payments varied from $0.5 billion in 2003 to $5.5 billion in 1999.

The US CTAMS has never exceeded the Bound Total AMS of $19.1 billion. It would have done so in some years without the non-product-specific *de minimis* exemption or if US fixed direct payments were included in the AMS as either non-product-specific or product-specific support. We discuss other subsidies that may be underreported, misclassified, or omitted from the notifications, some of which are also at issue in WTO dispute settlement cases. We note that tax credits and mandates related to ethanol production have been largely outside the disciplines of the Agreement and discuss arguments related to their inclusion as trade-distorting support.

We next provided an assessment of projected US support through 2016 and evaluated the extent to which the Agreement or new disciplines in the Doha draft modalities might limit future US policies. With projected high prices the Agreement hardly constrains US policies at all. Reclassified fixed direct payments, large ACRE revenue-guarantee payments, or ethanol tax credits could be accommodated without violating the Bound Total AMS. That is unlikely to be the case if the proposed new Doha disciplines were adopted since the room for maneuver would be more limited. With high prices, the unused support space within the Bound OTDS commitment is projected to be $4.3 billion by 2016 given the way that the US has notified its dairy support after implementing the 2008 FCE Act. If there were no ACRE revenue-guarantee payments, no reclassification of direct payments, and no inclusion of other subsidies, the US would have this limited flexibility to increase support – whether through higher loan rates or by increasing other forms of product-specific support included in the CTAMS, raising target prices for countercyclical payments in the blue box, or through expanding non-product-specific AMS while staying below the *de minimis* threshold. Additional redefinition of the dairy program with a corresponding further reduction in notified MPS could provide more flexibility for increasing loan rates for other commodities by opening additional space within the Bound Total AMS. However, if payments under the ACRE program become significant it seems unlikely that the United States would be able to stay within a reduced Bound Total AMS or meet other Doha commitments.

If the relatively high-price environment foreseen by the USDA continues to materialize, it appears that the United States would have to adapt to the Doha draft modalities by making modest downward adjustments in the support provided by some of its policies. Experience with farm legislation shows that such adjustments would not be easy to make nor politically painless. The proposed product-specific limits, in particular, could further constrain policy flexibility. Sugar poses problems for AMS commitments even if world prices are high because of the way MPS is calculated and notified. The redefinition of the dairy program in the FCE Act might signal that a similar attempt could be made to resolve this issue for sugar without substantive change in the degree of support provided to producers. The stringent modalities for cotton, if adopted, could prove challenging for meeting blue box commitments, even under projected high prices. Other product-specific caps, such as for AMS for corn, would limit support well below levels observed in the 2000s.

The price environment foreseen by USDA and incorporated into our projections may not materialize. Lower prices could prove a challenge. In that case, the Bound Total AMS and some product-specific AMS limits could well be exceeded under a Doha agreement, unless alternatives to current support policies were found. One option would be to use the green box to alter the composition of farm support. Green box support for farmers could be expanded, particularly under the environmental category, or under other categories such as decoupled income support payments or disaster relief payments that satisfy green box criteria. The future status of current US fixed direct payments is in doubt, but payment rules could be modified to ensure green box compliance.

In conclusion, the strengthened disciplines on domestic support in the Doha draft modalities would have the effect of reducing substantially the leeway in the amount of support that can be provided to US farmers while still meeting WTO commitments. A few commodities pose problems even with relatively high prices. The option of redefining support policies to reduce notified MPS further for dairy or for sugar and the possibility of there being some unused support space in other areas (blue box and non-product-specific AMS falling under *de minimis*) provide some amount of flexibility in meeting future WTO commitments. However, if prices were to fall substantially, so that major countercyclical, price support, or ACRE revenue-guarantee payments were triggered, the likelihood of meeting tighter WTO commitments on domestic support under a continuation of existing programs would be substantially reduced. Thus, the tighter Doha commitments could bring significant change in the design of future US domestic support policies for agriculture.

References

Blandford, D., and T. Josling. 2007. US and EU domestic support notifications, 2007–2012. Paper presented at a workshop of the German Marshall Fund of the United States, Washington, DC, September 11.

Blandford, D., D. Laborde, and W. Martin. 2008. Implications for the United States. ICTSD/IPC/IFFPRI Project on Draft Agricultural Modalities. Paper presented at a seminar in Geneva, March 12.

Chite, R. M. 2007. Farm bill budget and costs: 2002 vs. 2007. RS22694, Congressional Research Service. November 7.

Congressional Budget Office. 2008. H.R. 2419: The Food, Conservation, and Energy Act of 2008 – Conference agreement compared to March 2007 CBO baseline, May 12. www.cbo.gov (accessed June 8, 2008).

de Gorter, H., and D. R. Just. 2009. The economics of blend mandates for biofuels. *American Journal of Agricultural Economics* 91(3): 738–750.

Gardner, B. 2002. *American Agriculture in the Twentieth Century: How it Flourished and What it Cost*. Cambridge, MA: Harvard University Press.

2009. Distortions to agricultural incentives in the United States and Canada. In *Distortions to Agricultural Incentives: A Global Perspective 1955–2007*, ed. K. Anderson. London: Palgrave Macmillan, and Washington, DC: World Bank.

Hull, D., J. Langley, and G. Hitz. 2009. CBO March 2009 baseline for CCC & FCIC, February 20. www.cbo.gov (accessed March 10, 2009).

Josling, T. E., S. Tangermann, and T. K. Warley. 1996. *Agriculture in the GATT*. New York: St. Martin's Press Inc.

Orden, D., D. Blandford, and T. Josling. 2010. Determinants of farm policies in the United States, 1996–2008. In *The Political Economy of Distortions to Agricultural Incentives*, ed. K. Anderson. Cambridge University Press.

Orden, D., R. Paarlberg, and T. Roe. 1999. *Policy Reform in American Agriculture: Analysis and Prognosis*. University of Chicago Press.

Sumner, D. 2005. Boxed in: Conflicts between US farm policies and WTO obligations. Trade Policy Analysis No. 32, CATO Institute.

USDA (US Department of Agriculture). 2009a. Commodity Credit Corporation commodity estimates book FY 2010 mid-session review. Presentation 2010–02. Farm Service Agency, July.

2009b. USDA agricultural projections to 2017. Long-term projections report OCE-2008–1. Office of the Chief Economist, World Agricultural Outlook Board.

WTO. 2005. United States – Subsidies on upland cotton. Report of the Appellate Body. WT/DS267/AB/R, 3 March.

2007a. United States – Domestic support and export credit guarantees for agricultural products. Request for the establishment of a panel by Brazil. WT/DS365/13, 9 November.

2007b. United States – Subsidies and other domestic support for corn and other agricultural products. Request for the establishment of a panel by Canada. WT/DS357/12, 9 November.

2008. Revised draft modalities for agriculture. TN/AG/W/4/Rev.4, 6 December.

Zulauf, C., and D. Orden. 2010. The Revenue program option in the 2008 US farm bill: Evaluating performance characteristics of the ACRE program. *Agricultural and Resource Economics Review* 39(3): 517–533.

5

Japan

YOSHIHISA GODO AND DAISUKE TAKAHASHI

Japan's general approach toward agricultural domestic policy reform is one of strict compliance with the domestic support disciplines of the WTO. Japan reduced its AMS support by nearly 80 percent between 1995 and 2000. As a result, by 2000 its Current Total AMS had declined to less than 20 percent of its commitment under the Agreement. Japan launched an extensive agricultural subsidy reform in 2007 that partly reflected the principle of decoupling. An additional expansion of direct payments to farmers, the categorization of which will have to be taken into account in the future, was proposed in 2009 after a shift in control of the government.

This seemingly accommodating attitude on domestic agricultural policy contrasts with a less flexible attitude on border protection for agricultural commodities. Japan's nominal protection rate for agriculture is one of the highest among developed nations. Japan, which is surrounded by the ocean and poorly endowed with natural resources, relies heavily on trade. Nevertheless, its strong resistance to reductions in agricultural border protection has repeatedly hindered trade negotiations with other countries. During the Uruguay Round negotiations, Japan lobbied hard to maintain its rice autarky policy. An inflexible stance on rice imports almost resulted in Japan's failure to join the final agreements.

In consideration of this background, this chapter provides a comprehensive picture of Japan's agricultural policy. Farmland regulations are often manipulated in Japan, bringing financial benefits to farmland owners. The overwhelming majority of farmers are more concerned with the benefits gained from farmland regulations than earning profits from farming. The political manipulation of farmland regulations is

The authors express their thanks to Mr. Yuichi Otsuka and Mr. Kazuhiko Terao of the Ministry of Agriculture, Forestry and Fisheries (MAFF) for answering many questions about Japan's official WTO notification procedures.

a deep-seated problem and has been treated as a taboo subject for open discussion in Japanese society. Rice support also remains politically sacrosanct. In this chapter we overlook this taboo and elaborate on the dynamics of Japanese agricultural policy, including the future sanctity of rice policy.

The overall political economy of Japanese agriculture is discussed first, including the power of small farmers and the importance of farmland values. Rice support policy is then evaluated. This is followed by a brief discussion of the extensive agricultural policy reforms implemented in 2007 and thereafter. We examine Japan's notifications of domestic support to the WTO and evaluate projected support in light of the Agreement and the draft Doha modalities.

Political economy of the agricultural sector

It is useful to quickly review the geographical and ecological characteristics of Japan's farm sector before discussing related policy problems. Although Japan has substantial rainfall, water flows quickly to the ocean due to the mountainous topography. Thus, farmers need a highly sophisticated water control system. Japan's water usage system for rice paddy fields is unique compared to those found elsewhere in the developed world. A paddy field consists of many small plots of land. Water drawn from a floodgate of a river moves through all plots in a farming community in a set order (from upper plots to lower plots), slowly but continuously. Since farmers in a Japanese farming community share the same water, inappropriate water usage on one plot profoundly affects farming in other plots on the paddy field plain. Thus, the members in a farming community must collaborate with each other in the use of farmland and water.

A traditional farming community in Japan consists of about twenty households. Each farmer has several tiny plots of land at different locations in a paddy field plain. The average individual farm size is around 1.0 hectare. Therefore, farm ownership is expressed as a mosaic pattern. This structure is reasonable for traditional small-scale farming because each farmer's paddy field plots adjoin different farmers' plots at various points, allowing farmers to routinely observe each other's activities, making collaboration on farmland and water use easier.

After the development of labor-saving technology in the post-war period, this traditional farming community structure became less efficient. It has been estimated that the optimal farm size is over 15 hectares and that the production cost of rice could be halved if farmland was consolidated into large-scale farms (MAFF 1992). Thus, if the price mechanisms functioned properly in the farmland market, small-scale farmers would have been weeded out, and only large-scale farmers would have survived. In reality, however, the average farm size has not increased sufficiently to capture this economy of scale. Nearly 70 percent of Japan's farmland is still operated as inefficient-scale farms of less than 3 hectares. As of 2003, the average farm size was still around 1.4 hectares. While large-acreage farms that exceed 30 hectares have also emerged, the number is small.[1]

Small-scale farmers' agricultural productivity is low, so they hardly earn profits from farming. This does not mean, however, that small-scale farmers lead poverty-stricken lives. On the contrary, the average income (measured by household income per head) of small-scale farmers exceeds that of urban workers (Table 5.1). This is because small-scale farmers usually have stable non-agricultural income opportunities. Small-scale farmers earn their living mainly from their off-farm income. Many small-scale farmers are well-off salaried workers who own farmland as a side business. The side business includes not only farming but also taking advantage of farmland regulations. An overwhelming majority of farmland owners prefer to maintain the structure of traditional small-farming communities because it is favorable for keeping good connections (including informal connections) with government authorities and policymakers.

Small-scale farmers' political power

Why do small-scale farmers dominate Japanese agriculture while being inferior to large-scale farmers in terms of agricultural productivity? The answer to this question lies in the political dynamics of Japanese agriculture that prevent the price mechanisms from functioning properly in the farmland market.

Geographically, the amount of flat land is limited in Japan. In particular, high-quality farmland, which consists of flat and well-shaped plots of paddy fields, is extremely limited. If a farmer wants to enlarge his farm, he must purchase or lease farmland from other farmers. This means that the development of large-scale farming inevitably breaks the structure of traditional farming communities.

As a voting group, the traditional farming community has several characteristics attractive to politicians. Traditional small-scale farmers

[1] Only 555 farms exceed 30 hectares, less than 0.02 percent of the total number of farms (2.8 million).

Table 5.1 *Comparison of household income in Japan, 2003*

	Farm size	Number of farm households	Household income per head	Percentage of farm income in total household income
	Hectares	*Thousands*	*Thousand yen*	%
Commercial farm households				
	Below 0.5	436	1,693	19
	0.5–1.0	673	1,763	4
	1.0–1.5 }	498	1,786	8
	1.5–2.0 }		1,579	13
	2.0–3.0	159	1,684	22
	Over 3.0	144	1,561	34
Total		1,911	1,678	54
Salaried worker household			1,515	

Note: Commercial farm households are defined as having over 0.3 hectares of farmland, or agricultural revenue over 0.5 million yen.
Sources: Ministry of Agriculture, Forestry and Fisheries, *Statistical Survey on Farm Management and Economy*; Ministry of Internal Affairs and Communications, *Family Income and Expenditure Survey.*

have cultivated the same land for generations and have strong community ties. The need to share irrigation water leads farmers to cooperate on issues in which they have common interests. Farmers' voting rate is usually higher than that of non-farmers. These characteristics allow farmers to easily consolidate their support for politicians.

In addition, the number of registered voters per member of the Diet (parliament) is smaller in rural than in urban areas. While this rural–urban disparity was reduced to some degree in the 1994 reform of the electoral system, rural voters still have nearly three times the voting power of their urban counterparts. This disparity has maintained the influence of farmers' votes. Urban dwellers in Japan often show their sympathy towards farmers, and the Japanese mass media tend to describe farmers as honest and weak persons who need special protection by the government. It has therefore been in the interests of politicians to maintain the structure of traditional small-farming communities, and to obtain the electoral support of farmers. This has been the primary strategy of the Liberal Democratic Party (LDP), which has been in power for almost the entire post-war period.

The collusion between LDP politicians and farming communities also benefits the Japanese Ministry of Agriculture, Forestry and Fisheries (MAFF). MAFF has been chronically criticized for its extravagant personnel practices and budget.[2] In order to maintain its staff and budget, MAFF requires the support of LDP politicians.

The replacement of small-scale farmers by large-scale farmers is undesirable for MAFF as well as rural politicians. Thus, MAFF and these politicians need a special organization to impede the market mechanism that would lead to land consolidation, and this role has been filled by the agricultural cooperatives collectively known as Japan Agriculture (JA). JA not only lobbies politicians and provides services to farmers but also observes and controls members' activities, both directly and indirectly. JA also functions as a *de facto* sub-governmental body that helps MAFF create and enforce policy. Some of MAFF's subsidies for farmers (for example, low-interest loans) are distributed through JA. Thus, MAFF does not introduce policies without considering JA's interests.

The political dynamics among small-scale farmers, MAFF, politicians, and JA are summarized in Figure 5.1. Since this collusion has benefited these parties at a cost to society in general, great care is taken to ensure that their true objectives are obscured. MAFF has always favored small-scale farming communities in policymaking and policy enforcement, while simultaneously stating the promotion of large-scale farming as its objective. MAFF policies tend to be extremely complex and ambiguous. It is thus difficult for consumers (and other outside interests) to be fully informed of those policies' implications and effects. Likewise, JA's structural and operational complexity has been a strategy for camouflaging its real influence.

The Agricultural Cooperative Law guarantees farmers freedom in establishing agricultural cooperatives, stipulating that there is no obligation for an agricultural cooperative to join the JA system. Farmers are free to join or leave agricultural cooperatives as they see fit. However, under implicit pressures from MAFF and rural communities, almost all farmers join JA and renounce the establishment of other agricultural

[2] As of 2004, the number of personnel in MAFF was nearly five times that of the Ministry of Economy, Trade and Industry.

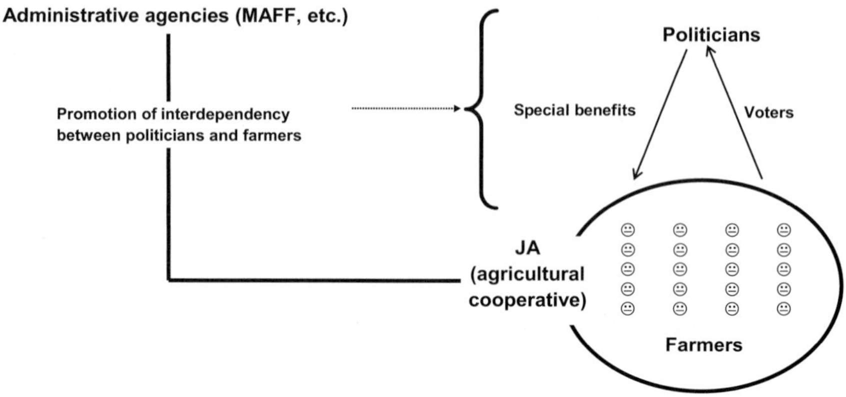

Figure 5.1 Political dynamics among Japan's farmers, politicians, MAFF and JA
Source: Authors' conceptualization.

cooperatives. Many JA businesses have enjoyed heavy protection, as well as regulation, by the government. For instance, JA was given a monopolistic position in the collection of rice and the sale of fertilizer.

JA's businesses are not limited to agriculture-related activities, such as operation of joint-use agricultural facilities, joint shipping of agricultural commodities, joint purchasing of agricultural inputs, and the establishment of agricultural machinery centers. JA also provides almost all services in rural life. JA's non-agricultural businesses include financial activities (banking and insurance), supermarkets, ceremony halls, gasoline stations, travel ticketing, and land development, and these have been increasing. In recent years, two-thirds of JA officers have been employed in non-agricultural activities.

Among JA's businesses, banking and insurance services are the most profitable. Banking and insurance businesses had been under heavy supervision of the Ministry of Finance (MOF) until the early 1990s. MOF's various regulations of the financial market prevented weak financial companies from collapsing. This is known as the "convoy" system. Under the convoy system, MOF provided particularly favorable treatment toward JA's financial activities. For example, JA was given more freedom than ordinary commercial banks about branch locations, its term-deposit interest rates, and insurance premiums. Because of MOF's favorable treatment, JA enjoyed stable profits from its banking and insurance ventures.

JA's farm services are convenient for small-scale farmers. Although entrepreneurial large-scale farmers have made efforts to develop their own supply and distribution channels, traditional small-scale farmers, who continue to make up the overwhelming majority of JA members, are dependent on its services. Thus, despite deregulation of the market for farm products and farm inputs in the 1980s and 1990s, JA has maintained its market-dominant position in the supply and distribution of these products and inputs.

The significance of farmland regulations

The largest source of benefits delivered to small-scale farmers by politicians comes from the manipulation of farmland regulations. This political use of regulations involves deep-seated issues. Its main features are described by Godo (2007), who raised concerns about its impact on society.

In Japan, land of high quality for farming in practice also means of high potential for farmland conversion. Favorable conditions for modern farming are flatness, abundance of sunlight, conveniently sized blocks of well-shaped plots, a good supply and drainage of water, and good access to roads. These five conditions are equally favorable for the conversion of farmland to non-agricultural uses for private or public facilities.

Because farmland has various externalities, such as prevention of floods, numerous laws have been written protecting and regulating the use of farmland. Among these, the Law Concerning the Construction of Agricultural Promotion Areas (LCAPA) is particularly important. The LCAPA authorizes municipal governments to designate zones of Exclusively Agricultural Areas (EAAs). Farmers in EAAs are responsible for using farmland for farming purposes only. Abandonment of farmland and conversion to non-agricultural uses are prohibited. Under MAFF's favorite slogan, to increase food self-sufficiency, MAFF allocates a large number of farmland improvement investments to EAAs. These investments increase not only agricultural productivity but also the potential for farmland conversion. In addition, farmland in EAAs receives favorable treatments in taxation and allocation of agricultural subsidies.

On the surface, the laws regarding farmland use appear strict. In practice, however, the implementation of those laws is problematic. Farmland-use regulations are often manipulated when the authorities are subject to political pressure. A small-scale farmer's ideal scenario is that his farmland is initially included in an EAA so that he can enjoy agricultural subsidies and MAFF farmland improvement investments, as well as a reduction in asset taxes. Then, when a farmland-conversion plan is implemented, the farmer's land will ideally be excluded from the EAA and the plan approved so that the farmer can enjoy capital gains.

In order to realize this scenario, small-scale farmers usually join forces to pressure local authorities and policymakers. Although farmers cannot control critical factors, such as when and how a farmland-conversion plan is approved, public construction projects provide the best conditions for land conversion. The public sector usually purchases farmland at a higher price than the private sector, and favorable tax treatment is granted when farmland is sold for public sector use. A large private development, such as a factory site or a shopping center, is the second-best scenario, because prices tend to increase for these large-scale developments. As opportunities for public construction projects or large private development plans are limited, politicians are not always able to deliver such desirable opportunities to their farming constituents. However, in the long run, the possibility of securing a desirable land conversion increases when these politicians continue their promotional efforts.

The ideal scenario also increases the national budget for farmland investments and public construction works, thus benefiting MAFF, which manages rural public construction works. Thus, MAFF welcomes this scenario and turns a blind eye to the manipulation of farmland-use regulations. Obviously the ideal scenario contradicts MAFF's objective to increase food self-sufficiency. MAFF needs to hide the realities of farmland-use regulations from public scrutiny; otherwise it will face difficulties maintaining its extravagant fiscal expenditures. Since the ideal scenario is based on extensive collusion between small-scale farmers and politicians, the expectation of the ideal scenario increases JA's weight in rural political dynamics. In addition, small-scale farmers usually deposit proceeds from the sale of farmland into JA accounts, producing more profit for JA's banking businesses. Thus, JA also encourages the ideal scenario.

When farmland is converted for non-agricultural land use, the farmland price is 30–140 times higher than its earning capacity under agricultural use (Figure 5.2). Even when used for farming, its selling value is 3–80 times higher than its farming-earning capacity. This reflects farmers' expectations of capital gains from farmland conversion: the market value of land is too high if agricultural production is the sole motivation of purchasers. In Japanese business practice, tenant farmers' rights are heavily protected. If a landowner rents his farmland to a tenant farmer, the landowner cannot sell the farmland without the tenant farmer's approval. Thus, small-scale farmers, who are expecting eventual farmland conversion, are reluctant to rent their farmland to large-scale farmers even if large-scale farmers offer relatively high rents based on agricultural use potential.

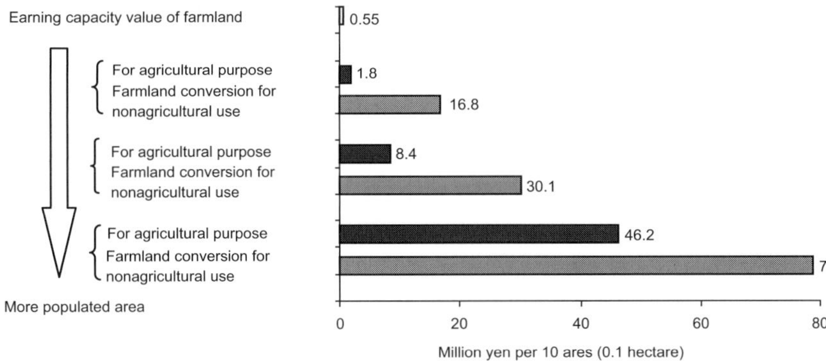

Figure 5.2 Market value of paddy fields for agricultural and non-agricultural uses in Japan
Source: Godo 2007.

Rice policy

Even if small-scale farmers do not earn profits from it, they still continue farming for two reasons. First, asset taxes are low as long as they are farming. Second, through their water usage they can maintain close relationships with other farmers in the rural community, which in turn is necessary to maintain their solidarity as a voting group.

Simultaneously, however, small-scale farmers tend not to devote a great deal of time to farming, because they earn their living mainly from off-farm income. Thus, small-scale farmers need a crop that can be grown with minimum labor inputs. In Japan, that crop is rice. Labor-saving technologies (such as agricultural machinery, agricultural chemicals, and irrigation systems) are developed mostly for rice farming. In addition, MAFF provides subsidies for JA's construction of joint-use facilities for rice processing. These facilities help part-time farmers, whose farms are too small to justify individual rice milling and storage facilities.

Government-led rice production cartel

Politicians demonstrate their allegiance to small-scale farmers by displaying their efforts to protect rice, thus explaining why Japanese politicians are extremely sensitive to rice policy. Rice receives high border protection and various subsidies. MAFF has operated a special program, the across-the-board land-use diversion program, aimed at supporting rice prices. This program, essentially a government-led rice production cartel, was first established in 1970. Every year, MAFF set a target acreage of paddy fields to be diverted from rice planting so as to curtail rice production. The target acreage was allocated among all villages in Japan. All farmers in the villages collaborated to achieve the allocated acreages under JA's guidance and supervision. Around one-third of the paddy fields were diverted from rice planting. Farmers grew alternative crops, such as wheat, soybeans, and vegetables, which were less profitable, in the diverted paddy fields. MAFF provided financial support to rice farmers according to the acreage diverted from rice planting. It did not fully compensate for the reduction of rice income at the farm household level. Yet in the aggregate, the cartel effect of the across-the-board diversion program benefited rice farmers by maintaining high rice prices. JA's ability to ensure the support of rice farmers was critically important to enacting the rice production-control program.

From 1970 to 1994, MAFF did not have any written laws for carrying out the diversion program. Instead of written laws, MAFF's administrative guidance, which had no formal legal standing, served the coordination role. The Staple Food Law of 1995 was the first written law that stipulated the diversion program.

For Japanese consumers, rice is the staple food. Although the average household spends only 1 percent of its expenditures on rice, it is included in every meal. Japanese eat rice steamed, without any spices or condiments. Because of this cooking style, Japanese consumers are sensitive to the quality of rice. Top-quality rice is often considered suitable as a gift and is sold as such in Japanese department stores, while low-quality rice is used for inexpensive meals.

Until 1995, the Food Control Law specified the distribution of rice. According to the Food Control Law, farmers had only two legal ways to sell rice. One was as "government rice" and the other was as "voluntary rice". The former was purchased by MAFF at government-set prices (which differ depending on the shape and weight of the grain). The latter was purchased by JA at market price. In both cases, market channels were strictly controlled under the law. Generally, high-quality rice was sold by farmers as voluntary rice and low-quality rice was sold as government rice. Since MAFF determined the procurement price for government rice before the harvest season, the percentage of government rice tended to increase in years of bumper harvests, when the market price sank.

Rice traders and rice market channels were required to be authorized under the Food Control Law. In practice, however, there was a significant amount of so-called "freed rice" that circumvented the law. This is

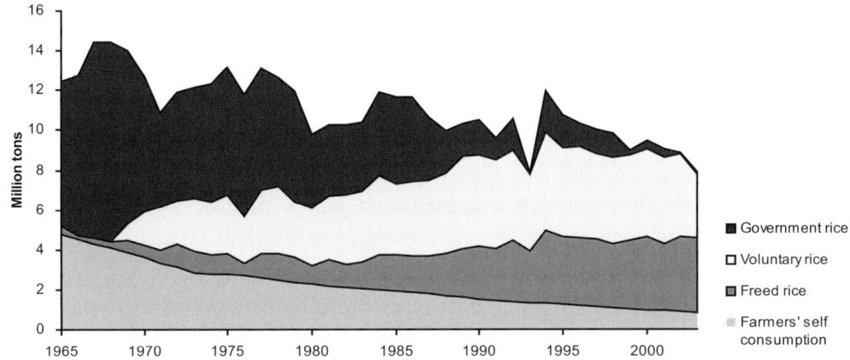

Figure 5.3 Japan's production and marketing of rice
Source: Seisansha-no Beikoku Genzaidala Chosa Kekka (Survey on Production and Stock of Rice).

because the legal rice-distribution system (as stipulated by the Food Control Law) was too rigid to meet consumers' changing preferences. In particular, top-quality rice sold at higher prices in the illegal rice market. A significant number of farmers and consumers ignored the Food Control Law in favor of illegal rice, and MAFF also turned a blind eye to its purchase and sale.

In 1995, the Staple Food Law legalized freed rice. The classifications of government rice, voluntary rice, and freed rice remained until 2004, when MAFF abolished these classifications altogether. While MAFF continued to procure rice for buffer stocks, distribution was allowed on a commercial basis without MAFF's administrative interventions. Figure 5.3 shows the volumes of the three types of rice. Government rice had been losing importance in the rice market since the introduction of voluntary rice in 1969. The percentage of government rice went down to less than 20 percent by the end of the 1980s.

The 2007 reform and a subsequent shift in political power

Until the early 1990s, the political ties between politicians, small-scale farmers, JA, and MAFF remained strong. However, there was a turning point in Japan's political dynamics in the middle of the 1990s, which was brought on by two factors.

First, JA's financial services faced an increasingly harsh business climate. MOF implemented financial market liberalization in the mid 1990s, which deprived JA's banking and insurance businesses of various privileges. As JA's banking and insurance businesses had been strongly protected in the financial markets, financial market liberalization damaged JA's profitability. Second, the reform of the lower house election system in 1994 reduced the voting power of JA. In the 1994 election reform, the former multi-seat system was replaced with the single-seat system. Before the reform, JA was proud of its techniques for dividing votes among different lawmakers in a single constituency. In the former multi-seat system, LDP needed to have a plural number of politicians elected in a single constituency in order to stay in power. Thus, JA's techniques for dividing votes were so attractive that LDP signaled its strong allegiance to JA. However, under the new single-seat system, JA's techniques became less useful. Accordingly, JA's political voice became less influential. In addition, the 1994 election reform allocated less seats to rural areas (Mulgan 2000). This also reduced JA's power.

These two factors seriously undermined JA's political influence and, accordingly, organizing ability. As a result, each year it became more difficult for JA to persuade rice farmers to join the across-the-board diversion program. It was thus only a matter of time before MAFF was forced to implement a comprehensive revision of its rice policy.

An extensive agricultural policy reform was ultimately implemented in 2007. The 2007 MAFF reform was characterized by two aspects. First, the diversion program was changed from the former compulsory across-the-board program to a voluntary program.[3] This revision left it entirely to individual farmers' discretion whether to participate in the diversion program in exchange for receiving subsidies or to grow rice freely but give up the subsidies.

Subsidies for wheat, barley, potatoes, soybeans, and sugar beets, the five primary farm products grown in paddy fields set aside from rice farming, were also replaced by a program with a new type of direct payments. Some of the new type payments were based on fixed average agricultural production in the base years 2004–06, while others were linked to annual agricultural production. The former corresponds to decoupled income support (in the green box) and the latter to non-exempt direct payments

[3] The shift to a voluntary diversion program was stipulated initially in the 2004 revision to the Staple Food Law. From 2004–06 the central and local governments gradually withdrew from allocating acreage diversion requirements to farmers.

(AMS support). The 2007 reform marked the first introduction of decoupled direct payment subsidies as a policy measure.

Moreover, the new type of direct payments are unique in that there is an additional prerequisite for recipients. These recipients must be "core" farmers. Core farmers are those designated by the municipal governments as the standard-bearers of local agriculture. More precisely, there are two types of core farmer: individual-type core farmers and group-type core farmers. The former are individual farm households whose farm size is over 4 hectares. The latter are agricultural farming groups composed of farmers in the same community who form over-20-hectare joint-farming groups. Theoretically, any economic entity is allowed to organize group-type core farmers: in practice, however, only JA does so.

According to its announcements, MAFF aims to raise agricultural productivity by promoting large-scale farming through the concentration of agricultural subsidies to core farmers. However, these announcements should be read with caution as discussed above. For example, it is unclear whether farming groups organized by JA are actually efficient. JA's farming groups are sometimes nothing more than patchworks of small-scale farmers. JA is known to organize small-scale farmers into farming groups without making substantial changes in farming practices for the sole purpose of receiving subsidies, to the benefit of both parties. Obviously, this is a case of mistaking the means (receiving subsidies) for the intended ends (creating efficient farming groups). In addition, JA deprives individual large-scale farmers of tenant farmland by persuading farmland owners who hitherto leased farmland to individual large-scale farmers to instead join JA's farming groups. This deprivation harms individual large-scale farmers who have higher productivity.

In sum, the 2007 reform supported JA's efforts to maintain its organizing ability by giving incentives to farmers to participate in farming groups organized by JA. Thus, it is unclear whether the 2007 reform will in fact improve the productivity of Japanese agriculture (Honma 2009).

The 2007 reform has another serious problem. There are good reasons to believe that it can stimulate agricultural production without efficiency gains, contradicting the original purpose of the reform. The 2007 reform stimulated rice production because farmers were clearly allowed to choose whether or not to participate in the diversion program. In particular, small-scale farmers who hold farmland in expectation of capital gains from farmland conversions, and therefore are unconcerned with farm income, surged into rice production because rice is the least labor-intensive crop. As a result, rice prices declined sharply in 2007. Even for farmers who joined the voluntary diversion program, the 2007 reform stimulated the production of wheat, barley, potatoes, soybeans, and sugar beets, because the farmers anticipated future shifts in the base years of production that determine the decoupled direct-payment subsidies. The average production of the three years 2004–06 was used for the decoupled direct-payment subsidies in the 2007 reform. However, farmers expect that the base year will be updated in the future, stimulating the production of these five crops in paddy fields diverted from growing rice.[4]

For 2007, MAFF allocated nearly 100 billion yen for the decoupled direct-payment subsidies for the five crops. For that, MAFF reduced non-exempt subsidies for the five crops. Hereby, the 2007 reform apparently suits the WTO's discipline of reducing trade-distorting domestic support.

The DPJ takes power in 2009

The lower house election in August in 2009 was a dramatic turning point of reorganization within Japanese politics. In this election, the Democratic Party of Japan (DPJ) recorded a landslide victory and took power from the LDP. The LDP receded from being the leading party for the first time since its establishment in 1955.

This DPJ's landslide victory is attributable partly to a drastic change in small-scale farmers' voting behavior. Throughout the election campaign, the DPJ promised increased farm subsidies. This DPJ's promise attracted the votes of small-scale farmers, who had once formed a solid support base for LDP politicians.

After taking power, based on its promises in the general election, the DPJ groped toward launching a new direct-payment program, called the Income Compensation Program (ICP). Under ICP, the government will provide compensation to farmers if production costs exceeds market prices.

ICP will be applied by agricultural commodity. It was proposed to be offered for rice first in 2010. The government estimated an annual budget of 560 billion yen for ICP for rice.[5] This would be a huge increase from any past level of payments in Japan. The DPJ also proposed that

[4] See Hart and Beghin (2006) for discussion of this effect in other contexts.

[5] The expenditure estimates for the ICP are quoted from www.dpj.or.jp/special/manifesto2009/pdf/manifesto_2009.pdf Japanese newspapers also expected the budget for the ICP to increase to 1 trillion yen. For example, see "*Kobetsu Shotoku Hosho, Kome, Rainendo Kara* (The Income Compensation Program will start in the 2010 fiscal year)" p. 2 in the evening paper of Nikkei, October 14, 2009.

in 2011 the ICP be extended to other major crops such as wheat and soybeans. The DPJ estimated that this extension would involve an additional annual expenditure of 440 billion yen. If such increased expenditures materialize, they will substantially alter the profile of Japan's domestic support.

Domestic support notifications and shadow notifications

The Japanese government had submitted notifications of its domestic agricultural support programs to the WTO for 1995–2006 as of December 2009. Japan's domestic support notifications have been submitted regularly but even so there is a lag of two or three years before the notification for a given year is available (see Table 1.1). The notifications are reviewed and we present estimates of Japan's likely notifications for 2007 and 2008 in order to trace Japan's agricultural policy reforms. We also make projections through 2015 to assess Japan's domestic support under the Agreement and the Doha draft modalities.

Notifications, 1995–2006

Table 5.2 and Figure 5.4 provide a summary of the notifications for 1995–2006 and shadow notifications for 2007 and 2008. Green box expenditures decline over time but nonetheless account for about 75 percent of total support in Japan after its notified CTAMS dropped sharply in 1998. Japan's CTAMS has been comprised primarily of market price support but also of non-exempt direct payments.

Japan had no blue box programs when the Agreement was concluded and has subsequently made only minimal use of the blue box. The *Inasaku Shotoku Kiban Kakuho Taisaku* (Rice Farming Income Stabilization Program (RFISP)), which was implemented in 1998, was Japan's first blue box program with initial expenditures of 50 billion yen. RFISP is a countercyclical program. It stipulated that MAFF would provide income support for farmers who joined the riceland diversion program if the market rice price fell below the average rice price of the previous three years. As described above, almost all rice farmers participated in the riceland diversion program in 1998. By that time, procurements of government rice accounted for only a limited portion of the rice market, which motivated the addition of the RFISP in conjunction with the diversion of land from rice production. A second blue box program, *Ninai-te Keiei Antei Taisaku* (Business Stabilization Policy

Table 5.2 *Summary of Japan's domestic support notifications and shadow notifications, 1995–2008*

	Notifications						
	1995	1996	1997	1998	1999	2000	2001
Type of support	*Billion yen*						
Green box	3,169.0	2,818.1	2,651.7	3,001.6	2,685.9	2,595.3	2,546.9
Blue box	—	—	—	50.2	92.7	92.7	91.1
Current Total AMS	3,507.5	3,329.9	3,170.9	766.3	748.0	708.5	666.8
of which, MPS	3,271.3	3,125.8	2,967.9	641.5	619.6	503.9	389.7
Total *de minimis*	36.6	37.3	36.1	75.5	32.6	31.7	32.1
Product-specific	12.5	11.4	11.7	53.1	10.4	10.8	12.0
Non-product-specific	24.1	25.9	24.4	22.4	22.2	20.9	20.1
Total support	6,713.1	6,185.3	5,858.7	3,893.6	3,559.2	3,428.2	3,336.9
Share of total support	%						
Green box	47	46	45	77	75	76	76
Blue box	—	—	—	1	3	3	3
CTAMS	52	54	54	20	21	21	20
Total *de minimis*	1	1	1	2	1	1	1
Total	100	100	100	100	100	100	100
Value of production (billion yen)	10,434.1	10,248.9	9,831.6	9,944.1	9,418.1	9,122.4	8,881.3
Bound Total AMS (billion yen)	4,800.6	4,635.0	4,469.5	4,304.0	4,138.4	3,972.9	3,972.9
CTAMS as share of binding (%)	73	72	71	18	18	18	17

Notes: Small differences in totals are due to rounding. — indicates zero.
Sources: Japan's notifications to WTO and authors' calculations.

					Shadow notifications	
2002	2003	2004	2005	2006	2007	2008
2,275.2	2,086.3	2,098.3	1,916.3	1,802.4	1,795.7	1,887.3
86.5	68.2	67.8	65.3	70.1	42.4	32.4
729.9	641.8	607.8	593.2	571.3	509.0	510.7
404.0	405.6	403.0	394.7	389.9	378.1	385.3
43.6	35.0	41.1	41.3	37.6	33.4	88.9
23.2	16.9	24.1	23.2	18.6	15.4	15.4
20.4	18.1	17.0	18.1	19.0	18.0	73.5
3,135.2	2,831.3	2,815.0	2,616.1	2,481.4	2,380.5	2,519.3
73	74	75	73	73	75	75
3	2	2	2	3	2	1
23	23	22	23	23	21	20
1	1	1	2	2	1	4
100	100	100	100	100	100	100
8,929.7	8,856.5	8,713.6	8,511.9	8,290.0	8,192.7	8,650.9
3,972.9	3,972.9	3,972.9	3,972.9	3,972.9	3,972.9	3,972.9
18	16	15	15	14	13	13

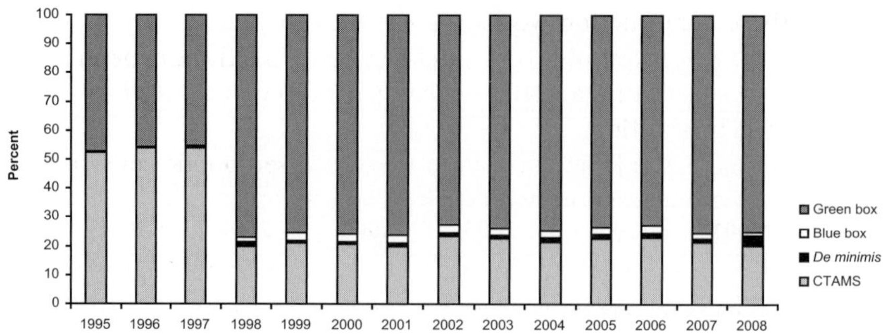

Figure 5.4 Japan's domestic support notifications and shadow notifications
Sources: Japan's notifications to WTO and authors' calculations.

for Farm Units with Approved Municipal Management Improvement Plans), was subsequently added.

Japan has also made only minimal use of product-specific and non-product-specific *de minimis* allowances. Product-specific *de minimis* AMS support has been claimed for such commodities as rice (*Kajo Mai Tanki Yushi Shikin Kashitsuke Kin*, a short-term loan program), eggs, fruits and vegetables. Local governments, in addition to MAFF, are engaged in price support for vegetables, which is accounted for in the notifications. Non-product-specific AMS support has resulted from agricultural insurance subsidies, and has been within the *de minimis* amount.

Green box

Green box expenditures are shown in Table 5.3. General services, particularly infrastructural services for the agricultural sector and rural areas, make up the largest portion of the green box. The infrastructure expenditures correspond to MAFF public construction works, such as farmland improvement investments and construction of rural roads.[6] As discussed

[6] Among programs in the national budget contributing to the infrastructure expenditures are *Noson Shinko-hi* (Rural Promotion Expenses), *Fusuigai tou Taisaku-hi* (Natural Disaster Policy), *Nogyo Seisan Kiban Seibi Jigyo tou Shido Kantoku-hi* (Instruction and Management for the Project for Improvement of Production Base), *Kaigan Jigyo-hi* (Expenses for Coastal Projects), *Nogyo Seisan Kiban Seibi Jigyo-hi* (Expenses for the Activities for Improvement of Production Base), *Gyuniku tou Kanze Zaigen Nogyo Seisan Kiban Seibi Jigyo-hi* (Expenses for the Activities for Improvement of Production Base financed by Beef Tariff) *Noson Seibi Jigyo-hi* (Expenses for Rural Areas Improvement),

above, these construction works are welcomed by small-scale farmers, who have expectations of future capital gains. With these expenditures, the green box subsidies amount to as much as 30 percent of the value of agricultural production.

Traditionally, the Japanese government has used public construction works as an anti-recession fiscal policy. Expenditure for infrastructural services for the agricultural sector and rural areas surged in 1998, when the Japanese economy plunged into the worst economic slump since the 1970s. In response to increased criticism of public construction by Japanese citizens, the national budgets for infrastructural services for the agricultural sector and rural areas have been decreasing since then. In particular, from 2001 to 2007 presidents Koizumi and Abe tried to gain popularity for the LDP as reformers and the budgets for rural public construction works were severely rolled back. The total amount of green box expenditures decreased during this period.

Other categories of green box support account for less than one-quarter of the total. Japan had not provided any decoupled income support or income insurance through 2006. There were small expenditures for disaster relief and structural adjustment. Interestingly, Japan reports some of the support it provides through its agricultural insurance scheme as support that meets the green box criteria for payments for relief from natural disasters, while the rest of the support through that scheme is reported as non-product-specific AMS. Expenditures on environmental programs in the green box more than doubled from their initial level but remained less than 200 billion yen.

Current Total AMS

The composition of Japan's CTAMS is shown in Table 5.4 and its levels are compared to Japan's Bound Total AMS under the Agreement and the final ceiling proposed in the Doha draft modalities in Figure 5.5. The Japanese government has provided AMS support above *de minimis* for rice, barley, wheat, soybeans, sugar, starch (potatoes), beef and veal, meat of swine, and silk-worm cocoons. A sub-governmental body, the Agricultural and Livestock Industries Corporation (ALIC), has also engaged in support

Nochi tou Hozen Kanri Jigyo-hi (Expenses for Farmland Maintenance), *Norin Gyogyo you Kihatsu-yu Zei Zaigen migawari Noson Seibi Jigyo-hi* (Expenses for Rural Road Construction Financed by Gasoline Tax), *Chiho Noseikyoku Kaigan Jigyo Koji Sho-hi* (Miscellaneous Expenses for Local Agricultural Office's Coastal Project), and *Chiho Noseikyoku Jisuberi Taisaku Jigyo Koji Sho-hi* (Miscellaneous Expenses for Local Agricultural Office's Landslide Prevention Project).

Table 5.3 *Composition of Japan's green box notifications and shadow notifications, 1995–2008*

	Notifications					
	1995	1996	1997	1998	1999	2000
	Billion yen					
General services	2,687.8	2,323.5	2,182.2	2,594.2	2,308.3	2,165.7
Infrastructure services	1,907.9	1,680.8	1,487.7	1,800.7	1,552.4	1,428.4
Public stockholding	59.9	61.5	67.3	56.6	46.8	46.4
Domestic food aid	28.1	27	26.4	13.8	9.3	5.4
Decoupled income support	—	—	—	—	—	—
Income insurance	—	—	—	—	—	—
Crop insurance/ disaster relief	68.3	65.8	62	58.6	57.9	55.5
Producer retirement	119.4	98.6	90.9	84.9	85.4	88.3
Resource retirement	7.9	0.5	0.5	0.5	0.5	0.5
Investment aids	116.9	107.9	89.5	77.4	54.3	55.2
Environmental payments	80.7	133.3	132.9	115.6	123.4	145.3
Regional assistance	—	—	—	—	—	33
Total	3,169.0	2,818.1	2,651.7	3,001.6	2,685.9	2,595.3

Notes: — indicates zero.

[a] Estimated on the assumption that the percentage of infrastructure service for agriculture and rural areas in General service is the same as that of 2006.

Sources: Japan's notifications to WTO and authors' calculations.

						Shadow notifications	
2001	2002	2003	2004	2005	2006	2007	2008
2,094.5	1,743.3	1,603.6	1,658.9	1,465.4	1,373.8	1,239.1	1,338.8
1,342.4	1,067.6	950.7	909.9	840.0	784.4	707.5[a]	764.4[a]
43.3	36.3	31.9	28.2	24.5	20.9	18.9	20.4
5.3	4.8	2.5	—	3.2	2.5	2.3	2.4
—	—	—	—	—	—	101.3	102.3
—	—	—	—	—	—	—	—
54.1	53.6	48.3	48	49	50.0	45.1	48.7
97.6	162.7	158.1	156.5	155.8	156.0	157.2	158.2
0.4	0.1	—	—	—	—	—	—
42.4	31.2	23.5	22.8	19.9	7.4	6.7	7.2
176.3	210.2	195.4	167.1	176.7	170.0	203.1	187.1
33	33	23	16.8	21.8	21.8	22.1	22.1
2,546.9	2,275.2	2,086.3	2,098.3	1,916.3	1,802.4	1,795.7	1,887.3

Table 5.4 *Composition of Japan's Current Total AMS notifications and shadow notifications, 1995–2008*

	Notifications					
	1995	1996	1997	1998	1999	2000
	Billion yen					
Market Price Support	3,271.3	3,125.8	2,967.9	641.5	619.6	503.9
Rice	2,560.7	2,464.5	2,315.3	—	—	—
Barley	23.6	25.2	20.2	14.9	21.1	1.2
Wheat	55.3	59.6	69.3	68.2	69.3	2.8
Soybeans	—	—	—	—	—	—
Sugar	58.9	49.0	53.8	59.8	54.6	53.4
Starch	21.6	17.6	20.8	20.4	16.4	15.7
Milk	114.4	115.1	110.1	107.3	105.8	95.9
Beef and veal	122.9	103.0	92.6	90.4	87.7	80.3
Meat of swine	312.8	291.8	285.8	280.5	264.7	254.6
Silk-worm cocoons	1.1	—	—	—	—	—
Non-exempt direct payments	236.2	204.1	203.0	124.8	128.4	204.6
Rice	100.8	93.0	82.2	—	—	—
Barley	0.9	0.9	0.9	0.9	0.9	10.2
Wheat	—	—	—	—	—	75.0
Soybeans	1.7	2.6	4.9	6.9	9.8	15.6
Sugar	—	—	—	—	—	0.6
Starch	—	—	—	—	—	—
Milk	37.4	38.2	39.5	40.6	36.4	34.5
Beef and veal	83.5	68.0	73.7	75.1	80.4	67.1
Meat of swine	10.5	—	—	—	—	—
Silk-worm cocoons	1.4	1.4	1.8	1.3	0.9	1.6
Current Total AMS	3,507.5	3,329.9	3,170.9	766.3	748.0	708.5

Notes: — indicates zero.
Sources: Japan's notifications to WTO and authors' calculations.

						Shadow notifications	
2001	2002	2003	2004	2005	2006	2007	2008
389.7	404.0	405.6	403.0	394.7	389.9	378.1	385.3
—	—	—	—	—	—	—	—
0.2	0.1	0.1	—	—	—	—	—
0.2	—	—	—	—	—	—	—
—	—	—	—	—	—	—	—
54.6	53.8	56.4	56.7	54.8	50.3	33.8	37.1
17.7	18.8	16.5	15.5	15.1	13.6	16.1	16.3
—	—	—	—	—	—	—	—
67.3	78.7	74.0	74.6	72.9	72.6	75.4	76.2
249.7	252.6	258.6	256.2	251.9	253.4	252.8	255.7
—	—	—	—	—	—		
277.1	325.9	236.2	204.8	198.5	181.4	130.9	125.4
—	—	—	—	—	—	—	—
10.5	10.8	14.0	11.1	10.0	11.1	5.9	5.6
81.5	84.9	102.8	94.7	94.6	92.6	49.4	47.0
18.5	26.6	28.1	27.6	26.4	25.5	13.6	13.0
0.6	1.2	1.5	2.0	2.5	1.5	0.8	0.8
—	—	—	—	—	—	—	—
36.0	53.6	30.8	26.9	26.9	28.5	29.8	22.0
126.1	147.4	57.8	41.1	37.1	21.4	31.0	37.0
2.5	—	—	0.3	—	—	—	—
1.4	1.4	1.2	1.1	1.0	0.8	0.4	—
666.8	729.9	641.8	607.8	593.2	571.3	509.0	510.7

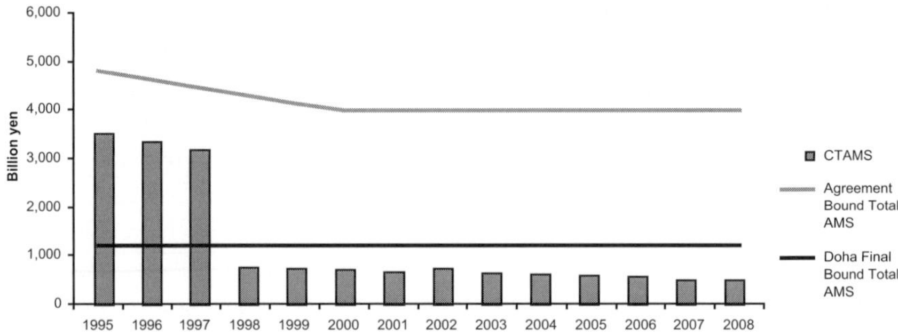

Figure 5.5 Japan's notifications of CTAMS compared with commitments agreed in the Uruguay Round and proposed in the Doha Round

programs for sugar, starch, milk, beef and veal, meat of swine and silkworm cocoons. From 1995 to 1997, Japan's CTAMS was closest to its commitment level – about 70 percent of the ceiling was utilized.

The most noticeable aspect of Japan's CTAMS is that it decreased sharply in 1998 because market price support for rice was no longer calculated. A program of small non-exempt direct payments to rice producers was also eliminated. Yet, there was no corresponding revision in the Staple Food Law. MAFF continued to procure rice from farmers after 1998. In its 1998 policy guideline, MAFF announced that government rice procurement should be limited to purchase of rice stocks for food security. The government has explained that the administered rice price has been abolished and purchases are made at market prices (WTO 2001). On this basis, Japan does not calculate a rice MPS as part of its AMS support for rice. In computing the rice AMS for 1995–97, Japan used the total production of rice as eligible production. In the latter half of the 1990s, however, government rice made up less than 5 percent of total rice distribution. It is clear that MAFF's intervention in the rice market became less effective after it introduced voluntary rice in 1969. MAFF's rice procurement had been decreasing throughout three decades, as shown above. Thus, even though there was not a clear-cut turning-point year (such as 1998), perhaps Japan could be justified in removing rice MPS from the CTAMS. Since a large rice MPS was part of the base from which Japan's Final Bound Total AMS commitment was derived, removing rice MPS created a significant amount of latitude under the ceiling on its CTAMS. In 1998, Japan's notified CTAMS fell to less than 20 percent of this commitment.

Nonetheless, the overwhelming majority of Japanese agricultural policy researchers are skeptical of whether MAFF's new rice policy guideline of 1998 had any practical meaning. Even after 1998, MAFF's procurement of rice has been occasionally undertaken for the political purpose of supporting the rice price. A typical example occurred as late as 2007. While MAFF's rice stock was already at a sufficient level for the purpose of food security, MAFF decided to increase rice stocks after receiving strong pressure from LDP politicians who wanted to curry favor with farmers.[7] In this case, MAFF's rice procurement can be seen as a *de facto* market price support measure. Thus, there is ground for controversy about whether a rice MPS since 1998 should still be included in the AMS.

Moreover, since Japan's rice is protected by prohibitively high tariffs, abandoning the administered price did not reduce economic protection for rice. Japan's complete elimination of MPS from its notifications to the WTO is an extreme example of the imperfect correspondence between this measurement in the notifications and an economic measurement of price support. The outcomes for rice for Japan are illustrated in Figure 5.6. Notified MPS drops to zero in 1998. The economic protection of rice, in contrast, does not change in 1998. The economic price support (OFCD MPS) exhibits a downward trend over time, but remains over 1,200 billion yen in 2007.

After the rice MPS was no longer calculated, about two-thirds of the remaining support in CTAMS has consisted of MPS for other products and one-third of non-exempt direct payments. MPS for milk was eliminated in 2001 as a consequence of abolishing the administered price, and the procured quantities of wheat and barley used as eligible production fell so low that these price support programs were also terminated. Small direct payments tied to production have continued for these commodities.[8] Market price support has been continued for sugar, starch, beef and veal, meat of swine and silk-worm cocoons. ALIC plays a role for these commodities. For sugar and starch, farmers receive a grant from ALIC in addition to their sales at the administered price. Since the difference between

[7] For example, see "*Norinsuisansho, Seifu Bichiku-mai Hyakumannton ni Tsumimashi-ni* (Government Stock of Rice will be increased to 1 million tons)" p. 5 in the morning paper of Nikkei, October 26, 2007.

[8] For wheat and barley the expenditures are for *Mugisaku Keiei Antei Taisaku* (Wheat and Barley Farming Income Stabilization Programs). For milk, the programs include MAFF's expenditures for *Shitei Seinyu-sha Dantai Kofukin* (Subsidy to Designated Milk Produce Organization) and ALIC's expenditures for *Kako Genryonyu Seisansha Keiei Antei Taisaku* (Business Stabilization Policy for Manufacturing Milk Producers), *Ekijo Nyuseihin Seisan Kakudai Jigyo* (Liquid Dairy Products Production Promotion Policy), *Rakuno Antei Tokubetsu Taisaku Jigyo* (Business Stabilization Special Policy for Dairy Farming), and *Juyo-ki Seinyu Seisan Suishin Taisaku* (Summertime Milk Production Promotion Policy).

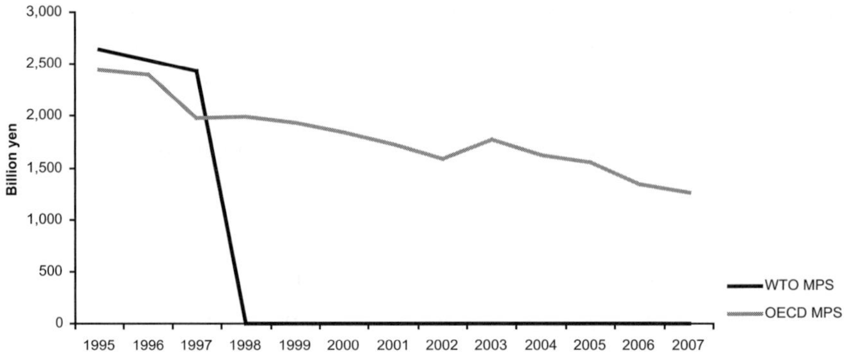

Figure 5.6 Japan's market price support for rice from notifications and OECD
Source: Authors' calculations based on WTO notifications and OECD statistics.

the fixed external reference price and the applied administered price does not capture the full support level an adjustment is made in computing the notified MPS. For beef and veal, ALIC sets lower and upper boundary prices, buying when the market price falls below the lower boundary price, and selling when the market price exceeds the upper boundary price. The eligible production is the total amount of dressed carcass from adult beef cattle, veal calves and dairy veal calves. Sugar, beef and veal, silk-worm cocoons, and also soybeans, have continued to receive small amounts of non-exempt direct payments.[9]

Shadow notifications, 2007 and 2008

In constructing the shadow notifications, we first replicated the latest notification available at the time. The notification documents provide little information on data sources and details of calculation. Thus, we had to make best guesses based on the financial statements of the

[9] The non-exempt direct payment programs are as follows: For sugar in the national budget *Nogyo Keiei Kiban Kyoka Tokubetsu Taisaku* (Agricultural Management Framework Reinforcement Special Policy), for beef and veal ALIC programs *Nikuyo Koushi Seisansha Hokyukin Seido* (Subsidy Program for Beef Calf Farmers) and *Nikuyogyu Hi-iku Keiei Antei Taisaku* (Business Stabilization Policy), for silk-worm cocoons reported by ALIC *Sanshi-gyo Keiei Antei Taisaku* (Sericulture Business Stabilization Policy), and for soybeans in the national budget *Daizusaku Keiei Antei Taisaku* (Soybean Farming Income Stabilization Program) and the *Kokunai Daizu Seisan Antei Taisaku* (Subsidy Program for Soybean Producers).

government and relevant extra-governmental organizations. In order to clarify the details of the notification computation process, we conducted interviews with officers of the MAFF Kokusai-bu (Department of International Relations), the contact department for WTO notifications. The Kokusai-bu is not directly responsible for computing monetary values of domestic support measures; instead, it allocates computation to the various MAFF departments that manage fiscal expenditures. The Kokusai-bu then collects and compiles these results to conform to the WTO notification format. The details of MAFF's computation procedures are difficult to access even for Kokusai-bu officers, and are thus effectively unavailable to the public.[10]

We initially succeeded in replicating the notified CTAMS, *de minimis* AMSs, and blue box payments almost perfectly for 2004.[11] Our subsequent estimates closely matched the notifications for the years 2005 and 2006 submitted by Japan in 2008. Estimation of shadow notifications for 2007 and 2008, however, was somewhat more problematic. One problem arose in the treatment of the new direct payments introduced in the 2007 reform. The Japanese government had not made any announcements on how the new subsidies would be classified. As described above, some are determined by base-year production and might qualify for inclusion in the blue box, while some are based on annual production and should be counted in the AMS. We made a best guess on the classification of these subsidies based on various governmental documents. However, the estimates for 2007 and 2008 are likely to be less accurate than were our replications for 2005 and 2006.

The green box was more difficult to replicate. From the government report on the national budget, we found items of expenditure that seem to correspond to the components in the 2004–06 notifications. However, there were many gaps. For example, in the national budget the expenditures for extension and advisory services, research programs and infrastructural services for technological improvement of agricultural production exceed the corresponding category in the notification by 44 percent. We concluded this was because the former includes the

[10] Our interview with *Kokusa-bu* officers also revealed that the notifications are based on the initial budgets of the national treasury. For the purpose of computing monetary values of domestic support programs, the settled account data should be more suitable than the initial budget data. However, this is not considered a serious problem because the gap between MAFF's initial budget and settled account is generally small.

[11] Godo and Takahashi (2008) provide details of our initial shadow assessments. Description of subsequent assumptions is available from the authors.

personnel expenses of officers who are not engaged in extension services. The Japanese government calculates the notified components of the green box from national budget data available to the government only. Moreover, reflecting MAFF reforms, formatting of some parts of the government report on the national budgetary changed markedly in 2007. We estimated the components of the green box for 2007 and 2008 based on information gathered in interviews and review of official documents.

The resulting shadow notifications for 2007 and 2008 are shown in Tables 5.2 to 5.4. Total green box expenditures are estimated to remain near earlier levels. As a result of the 2007 reform, we estimate yearly payments of 100 billion yen as decoupled income support in 2007 and 2008. Correspondingly, non-exempt direct payments in the CTAMS for barley, wheat, soybeans and sugar decline by 60.9 billion yen from 130.7 billion yen in 2006 to an estimated 69.7 billion yen in 2007. Expenditures for environmental programs in the green box also increase by 33 billion yen in 2007 as a result of the reforms. These expenditures are for environmental programs related to rice production, so they complement the blue box support for rice producers. The two blue box programs for rice were consolidated into a single program *Inasaku Kozo Kaikaku Sokushin Kofu-kin* (Subsidies for Promotion for Rice Farming Structural Reform) which was scheduled to terminate in 2010. According to the national budget, MAFF disbursed 29 billion yen for the new blue box program in 2007 and an additional 13.3 billion yen were disbursed by the earlier programs, leading to an estimated net decline in blue box expenditures (Table 5.2). Non-exempt direct payments accounted for in *de minimis* AMSs are estimated to remain nearly constant in 2007. In 2008 MAFF launched a new non-product-specific program *Shunyu Gensho Hoten* (Compensation for Reduction of Farm Income) with a budget of 55.5 billion yen for the first year. Although significantly larger than in earlier years, non-product-specific AMS would nevertheless remain *de minimis*.

Projections of domestic support notifications, 2009–2015

Our projections for domestic support of Japan from 2009 through 2015 are presented in Table 5.5. Understandably, it is difficult to make projections of domestic policy several years into the future. We estimated some of Japan's future expenditures for domestic agricultural support by taking trends and/or the average of past expenditures. For expenditures that are under strong pressure of cutbacks from the Ministry of Finance,

Table 5.5 *Projected levels of Japan's domestic support, 2009–15*

	2009	2010	2011	2012	2013	2014	2015
	Billion yen						
Green box	1,913	1,650	1,629	1,603	1,577	1,552	1,526
General services	1,351	1,090	1,071	1,046	1,022	998	974
Public stockholding	28	28	28	28	28	28	28
Domestic food aid	3	3	3	3	3	3	3
Decoupled income support	102	102	102	102	102	102	102
Income insurance	—	—	—	—	—	—	—
Crop insurance/ disaster relief	43	41	39	38	36	35	33
Producer retirement	158	158	158	158	158	158	158
Resource retirement	—	—	—	—	—	—	—
Investment aids	21	21	21	21	21	21	21
Environmental payments	184	184	184	184	184	184	184
Regional assistance	23	23	23	23	23	23	23
OTDS	605	1,131	1,569	1,566	1,564	1,561	1,558
Blue box	31	560	560	560	560	560	560
CTAMS	485	483	920	917	915	912	909
MPS	350	348	345	343	340	337	334
Non-exempt direct payments	135	135	575	575	575	575	575
Total *de minimis*	89	89	89	89	89	89	89
Total support	2,518	2,781	3,198	3,169	3,141	3,113	3,084

Note: — indicates zero.
Source: Authors' calculations.

we extrapolated by taking five-year trends for 2002–06. For others, we assume that annual expenditures for 2009–15 will be the same as the averages of 2002–06. In cases of recent policy change or announced changes, the projections reflect their effects.

Total green box expenditures are projected to decline between 2009 and 2015, although political pressure may prevent this from occurring. The projected decline is due primarily to reductions in anticipated expenditures for infrastructure services for agriculture and rural areas. The DPJ announced in 2009 that MAFF's public construction expenditures in this category would be reduced by 250 billion yen in 2010.[12] We include this reduction in our projections and assume that further declines occur thereafter at the slower pace observed in the five-year period 2002–06.

As discussed above, if fully implemented the new ICP announced by the DPJ in 2009 will cause significant increases in Japan's domestic support. How ICP payments will be reported to the WTO is uncertain. There were no initial announcements from MAFF on the treatment of ICP in domestic support notifications. ICP for rice requires recipient farmers to participate in the rice diversion program. Thus, if the ICP for rice can be shown to meet the relevant criteria, it might be reported as a blue box policy. However, ICP for the other crops seem not to meet the blue box criteria and these payments may need to be reported as AMS support.

The DPJ's landslide victory in 2009 reflects its campaign promises and the strong support of small-scale farmers in the election. In this political atmosphere, Japan's support expenditures under blue box and AMS measures are likely to increase at least for several years. However, there is also the possibility that the DPJ reconsiders the ICP. The ICP will impose a heavy fiscal burden on Japan's national treasury. Both IMF (2009) and OECD (2009) estimate that Japan's fiscal condition is among the worst for the major developed countries. In this macroeconomic context, it could happen that the DPJ government will have to moderate its planned development of ICP due to budget considerations. Nonetheless, we assumed ICP for rice is fully implemented in 2010 with an annual budget of 560 billion yen and is categorized in the blue box. We also assumed the expenditure level is continued through 2015. The small expenditures on other blue box programs are scheduled for a phase-out in 2010.

AMS support (CTAMS plus *de minimis*) includes several projections. For MPS, we assumed that administered and external reference prices for 2009–15 are the same as the average of 2002–06. We estimated

[12] This reduction is alleged to be a part of the DPJ's election tactics for the 2011 upper house election. An overwhelming majority of the construction companies engaged in infrastructural services for the agricultural sector and rural areas had supported the LDP. The proposed reduction will weaken the LDP's vote-getting power.

eligible production by taking log-linear extrapolations from five-year production data. Resulting MPS remains nearly constant. Similarly, we assumed that product-specific and non-product-specific *de minimis* support remains constant at recent levels. Most of the non-product-specific AMS has consisted of those payments under the agricultural insurance scheme that do not meet the green box criteria. It is obviously impossible to predict whether such support would decrease or increase in the future.

A more dramatic change is evident in our projections for the non-exempt direct payments in the CTAMS. We assumed that ICP for crops other than rice will be categorized as AMS support. Payments will be product-specific and large enough to make the AMSs for the relevant crops exceed their *de minimis* thresholds, so these projected expenditures are included in the CTAMS. Projected expenditures included in CTAMS prior to 2011 arise from a continuation of existing support programs at essentially a constant nominal level. These programs are projected to continue through 2015 at similar funding levels.

Constraints on projected support under the Agreement and Doha draft modalities

While our projected domestic support for Japan shows increases due to the proposed ICP, the projected CTAMS remains well under Japan's Final Bound Total AMS commitment of 3,973 billion yen. Thus, Japan would not face any compliance problems under the Agreement for the level and nature of our projected support.

Japan's potential commitments under the December 2008 Doha draft modalities are shown in Table 5.6. Japan's Base OTDS of 5,448 billion yen is the sum of its Final Bound Total AMS under the Agreement plus 15 percent of its average value of agricultural production during 1995–2000. Its OTDS ceiling would be reduced by 75 percent to 1,362 billion yen once the new commitments were fully phased in over five years. This assumes Japan falls into the middle tier in the modalities for OTDS cuts but requires extra effort because its Base OTDS exceeds 40 percent of its value of production in the base period (see Table 2.2). Final Bound Total AMS would decline by 70 percent to 1,192 billion yen once the new commitments were fully phased in (Japan is in the top tier for cuts to Final Bound Total AMS). Immediately upon implementation, the cap on overall blue box payments would be 2.5 percent of the value of agricultural production during 1995–2000 (245 billion yen)

Table 5.6 *OTDS, CTAMS and blue box limits and the* de minimis *allowance for Japan under the Doha draft modalities*

	Billion yen
Final Bound Total AMS	3,972.9
Value of production (average 1995–2000)	9,833.2
10 percent value of production	983.3
5 percent value of production[a]	491.7
Base OTDS	5,447.9
Base OTDS as share of value of production (1995–2000)[b]	55.4%
Final Bound OTDS (after 75 percent reduction)	1,362.0
Final Bound Total AMS (after 70 percent reduction)	1,191.9
Blue box limit (2.5 percent value of production 1995–2000)	245.8
De minimis	
50 percent immediate reduction	2.5%

Notes: See Table 2.2 and Appendix B regarding all notes.

[a] Paragraph 1(c) condition: 5 percent of production value included in OTDS if blue box less than that amount.

[b] Tests for application of paragraph 4: exceeds 40 percent so additional effort required.

Source: Authors' calculations based on WTO (2008).

and the *de minimis* thresholds would fall to 2.5 percent of annual value of production.[13]

In our projections, Japan's annual CTAMS remains below 900 billion yen through 2015 so Japan would not be constrained by the Final Bound Total AMS from the Doha draft modalities. However, if ICP funding materializes as projected, Japan's OTDS would exceed 1,500 billion yen. This means that Japan's OTDS would exceed the OTDS limit implied

[13] Another major uncertain element is the possibility of a drastic reduction in border protection for agricultural commodities. Lower border protection can require reductions in domestic support, particularly MPS. Alternatively, if the Japanese government concludes an international agreement reducing border protection for agricultural products, Japanese farmers, who form one of the strongest voting groups, will press the government for compensation programs. This could result in increased fiscal expenditures. However, this uncertain element of the effects of lower tariff protection on domestic support is so difficult to predict that we did not try to incorporate it into our analysis.

by the Doha draft modalities of December 2008 once fully phased in.[14] While Japan would have had a large margin below the OTDS limit up until 2009, the new ICP policy would increase Japan's applied OTDS support significantly. With fully funded IPC payments for rice categorized in the blue box, Japan would also exceed its overall blue box limit under the Doha draft modalities.

Another problem is that ICP at the proposed levels would not be consistent with product-specific AMS and product-specific blue box limits. However, neither the DPJ nor MAFF made any announcements about the inconsistency between ICP and the Doha negotiations when the program was proposed. We have deep concerns that Japan's ICP could cause a serious conflict in the Doha negotiations. Alternatively, Japan could expand its support in the green box, and member countries of the WTO may put pressure on Japan to replace ICP by green box measures.

Summary and conclusions

We began this chapter by highlighting the difference in scale of operations of agriculture in Japan compared to the rest of the developed world. Seventy percent of the farmland in Japan is still contained in farms of less than 3 hectares that are too small to be efficient. We argue that political pressure has precluded emergence of larger farms that would achieve scale economies. Failure of the price mechanism to function properly in farmland markets is at the heart of the farm size and productivity impasse. This failure arises from an extensive set of farmland regulations and government investments that subsidize and sustain land in farming, enhance its value through infrastructure investments, and eventually determine the capital gains associated with converting land to non-farm uses. The political economy of these policies involves politicians courting rural voters, benefits to MAFF and the privileged position of the JA cooperatives. Small-scale farmers retain possession and use of farmland not for the purpose of earning farm income but in the hope of capital gains received through the manipulation of farmland regulations.

Associated with this nexus of farmland policies, rice production has been highly protected and regulated. Japan has had ample room for

[14] During the five-year phase-in period, allowed OTDS would be greater than our projected levels of annual OTDS.

managing domestic prices under its high border protection. Administered prices were set in this context and a rice production-control program was implemented through JA, with about one-third of riceland diverted to other crops to avoid excess rice supplies at the established price. By the early 1990s, *de facto* deregulation of rice marketing had occurred and government rice procurements had fallen to less than one-fifth of production. A new Staple Food Law liberalized domestic rice marketing in 1995 but retained a program for riceland diversion that MAFF and JA continued to administer.

Japan's domestic support notifications have been submitted regularly. They give an impression of Japan as a model of compliance. We have contrasted Japan's *prima facie* compliance with WTO domestic support disciplines with its less flexible attitude toward border protection, particularly its resistance to opening the domestic rice market.

The dominant green box expenditures for Japan are for infrastructure services for agriculture and rural areas, corresponding to MAFF irrigation, road and other rural construction projects. This category of green box expenditures, which does not appear in the notifications for the EU or US, is tied to the political economy of farmland regulation and conversion of farmland to non-agricultural uses.

In determining its Final Bound Total AMS, and in the notifications of CTAMS for 1995–97, Japan reported MPS for rice based on total production, despite limited government procurement by that time. The rice MPS dominated Japan's CTAMS during these years and the notified values exceeded 70 percent of the ceiling. Subsequently, in 1998 MAFF announced guidelines that rice procurements would be made only for food security purposes. It also ceased applying a government-set or administered price. As a consequence, Japan ceased reporting MPS for rice in its CTAMS, which fell to just 18 percent of the commitment and has remained at that low level. Essentially this single change (or reinterpretation) of policy allowed Japan to exclude itself from any binding constraint on the amount of AMS support it provided. Being compliant on domestic support with the Agreement proved easy, but economic protection of rice did not change. In 1998 Japan also implemented a new policy of payments to rice farmers for participating in the riceland diversion program. The expenditures were notified under the blue box and are arguably consistent with the objective of guiding countries toward less trade-distorting policies. But with so much latitude created by the modification of the notifications for rice, one can hardly argue that this reform resulted from pressure of the WTO commitment on domestic support.

In 2007 Japan undertook additional agricultural policy reforms that are consistent to some extent with the decoupling of support encouraged by WTO rules. Price supports for five crops grown on riceland (wheat, barley, potatoes, soybeans and sugar beets) were replaced by direct payments – some based on a fixed production base from 2004–06, which we believe will be notified in the green box, and others linked to annual production which we anticipate being notified as product-specific AMS support. We are skeptical that these reforms have lessened production incentives given the existing structure of farmland holdings. We are also skeptical that the new policies will alter the past political economy of farmland policies and lead to increased efficiency of Japan's agriculture, which would provide a constructive avenue to higher output.

In addition, we have highlighted proposals for Japan's new direct payment program, called ICP, which will increase Japan's OTDS very significantly. The DPJ, which took power in September 2009, announced that ICP would start for rice first in 2010 and then extend to other agricultural products in 2011. If fully funded as announced, the ICP may conflict with the revised Doha draft modalities in agriculture of December 2008. Thus, how to cope with ICP could become one of the major concerns for the Japanese government in the Doha round negotiations.

References

Godo, Y. 2007. The puzzle of small farming in Japan. Pacific Economic Papers No. 365. Australian National University, Australia–Japan Research Centre. www.crawford.anu.edu.au/pdf/pep/pep-365.pdf.

Godo, Y., and D. Takahashi. 2008. Japan: Shadow WTO agricultural domestic support. IFPRI Discussion Paper 822.

Hart, C. E., and J. C. Beghin. 2006. Rethinking agricultural domestic support under the World Trade Organization. In *Agricultural Trade Reform and the Doha Development Agenda*, ed. K. Anderson and W. Martin. New York: Palgrave Macmillan, and Washington, DC: World Bank.

Honma, M. 2009. Agricultural trade policy reform in Japan. In *Agricultural Subsidies in the WTO Green Box: Ensuring Coherence with Sustainable Development Goals,* ed. R. Meléndez-Ortiz, C. Bellmann, and J. Hepburn. Cambridge University Press.

IMF (International Monetary Fund). 2009. *IMF World Economic Outlook – Sustaining the Recovery.* Washington, DC.

MAFF (Ministry of Agriculture, Forestry and Fisheries). 1992. *Atarashii Shokuryo Nogyo Noson Seisaku no Hoko* (New Policy Direction of Food, Agriculture and Rural Policies). Tokyo.

Mulgan, A. G. 2000. *Japan's Interventionist State*. London: Routledge.

OECD. 2009. *Economic Outlook*, Paris.

WTO. 2001. Summary report of the WTO Committee on Agriculture. 26th meeting, 29–30 March. G/AG/R/26.

6

Norway

IVAR GAASLAND, ROBERTO GARCIA AND ERLING VÅRDAL

Norway is an economically advanced country in northwestern Europe. The World Bank (2010) has estimated that the country's per capita gross national income was $58,500 in 2008, the second highest in the world. Agriculture's contribution to gross domestic product (GDP) is less than 1 percent and, together with forestry, the sector accounts for roughly 3 percent of employment measured in standard person–years of labor. Less than 3 percent of the land area in Norway is suitable for crops, and of this only one-third is suitable for food grains. Low temperatures and a short growing season produce low yields per hectare. Wheat and potato yields, for example, are only 60 percent of the averages obtained in central Europe. Farmland is scattered around the country. Plots are relatively small and have very steep slopes in some regions. In general, it is difficult for Norwegian agriculture to compete with countries that have a more favorable climate and geography.

Dual objectives of maintaining self-sufficiency in basic products and sustaining small-scale farming throughout the country have long been central to Norwegian agricultural policy. Due to the difficult production conditions, substantial government support is necessary to pursue these objectives. A widely recognized international measure of the support provided to agriculture is the OECD's producer support estimate (PSE). The percentage PSE (value of support divided by the value of farm production) was 62 percent for Norway in 2008, the highest among the Organization's

We thank Rune Mjørlund for providing indispensable assistance with detailed data on the Norwegian support system for farmers. We are indebted to Klaus Mittenzwei of the Norwegian Agricultural Economics Research Institute, and Lasse Erdal of the Norwegian Agricultural Authority, for clarifying issues on Norwegian support arrangements. These individuals should not be held responsible for any errors of interpretation in this chapter. Ivar Gaasland gratefully acknowledges financial support from the Research Council of Norway's program Area and Nature-based Industrial Development (AREAL).

member countries (OECD 2009). Roughly 60 percent of the support is provided through budgetary measures, while the rest is through market price support buttressed by import tariffs for major products in the range of 190–430 percent. According to OECD estimates more than 50 percent of support is directly attached to the volume of production (i.e., market price support or output-related subsidies). Norway is self-sufficient in dairy products, meat products and eggs; the equivalent of 10 percent of the milk produced is exported with export subsidies. Given climatic disadvantages, some grain has to be imported, as well as products of tropical or sub-tropical origin.

This brief review of Norwegian agriculture suggests that it would suffer severely from a substantial reduction in agricultural support and from trade liberalization. As a member of the G10 of importing countries in the WTO, Norway has resisted efforts to liberalize agricultural trade in the Doha Round of negotiations. In addition, as we shall demonstrate, Norway has already made strategic changes to its notifications of domestic support to avoid pressures for policy reform from WTO commitments.

The purpose of this chapter is three-fold: to assess whether support provided by Norwegian agricultural programs and policies since 1995 has complied with WTO commitments; to analyze the effects of applying new commitments in the Doha draft modalities; and to examine likely policy responses to potential Doha commitments.

The chapter is comprised of five sections. First, we provide a review of key elements of domestic agricultural policy. Norway's notifications of agricultural support to the WTO for the period 1995–2007 and estimates of a shadow notification for 2008 based on available statistical data are presented, and compliance with commitments is assessed. We next provide alternative domestic support notifications for 1995–2007 that we argue are more consistent with WTO definitions. Looking ahead, proposed reduction commitments in the 2008 Doha draft modalities are analyzed. An economic model of Norwegian agriculture is used to assess potential impacts on production and trade. We employ assumptions about the likely policy responses of the government of Norway to new WTO commitments under the primary objective of minimizing their impact on current agricultural activity. Our conclusions are presented in the final section.

Domestic agricultural policy

To meet its agricultural policy objectives, Norway's domestic support programs have been accompanied by a restrictive trade policy. Direct support is provided through various price and income support instruments, production subsidies and investment measures. Direct payments are differentiated to account for farm size and geographical differences (NILF 2007). Regulatory and other policy measures that aim to stabilize and support domestic market prices feature prominently. Trade instruments (i.e., tariffs, tariff-rate quotas and export subsidies) provide the backbone for domestic price support.

Target prices have traditionally been an important element in Norway's market regulation. These are determined annually for the main agricultural products (i.e., dairy, meat products and eggs) in negotiations between the Norwegian government and the two farmers' unions.[1] Farmer-owned cooperatives are assigned the responsibility of regulating sales in domestic agricultural markets to ensure that farmgate prices stay close to target prices (NILF 2007).

There are several institutional and regulatory arrangements that contribute to ensuring that objectives are met. First, market access restrictions provide the necessary protection to enable domestic prices to be maintained above those at the border. Prohibitive MFN tariffs mean that imports are limited to relatively small tariff-rate quotas (with in-quota tariffs that are typically above 100 percent). Second, the cooperatives, being responsible for regulating the markets, are exempt from anti-trust laws relating to pricing practices and market concentration and, consequently, have relatively high market shares.[2] Third, any farmer who is not a member of a cooperative is legally obliged to contribute to the financing of their marketing functions, e.g., storage or export. Finally, the Norwegian Agricultural Authority (NAA) is charged with temporarily reducing applied tariffs whenever a market price exceeds the corresponding target price by more than a specified amount for two consecutive weeks.[3] There have been times when the applied tariff has been lowered to keep market prices below an upper limit (NILF 2007). In addition to subsidized exports of cheese, which take place on a regular

[1] The largest is Norges Bondelag (the Norwegian Farmers' Union), but another, Norsk Bonde-og Småbrukarlag (the Norwegian Farmers' and Smallholders' Union), attracts small-scale farmers.

[2] For some products, e.g., dairy, the market share of the cooperative exceeds 90 percent. However, in other commodity categories, particularly fruits and vegetables, market shares are below 50 percent.

[3] The NAA is an agency of the Ministry of Agriculture and Food, which is responsible for ensuring that all agricultural schemes and regulations are administered uniformly across the country.

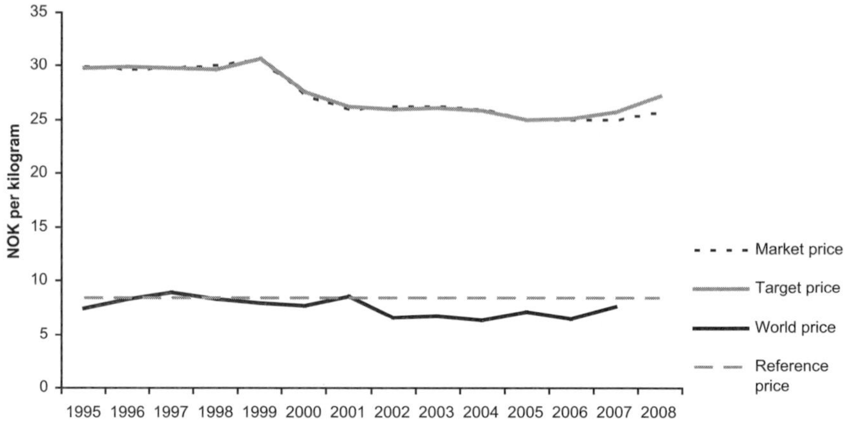

Figure 6.1 Poultry prices in Norway and on world markets
Source: Authors' calculations based on NAA (2009) and OECD statistics (2009).

basis, export subsidies have been employed to prevent domestic prices of other products (primarily other dairy products and meat) from falling too far below target levels.

To illustrate the typical pattern in the domestic market, data for poultry prices for 1995–2008 are presented in Figure 6.1. The domestic market price has moved in lockstep with the annually negotiated target price. At the bottom of the chart are the corresponding border price and the fixed 1986–88 reference price used in establishing Norway's Uruguay Round domestic support commitments.[4]

Figure 6.1 shows that the domestic price is far higher than the border price (by 250–300 percent), which is made possible by a prohibitive tariff (425 percent). Furthermore, it is apparent that there is a very high correlation between the target price and the market price. Although the graph only illustrates the pattern for poultry, the situation is similar for most other regulated markets. There is a general tendency for a high degree of correlation between the market price and the target price. The correlation is perfect for grains. It is very high for the various meat products

[4] The border price of poultry is comparable with the domestic price and is taken from the OECD PSE database, Table 4.6 – the "border reference price (f.o.b.)", referred to as line VII.1 in the table. This price includes processing costs.

and milk, but it is weaker for fruits and vegetables due to the somewhat greater price variability associated with these products.

Domestic support notifications

Norway's domestic support notifications are summarized in Table 6.1. The data for 1995–2007 are from notifications, and those for 2008 are estimates.[5] Support is notified in Norwegian krone (NOK), which is also the currency of our computations. The approximate exchange rate against the US dollar in April 2010 was NOK 6. This was relatively low; a more representative value is given by the average over the last thirty-five years, which is approximately NOK 7.5. Since the inflation rates in the two countries have been about the same over this time span, we can interpret NOK 7.5 as the purchasing power parity value between the NOK and the US dollar. In the Uruguay Round negotiations, Norway established a base commitment for its Bound Total AMS of NOK 14.3 billion. With the required 20 percent reduction over the implementation period (1995–2000) the Final Bound Total AMS is NOK 11.4 billion. The notified CTAMS has ranged between NOK 9.8 billion and NOK 10.9 billion, below the ceiling but much closer to the limit than in many other countries.

Total support in Table 6.1 is the sum of green and blue box support, CTAMS, and *de minimis*. Given that the green box is supposed to be comprised of support provided through non-trade-distorting programs, total notified trade-distorting support (OTDS) is the sum of blue box support, CTAMS, and *de minimis*. Defined in this way, trade-distorting support averaged about 80 percent of the total to agriculture between 1995 and 2004, but was reduced to less than 70 percent after 2004 when some support was shifted from the blue box to the green box. Figure 6.2 illustrates the composition of total domestic support.[6] The CTAMS, the highest section of the bars, has been stable throughout 1995–2008 (at about 49 percent of the total), as is also the case for total value of support. Since 2005, however, the blue-box amount has been reduced due to the reporting of more programs in the green box. The share of blue box support fell from roughly one-third of the total before 2005 to 18 percent after box-shifting. The value

[5] Domestic support notifications submitted by Norway can be accessed through the WTO's Documents On-line database, http://docsonline.wto.org. The documents have the symbol G/AG/N/NOR/*.

[6] The *de minimis* is not included because of small numbers.

Table 6.1 *Summary of Norway's domestic support notifications and shadow notification, 1995–2008*

	Notifications						
	1995	1996	1997	1998	1999	2000	2001
Type of support	*Billion NOK*						
Green box	4.1	4.1	3.7	3.9	4.3	5.0	4.3
Blue box	7.1	7.2	7.4	7.9	7.7	7.7	7.3
Current Total AMS	9.8	10.5	10.5	10.9	10.8	10.3	10.7
of which, MPS	10.1	10.8	11.0	11.3	11.4	10.6	10.9
Total *de minimis*	—	—	—	—	—	—	—
Product-specific	—	—	—	—	—	—	—
Non-product-specific	—	—	—	—	—	—	—
Total support	21.0	21.8	21.6	22.7	22.8	23.0	22.3
Share of total support	%						
Green box	20	19	17	17	19	22	19
Blue box	34	33	34	35	34	33	33
CTAMS	47	48	49	48	47	45	48
Total *de minimis*	—	—	—	—	—	—	—
Total	100	100	100	100	100	100	100
Value of production (billion NOK)[a]	22.6	22.9	22.6	23.1	22.5	22.2	21.9
Bound Total AMS (billion NOK)	13.8	13.4	12.9	12.4	11.9	11.4	11.4
CTAMS as share of binding (%)	71	79	82	88	91	90	94

Notes: Small differences in totals are due to rounding. — indicates zero.

[a] Value of production at the farmgate, excluding direct payments.

Sources: Norway's notifications to WTO, NILF (2008) and authors' calculations.

						Shadow notification
2002	2003	2004	2005	2006	2007	2008
4.3	3.9	4.0	5.9	6.2	6.7	6.9
7.5	7.4	7.4	3.9	3.8	3.7	3.7
10.4	10.8	10.7	10.9	10.8	10.4	11.1
11.1	11.6	11.5	11.6	11.4	11.1	11.9
0.1	0.1	0.1	0.2	0.2	0.2	0.2
0.1	0.1	0.1	0.1	0.1	0.1	0.1
—	—	—	0.2	0.1	0.1	0.1
22.3	22.1	22.1	20.9	20.9	21.0	21.9
19	18	18	28	30	32	32
34	33	33	19	18	18	17
47	49	48	52	51	50	51
—	—	—	1	1	1	1
100	100	100	100	100	100	100
22.1	22.6	22.3	22.8	23.1	24.3	24.8
11.4	11.4	11.4	11.4	11.4	11.4	11.4
91	94	94	96	94	92	98

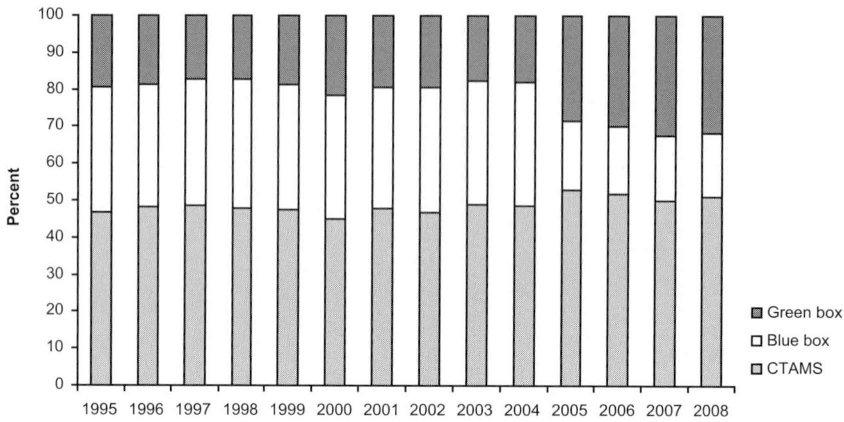

Figure 6.2 Norway's domestic support notifications and shadow notification
Source: Norway's notifications to WTO and authors' calculations based on SN (2008).

of the CTAMS relative to the ceiling commitment is shown graphically in Figure 6.3. As may be seen, the CTAMS has been consistently below the ceiling but the gap has narrowed, particularly since 2000, suggesting that the bound level has become increasingly close to being binding.

Green box

Table 6.2 shows the value of green box support under the major categories identified in Annex 2 of the Agreement. For 1995–2004 Norway's largest single green box item was the vacation and replacement scheme. This covers expenses incurred in finding a replacement due to illness or when taking a vacation and is a part of a series of welfare provisions for farmers. Since this type of support does not fit into the categories listed in Annex 2, Norway has notified it under the heading of "other". The amount of support under the scheme is substantial and has been fairly steady throughout the reporting period. For 1995–2004 it constituted about one-third of the total value of notified green box support. Since the scheme provides a subsidy for the employment of farm labor, it can be argued that it has the potential to stimulate production and does not conform to the production-neutrality requirement of Annex 2. In addition, because the size of payments under the scheme is based either on the number of animals or the acreage in production on a given farm, it also appears inconsistent with the neutrality requirement.

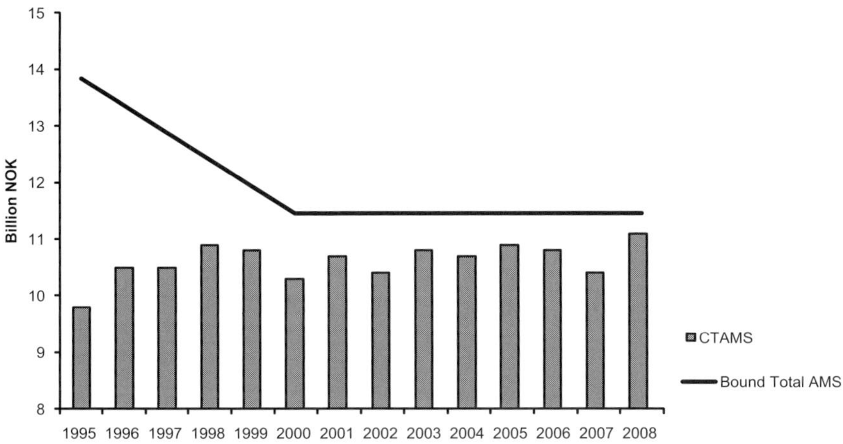

Figure 6.3 Norway's notifications of CTAMS compared with commitment agreed in the Uruguay Round

Another questionable green box item is the grain price support program notified under the Annex 2 heading of public stockholding for food security purposes. During 1995–2004, *per kilogram* payments were provided to processing industries that use Norwegian grain, which constituted a price-reducing subsidy. A second item notified under the public stockholding heading was government expenses incurred in regulating the grain price. Neither of these items complies with the Annex 2 criteria for public stockholding for food security purposes.[7] In the latest notifications by the Norwegian government (2005–07), grain price support has been removed from the green box.[8]

Since 2005 environmental payments have become the largest green box category for Norway. These consist primarily of payments under the acreage and cultural landscape scheme, but also include smaller programs

[7] "Expenditures (or revenue foregone) in relation to the accumulation and holding of stocks of products which form an integral part of a food security programme identified in national legislation. This may include government aid to private storage of products as part of such a programme. Food purchases by the government shall be made at current market prices and sales from food security stocks shall be made at no less than the current domestic market price for the product and quality in question" (WTO 1995, see Appendix A).

[8] Since 2005 some of the additional support provided for the use of domestically produced grain has been notified as non-product-specific AMS under the heading of a feed-transport subsidy. However, since the non-product-specific AMS is *de minimis*, it does not count towards the CTAMS.

Table 6.2 *Composition of Norway's green box notifications and shadow notification, 1995–2008*

	Notifications						
	1995	1996	1997	1998	1999	2000	2001
	Million NOK						
General services	1,023	971	707	828	880	909	899
Public stockholding	506	694	747	725	633	701	718
Grain price support	504	690	741	724	626	694	711
Domestic food aid	—	—	—	—	—	—	—
Decoupled income support	—	—	—	—	—	—	—
Income insurance	—	—	—	—	—	—	—
Crop insurance/ disaster relief	125	20	30	30	31	28	14
Producer retirement	—	—	—	—	30	63	86
Resource retirement	—	—	—	—	149	721	—
Investment aids	741	763	654	713	849	771	858
Environmental payments	180	161	180	188	217	264	264
Regional assistance	11	11	11	16	11	10	10
Other	1,514	1,496	1,347	1,390	1,477	1,545	1,467
Vacation and replacement scheme	1,436	1,413	1,281	1,326	1,394	1,480	1,400
Total	4,100	4,116	3,676	3,890	4,277	5,012	4,316

Note: — indicates zero.

Sources: Norway's notifications to WTO and authors' calculations.

						Shadow notification
2002	2003	2004	2005	2006	2007	2008
803	875	990	557	627	829	870
540	529	671	7	6	7	—
533	523	671	—	—	—	—
—	—	—	—	—	—	—
—	—	—	—	—	—	—
—	—	—	—	—	—	—
33	50	43	3	13	28	30
104	116	119	121	114	105	100
90	159	—	—	—	—	0
853	632	664	599	613	632	650
318	292	249	3,395	3,613	3,943	4,000
10	10	10	—	—	—	—
1,587	1,219	1,240	1,183	1,202	1,174	1,200
1,539	1,161	1,191	1,183	1,202	1,174	1,200
4,338	3,882	3,986	5,865	6,188	6,718	6,850

such as a subsidy for organic production. Earlier, payments under the acreage and cultural landscape scheme were notified in the blue box, but in 2005 they were included in the existing National Environmental Program. Participants in this program must implement an environmental plan and land must be managed in an environmentally friendly manner. A farmer receives a specified payment per hectare as a reward for compliance. In addition, payments are provided on an activity-specific basis to help cover the costs of implementing approved production techniques. The NAA claims that the acreage and cultural landscape scheme complies with green box criteria. However, this is questionable. First, in order for farmers to receive support, production (active farming) is necessary. Second, to be classified as an environmental payment under the Agreement, the amount provided should be limited to the loss of income or additional costs involved in compliance. The payments in this case do not seem to be related to additional costs or income foregone.

In 2007 a further budgetary change was made by the Ministry of Agriculture and Food (MAF 2006) under which support for grazing livestock paid on a headage basis, notified earlier under the blue box, was included in the funding for the National Environmental Program and notified under environmental payments in the green box. Additional payments under a regional environmental program cover expenses for maintaining agricultural structures (e.g., field boundaries). Administrators at the county level are responsible for disbursing these funds.[9]

Investment aid provided through the Agricultural Development Fund is notified under the structural adjustment assistance heading in the green box. Norway indicates that this aid is for structural adjustment and rural development services. Increasingly, the funds have been redirected towards stimulating new business activities in rural areas. Consequently, less of the support has been directed towards investment in traditional agricultural activities (NILF 2007). The item accounts for 10–20 percent of total notified green box support. An important dimension of the WTO criteria for this type of support is that it should not be related to the current or future output of any particular product. The payment should only compensate for or assist in the financial or physical restructuring of a producer's operations to correct structural disadvantages, and may only be

[9] In 2007, as shown in Table 6.2, subsidies notified as environmental payments amounted to NOK 3,943 million. Of this NOK 3,134 was under the acreage and cultural landscape scheme, NOK 352 under headage support, NOK 383 under the regional environmental programme, and NOK 74 for organic production.

given for the period necessary for the realization of the investment (WTO 1995). Whether Norway's notified expenditures under this heading comply with such conditions is open to interpretation.

Finally, services provided by the government to support and facilitate agricultural marketing (such as research and development, pest and disease control, and extension) are categorized as general services in Annex 2. The conditions in the Agreement are that expenditures on general services should not involve direct payments to producers or processors. The program activities under general services amounted to about 11 percent of total green box support in 2004, prior to the expansion of the environment programs. Their conformity with the requirements of Annex 2 is not contested.

Blue box

Support classified under the blue box in the Agreement falls under three types: payments based on fixed area and yields; payments made on 85 percent or less of the base level of production; and livestock payments made on a fixed number of animals. Blue box support is not subject to a limit or to a reduction commitment in the Agreement. Table 6.3 lists all programs under the blue box as notified by Norway from 1995–2007 and a shadow notification for 2008.

The acreage and cultural landscape scheme discussed above provided the largest payments under the blue box category until 2005. This support is supposed to equalize differences in profitability among different types of production and farms of different sizes. Together with part of the headage support, the program was included in the National Environmental Program in 2004, and was reclassified as green box from 2005 onwards (MGAL 2004; MLSA 2005). This reclassification resulted in a decrease in blue box support from an annual average of roughly NOK 7.5 billion during 1995–2004 to less than NOK 4 billion from 2005 onwards. The reclassification is an example of box-shifting with little evidence of significant change in the economic characteristics of a program. The main modification was the adoption of an administrative vehicle under which cultural landscape payments could conveniently be placed.

Norway notifies structural income support to dairy farmers and regional deficiency payments for milk and meat production as payments on 85 percent or less of base level production. The aim of the deficiency payments is to even out differences in profitability and income between farmers in remote areas and those located closer to urban markets. This support has been declining over time.

Table 6.3 *Composition of Norway's blue box notifications and shadow notification, 1995–2008*

	Notifications					
	1995	1996	1997	1998	1999	2000
	Million NOK					
Acreage and cultural landscape	2,751	3,209	3,305	3,752	3,176	3,123
Structural income support, dairy	1,539	1,483	1,443	1,425	1,394	1,330
Deficiency payment, milk	450	432	434	433	450	428
Deficiency payment, meat	506	512	516	523	512	473
Headage support	1,871	1,611	1,678	1,748	2,142	2,317
Total	7,117	7,247	7,376	7,881	7,674	7,671

Note: — indicates zero.
Sources: Norway's notifications to WTO and authors' calculations.

Current Total AMS and de minimis

The CTAMS should include support through programs that encourage production by subsidizing the cost of inputs or by supporting prices for agricultural outputs. A summary of the principal programs that comprise the CTAMS for Norway is given in Table 6.4. The CTAMS is the addition of all product-specific and non-product-specific AMS support excluding that identified as *de minimis.*

By far the largest item in the AMS category is market price support (MPS), which is the value of product-specific price support aggregated across all commodities. In 2005–2006, twelve commodities (four types of grain, oilseeds, cows' and goats' milk, four types of meat, and eggs) were notified as receiving MPS. Bovine milk and meat production received more than 80 percent of the total. The second largest item in the AMS category, in absolute value, is other product-specific support. This includes transportation subsidies for meat and eggs, and a farm-feed adjustment value. The latter is an estimate of the additional costs incurred by livestock and milk producers due to the higher prices for

							Shadow notification
2001	2002	2003	2004	2005	2006	2007	2008
2,969	3,023	2,976	3,003	—	—	—	—
1,176	1,306	1,214	1,175	1,067	1,008	951	950
382	414	416	421	409	380	431	450
539	537	518	540	564	539	471	450
2,265	2,251	2,236	2,295	1,874	1,866	1,872	1,850
7,331	7,531	7,360	7,434	3,914	3,793	3,725	3,700

concentrated feed caused by MPS for grains and oilseeds. Consequently, other product-specific support is negative because the net effect is a tax (i.e., reported as associated fees or levies), consistent with the way Norway calculated its base-period AMS support and consequently its Bound Total AMS.[10] Non-exempt direct payments include relatively small income payments that encourage milk, bovine and sheep production. The programs listed under equivalent support measurement include subsidies related to the marketing, storage, and transportation of fruits, berries, vegetables and potatoes. Non-product-specific support includes insemination subsidies and taxes on fertilizers and pesticides. As highlighted in Table 6.5, beginning in 2002, support provided to fruits, berries and vegetables was designated as product-specific *de minimis*, and from 2005 non-product-specific subsidies for insemination and feed transport were also covered by the *de minimis* provision.

[10] A similar approach is used by the OECD to adjust the MPS for livestock commodities by subtracting an amount for excess feed cost. However, paralleling differences in methodology for estimating MPS, the feed adjustment amounts are also different.

Table 6.4 *Composition of Norway's Current Total AMS notifications and shadow notification, 1995–2008*

	Notifications						
	1995	1996	1997	1998	1999	2000	2001
	Million NOK						
Market Price Support	10,135	10,827	10,973	11,276	11,428	10,574	10,887
Barley	698	769	732	708	742	596	576
Wheat	493	372	362	488	336	428	337
Oats	371	410	354	396	400	357	330
Rye	—	—	—	—	—	—	—
Oilseeds	—	—	—	—	—	—	—
Milk	3,510	3,837	3,879	4,025	4,085	4,113	4,035
Goat milk	—	—	—	—	—	—	—
Eggs	389	394	443	449	463	401	342
Beef and veal	1,690	1,815	1,978	1,996	1,985	1,682	1,735
Pork	1,704	1,880	1,852	1,900	1,869	1,466	1,993
Sheep	650	671	633	586	673	678	733
Poultry	458	513	557	669	789	779	715
Potatoes	173	167	185	60	85	74	91
Non-exempt direct payments	1,061	954	847	733	673	599	540
Milk	432	345	258	173	124	93	82
Goat milk	—	—	—	—	—	—	—
Eggs	28	14	1	—	—	—	—
Beef and veal	252	264	273	263	266	259	217
Sheep	308	277	274	278	276	247	241
Potatoes	39	54	41	20	6	—	—
Other product-specific support	−1,417	−1,236	−1,236	−1,049	−1,287	−942	−810
Milk	−699	−450	−470	−412	−502	−373	−314
Goat milk	—	—	—	—	—	—	—
Eggs	−128	−105	−97	−88	−102	−75	−68
Beef and veal	−156	−191	−198	−162	−197	−136	−116
Pork	−360	−312	−309	−259	−321	−221	−194
Sheep	−12	−51	−48	−37	−50	−38	−74

						Shadow notification
2002	2003	2004	2005	2006	2007	2008
11,085	11,592	11,519	11,570	11,439	11,110	11,902
582	541	568	491	544	511	623
266	399	399	394	248	327	528
267	315	326	235	212	212	284
—	—	—	25	19	26	20
—	—	—	33	28	27	20
4,250	4,289	3,941	4,079	4,007	4,367	4,229
—	—	—	56	52	54	54
330	356	367	341	357	399	423
1,837	2,016	2,020	2,145	2,137	2,287	2,390
1,968	2,035	2,137	2,051	1,989	2,018	2,335
799	786	831	804	822	881	996
786	855	932	917	1,024	—	
—	—	—	—	—	—	—
523	366	258	298	296	269	203
—	—	—	—	—		
—	—	—	44	46	49	50
—	—	—	—	—	—	
247	101	—	—	—		
276	264	258	255	249	219	153
—	—	—	—	—	—	
−1,210	−1,193	−1,088	−976	−1,001	−969	−1,011
−439	−423	−374	−332	−334	−374	−351
—	—	—	−5	−4	−5	−5
−85	−88	−82	−71	−71	−86	−95
−185	−183	−169	−153	−157	−167	−174
−323	−322	−295	−265	−270	−295	−332
−51	−51	−43	−35	−38	−42	−53

Table 6.4 *(cont.)*

	Notifications						
	1995	1996	1997	1998	1999	2000	2001
	Million NOK						
Poultry	–62	–129	–114	–91	–115	–99	–44
Equivalent measurement of support[a]	87	65	64	52	48	50	51
Fruit and Vegetables	87	65	64	52	48	50	51
Potatoes	—	—	—	—	—	—	—
Non-product-specific AMS[b]	–79	–80	–123	–126	–75	12	32
Current Total AMS	9,786	10,529	10,526	10,886	10,787	10,293	10,700

Notes: — indicates zero.

[a] From 1995 to 2001 Norway notified EMS for potatoes as *de minimis*, and subsequently in CTAMS. Conversely, EMS for fruits and vegetables was notified in CTAMS until 2001, then as *de minimis*.

[b] From 1995 to 2004 Norway notified non-product-specific AMS, whether positive or negative, in CTAMS and subsequently has claimed it as *de minimis*.

Sources: Norway's notifications to WTO and authors' calculations.

Table 6.5 shows the combined total of all AMS support (CTAMS and *de minimis*) and the levels of product-specific and non-product-specific *de minimis* for Norway.

The WTO MPS construct is defined as the difference between a product's administered price and its external reference price, multiplied by the eligible volume of production. Norway has consistently notified its target prices as administered prices. The external reference prices are 1986–88 average border prices, used to establish Norway's Uruguay Round commitments. The notified eligible volume of production is generally close to the actual volume of production, published by Statistics Norway. Using

						Shadow notification
2002	2003	2004	2005	2006	2007	2008
–127	–126	–124	–116	–127	—	—
30	31	31	33	32	32	32
—	—	—	—	—	—	—
30	31	31	33	32	32	32
–29	–34	–56	—	—	—	—
10,399	10,761	10,665	10,925	10,765	10,442	11,126

poultry as an example, Figure 6.1 showed that the administered (target) price is well above the reference price. As noted earlier, this is not only the case for poultry, but reflects the situation for all major Norwegian agricultural products. Since high market prices are made possible by high import tariffs, the CTAMS is mostly a reflection of border support, i.e., support that consumers provide by paying high food prices. But within its regime of prohibitive tariffs, TRQs and discretionary import policies, the target prices become a focal point for pricing policy and implementation of border measures.

Over the years there has been considerable pressure from farmers to increase target prices. In 2007 this resulted in an increase for most products. In order not to exceed the Bound Total AMS ceiling, the poultry MPS was removed from the notification. Norway achieved this by abolishing the administered price and dropping the calculation of MPS from its notification. The target price was renamed a “reference price” but continues to serve as a guiding parameter for domestic policy purposes; because the poultry market is protected by high tariffs, economic market price support was maintained. This administrative maneuver resulted in

Table 6.5 De minimis *exemptions from CTAMS in Norway's notifications and shadow notification, 1995–2008*

	Notifications						
	1995	1996	1997	1998	1999	2000	2001
	Million NOK						
Sum of AMS support (amber box)	9,786	10,529	10,526	10,886	10,787	10,293	10,700
Total *de minimis*	—	—	—	—	—	—	—
Product-specific	—	—	—	—	—	—	—
Non-product-specific	—	—	—	—	—	—	—
	5% of value of production (million NOK)						
Non-product-specific threshold	1,130	1,145	1,130	1,155	1,125	1,110	1,095

Note: — indicates zero.
Sources: Norway's notifications to WTO and authors' calculations.

a reduction in the Norway's CTAMS without any major economic reform or market liberalization.[11]

In the May 2008 negotiations between the farmers' unions and the Ministry of Agriculture and Food, it was agreed to increase prices on most agricultural products, an action that most likely would have raised notified support above the Bound Total AMS ceiling. Following the approach adopted for poultry, the MPS calculation for sows, boars and mutton was dropped by eliminating the administered (target) prices and redefining these as reference prices. Since the market price support component of the CTAMS was NOK 11.1 billion in 2007, Norway has plenty of space to

[11] Japan was the first country to follow this strategy when it redefined its rice procurement program as being for the purpose of adjustment of rice stocks for food security in 1998; see Chapter 5.

						Shadow notification
2002	2003	2004	2005	2006	2007	2008
10,452	10,831	10,724	11,143	10,938	10,620	11,314
53	70	59	218	173	178	188
53	70	59	62	54	67	58
—	—	—	157	118	112	130
1,105	1,130	1,115	1,140	1,155	1,215	1,240

pursue a strategy of eliminating administered prices for other products in order to lower notified support in future years.

As discussed in Chapters 1 and 2, the MPS used in the WTO notifications will often deviate from that in OECD estimates, which are intended to measure border protection. In contrast to the OECD MPS, the WTO MPS calculation uses fixed world market prices for 1986–1988 rather than annual world market prices. Furthermore, the MPS is based on eligible rather than current production. Finally, the MPS employs administered prices, which may deviate from market prices.

A comparison of the value of the WTO MPS and OECD MPS for poultry is given in Figure 6.4 and for barley in Figure 6.5. For both products, the two measures differ, although by a relatively small amount in most years.[12] Nevertheless, the WTO MPS for poultry consistently

[12] Poultry was highlighted in Figure 6.1 through 2008. As noted, 2006 is the last year that its MPS was notified. This is the reason why the comparison between OECD MPS and the WTO MPS for poultry in Figure 6.4 ends in that year.

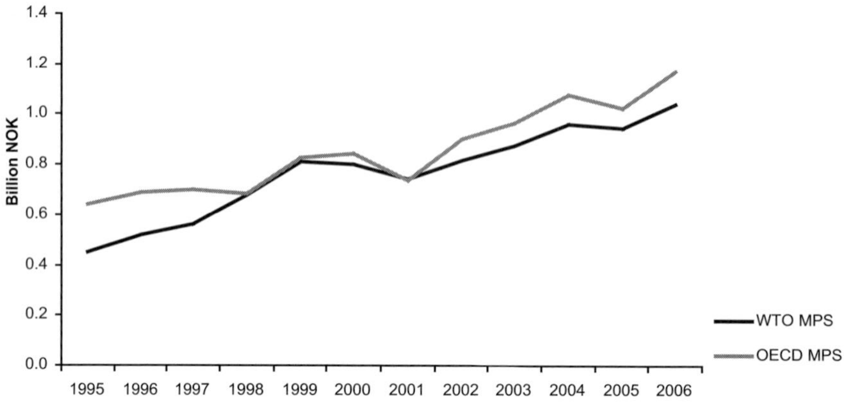

Figure 6.4 Norway's market price support for poultry from notifications and OECD
Source: Authors' calculations based on WTO notifications and OECD statistics.

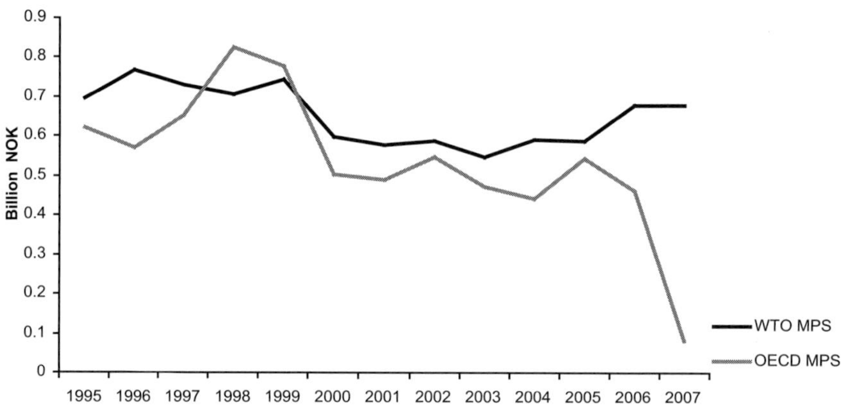

Figure 6.5 Norway's market price support for barley from notifications and OECD
Source: Authors' calculations based on WTO notifications and OECD statistics.

underestimates border support. During the first three years, the reported eligible quantity in the WTO MPS calculation was lower than the actual quantity produced, lowering the reported value relative to the OECD figures. In recent years the world market price for poultry, as reported by the OECD, was lower than the WTO reference price. For barley, the picture is mixed. Up to 2005, the measures are close to each other. However, in the last two years the WTO MPS has overestimated border support significantly. The cause is a spike in the world market price for grains, including barley, which occurred in 2007, pushing those prices well above the fixed external reference price.

Alternative notifications

In the previous section it was argued that the grain price support, the vacation and replacement scheme and the acreage and cultural landscape scheme are inconsistent with green box criteria because these programs either provide price support, or are closely tied to output or the use of primary production factors. Since the first two of these items do not appear to satisfy the criteria for blue box support, they should be included in the CTAMS. As noted in the previous section, the Norwegian authorities have notified grain price support in the CTAMS from 2005 onwards. An alternative notification would do this consistently for 1995–2007. With respect to the acreage and cultural landscape scheme, we contest the appropriateness of shifting the support provided under this program to the green box and argue that it belongs in the blue box.

Table 6.6 provides alternative notifications consistent with our interpretation of the grain-price support and the vacation and replacement scheme in the calculation of the CTAMS, while the acreage and cultural landscape scheme is retained in the blue box. The alternative notification is compared to the notifications for 1995–2007 and, for CTAMS, the ceiling under the Agreement.

According to our interpretation, notifications of the CTAMS consistently undervalue support. There are implications for compliance with WTO obligations starting in 1998. Norway's notifications suggest that the CTAMS has been close to the Bound Total AMS. Hence, any challenge to support notified under the green box as belonging in CTAMS would be problematic in terms of Norway's WTO compliance. As for the shifting of support between the blue and green box, differences in interpretation of the programs have no implications for the Uruguay Round commitments because the Agreement sets no limits on blue box or green box payments. The box shifting is, however, merely a strategic step towards meeting future obligations since the Doha Round proposals will impose a limit on Norway's blue box support and reduce the allowable amount.

To illustrate the relevance of the differing interpretations, the notified and alternative CTAMS values in Table 6.6 are highlighted in Figure 6.6.

Table 6.6 *Alternative notifications of Norway's domestic support, 1995–2007*

Type of support		1995	1996	1997	1998	1999
	Million NOK					
Green box	Notification	4,100	4,116	3,676	3,890	4,277
	Alternative	2,161	2,013	1,653	1,839	2,255
Blue box	Notification	7,117	7,247	7,376	7,881	7,674
	Alternative	7,117	7,246	7,375	7,880	7,674
CTAMS	Notification	9,786	10,529	10,526	10,886	10,787
	Alternative	11,726	12,632	12,548	12,936	12,807
	Commitment	13,834	13,357	12,880	12,403	11,926

Sources: Norway's notifications to WTO and authors' estimates.

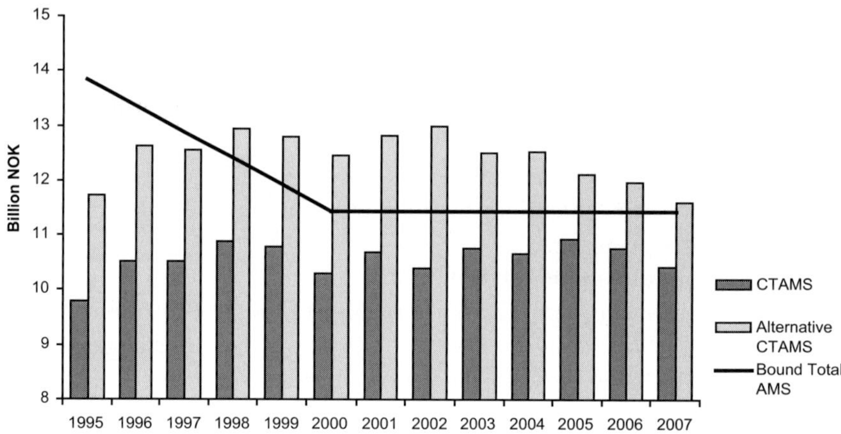

Figure 6.6 Alternative notifications of Norway's CTAMS
Sources: Norway's notification to WTO and authors' estimates.

According to our alternative interpretation, Norway has exceeded its Bound Total AMS ceiling since 1998. However the alternative CTAMS declined in 2007 and is closer to satisfying the current commitment. The reason for this development is the removal of poultry from the MPS calculation of the CTAMS.

2000	2001	2002	2003	2004	2005	2006	2007
5,012	4,316	4,338	3,882	3,986	5,865	6,188	6,718
2,838	2,205	2,265	2,197	2,124	1,670	1,997	2,410
7,671	7,331	7,531	7,360	7,434	3,914	3,793	3,725
7,669	7,330	7,531	7,360	7,434	6,927	6,782	6,859
10,293	10,700	10,399	10,761	10,665	10,925	10,765	10,442
12,467	12,811	12,997	12,515	12,527	12,108	11,967	11,615
11,449	11,449	11,449	11,449	11,449	11,449	11,449	11,449

Doha commitments and policy options for Norway

In this section,[13] the Doha draft modalities are translated into specific commitments with respect to domestic support, market access and export subsidies for Norway. It seems clear that tighter restrictions will require policy change. In contrast to countries discussed in other chapters of this book, this is likely to take place during the period of implementation of new constraints. As a consequence, we have attempted to make a quantitative link between these constraints, the reaction of policymakers, and subsequent domestic support notifications. Using assumptions of likely policy responses by the government, a sector model of Norwegian agriculture is employed to analyze the potential economic effects of meeting future reduction commitments in the Doha modalities (as drafted in 2008) on agricultural production and trade, and their budgetary and economic welfare implications. It is assumed that the primary objective of the Norwegian authorities will be to minimize the effects of commitments under the WTO modalities on agricultural activity. In summary, simulations of the reduction commitments, support values and budgetary outlays are based on our interpretations of likely Norwegian policy response rather than extrapolations of current policies and spending.

[13] This section is based on Blandford *et al.* (2010).

Table 6.7 *Base rates of support and proposed Doha commitments for Norway*

Domestic support	Base level	Proposed Doha final commitment
	Billion NOK	
Bound Total AMS	11.4	5.4
Blue box	7.5	3.6
10 percent value of production (1995–2000)	2.3	
OTDS	21.2	9.5

Source: Author's calculations from WTO (2008).

Doha commitments

Table 6.7 summarizes proposed commitments on Norwegian domestic support, based on the 2008 draft on domestic support modalities reviewed in Chapter 2 (see Table 2.2 and WTO 2008). The Base OTDS for Norway is NOK 21.2 billion, which is the sum of the Bound Total AMS, 10 percent of the average value of total agricultural production during 1995–2000 and the average value of Norway's blue box payments during 1995–2000. The blue box payments were greater than 5 percent of total value of production, which allows Norway to use this larger amount in establishing its Base OTDS (paragraph 1(c) of the draft modalities; see Appendix B of this book).

Since Norway's Bound Total AMS is less than US$15 billion (applying exchange rates in 2008), its reduction commitment would be 45 percent. However, for countries where the Final Bound Total AMS constitutes a large share of the total value of production (above 40 percent) an additional reduction of 7.5 percent is required. This applies to Norway. The resulting total reduction requirement of 52.5 percent means that Norway's Final Bound Total AMS would be cut from NOK 11.4 billion to NOK 5.4 billion. Given that as much as 40 percent of Norway's trade-distorting support during 1995–2000 was through blue box measures, the overall blue box limit is derived by reducing the average level of historical blue box payments by the same percentage as the reduction in the Bound Total AMS.[14]

[14] This follows from paragraph 39 in the draft modalities, known as the "Norway clause" (see Appendix B, paragraph 39).

This would establish the maximum value of blue box support at NOK 3.6 billion, which is 52.5 percent below the base period average of NOK 7.5 billion. Since Norway's Base OTDS is less than US$10 billion, its OTDS ceiling commitment would be NOK 9.5 billion, the result of a 55 percent reduction from the Base OTDS.

In assessing policy options for complying with the domestic support commitments in Table 6.7, it is important to take into account that Norway would also have to meet new market access and export subsidy commitments. The changes involved could limit Norway's ability to provide support to its farmers through current policy mechanisms. The Doha draft modalities specify that export subsidies are to be abolished. With respect to market access, Norway's MFN tariffs for products not declared to be sensitive are subject to a 70 percent reduction with a 100 percent ceiling on the final tariff. For the principal Norwegian products, the 100 percent ceiling would be binding.

Since all the main Norwegian products such as grain, meat and milk products could be defined as sensitive products, the 100 percent ceiling may not apply. Norway's MFN tariffs for sensitive products will be subject to a 23.33 percent reduction, which results in tariffs of over 100 percent. In return, Norway has to establish new market access opportunities through higher TRQs. These concessions would need to lead to in-quota import volumes equivalent to 6.5 percent of domestic consumption. We assume that Norway will attempt to achieve a quota fill rate of 65 percent, since if it were to fall below that level one could expect challenges from other WTO members. Further details on the market access assumptions for Norway are given in Blandford *et al.* (2010).

Projections and policy options

By comparing the proposed Doha commitments to the base levels in Table 6.7, it would be reasonable to suggest that the Norwegian agricultural sector will face substantial changes if the proposed Doha Round commitments are implemented. Amplifying this suggestion is the required elimination of export subsidies, which currently absorb 12 percent of the milk production and the expansion of the TRQ volumes across all commodities, which will imply higher imports.

To assess the impact of these policy changes a sector model of Norwegian agriculture was used to analyze potential impacts of the proposed Doha commitments on agricultural production and trade

Table 6.8 *Norway's projected notifications of domestic support to comply with proposed Doha commitments under base solution and alternative policy scenarios*

	Base solution	Box shifting	Export subsidy commitment	Market access commitment	Domestic support commitment[a]
Share of commitments					
Commitment = 100					
CTAMS	199	199	191	162	56
Blue box	209	114	119	95	100
OTDS	192	157	155	129	69
Index compared with base solution					
Base solution = 100					
Production value	100	100	99	78	93
Economic welfare	100	100	105	132	113

[a] Through the elimination of administered prices.
Source: Blandford *et al.* (2010).

(Blandford *et al.* 2010).[15] The base year in the model is 2003. Since the structure and size of agricultural production, as well as agricultural support, has been relatively stable over the last decade, this can be viewed as a representative year. Note that the base year predates any moves to minimize future adverse effects of the Doha Round, i.e., box-shifting and elimination of administered prices for some products. Thus, the analysis allows us to illuminate the importance of such moves.

The first column in Table 6.8 shows that domestic support in the base year was far above the ceilings implied by the Doha reduction commitments in Table 6.7. The CTAMS exceeded the proposed Bound Total AMS by 99 percent, the proposed blue box support ceiling was exceeded by 109 percent, and the proposed OTDS ceiling by 92 percent. The first strategy

[15] The model includes the most important commodities produced by the Norwegian agricultural sector but not all the commodities for which support is notified to the WTO. For given input costs, demand functions and support systems, the model computes market clearing prices and quantities. The model includes all major agricultural policies and generates estimates of production, use of inputs, domestic consumption and prices, imports and exports, measures of notified support, and economic surplus measured as the sum of producers' and consumers' surplus. More details and further references can be found in Brunstad *et al.* (2005).

of the government, if it is to minimize the impact of the new commitments on agricultural activity, would be to transfer subsidies from the blue box to the green box. As noted earlier this strategy has already been employed.

As discussed above, two years after the base year of our analysis (in 2005) roughly NOK 3.4 billion previously included in the acreage and cultural landscape (NOK 3 billion) and the headage support (NOK 0.4 billion) schemes were shifted from the blue box to the green box without any major change in policy implementation. The second column in Table 6.8 reflects this move. While the value of production and economic welfare are unchanged, the amount of blue box support and the imputed OTDS decrease substantially, with blue box support now only 14 percent above the ceiling.

The next issue is whether compliance with the market access commitments and the elimination of export subsidies would be sufficient to reduce notified domestic support below the Doha ceilings. The effect of eliminating export subsidies is shown in the third column of Table 6.8. The current practice of subsidizing exports of cheese through levies on domestic sales of fluid milk is assumed to be abolished. The implication is lower milk production caused by a cut in the farmgate price of milk. Since that price, interpreted as an administered price, enters into the market price support component of the CTAMS, both the CTAMS and the OTDS are reduced (by 4 percent and 1 percent, respectively). Lower milk production and farmgate prices lead to a 1 percent decline in the total value of agricultural production. However, the 5 percent increase in economic welfare is indicative of the economic cost of the current policy regime.

If we introduce the implementation of the proposed market access commitments, we generate the results in the fourth column of Table 6.8. While blue box support is now below the ceiling, the CTAMS and the OTDS still exceed Doha commitments by 62 percent and 29 percent, respectively. In other words, even if Norway complies with the market access and export subsidy commitments, the CTAMS and the OTDS values would violate their respective ceilings. Also note that the volume of agricultural production would be 22 percent below the base period level, which suggests that achieving further reductions in the CTAMS and the OTDS would have a major impact on Norwegian agriculture.

To minimize such effects, an obvious strategy would be to abolish all remaining administered prices, which, as explained above, will remove market price support as defined by the Agreement from the calculation of the CTAMS. Since 98 percent of Norway's CTAMS is market price

Table 6.9 *Projected composition of Norway's support for agriculture under base and Doha scenarios*

	Base solution	Doha solution
	Billion NOK	
Budget support	11.3	13.7
Market price support (OECD's economic definition)	8.6	5.4
Total support	19.9	19.1

Source: Blandford *et al.* (2010).

support, this would provide substantial flexibility for compensating producers for any reduction in market prices through non-exempt direct payments within the NOK 5.4 billion Bound Total AMS ceiling specified in Table 6.7. The results in the last column of Table 6.8 show that it would be possible to maintain more than 90 percent of the base level of agricultural production by using such non-exempt direct payments, while meeting Doha commitments within safe margins. However, such a policy would be costly for the economy since it would substitute expensive Norwegian agricultural production for cheaper imports. This is reflected by the drop in economic welfare from 132 percent of the base level in the fourth column to 113 percent in the fifth column of the table.

On the basis of these results we can conclude that while the proposed Doha commitments would allow Norway to maintain most of its current agricultural activity the nature of agricultural policy would have to change. The present system of domestic market regulation will be put under pressure if administered prices and export subsidies are eliminated and imports increase. Furthermore, cuts in import tariffs and higher TRQs imply lower farmgate prices, and, consequently, lower market price support. It follows that relatively more of the support for agriculture will have to be provided by taxpayers. Table 6.9 shows that budgetary support increases, in absolute terms, by NOK 2.4 billion, while market price support decreases by NOK 3.2 billion. As a result total support is only NOK 0.8 billion below the base year level.[16]

[16] Total support in this table differs from that in Table 6.1 primarily because economic price support, rather than the notified MPS, is used to evaluate the implications of a Doha agreement. The aggregate MPS, computed using the OECD methodology, for the commodities included in the model was below the equivalent notified MPS in 2003.

Conclusions

According to its agricultural support notifications to the WTO for 1995–2007 and our estimates for 2008, Norway has complied with its domestic support commitments under the Agreement. The ceiling on CTAMS has not affected Norwegian agricultural policy or programs. Norway has, in fact, managed to expand agricultural output relative to the base period of 1986–88, and the CTAMS and total support across all categories have remained relatively stable. The Uruguay Round reduction commitment merely involved a reduction in the "water" in an inflated Bound Total AMS during the implementation period of the Agreement in 1995–2000. Nevertheless, since 2000 the gap between the Bound Total AMS and Norway's notified CTAMS has narrowed, and seems to have completely closed by 2008.

Although Norway's WTO notifications indicate compliance with commitments, we argue that several of the green box entries are questionable. The vacation and replacement scheme seems to be amber box support rather than green box support, as claimed in the notifications. Also, it is an open question as to whether the acreage and cultural landscape scheme complies with the Annex 2 of the Agreement, which states that a payment can only compensate for the additional costs incurred or the loss of income involved in complying with an environmental program.

In 2007 Norway was close to surpassing its Bound Total AMS under the Agreement. Its response was to abolish administered prices for poultry, thereby excluding the corresponding market price support from the calculation of the CTAMS. In 2008, this practice was extended to other minor products. In this way, Norway has been able to meet its commitment under the Agreement, while maintaining the real support for production and forestalling policy reform and agricultural restructuring.

The 2008 proposed Doha modalities imply far more stringent commitments on domestic support, a reduction in border protection and the elimination of export subsidies. These commitments appear to have significant consequences for domestic prices and production. Nevertheless, by repackaging current domestic support (making changes to amber-box subsidies so as to notify payments in the green box) or by removing administrative prices and substituting budgetary support for market price support much of the agricultural restructuring that would otherwise be necessary could be avoided.

To maintain current activity and production levels, budgetary support, which is more transparent and subject to greater public scrutiny than market price support, will have to be increased. Also, a substantial part of the budgetary support would have to qualify for the green box. Since much of the support that Norway notifies or plans to notify as green box seems to be linked to production, this strategy may be subject to challenge in the WTO. If Norway were to lose such a challenge, it might be required to make real reforms in its agricultural policies rather than cosmetic ones.

References

Blandford, D., I. Gaasland, R. Garcia, and E. Vårdal. 2010. How effective are WTO disciplines on domestic support and market access for agriculture? *The World Economy* 33(11): 1470–1485.

Brunstad, R. J., I. Gaasland, and E. Vårdal. 2005. Multifunctionality of agriculture: An inquiry into the complementarity between landscape preservation and food security. *European Review of Agricultural Economics* 32(4): 469–488.

MAF (Ministry of Agriculture and Food). 2006. Proposition to the Parliament, No. 68 (2005–06), June.

MGAL (Ministry of Government Administration and Labor). 2004. Proposition to the Parliament. No. 66 (2003–04), May.

MLSA (Ministry of Labor and Social Affairs). 2005. Proposition to the Parliament No. 69 (2004–05), May.

NAA (Norwegian Agricultural Authority). 2009. Home page. www.slf.dep.no (accessed January–May 2008).

NILF (Norwegian Agricultural Economics Research Institute). 2007. Norwegian agriculture: Status and trends. Centre for Food Policy, July.

2008. Budsjettnemnda for jordbruket: Jordbrukets totalregnskap, 1959–2007 (Budget committee for agriculture: Economic accounts for agriculture, 1959–2007). July.

OECD. 2009. *Agricultural Policies in OECD Countries: Monitoring and Evaluation*. Paris.

SN (Statistics Norway). Various years. Agricultural statistics. www.ssb.no/jordbruk_en/ (accessed January–May 2008).

World Bank. 2010. Data and statistics – quick reference tables. www.worldbank.org (accessed April 7, 2010).

WTO. 1995. *Results of the Uruguay Round of Multilateral Trade Negotiations – The Legal Texts*. Geneva.

2008. Revised draft modalities for agriculture. TN/AG/W/4/Rev.4. 6 December.

PART III

Developing countries: will low levels of support rise?

7

Brazil

ANDRÉ NASSAR

Trade-distorting domestic support for agricultural products is among the most contentious issues in the Doha Round. It is not a stretch to assert that disciplining domestic support became the central shared offensive interest among developing countries; it acted as the glue that kept the G20 an active coalition in the negotiations. Although there is a consensus that domestic support disciplines must be strengthened, the concrete implications in terms of commitments and the allocation of subsidies among the various boxes remain controversial. The issue of disciplining domestic support is broader than the Doha Round because it also involves other spheres of the WTO, such as the Dispute Settlement Body (DSB) and the work of the Committee on Agriculture.

The agricultural sector is like no other sector of the Brazilian economy. It is at the heart of political attention because farm productivity has recently increased markedly due to technological modernization. Brazil has grown, in only a few years, to become among the top agricultural exporters. Consequently, trade liberalization is a key issue of importance for the sustainability of Brazilian agriculture. Constraining domestic support among its competitors and trade partners, together with gaining improved market access conditions, are critical to Brazilian agriculture's future. Stronger disciplines and tighter commitments, along with transparency, are goals of Brazil in the multilateral negotiations. Brazil has also emerged in recent years as a major player seeking to strengthen the disciplines for trade-distorting domestic support through the WTO legal system. In terms of its own policies, Brazil has decided to be transparent. It has opened to public scrutiny information related to its agricultural

The author is very grateful for the personal help provided by Renato Antonio Henz, Savio Rafael Pereira and Luiz Claudio Carmona from the Ministry of Agriculture and Livestock in clarifying how Brazilian agricultural policies are notified to the World Trade Organization and also for the insightful technical comments from Lars Brink and David Orden.

support programs. In contrast to many developing countries, Brazil has regularly updated its WTO domestic support notifications (through 2005/06 as of June 2010). Its policies have been submitted to the OECD for evaluation since 2005. The OECD's analysis confirms that Brazil has low levels of support. Among China, Russia, South Africa, and Ukraine, non-OECD members that have been monitored by the OECD, Brazil is the lowest in terms of the percentage Producer Support Estimate (PSE).

This chapter addresses Brazilian agricultural policy with a focus on programs of the government that could be considered distortive to trade. Domestic support programs with trade-distorting effects, as understood within the WTO legal system and more specifically the Agreement on Agriculture, are examined in detail. The specific instruments of Brazil's agricultural support programs are described, how they are notified to the WTO is assessed, and the levels of support are presented. Shadow notifications are calculated through 2007/08 and projections of policies and product-specific support are made through 2018.

The main objective of the chapter is to provide consistent information with respect to support policies in Brazil as a basis for understanding the outcomes it seeks from the Doha Round. Brazilian notifications, however, are not immune from critical assessment. Alternative approaches to measuring the support provided in Brazil are examined. These alternative approaches do not change the conclusion that Brazilian support is relatively low in relation to total agricultural output or on a product-specific basis for those crops targeted for support. We show that Brazil is in a comfortable position to accept the tighter disciplines on domestic support it would face under the proposed Doha modalities.

In updating the notifications and projecting government support to the agricultural sector most information regarding agricultural policies and expenditures was publicly available at Brazilian government websites. An exception is the subsidies related to debt rescheduling programs, which have become a key support policy. Those programs were the most difficult to trace and interpret in terms of the data and methodologies used by the government to measure support levels and prepare the notifications.

There also remain unresolved questions for Brazil related to the WTO disciplines for domestic support, in particular the treatment of biofuels in the WTO. Although agricultural-based biofuels production has increased at rapid rates in the US, EU and Brazil, it is still not clear how to classify ethanol and biodiesel policies within the WTO context. Certain support policies are being notified to the WTO by these countries. However, the two biggest policies, tax exemptions and credits and blending mandates, are not notified to the WTO as agricultural domestic support by Brazil or other countries. I provide a brief discussion on the ethanol policies in place in Brazil and a few alternatives that could be used for notifying biofuels policies.

Brazil's agricultural support policies

With regard to the rural sector, Brazilian policies are organized in two general frameworks: agrarian policy and agricultural policy (Chaddad and Jank 2006). The agrarian policy comprises programs related to land reform and settlement projects. Agrarian reform programs are notified in the green box as general services. They address primarily the challenge of reducing rural poverty not increasing national agricultural production.

Agricultural policy in Brazil benefits two groups: commercial farmers and family farmers. The classification and division between these two groups was developed based on the 1996 Agricultural Census. The Ministry of Agriculture and Livestock (MAPA) manages the policies for commercial farmers, and the Ministry of Agrarian Development (MDA) manages both the agricultural programs for family farming and the agrarian reform programs. In some cases, policies are implemented for commercial and family farmers by the same government agency. That is the case with output market support programs, which are implemented by the National Food Supply Company (CONAB). In other cases, the nature of the policies for commercial farmers and family farmers are similar even if the administrative channels differ. However, the government makes a clear distinction between commercial and family farmers, and this is reflected in the types and levels of support provided. This distinction as a basis for policy is a relatively new development in Brazil. The political focus has moved toward a developmental objective, addressing the needs of low-income and small farms.

Within the framework of distinguishing between commercial and family farmers, the Brazilian federal government follows five main agricultural policy strategies (Damico and Nassar 2007). These strategies are primarily based on two main tools: various rural credit programs available to commercial and family farmers with preferential interest rates and output (price and income) support programs for specific products. Debt management and rescheduling programs are, in essence, based on the preferential credit. Income insurance is a relatively new strategy of the federal government. A recent agricultural risk insurance program based on subsidized insurance rate premiums launched in 2005 remains small in terms of production coverage and its availability to producers, although it has shown an increasing trend.

Production, marketing and investment credit programs

One main component of Brazilian agricultural support policies is based on providing credit lines with reduced interest rates to both commercial and family farmers. The rationale behind the preferential credit policies in Brazil derives from the high interest rates that have prevailed in the country and agriculture production being a risky economic activity requiring seasonal financing. Credit policy is directed toward the farming community directly via government sourcing and indirectly through financial institutions. The federal government requires banks to keep a total of 25 percent of deposits available for farm credit. Moreover, rural savings, the National Development Bank (BNDES) and the Workers Support Fund complement the other source of funding for agricultural credit.[1]

In order to implement credit policies based on preferential interest rates, the government has developed the National System of Rural Credit (SNCR). The SNCR has adopted many changes since its creation in the late 1960s. The basic principle of the system, however, remains the same: to organize various sources of funding that are devoted to rural credit and to allocate funds among several agencies that are responsible for lending. The allocation is made according to the different credit programs defined by the federal government. There are programs in place for production credit, marketing credit, and investment credit. Production credit and marketing loans, also known as EGF (federal government loans), are both short-term credit. The first provides credit usually taken for nine months to cover cropping activities (acquisition of seeds and fertilizers) and variable costs associated with production. Marketing loans are oriented to after-harvesting activities, such as storage, and usually have a duration of six months. Investment credit is focused on medium-term loans for capital goods acquisitions.

Until 1996 credit programs did not distinguish between classifications of farmers. With the creation of PRONAF (Family Farmers Special Program), production and investment credit started to be channelled

[1] Data on amount of preferential credit available to producers as well as explanations of the sources of funds can be obtained in the Rural Credit Yearbook published annually by the Brazilian Central Bank (BACEN).

with special conditions (usually lower interest rates) to family farmers. Credit for family farmers is concentrated in production and investment credit and, until 2007, without provisions for marketing loans. PRONAF remains a set of policies predominantly based on short-term and investment credit and is discussed separately below.

In the 1970s, credit policies were the main instruments used by the government to stimulate the expansion of agricultural production. Stated objectives included to guarantee food security and to promote the occupation of the Brazilian territory. During the 1970s and 1980s, real interest rates were negative, and there was no restriction on the availability of subsidized credit to individual farmers.

The purpose and scope of the credit policies changed in the 1990s. As a consequence of Brazil addressing its balance-of-payments crisis and hyperinflation, preferential credit policies, especially for production and marketing loans, lost some of their importance as a mechanism to promote increased output. The amount of available credit decreased in real terms during that period and limits were placed on the levels of borrowing allowed per farmer. It was only in 2003 that the amount of credit began to grow once again, as shown in Figure 7.1.

Limited availability of credit has at certain times constrained the performance of Brazilian agriculture. Figure 7.1 shows that official credit availability and agricultural output measured by the value of production follow a similar trend. In the period between 1999 and 2003, the value of production decreased following a reduction in available credit as well as lower world prices for agricultural commodities. The reduction of subsidized credit as a percentage of output value during this period is explained not only by the low availability of resources for credit but also by a high level of credit default that prevented farmers from obtaining new loans. Among other factors, the balance of credit started to grow again in 2003 as a response to the debt rescheduling programs that were implemented. Although the availability of credit has been increasing since 2003, the ratio between credit and total value of production remains flat over the last few years (2005–09), indicating that the importance of subsidized credit in financing production had stabilized.

The amount of capital for production and marketing activities channeled through the SNCR represents only a portion of the total use of credit in the agricultural sector. The SNCR credit is less than 40 percent of the value of production for most crops. Production credit (primarily to finance planting costs) is generally below 25 percent of the value of production. For this reason, field crop production in Brazil, especially for

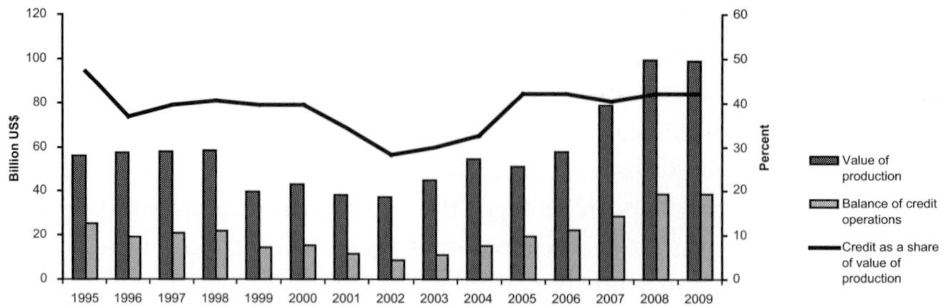

Figure 7.1 Availability of subsidized credit and value of agricultural production in Brazil

Note: Balance of credit operations on December 31 each year.

Sources: IBGE and BACEN.

soybeans and cotton, is also dependent on private, unsubsidized credit supplied by trading companies and producers.

The production and marketing credit programs function under similar administrative procedures and interest rates. Both impose limits on borrowing per participant. Both are notified to the WTO as product-specific support because the producer has to specify the product for which the credit will be used. However, the distribution of resources among products is not predefined and depends on demand from producers.

Investment credit

Government-supported investment credit has a complex structure, as there are many programs with different objectives. The largest among the investment credit programs provided by the BNDES is the Program for the Modernization of Agricultural Machinery (MODERFROTA). It provides investment credit to medium- and large-scale producers to finance purchases of equipment such as tractors and other agricultural machinery. There are seven other specific credit programs provided by the BNDES as part of the SNCR: Incentives Program for Irrigation and Storage (MODERINFRA), Cooperative Development Program for the Enhancement of Agricultural Value Added (PRODECOOP), Program for the Modernization of Agriculture and the Conservation of Natural Resources (MODERAGRO), Agri-business Development Program (PRODEAGRO), Fruit Industry Development Program (PRODEFRUTA), Milk Production Mechanization and Transportation Incentive Program (PROLEITE), and the Program of Commercial Planting and Recovery Forest (PROPFLORA). Together the investment credit programs account for about 10 percent of the financing provided annually through the SNCR. Each of these credit programs has specific eligibility criteria, borrowing limits and repayment terms and conditions.[2]

The MODERFROTA as well as the seven other investment credit programs from the BNDES are considered by the Brazilian government to be development programs. They are notified to the WTO under Article 6.2 of the Agreement as exempt from any ceiling on support.

Output support programs

There are two groups of price and income support programs oriented to commercial farmers. The first are programs with instruments under which the supported crop ends up in government stocks (Federal Government Acquisitions (AGF) and Contract Options Acquisitions (COA)). The AGF and COA programs are notified to the WTO as market price support (MPS). The second are programs with instruments that aim to facilitate the distribution of the product through market channels while providing support based on payment of price equalization premiums, without the government acquiring stocks (Premium to Commercial Buyers (PEP), Premium to Commercial Buyers Under a Private Sell Option Contract (PROP), and Equalization Premium to Farmers (PEPRO)). The price equalization programs are notified as product-specific AMS budgetary outlays. I refer to these programs of price and income support together as output support.

Brazil's output support programs are inherited from its earlier Policy of Guaranteed Minimum Prices (PGPM) which was widely used by the federal government during the 1970s and 1980s to intervene in markets to control prices and stimulate production through stocks management (OECD 2005). Through the AGF mechanism, the government used intervention stocks to regulate the market supply, purchasing agricultural products to support market prices (CONAB 2008). The subsidized marketing credit under EGF complemented the AGF by allowing producers to withhold the sale of commodities for a certain period in anticipation of higher prices. Prior to 1996, EGF operated explicitly as price support because borrowers could choose to relinquish the pledged product instead of repaying the loan.

[2] See Nassar and Ures (2009) for further discussion of the investment credit programs. Detailed information about BNDES operated agricultural investments programs can be obtained at http://inter.bndes.gov.br/english/programs.asp#agro.

Due to this policy, the federal government accumulated large stocks of products such as wheat, rice, maize, and dry beans during some crop seasons. This government stockholding became unsustainable and Brazilian policy shifted toward operations that were more market-oriented in the early 1990s. Remaining AGFs were used mainly for purchases from family farmers, reflecting the shift in focus of Brazilian agricultural policy. The objective of supporting prices to promote food security gave way to providing targeted income support (Chaddad and Jank 2006; CONAB 2008a).

Federal government purchases as a mechanism to sustain prices for producers are still utilized for certain crops in some years under the COA programs (CONAB 2008b, CONAB 2008c). In one such program, options contracts are auctioned at the start of the crop season, guaranteeing the holder a future sale at a fixed execution price. If the holder decides to exercise the option, which tends to occur when market prices are low, then the government may purchase the product or, if the government is not interested in acquiring the product, it can either buy back the contract before the option expires and pay a premium to producers or it may transfer its purchasing rights to private agents. If the government decides to buy the product, the farmer delivers the production under the contract to the government and receives the execution price. Under the transfer of purchasing rights to private agents, the product will be delivered to private companies that will pay the execution price and receive the difference from the market price as a payment from the government. The utilization of the COA has shown that the government has been opting for transferring purchase rights to private agents in order to avoid stockpiling. When the AGF and COA programs lead to the government withdrawing production from the market, they potentially shift prices upward and subsidize the whole stored production.

Support programs based on price equalization premiums were also put in place during Brazil's agricultural policy reform in the early 1990s. There are two aspects to the operation of these programs: a reference price for the farmer and an equalization premium that is sold at auction to private agents (either producers or wholesale buyers). The government sets the reference price and sells the premium in an auction. The equalization premium, which is the subsidy, is in general lower than the difference between the market price and the reference price and is sometimes subject to a maximum set by the government. The government sets the amount of product for which the premiums will be available in the auction. This means that the equalization premium programs are not generally available for the whole of production. They are usually targeted to least-developed regions, where the price at the farm level tends to be lower as it is disadvantaged by transportation costs (CONAB 2008d, CONAB 2008e, CONAB 2008f). Their effect is primarily to alter the location of production in the country, although raising the prices received by producers in remote and disadvantaged areas can also increase national output.

Table 7.1 presents the amount of production benefiting from output support programs in comparison with the total quantity of production from 2004/05 through 2008/09. The amount of production benefiting from support varies according to the crop season. There is no predefined rule for the decision of the government in terms of implementing the support instruments or setting their parameters such as reference price or equalization premiums. These decisions are made by the government based on the situation of prices during each marketing period (March to December). The AGF and COA instruments were used primarily for rice and maize. Overall, higher prices in 2008 interrupted any upward trends in the use of the support mechanisms observed from 2005 to 2007, except in the case of cotton for which almost two-thirds of production received the premiums in 2007/08, with support rising for maize in 2008/09.

Rural development and family farming support

With the creation of MDA in the 1990s to support rural development the government started to channel funds from the SNCR to family farmers through PRONAF. This program gained relevance in the SNCR, not only in terms of the amount of credit made available but also in terms of subsidization levels, which are considerably higher than for commercial farmers.

According to the 2006 Agricultural Census, out of the 5.2 million rural households in Brazil, 84.4 percent are classified as households engaged in family farming. Criteria to classify family farms are: size of the rural household; utilization of predominantly family labor; and family income generated from own-household economic activities of the family. PRONAF can be classified as a different policy strategy from other credit programs because it targets farmers with low income and with few available resources. PRONAF's main objective is to provide the financial liquidity to allow family farmers and agrarian reform settlers to remain in rural areas. PRONAF provides both short-term production and investment credit through its programs. There are several investment programs

Table 7.1 *Brazil's production benefiting from price and income support programs, 2004/05–2008/09*

	2004/05	2005/06	2006/07	2007/08	2008/09
	Thousand tons				
Cotton					
Production	1,299	1,038	1,524	1,602	1,214
AGF/COA	5	—	1	—	—
Equalization premium	470	464	729	1,024	792
Rice					
Production	13,227	11,722	11,316	12,074	12,603
AGF/COA	917	308	920	—	669
Equalization premium	328	699	158	—	—
Edible beans					
Production	3,044	3,471	3,340	3,521	3,491
AGF/COA	—	3	36	—	150
Equalization premium	—	—	125	—	67
Maize					
Production	34,977	42,515	51,370	58,652	51,004
AGF/COA	637	2,224	273	—	3,858
Equalization premium	874	5,586	4,936	165	4,875
Cassava					
Production	25,872	26,639	26,804	27,378	26,614
AGF/COA	—	—	—	—	—
Equalization premium	76	189	—	—	—
Soybean					
Production	52,305	55,027	58,392	60,018	57,166
AGF/COA	—	15	—	—	—
Equalization premium	—	11,953	5,354	—	—
Wheat					
Production	5,846	4,873	2,234	4,097	5,884
AGF/COA	483	32	—	1,339	21
Equalization premium	1,345	240	—	309	1,395

Table 7.1 *(cont.)*

	2004/05	2005/06	2006/07	2007/08	2008/09
Coffee					
Production	2,140	2,573	2,160	2,491	2,434
AGF/COA	—	—	—	—	180
Equalization premium	—	—	300	—	—

Notes: AGF is Federal Government Acquisitions; COA is Contract Option Acquisitions. — indicates zero.
Source: CONAB.

with different objectives and credit lines. In 2000, PRONAF loans totaled US$1 billion, 86 percent for short-term credit and 14 percent for investment.[3] For the 2008/09 crop season, US$5.6 billion were available for PRONAF loans, with 51 percent designated for investment programs.

PRONAF beneficiaries are divided into five groups depending on the size of the farm, the number of people employed, production, and the income of the farmer (MDA 2007). PRONAF credit lines and interest rates are defined progressively according to the income of the beneficiary group. For example, agrarian reform settlers, who are among the poorest farmers, could borrow for investments at an interest rate of 1.5 percent in 2009, while eligible farmers showing evidence of commercial production, using both family and contract labor and earning at least 80 percent of their income from agriculture, paid an interest rate of 5.5 percent.

As an instrument to guarantee food supplies for the anti-poverty Zero Hunger Program, the Program of Acquisition of Agricultural Products from Family Farming (Programa de Aquisição de Alimentos – PAA) was created in 2003 (MDA 2010). The PAA guarantees supplies through CONAB's acquisitions of food from family farmers. Acquisitions, however, are made at market prices. According to CONAB's management report, expenditures in PAA totalled US$157.3 million for the acquisition of 174.7 thousand tons of food products from 92,071 family farmers in 2008 (CONAB 2008g).

A marketing loan program specifically for family farmers was established at the end of 2006 (Programa de Garantia de Preços para a Agricultura Familiar – PGPAF). PGPAF is a price support program

[3] In this chapter US dollars are distinguished from Brazilian Real using US$ and R$, respectively.

that works similarly to price support programs for commercial farmers. PGPAF is linked to production credit and grants discount bonuses for farmers in the liquidation of the credit offered by PRONAF if the market price of a product is below a guaranteed price. Bonuses are calculated as the difference between market price and guaranteed price. Market prices and bonuses are calculated and announced monthly by MDA. Guaranteed prices are calculated based on the average regional production cost (OECD 2009). The limit for the bonuses, which is ultimately the amount of subsidy, is R$3,500 (US$1,800) per beneficiary for each crop.

Debt management programs

The credit-based programs that dominate agricultural policy in Brazil are not exempt from complications. The major complication is that the government becomes directly involved in management of the level of indebtedness of the rural sector. Producers have not always repaid their loans for several reasons, resulting in increased levels of indebtedness and constraints on the performance of Brazilian agriculture. Credit subsidy policies themselves can lead to overinvestment in production capacity with immobilization of capital in land and machinery, depressing repayment capability. Among other reasons contributing to defaults on the loans have been crop losses due to poor weather conditions or emergence of new diseases (e.g., soybean rust in 2005), income loss due to high transportation costs, and effects on agriculture from changes in macroeconomic policy such as measures implemented to control inflation and resulting in appreciation of the Brazilian Real.

Under these circumstances, debt rescheduling and management programs have come to play an important role in Brazilian agricultural policy. These programs have become the most important source of subsidies for Brazilian commercial producers.

Debt management became an objective of Brazilian agricultural policy when the government decided to renegotiate the overdue rural credit, intended to allow producers to receive new loans and roll over the old ones. The majority of the renegotiated debts were acquired during the 1980s and early 1990s. All main credit programs have, since 1995, benefited from rescheduling conditions. The most important arrangements were the rural debt securitizations in November 1995 and April 2002, the Financial Assets Rehabilitation Program (Programa Especial de Saneamento de Ativos – PESA) in February 1998, and the renegotiation of debts from family farming programs. In September 2008, the government took another step with debt rescheduling programs, through the Law 11775 of September 17, 2008 (the 2008 debt settlement package as it is called in OECD 2009). The debts remaining from the previous arrangements were to be renegotiated and new debts obtained after the implementation of these arrangements were also to be addressed in this renegotiation.

The government uses December 2002 as the base period for calculating the subsidy provided by the debt rescheduling program as notified to the WTO. The balance of overdue credit at that time totalled R$29.2 billion (US$10 billion), which corresponded to 84 percent of the total balance of debts. More than 50 percent of the outstanding debt was associated with the earlier securitization and PESA rescheduling programs.

The general principle of the rescheduling programs before 2008 was to offer interest rates lower than the original rates and prolong the period of repayment. The subsidy burden for the Brazilian government depends on the present value of the overdue debt, the difference in interest rates, and the renegotiated payment schedule (twenty-four years for the securitization program and twenty years for the PESA) compared to the initial repayment period.

Although the securitization program had been in place since the end of 1995, the government began notifying debt rescheduling to the WTO for 1998/99. Assessing the debt rescheduling subsidies was facilitated by OECD's evaluation of Brazilian policies and calculation of the Brazilian PSEs (OECD 2005). In order to supply information regarding the rescheduling programs to the OECD, the government gathered data that were located in different ministries and banks and, by doing so, created a database from which the aggregate cost could be measured.

Many factors contributed to the announcement of the 2008 debt rescheduling. According to the Ministry of Finance, by August 2007, the balance of overdue credit was R$87.8 billion (US$45.1 billion).[4] This balance of credit was nearly double that of 2002 as a percentage of the value of agricultural production: in 2002 it was 27 percent of the total value of production and it had reached 57 percent in 2007. Farmers' incomes, however, had not achieved the expected performance and the solvency of producers, in particular in the state of Mato Grosso, was compromised.

[4] This amount is distributed as follows: R$27.4 billion under renegotiation programs; R$10.5 billion under new production credit; R$17.3 billion under new investment and marketing credit; R$12 billion under constitutional funds that were not subjected to rescheduling programs; and R$7.1 billion under execution by the Brazilian treasury and that originated from rescheduled debt not paid (MF 2008 and MF 2008a). It is necessary to add also R$13.4 billion of overdue credit originating from programs for family farming.

Thus, the farm sector and the government negotiated the 2008 rural debt management policy.

The 2008 debt renegotiation process is, in concept, different from the others. This program is based on providing incentives for farmers to pay the debts with rebates and discounts on the interest rate. The new policy is more of a debt liquidation and regularization – for the delinquent renegotiated debts covered by the previous programs – than a rescheduling program, as previous programs were. The amount of credit to be renegotiated was subjected to negotiations among the government, the congress, and lobbying organizations of commercial and family farmers. Depending on the level of engagement by farmers under this regulation, it will eventually replace the earlier debt management programs. The specific conditions of each debt modality in terms of payment schedule, interest rates, and the debt balance covered makes the calculation in advance of the subsidies associated with this debt rescheduling a difficult task.

Agricultural risk insurance

Production insurance is a relatively new strategy within Brazilian agricultural policy. There is a common perception among policymakers and producers that the country must develop a comprehensive national insurance policy to reduce the risks associated with climate, pests, and diseases that negatively affect crop yields and, consequently, farmers' incomes. This insurance policy is seen as one solution to avoid problems with debt defaults in the future.

A new agricultural risk insurance program was created in 2005 and introduced in 2006 by the federal government. Benefits were relatively limited in its initial phase. The amount of collateral paid in (mainly by the government) is small and consequently the insurance program covers only a small portion of production. The value of output each producer can insure is capped, limiting further the scope of the program.

Domestic support notifications and shadow notifications

Brazil had notified its domestic support to the WTO for 1994/95 through 2005/06 as of June 2010. A summary of the notifications, together with shadow notifications through 2008/09, is presented in Table 7.2. Unlike many developing countries, Brazil has a positive Bound Total AMS. This commitment arose because of product-specific support above the *de minimis* threshold that Brazil provided for rice, wheat and coffee under its production and marketing credit and output market support policies during the 1986–88 base period of the Agreement. Brazil's Final Bound Total AMS of US$912.1 million is very small compared to the total production value of Brazilian agriculture (around 0.8 percent). Nonetheless, it has provided Brazil with more flexibility for support within the WTO disciplines than is available to developing countries without a positive Bound Total AMS, whose AMS support must not exceed *de minimis* thresholds. Brazil notifies its support in US dollars, so the nominal levels are affected by movements in the exchange rate of the Brazilian Real against the dollar.

Notifications, 1994/94–2005/06

Product-specific AMS support notified by Brazil has mostly been under its *de minimis* thresholds, but in several years support has exceeded those thresholds for one or more commodities resulting in notification of a CTAMS, as summarized in Table 7.2. Brazil has notified non-product-specific AMS support as *de minimis*. It has also made use of Article 6.2 development programs but has not reported any blue box payments. Brazil falls in the middle of the range among developing countries in terms of its average green box expenditures as a percentage of agricultural GDP (Nassar *et al.* 2009). However, Brazil's green box expenditure levels have declined over time, reaching a trough during 2002/03 to 2004/05.

Green box

The components of Brazil's green box notifications are shown in Table 7.3. General services, including research, training, advisory, inspection, marketing and promotion, infrastructure services and agrarian reform programs, comprise more than half of Brazil's green box support, peaking as a percentage of the total in the late 1990s. Green box expenditures started to increase in 2004/05, reversing the trend observed in previous years, especially in the case of general services. Increasing expenditures in general services are explained by the agrarian reform programs, including the purchase of land for resettlement. Policies related to agrarian reform are managed by the National Institute for Colonization and Agrarian Reform (INCRA) and supervised by MDA. INCRA's programs vary from infrastructure development to provision of credit. All of these expenditures are notified in the general services category. Brazil has also notified insignificant expenditures for its agricultural crop insurance and disaster relief programs in the green box, without indicating which

Table 7.2 *Summary of Brazil's domestic support notifications and shadow notifications, 1994/95–2007/08*

	Notifications						
	1994/95	1995/96	1996/97	1997/98	1998/99	1999/2000	2000/01
Type of support	*Million US dollars*						
Green box	4,883.2	2,600.3	3,458.2	2,420.2	1,568.0	1,486.8	1,462.0
Development programs	358.9	269.3	280.7	372.9	156.0	309.7	331.5
Blue box	—	—	—	—	—	—	—
Current Total AMS	—	—	—	82.8	—	—	—
Total *de minimis*	399.6	363.3	306.8	410.2	1,247.0	1,053.0	975.7
Product-specific	381.2	283.5	236.7	305.0	409.1	230.4	235.8
Non-product-specific	18.4	79.8	70.1	105.2	837.9	822.6	739.9
Total support	5,641.7	3,232.9	4,045.8	3,286.1	2,970.9	2,849.5	2,769.2
Share of total support	%						
Green box	86	80	85	74	53	52	53
Development programs	6	8	7	11	5	11	12
Current Total AMS	—	—	—	3	—	—	—
De minimis	7	11	8	12	42	37	35
Total	100	100	100	100	100	100	100
Value of production (million US dollars)	56,124.6	57,464.2	57,628.3	58,262.3	39,724.8	42,909.7	38,409.2
Bound Total AMS (million US dollars)	1,039.1	1,025.0	1,010.9	996.8	982.7	968.6	954.4
CTAMS as share of binding (%)	—	—	—	8.3	—	—	—

Notes: Small differences in totals are due to rounding. — indicates zero.
Sources: WTO notifications and author's calculations.

					Shadow notifications	
2001/02	2002/03	2003/04	2004/05	2005/06	2006/07	2007/08
892.6	820.1	885.1	1,920.4	2,421.9	2,217.3	2,186.8
392.8	494.5	394.3	626.0	764.2	400.5	1,031.9
—	—	—	—	—	—	—
—	—	—	117.0	—	285.9	532.8
1,015.3	1,318.6	1,129.3	1,262.8	1,652.3	2,036.6	2,138.2
211.8	249.5	278.6	69.4	309.3	561.2	48.9
803.5	1,069.1	850.7	1,193.4	1,343.0	1,475.4	2,089.2
2,300.7	2,633.3	2,408.7	3,926.2	4,838.4	4,940.4	5,889.8
39	31	37	49	50	45	37
17	19	16	16	16	8	18
—	—	—	3	—	6	9
44	50	47	33	34	41	36
100	100	100	100	100	100	100
37,276.6	44,940.3	54,419.4	50,969.8	57,899.4	78,791.0	99,435.9
940.3	926.2	912.1	912.1	912.1	912.1	912.1
—	—	—	12.8	—	31.3	58.4

Table 7.3 *Composition of Brazil's green box notifications and shadow notifications, 1994/95–2007/08*

	Notifications					
	1994/95	1995/96	1996/97	1997/98	1998/1999	1999/2000
	Million US dollars					
General services	2,444.7	1,953.6	2,704.2	1,985.6	1,213.7	856.5
Public stockholding	451.7	495.1	338.2	—	140.6	40.8
Domestic food aid	1,590.6	151.6	325.7	434.6	185.8	589.2
Decoupled income support	—	—	—	—	—	—
Income insurance	—	—	—	—	—	—
Crop insurance/ disaster relief	—	—	90.0	—	27.8	0.4
Producer retirement	24.1	—	—	—	—	—
Resource retirement	—	—	—	—	—	—
Investment aids	—	—	—	—	—	—
Environmental payments	—	—	—	—	—	—
Regional assistance	—	—	—	—	—	—
Other	372.1	—	—	—	—	—
Total	4,883.2	2,600.3	3,458.2	2,420.2	1,568.0	1,486.8

Note: — indicates zero.
Sources: WTO notifications to WTO and author's calculations.

						Shadow notifications	
2000/01	2001/02	2002/03	2003/04	2004/05	2005/06	2006/07	2007/08
959.9	553.1	446.1	472.1	1,252.8	1,558.6	1,522.7	1,481.6
71.7	45.1	6.0	65.3	147.9	156.7	176.2	262.8
430.1	293.7	355.4	347.8	503.5	680.5	476.6	374.9
—	—	—	—	—	—	—	—
—	—	—	—	—	—	—	—
0.3	0.8	12.7	—	16.1	26.0	41.9	67.4
—	—	—	—	—	—	—	—
—	—	—	—	—	—	—	—
—	—	—	—	—	—	—	—
—	—	—	—	—	—	—	—
—	—	—	—	—	—	—	—
—	—	—	—	—	—	—	—
1,462.0	892.6	820.1	885.1	1,920.4	2,421.9	2,217.3	2,186.8

Table 7.4 *Composition of Brazil's development program notifications and shadow notifications, 1994/95–2007/08*

	Notifications						
	1994/95	1995/96	1996/97	1997/98	1998/99	1999/2000	2000/01
	Million US dollars						
Production Credit (family)	196.5	84.0	98.6	157.1	12.5	105.4	92.4
Investment Credit (all)	162.4	185.3	182.1	215.8	129.3	188.9	225.9
Debt Rescheduling (family)	—	—	—	—	14.1	15.4	13.2
Total	358.9	269.3	280.7	372.9	156.0	309.7	331.5

Note: — indicates zero.
Sources: WTO notifications and author's calculations.

green box provisions the programs are claimed to satisfy (such as income and income safety nets or relief from natural disasters, including crop insurance).

Public stockholding and food aid programs are directed toward consumers and family farmers and increased in relative importance in the early 2000s. Expenditures have increased due to PAA. Domestic food aid is also receiving more attention by the government and expenditures have increased since 2000/01.

Development programs

Brazil uses Article 6.2 for development programs to notify subsidies for production credit and debt rescheduling for family farmers and investment credit for both family and commercial farmers. The levels of these subsidies are shown in Table 7.4. Overall, the level of credit subsidies does not display a marked trend, with 1998/99 an outlier of relatively low credit availability. Debt rescheduling for family farmers was first notified for that year and remains below US$25 million through 2005/06. The largest expenditures are for investment credit to family and commercial farmers.

Brazil's overall spending on subsidy programs for family farms shows an increasing trend that reflects its importance in the policy

					Shadow notifications	
2001/02	2002/03	2003/04	2004/05	2005/06	2006/07	2007/08
95.8	117.8	97.6	149.7	98.8	83.0	150.8
283.6	362.9	280.4	456.5	642.4	289.7	849.0
13.3	13.8	16.3	19.8	23.0	27.7	32.1
392.8	494.5	394.3	626.0	764.2	400.5	1,031.9

decision-making process in recent years. Figure 7.2 illustrates this shift. It shows the subsidies channelled to family farmers through PRONAF from 1999–2008 (this excludes investment credit to commercial farmers included in Table 7.4) based on Brazil's notifications to the WTO through 2005/06 and estimates of these subsidies for three subsequent years.

Product-specific AMS support: *de minimis* and CTAMS

The components of Brazil's product-specific support notified as *de minimis* and its positive CTAMS in two years (1997/98 and 2004/05) are shown in detail in Table 7.5. Product-specific AMS support is broken down into its components both in full (the sum for all products) and for five specific crops. The five crops presented individually in the table (maize, rice, wheat, cotton, and soybeans) were chosen because they are the largest beneficiaries of market price support and price equalization premiums. The components of non-product-specific AMS support are also shown, along with product-specific and non-product-specific *de minimis* thresholds.

Brazil notified CTAMS of US$82.8 million for 1997/98 and also notified an additional US$305 million of product-specific AMS support as *de minimis* for that year, resulting in total product-specific AMS support of US$387.8 million. In 2004/05 Brazil notified CTAMS of US$117 million and *de minimis* product-specific support of US$69.9 million.

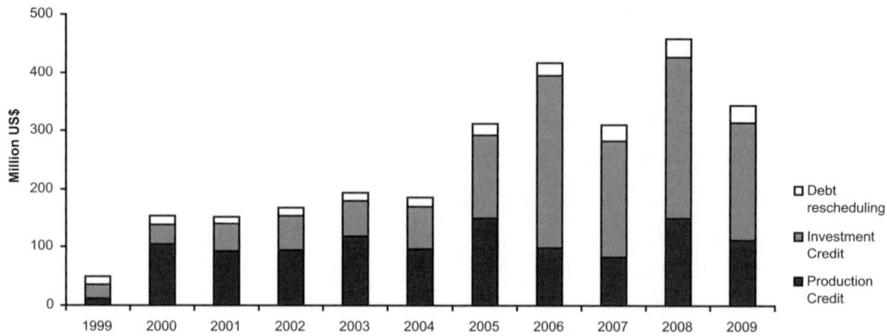

Figure 7.2 Brazil's PRONAF credit and debt rescheduling subsidies
Sources: Brazil's notifications to the WTO and authors' calculations

Brazil's notified product-specific AMS support did not change much from 1994/95 to 2005/06. Support for cotton and wheat (at 11.5 percent and 10.1 percent of the value of production, respectively) exceeded Brazil's 10 percent of value of production *de minimis* thresholds in 1997/98 resulting in the small positive CTAMS. However, for both cotton and wheat the levels of AMS support fell in subsequent years to rates well below the thresholds, with exception of wheat in 2004/05. Additionally, for six other important crops (including also sugarcane, coffee, and dry beans not shown separately in Table 7.5), and for various minor commodities, the Brazilian government has provided AMS support at levels far below the allowed *de minimis*.[5]

In calculating the MPS notified for the AGF/COA programs, the eligible quantities are the amounts of each commodity procured by the government. Subsidies arising as price equalization premiums are notified as budget expenditures. Brazil has also notified non-exempt direct payments from 1997/98 to 2001/02 due to a specific program for sugarcane. The calculated MPS has been negative for some crops in certain years (all years for maize). Negative MPS is shown in the notifications but counted as zero within each notified product-specific AMS of Brazil.

More complicated to assess are the subsidies associated with production and marketing credit that were reported as product-specific until 2003/04 and with production and investment credits notified as non-product-specific AMS support or under Article 6.2. As a general

[5] Although small in magnitude, minor crops that have received support notified as *de minimis* include cassava, wine/winery, oats, sorghum and barley.

principle, credit subsidies are computed by subtracting the preferential rate available under a credit program from the market-based interest rate, and multiplying by the amount borrowed through the SNCR to derive the forgone revenue of the government. Although the methodology is the same for all credit subsidies, there are differences in the calculations for production and marketing credit for commercial farmers, production credit for family farmers, and investment credit, as described above. In the case of production and marketing credit for commercial farmers, the subsidies are product-specific. There is no breakdown by product in the case of production credit for family farming. Investment credit subsidies are calculated according to the specific conditions of each program. In each case, the total subsidy reported to the WTO in each category of the notifications is the sum of the subsidies for those credit programs fitting that category from all of the various credit programs. It is interesting to note in Table 7.5 that production and marketing credit subsidies were not notified as product-specific in the last two notifications submitted for 2004/05 and 2005/06 in April 2010. The Brazilian government, differently from previous years, notified as product-specific AMS support only MPS and programs with budget expenditures, such as equalization premiums. From 2004/05, production and marketing credit subsidies were entirely notified as non-product-specific support. Two reasons justify the option taken by the government: the preferential rates are the same independently of the product; and given that there is no predefined product-specific allocation for the credit, the distribution of available credit among products is known only after the credit is borrowed.

Interest rate movements affect the level of credit subsides provided. The market interest rate and the rate for the production and marketing credit programs are shown in Figure 7.3 for the period 2002–2009. The preferential rate given by the government does not follow the pattern of the market rate, and remained unchanged through 2007. With the preferential rate constant, as the market rate rises or falls, the rate of the subsidy also increases or decreases. In 2007, after some pressure by agricultural lobbyists, the government lowered the preferential rate by a small amount and by doing so increased the level of support for any given market interest rate.

Non-product-specific *de minimis* AMS support

Non-product-specific AMS support notified by Brazil increased from US$18.4 million in 1994/95 to a peak over US$1.1 billion in 2004/05 and

Table 7.5 *Composition of Brazil's AMS notifications and shadow notifications, 1994/95–2007/08*

	Notifications					
	1994/95	1995/96	1996/97	1997/98	1998/99	1999/2000
	Million US dollars					
Total product-specific AMS	381.2	283.5	236.7	387.8	409.1	230.4
Market Price Support[a]	136.9	12.8	2.7	11.4	—	—
Non-exempt direct payments	—	—	—	75.3	15.5	45.1
Other product-specific support	244.3	270.7	234.0	301.1	382.3	177.4
Production and marketing credit	139.6	240.2	181.3	255.1	378.1	146.2
Price equalization premiums[b]	—	30.6	52.7	46.1	4.3	31.2
Other not included in above programs	104.7	—	—	—	11.2	7.9
CTAMS	—	—	—	82.8	—	—
Product-specific AMS (selected commodities)						
Maize	26.9	73.1	88.5	47.9	86.8	36.9
Market Price Support	-68.8	-19.7	-74.8	-10.1	-33.8	-24.9
Non-exempt direct payments	—	—	—	—	—	—

						Shadow notifications	
2000/01	2001/02	2002/03	2003/04	2004/05	2005/06	2006/07	2007/08
235.8	211.8	249.5	278.6	186.4	309.3	847.1	581.8
—	—	9.9	16.0	19.3	23.8	90.9	209.1
45.2	47.5	—	—	—	—	—	—
190.5	164.2	233.5	262.6	167.1	285.4	756.2	372.7
138.3	155.2	233.5	217.2	8.2	—	—	—
52.2	9.0	—	45.4	158.9	285.4	756.2	372.7
—	—	6.2	—	—	—	—	—
—	—	—	—	117.0	—	285.9	532.8
56.3	39.1	67.4	71.4	14.0	129.1	126.7	36.4
-225.9	-99.7	-56.8	-36.4	-15.4	-42.2	-8.1	-1.3
—	—	—	—	—	—	—	—

Table 7.5 (*cont.*)

	Notifications					
	1994/95	1995/96	1996/97	1997/98	1998/99	1999/2000
Production and marketing credit	26.9	73.1	47.2	45.1	82.6	36.9
Price equalization premiums	—	—	41.2	2.8	4.2	0.0
Rice	109.9	46.7	21.7	27.9	49.7	17.0
Market Price Support	95.1	12.7	2.7	1.5	–30.2	–61.0
Non-exempt direct payments	—	—	—	—	—	—
Production and marketing credit	14.8	34.0	19.1	26.4	49.7	17.0
Price equalization premiums	—	—	—	—	—	—
Wheat	18.6	40.6	25.9	27.4	8.3	7.4
Market Price Support	7.9	–0.5	–1.3	—	—	–4.3
Non-exempt direct payments	—	—	—	—	—	—
Production and marketing credit	10.7	10.1	14.5	10.3	8.3	7.4
Price equalization premiums	—	30.6	11.4	17.1	—	—
Cotton	46.4	12.8	10.3	55.4	35.1	55.3
Market Price Support	33.9	—	—	9.9	–4.9	–4.9
Non-exempt direct payments	—	—	—	—	—	—

						Shadow notifications	
2000/01	2001/02	2002/03	2003/04	2004/05	2005/06	2006/07	2007/08
36.5	39.1	61.2	57.3	—	—	—	—
19.8	—	6.2	14.0	14.0	129.1	126.7	36.4
13.3	14.3	18.3	20.2	2.1	57.9	92.4	—
-22.3	-14.7	—	—	-3.1	21.7	83.7	—
—	—	—	—	—	—	—	—
13.3	14.1	18.3	20.2	—	—	—	—
—	0.1	—	—	2.1	36.2	8.7	—
10.3	13.5	32.8	54.3	117.0	22.4	—	236.1
—	—	9.9	16.0	19.3	1.7	—	207.0
—	—	—	—	—	—	—	—
10.3	13.5	22.9	18.7	—	—	—	—
—	—	—	19.6	97.7	20.6	—	29.0
52.1	27.7	18.1	27.4	44.3	82.7	285.9	296.8
-20.4	-0.4	—	—	—	0.3	0.3	—
—	—	—	—	—	—	—	—

Table 7.5 (*cont.*)

	Notifications					
	1994/95	1995/96	1996/97	1997/98	1998/99	1999/2000
Production and marketing credit	12.6	12.7	10.3	19.3	23.8	16.2
Price equalization premiums	—	—	—	26.2	11.3	39.1
Soybean	144.8	59.3	44.7	87.3	134.0	38.5
Market Price Support	-189.3	-3.2	-0.04	—	-0.1	—
Non-exempt direct payments	—	—	—	—	—	—
Production and marketing credit	40.2	59.3	44.7	87.3	134.0	38.5
Price equalization premiums	104.7	—	—	—	—	—
Total (five crops)	346.7	232.5	191.1	245.9	313.9	155.1
Market Price Support[a]	136.9	12.8	2.7	11.4	—	—
Non-exempt direct payments	—	—	—	—	—	—
Production and marketing credit	105.2	189.2	135.7	188.5	298.4	115.9
Price equalization premiums[b]	104.7	30.6	52.7	46.1	15.5	39.1

						Shadow notifications	
2000/01	2001/02	2002/03	2003/04	2004/05	2005/06	2006/07	2007/08
19.7	18.7	18.1	15.7	—	—	—	—
32.4	9.0	—	11.8	44.3	82.4	285.6	296.8
33.1	44.8	78.2	64.3	—	14.1	226.2	—
—	—	—	—	—	—	1.8	—
—	—	—	—	—	—	—	—
33.1	44.8	78.2	64.3	—	—	—	—
—	—	—	—	—	14.1	224.5	—
165.2	139.3	214.8	237.6	177.5	306.2	731.2	569.3
—	—	9.9	16.0	19.3	23.8	85.7	207.0
—	—	—	—	—	—	—	—
113.0	130.1	198.7	176.2	—	—	—	—
52.2	9.2	6.2	45.4	158.3	282.4	645.5	362.2

Table 7.5 (*cont.*)

	Notifications					
	1994/95	1995/96	1996/97	1997/98	1998/99	1999/2000
Product-specific *de minimis* threshold	*10% of value of production (million US dollars)*					
Maize	394.9	376.5	348.5	334.1	265.7	330.0
Rice	215.0	174.4	175.0	193.8	171.8	141.4
Wheat	25.3	47.9	31.4	27.2	26.0	19.1
Cotton	63.2	42.3	43.0	48.3	49.1	69.9
Soybean	386.4	480.4	597.7	560.1	404.4	497.8
Non-product-specific AMS	18.4	79.8	70.1	105.2	837.9	822.6
Production credit	13.2	78.2	60.7	98.6	241.9	176.0
Marketing credit	5.3	1.6	9.4	6.7	6.6	3.9
Debt rescheduling	—	—	—	—	589.4	642.6
Risk minimizing agribusiness program	—	—	—	—	—	—
	10% of value of production (million US dollars)					
Non-product-specific threshold	5,612.5	5,746.4	5,762.8	5,826.2	3,972.5	4,291.0

Notes: — indicates zero.

[a] Includes Federal Government Acquisitions (AGF) and Contract Options Acquisitions (COA). Any negative MPS reported as zero by Brazil.

[b] Includes PEP, PROP and PEPRO (see text).

Sources: WTO notifications and author's calculations.

2005/06 (Table 7.5). The two main components of Brazil's AMS support notified as non-product-specific are production and marketing credit subsidies (until 2004/05 only those for a select group of products, animal breeding, seeds, and packaging) and subsidies associated with debt rescheduling. Both components have increased significantly; the first as

						Shadow notifications	
2000/01	2001/02	2002/03	2003/04	2004/05	2005/06	2006/07	2007/08
268.9	305.2	439.4	396.4	388.6	457.6	802.1	1,131.4
127.6	131.0	191.5	251.8	206.0	197.9	234.8	381.6
36.3	47.8	79.9	71.9	58.1	45.9	99.4	147.4
79.0	55.7	87.5	177.4	249.5	130.2	204.9	214.2
619.3	590.3	928.8	1,060.2	893.5	849.1	1,324.8	2,112.0
739.9	803.5	1,069.1	850.7	1,193.4	1,343.0	1,475.4	2,089.2
183.0	241.8	485.6	162.3	253.6	259.6	186.9	454.9
4.7	4.9	9.3	9.4	102.5	98.8	57.1	145.3
552.2	556.7	574.2	679.0	826.0	959.8	1,157.0	1,340.4
—	—	—	—	11.4	24.8	80.5	148.7
3,840.9	3,727.7	4,494.0	5,441.9	5,097.0	5,789.9	7,879.1	9,943.6

a consequence of the changes in credit policies and the inclusion since 2004/05 of credit subsidies notified earlier as product-specific, and the second as a result of creation of the debt management programs. Debt rescheduling has become the largest source of notified non-product-specific support since 1998/99. This subsidy includes support provided through rescheduling of production and marketing credit that was initially extended on a product-specific basis.

As has been noted, calculation of the subsidies associated with debt rescheduling is complex. The mechanics of the government's calculations

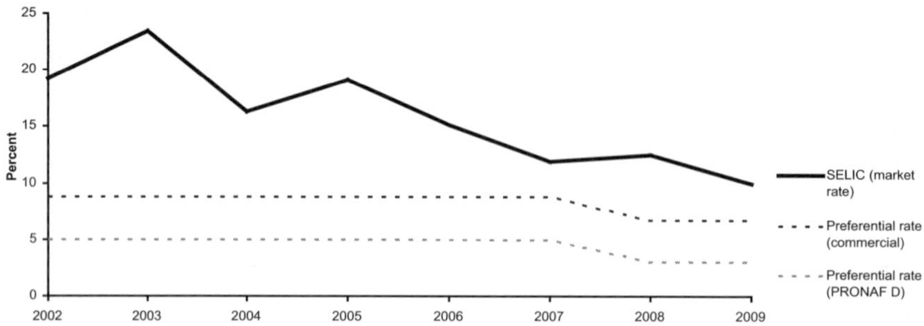

Figure 7.3 Comparison between Brazil's market-based and subsidized interest rates for production and marketing credit
Sources: BACEN and MAPA.

for the notified subsidies are not clear because the government has not published any document explaining the methodology used. It is important to note that the debt settlement package announced in 2008 was not subjected to quantitative evaluation in this analysis due to the lack of available information.

Information was gathered on the debt rescheduling programs from interviews with government officials at a technical level together with an internal government document (dated 2004) that provided some explanation about how the government prepared the notifications.[6] According to these sources, the level of subsidies for the debt rescheduling program was calculated by following a particular methodology to compare the cost to the government of the original loans with the cost of the rescheduled loans. The methodology measured the subsidization as the difference of the present value of the original and rescheduled loans, with December 2002 as the base point in time. This calculation had to be done for each program and then aggregated because interest rates and scheduled repayment periods were different among programs. The level of subsidization

[6] With the exception of the work done by OECD (2005 and 2009), there is no public document available explaining the methodologies used by the different government agencies to calculate the subsidy components of the debt rescheduling programs. Part of the complexity is associated with putting together information on all of the credit programs, which involves not only official banks such as Banco do Brasil and BNDES but also private banks. In interviews with technical professionals involved with this topic it was possible to gather almost all of the information needed to replicate the notified subsidies for debt rescheduling and to estimate these subsidies up to 2008. However, I am of the view that the government should make an effort to be more transparent in disclosing information on the debit renegotiation programs.

calculated for 2002 was divided by the lifetime of the rescheduled loan, to derive a base-level of annual subsidy for each program. An aggregated annual subsidy value was then calculated for 2002. The debt rescheduling program was notified for each year starting in 1998/99 when notifications for 1998/99 to 2002/03 were submitted in May 2005. Annual debt rescheduling subsidy levels for years prior to and after 2002 were adjusted for inflation using the price index IGP-DI from Fundação Getulio Vargas. From 1998/99 to 2000/01 annual inflation was discounted and for 2002/03 (and later for 2004/05 and 2005/06) the amount of subsidy was inflated. After adjusting for inflation the total was converted to US dollars using the appropriate exchange rate for each year.

The implementation of the rescheduling programs had shown by the time Brazil made its notifications that many farmers had failed to make even the rescheduled payments, so part of the rescheduled loans had not been liquidated as designed. Due to the fact that a share of the annual installments had not been paid by farmers, the government initiated changes in the debt rescheduling policies, prolonging the length of the loans and reducing interest rates. This consequently led to a higher level of subsidization. According to government officials, the notifications for 1998/99 to 2001/02 were able to capture those changes. However, for 2003/04 to 2005/06, at the times the notifications were made the government did not have data available on loan repayment delinquencies or the government decided to notify defaults on later notifications, together with the implementation of the 2008 debt settlement package. Hence, the option used was to assume zero default on the annual payments as they were due. With this methodology adopted by the government, the subsidies associated with overdue payments in the debt rescheduling programs are captured only when a new program is launched. The benefits received by producers because they did not pay the annual installments as due on their rescheduled loans are not captured unless a new rescheduling occurs.[7]

The insurance program under the nomenclature Risk Minimizing Agribusiness Program was first notified as non-product-specific AMS support by the Brazilian government in 2004/05. The reason why the program was not notified as product-specific is that there is no pre-defined

[7] In order to check my understanding of the government's methodology, the level of subsidies associated with debt rescheduling for 2002 were recalculated using unpublished and unofficial information gathered from government officials. According to these calculations the subsidy in that year amounted to R$1.86 billion. The notified value was R$1.66 billion (US$570 million, converted using R$2.92/US$ exchange rate). Although the results are not exactly the same, they are reasonably close.

product-specific allocation and, therefore, demand for insurance by commodity is market driven. Table 7.5 shows that, although the program remains small compared with debt rescheduling (even for the period of shadow notifications) expenditures follow an upward trend.

Shadow notifications, 2006/07 and 2007/08

Shadow notifications for the years 2006/07 and 2007/08 are also shown in Tables 7.2–7.5. I followed the same classification of programs as the Brazilian government in terms of placing various measures in different categories. With the exception of some unpublished data regarding the debt rescheduling programs, our assumptions and calculations were made based on accessible online information in various government databases. The focus is on the AMSs, for both product-specific and non-product-specific support, as well as checking conformity with *de minimis* thresholds and paying attention to benefits granted under Article 6.2 of the Agreement. Green box expenditures were estimated based on reports of the official budget of the Federal Government.[8] Calculations were made in domestic currency then converted to US dollars.

Data was available to calculate market price support under the AGF/COA programs and government costs for the price equalization premium programs similarly to the notifications. Value of production data was available from the Brazilian Institute of Geography and Statistics (IBGE).

More difficult to calculate were the subsidies from credit programs and debt rescheduling. For credit subsidies, the same method as used by the federal government was used to calculate the shadow notification estimates. The government did not notify product-specific production and marketing credit subsidies for 2004/05 and 2005/06 but this support was tracked from available statistics and added to the shadow estimates of non-product-specific credit subsidies. For all credit subsidies, the market interest rate used in the calculations was the short-term government reference interest rate, which is the SELIC rate. The preferential interest rate varied from program to program. Production and investment credit for commercial and family farmers, as well as marketing credit, were calculated with information provided by the BACEN database.

The methodology applied for the shadow notifications to calculate production and marketing credit subsidies also differs in several respects

[8] Because there is no publicly available data for bonuses granted by PGPAF it was not possible to estimate shadow notifications for this program which is expected to be notified as an Article 6.2 development program.

from the methodology used by the government. The government has access to loan information on a monthly basis and the subsidy is calculated by month and summed to an annual value. Besides that, the government is also informed about the amount of loans made with subsidized interest rates, which is smaller than the total loans released by the Brazilian Central Bank and listed in the reports used in this study to calculate the shadow notifications. For production and marketing credit programs, product-specific data on loans released by the Brazilian Central Bank, which are the ones I had available, are annual and the calculations are on an annual basis. In order to check the accuracy of the shadow notifications, the subsidy levels of past years were recalculated using the annual data available and the results were compared with the notified levels. Although the results were always higher than the government's notifications (as expected due to the fact that the Brazilian Central Bank reports total rural credit and not only subsidized rural credit) they followed the same trends.

A similar methodology was used for shadow notifications on investment credit. However, interest rates vary among the programs, which is different from production credit where interest rates only vary between commercial and family farmers. Due to the existence of several investment programs for commercial and family farmers and, as a consequence, several interest rates and loan conditions, a representative one was used based on the interest rates associated with the largest programs: 5 percent a year for family farmers for 2006/07 and 3 percent a year for 2007/08; and 11 percent and 8.5 percent a year for the same period for commercial farmers. Again, results for past years were used to confirm that the calculations gave reasonable estimates for the shadow notifications.

For debt rescheduling subsidies I followed the procedures utilized by the government. The calculation of the subsidies associated with the debt rescheduling program was the most complex task. Even when the Brazilian government makes available information regarding the stock of debt, as done by the Ministry of Finance in 2008, information on interest rates of the original loan are quite difficult to obtain. In these and other calculations, consultations with government officials from MAPA provided insights into how calculations and therefore the notifications were made. Such information was necessary in order to understand the complex system of debt rescheduling support and how it is organized and presented.

In order to calculate green box shadow notifications, I compared several headings of the 2006 federal government official budget with notifications for 2005/06. Once a coherent connection was established between the headings and the notifications, comparing headings' names and the amount of expenditures declared, 2007 and 2008 official budget reports were used to estimate shadow green box support.

Support levels

In the shadow notifications, estimated green box expenditures show a reduction in comparison to 2005/06. Expenditures on domestic food aid were lower both in 2006/07 and 2007/08. Expenditures on agrarian reform programmes also decreased, especially in 2007/08. There is a decline in subsidies under Article 6.2 development programs during 2006/07 due to a sharp decrease of the SELIC rate (from 15.09 percent a year in 2006 to 11.88 percent a year in 2007, as shown in Figure 7.3). However, in 2007/08 estimated development program support increases to its highest nominal level. The increase, as already indicated in the last notified year (2005/06), arises primarily from expanded subsidies for investment credit. This represents a change in policy by the Brazilian government. Prior to 2004/05 the majority of the investment credit was channeled to commercial farmers (around 90 percent). From 2004/05 onward, not only did the total amount of credit increase but the share of PRONAF investment credit also increased to around 30 percent of the total directed to family farmers.

Estimated non-product-specific AMS subsidies also increase in the shadow notifications, confirming the upward trend observed in the recent notifications, rising from US$1,343 million notified for 2005/06 to US$2,089 billion estimated for 2007/08. This increase primarily reflects an estimated increase in subsidies from debt rescheduling based on past rescheduling programs. Despite the increase in estimated subsidy in US dollars, in percentage terms the non-product-specific subsidies remain far below the *de minimis* threshold and fall slightly from 2.3 percent of the total value of production to 2.1 percent.

Our shadow notifications also indicate an increase in the sum of product-specific AMS support for the five crops presented individually in Table 7.5. Only cotton shows a consistent increase of product-specific support compared with the previous years. For the other crops, product-specific support oscillates between the two years. The importance of the specific policies also continues to differ among the crops. For maize, cotton and soybeans price equalization premiums dominate the product-specific support in the shadow notifications. For rice, MPS is more relevant and for wheat both are relevant. For the five crops together, and for the sum of all products, price equalization policies provide more support than MPS policies. In all five cases, however, the highest annual product-specific support in the shadow notifications is higher than any notified value, indicating that MPS and price equalization premiums have been used more intensively in these two years. Positive CTAMS is estimated because the *de minimis* threshold is exceeded for cotton in both years and for wheat in 2007/08.

Cotton is a special case among the crops granted product-specific support, with essentially all from price equalization premiums. There are several reasons for the increased support for cotton. The continuous overvaluation of the Brazilian currency since 2004 has reduced the competitiveness of Brazilian cotton production which faces domestic prices determined by world prices. The level of competitiveness is also strongly affected by transportation costs. There are two main cotton-producing regions in Brazil: the state of Mato Grosso in the midwest cerrados, and the state of Bahia in the northeast cerrados. Together they are responsible for 80 percent of the total production. Neither region is endowed with good transportation infrastructure, causing farmgate prices to be lower and transportation costs higher than otherwise. In the medium-run, with the extension of the South–North Railway under the federal government's growth acceleration program (Programa de Aceleração do Crescimento), transportation costs in Bahia should drop, benefiting producers. The prospect for Mato Grosso, however, is not as promising for improved infrastructure.

The shadow notifications follow Brazil's government's previous notification and do not include subsidies for product-specific production and marketing credit. My estimates are that these subsidies add an average of US$268 million to non-product-specific AMS support during the last two notified years and US$255 million to the shadow notifications. As in previous years, this credit ends up being used mainly for maize and soybeans (an average of US$71 million and US$63 million over the four years, respectively).

Taking these results together, Brazil's AMS support has for the most part stayed within its product-specific and non-product-specific *de minimis* allowances. In only a few cases was CTAMS positive, and that was due only to support for cotton and wheat. The reason subsidies for cotton and wheat have in some years exceeded the *de minimis* thresholds is the output support programs. The situation of cotton in 2006–08 illustrates this effect: in those years, the government decided to increase the share of the total production that benefited from price-equalization income support, leading to an increase in the level of subsidies. The depreciation of the US dollar also contributed to an increase in the level of subsidies.

Alternatives to the notifications in relation to the WTO rules

The low subsidization level of Brazilian policies for agriculture provides the country with a considerable amount of policy flexibility while complying with the WTO rules. This section discusses several alternatives that could be applied to assessing Brazil's support and the effects of these alternatives in terms of possible notifications.

Reallocate Article 6.2 investment subsidies to non-product-specific AMS support

The reason the government has notified investment subsidies as development programs is that these are generally available to the agricultural sector, as specified in the Article 6.2 provisions. However, for the sake of consistency, given that the government draws a clear distinction between commercial and family farmers, the same distinction could be undertaken for investment subsidies. In terms of its CTAMS, however, shifting investment subsidies for commercial farmers to non-product-specific AMS would not make a difference since this AMS support remains below the *de minimis* threshold.

A further point of discussion is related to the methodology applied to the calculation of investment credit subsidies. The government calculates interest rate differentials by comparing the investment program interest rate with the short-term SELIC rate. This rate has generally been higher than the long-run interest rate in Brazil. The calculated amount of investment subsidies is, therefore, intentionally overstated by the government. Given that the methodology used by the government already leads to Brazil remaining under the non-product-specific *de minimis* threshold, there is no compelling reason to recalculate the investment subsidies using the long-term interest rate.

Another factor affects the calculation of credit subsidies as notified using preferential interest rates compared with market interest rates. For a few sources of funding, the preferential rate is even lower than the cost of the sources of SNCR and the government uses budgetary resources to make up the difference. In Brazil, this operation is called interest rate equalization or compensation to the lenders for the interest foregone due to interest rate control (OECD 2005). This is the case for several credit programs. In addition, the government also may cover banks' fixed costs to administer PRONAF contracts. The majority of the PRONAF contracts are operated by the Banco do Brasil, Brazil's official retail bank.

Although the equalization is not a direct subsidy to the farmer, it is incurred as a budgetary expense. In the case of all credit lines, therefore, an alternative methodology would be to notify budgetary expenses rather than the subsidies based on interest rate differentials. Taking PRONAF as an example, the estimated notified subsidy value for production credit for 2007/08 was US$150.8 million (Table 7.4). It would be US$341 million under the budgetary expense approach. Although the subsidy increases, given that PRONAF is notified under Article 6.2 a change in the methodology would not affect Brazil's WTO compliance.

Apply developed country rules to Brazil

If Brazil were to be subject to developed country rules it would not be allowed to use Article 6.2, and the *de minimis* threshold would be 5 percent of the value of production, rather than 10 percent. The Article 6.2 subsidies would be added to the non-product-specific AMS. CTAMS would be calculated using the lower *de minimis* threshold. If Brazil had calculated the same Base Total AMS for 1986–88 as it did as a developing country, its Final Bound Total AMS would have been US$842.6 million in 2000 based on a 20 percent reduction from base level.[9]

The results of applying the developed country rules to Brazil are presented in Table 7.6. Although positive CTAMS would be notified at higher levels and for additional years Brazil would remain in compliance with the assumed commitment. Non-product-specific AMS support remains below the 5 percent *de minimis* threshold. Thus, if Brazil was treated as a developed country its past support would stay within the limits established by the WTO under the Agreement.

Recalculate MPS using total production rather than government procurement

Although paragraph 8 of Annex 3 of the Agreement is clear regarding the use of eligible production, not necessarily the whole production, in the calculation of MPS, there has been some discussion in Brazil of the

[9] Brazil's Base Total AMS might have been as much as US$2.5 billion if it had been treated as a developed country in the Uruguay Round, mainly because non-product-specific AMS might not have been *de minimis* and then would have counted in the base level.

Table 7.6 *Alternative subsidy measurement with Brazil treated as a developed country, 1994/95–2007/08*

	1994/95	1995/96	1996/97	1997/98	1998/99	1999/2000	2000/01	2001/02	2002/03	2003/04	2004/05	2005/06	2006/07	2007/08
	Million US dollars													
Total Bound AMS	1,018.1	983.0	947.9	912.8	877.7	842.6	842.6	842.6	842.6	842.6	842.6	842.6	842.6	842.6
Current Total AMS	175.0	40.6	33.2	86.8	35.1	55.3	52.1	—	—	54.3	117.0	82.7	285.9	532.8
Non-product-specific AMS support	377.3	349.1	350.9	478.1	993.9	1,132.2	1,071.4	1,196.3	1,563.6	1,245.0	1,819.4	2,107.2	1,875.9	3,121.2
As share of value of production (%)	0.7	0.6	0.6	0.8	2.5	2.6	2.8	3.2	3.5	2.3	3.6	3.6	2.4	3.1

Note: — indicates zero.
Sources: Brazil's notifications and author's calculations.

economic implications of this legal provision. The issue is that the quantity of government procurement, once withdrawn from the market, may impact domestic prices, which benefits the whole production or at least the production marketed after the government intervention. Using only the quantity of government procurement thus may underestimate the amount of support provided.

From 2004 to 2009, AGF was almost negligible in terms of purchased volumes (Table 7.1). COA was important, mainly for rice. The market situation for rice in Brazil in 2004/05 and 2006/07 confirms that although the COA directly benefits only a share of the total production, the program is able to affect prices. Government procurement for the 2004/05 and 2006/07 farming seasons was 7 percent and 8 percent, respectively, of the total production, and in both seasons prices responded positively to the government intervention. Had MPS for rice been calculated based on total production, it would have been close to US$1 billion in 2006/07. However, higher prices did not necessarily benefit the whole production of rice.

One reason is that government procurement in both years took place during the marketing season and it is very difficult to capture the share of the production that was already sold by the time the intervention started. Before planting, the producer is informed of the level of minimum prices, which is the reference price for the implementation of policies; however, the amount of production enrolled in the program is defined by the government in the marketing period of the season. Despite the fact that minimum prices are established before planting, there is no provision regarding volumes of government procurement and no guarantee that the government will intervene sufficiently to sustain the announced minimum prices.

A second reason is related to the way COA is operated. As discussed previously, COA is not used as a program to stockpile products in the hands of the government. The government eventually either buys back the contract before the option expires paying a premium for producers or transfers its purchasing rights to private agents to avoid stockpiling. Products traded through the COA, therefore, end up in the market rather than being stored by the government, and hence have less effect on market prices.

Alternative approaches to notifying the debt rescheduling programs

Given the different nature of the 2008 debt settlement package in comparison with the earlier debt rescheduling program, new methodologies will be needed to calculate debt rescheduling subsidies from 2008 onward. An update is also necessary to evaluate the subsidy component arising from payments in arrears or default under the debt rescheduling programs since 2002. The notifications and shadow notifications of debt repayment subsidies presented through 2008 are low estimates because the default aspect has not been included in the calculations and data to do so is not publicly available.

An alternative way to capture the subsidy equivalent related to overdue payments is to associate them with an opportunity cost. The delinquent amount has an opportunity cost that is appropriated by the indebted producers. The value of this opportunity cost could be added to the notified value of the subsidies. Unfortunately, the government does not make available to the public the records for overdue debt repayment.

Although I have not included an estimate of the 2008 debt settlement in the shadow notification, a sense of its likely magnitude can be provided. The total debt balance under negotiation is estimated to be in R$74.4 billion (US$38.2 billion). The level of new subsidization will depend on the parameters negotiated under the program. Sources from the government indicated that the additional subsidies, at 2007 value, would be around R$10 billion (US$5.7 billion). Assuming a lifetime of the rescheduled debt of fifteen years, this amount would imply US$380 million in addition to the notified value in 2008 of US$1.4 billion.

One can also take the term structure of repayment into account differently than does the government in calculating the annual subsidy cost. One idea, first pursued but later abandoned by the OECD, was to calculate the Brazilian PSE assuming that 100 percent of the debt rescheduling subsidy should be notified in one instalment. That option would put Brazil in a delicate position because the present value of the subsidy in 2002 would have been US$9.5 billion, which exceeds the US$3.7 billion non-product-specific *de minimis* threshold in 2001/02 and Brazil's Bound Total AMS.

A second possibility is to recalculate the annual subsidies assuming a repayment schedule that follows a financial cash flow similar to a mortgage loan. With this methodology, interest is front-loaded, while the principal is divided equally in the schedule of payments, increasing the initial payments and reducing the final payments.

To examine this option for the past debt renegotiations, the notified values were recalculated from 1998/99 to 2007/08, assuming a fifteen-year payment period. From the total of fifteen payments, which is equivalent to principal payments of 6.67 percent per payment in equal installments, the first payment moved up to 8.5 percent out of 100 percent of the total payments and the last payment moved down to 4.5 percent. The calculation based on distribution of the subsidy component over time using front-loaded interest payments shows annual results similar to the methodology used in the notifications, although with slightly higher subsidies in the early years and lower in the later years. The short assumed period of repayment, years, explains why these results are similar.

Even when one assumes that the government is using the best methodology available to calculate the subsidies notified for the debt rescheduling program, the economic impacts of this program are not captured by the notifications. It is clear that Brazilian farmers respond with increased production when the solvency problem is solved. Any rescheduling program will, therefore, stimulate new investments and push production up. In my view, Brazilian policymakers should pay more attention to this evidence when negotiating debt rescheduling. The government should act to minimize the adverse consequence of stimulating farmers to act as risk takers and overinvest in agricultural production. This is essentially a domestic policy consideration as long as Brazil is including the debt rescheduling program within its WTO support calculations.

Alternative approaches to notifying the Risk Minimizing Agribusiness Program

As presented in Table 7.5, the insurance program (Risk Minimizing Agribusiness Program) was first notified in 2004/05 as non-product-specific support. The nature of this program, in my opinion, indicates that it should have been notified as product-specific support. The program consists of the subsidization of a portion of the premium owed by the farmer when the insurance is contracted. Although a farmer can contract several insurance policies, they are denominated according to the beneficiary product. Additionally, the subsidy (the portion of the premium to be covered by the government) is defined on a product basis, indicating that the effect of the insurance is on the income specifically associated with a product.

Given that the program is still very small, especially because there is a very tight limit on the maximum amount of subsidy per insurance policy and per farmer, shifting the support under the program from non-product-specific AMS to product-specific would not change the compliance situation. Depending how the program evolves in the future, notifying it as product-specific support might contribute to some products exceeding their AMS *de minimis* thresholds.

Ethanol policies and the WTO rules

Recognition that biofuels policies contributed to the rise in agricultural commodities prices observed during 2007 and 2008 encouraged debate concerning the distortive effects of these policies. From an economic perspective, biofuels policies have real impacts on the world market of agricultural products, and as a consequence, they should be subjected to multilateral disciplines. Why not fit them into the WTO framework? In particular, why not notify them as any other agricultural domestic support? Although these questions are appropriate, answers are not that straightforward. Many questions arise concerning the notification of biofuels policies as agricultural domestic support policies. Are they targeted toward agricultural products? Who is the final beneficiary: farmers, blenders or consumers? Are domestic policies available only for the domestically produced biofuels and discriminatory against imported biofuels? What policies should be notified: specific subsidies, tax credits/tax exemption, blending mandates?

Brazilian policies for ethanol include the following instruments:

1. Twenty to twenty-five percent mandatory blend of anhydrous ethanol in gasoline A (pure gasoline). The gasoline blended with ethanol and sold at the pump is called gasoline C. Gasoline A is supplied by Petrobras (Brazilian oil company) to private distributors, which in turn blend the ethanol and distribute the gasoline C.
2. Tax exemption of Contribution to Intervention in the Economic Dominion (CIDE). The CIDE fee is set at R$0.18/liter (about US$0.09/liter). Both anhydrous and hydrous ethanol (E100 ethanol) are exempted.
3. Differential levy on the state tax (ICMS). In some states, like Sao Paulo, the ICMS fee for hydrous ethanol (12 percent) is lower than for gasoline (25 percent). However, given that ICMS is collected by gas stations, anhydrous ethanol is taxed at 25 percent as gasoline C. In other states the ICMS fee is the same for gasoline and hydrous ethanol.
4. Subsidized credit for ethanol storage (preferential rates). This program was included in the last two notifications by Brazil and classified as a sugarcane subsidy.
5. Partial exemption of the tax on industrialized products for flex-fuel cars.

The questions raised above are relevant to consideration of notifying the Brazilian policies as agricultural domestic support. One approach would be to notify the revenue forgone by the government with tax credit and exemption policies, mandate or not. But following the argument of de

Gorter and Just (2008), in a presence of a blending mandate the tax credit policies become a source of subsidy to consumption not production. Another issue for tax credit/exemption policies is that although they are not necessarily discriminatory against imported biofuels, in the presence of border protection, in effect they are. If there were no tariffs blocking ethanol trade, ethanol from different origins would receive similar benefits in countries that adopted tax credit policies. Although a free market would not resolve the issue of subsidizing consumption, at least the allocation of biofuel production among regions would be more efficient.

An alternative approach would be to focus on the mandate itself as a policy affecting prices. The mandate in Brazil is increasing the consumption of anhydrous ethanol, which follows the consumption of gasoline. However, the main consumption growth of ethanol in Brazil is taking place with hydrous ethanol. The mandate in Brazil, therefore, has a very different role from the mandate in the US or in the European countries in terms of subsidizing the production of ethanol. This particular situation in Brazil makes it even more difficult to find a common methodology to notify biofuels subsidies in the WTO as agricultural support.

Projected notifications through 2018

The notifications from 1994/95 to 2005/06 and shadow notifications through 2007/08 show that there are three programs that should be monitored most carefully in the future: output support programs, debt management programs and agricultural risk insurance. With respect to the latter two, and due to the reasons discussed above, I do not provide any projections, despite the fact that with the 2008 debt settlement package Brazil will provide additional debt rescheduling subsides and that agricultural risk insurance expenditures have shown an upward trend. The largest share of the value of production reached by non-product-specific *de minimis* support was 2.4 percent in 2002/03, compared to the *de minimis* threshold of 10 percent. Even without explicit projections, we can expect that the new debt management policies and any increase in agricultural risk insurance support, together with support from the other measures being notified as non-product-specific will fit within *de minimis*. The projections therefore focused on product-specific price and income support. Projections were made for four main commodities, cotton, rice, maize and wheat. These four crops account for more than 50 percent of the product-specific AMS support that Brazil provided in the recent years and include the only crops for which past AMS support has exceeded the *de minimis* threshold in one or more years.

The support projected for 2008/9–18/19 is presented in Table 7.7. Value of production was calculated using production and prices (real prices for 2009) projected by the Brazilian Land Use Model (BLUM) (ICONE 2010), assuming Brazil as a price taker and using world prices from FAPRI 2010 Outlook (FAPRI 2010). Our projected subsidies in Reals were converted to US dollars using the appropriate projected exchange rates.

The projections for product-specific AMS support assume that only COA and price equalization premium instruments will be used in the future. Because the market prices are projected in real terms, the minimum prices in Brazil were held constant at the 2009 nominal levels. The unitary subsidy is calculated by the difference between the estimated domestic price solved by BLUM and the COA reference price when the latter is above the former. In the projections, I assumed the share of output eligible for the price equalization premiums remained fixed for the projection period at about the highest share between the benefited volume and the production observed from 2004/05 to 2007/08: 65 percent for cotton, 10 for rice, 20 for maize, and 40 for wheat (see Table 7.1). Differently from the rest of the years, results for 2008/09 are calculated given that prices and COA and price equalization premium expenditures were available.

Under these assumptions, output support is projected to continue to be provided for cotton but at levels lower than during the years 2006/07, 2007/08 and 2008/09. Wheat is also projected to continue to receive output support. The projections indicate that the total support for cotton and wheat will fluctuate around 4 to 7 percent of the projected value of production. Thus, it is not expected that cotton and wheat support will exceed the *de minimis* threshold of the Agreement, with the exception of 2008/09 for cotton and 2010/11 for wheat.

Possible Doha commitments

Brazil's past and projected levels of support are well below its commitments under the Agreement on Agriculture. Its product-specific AMS support has been below the relevant *de minimis* threshold for most crops in most years. Even the sum of all of its product-specific AMSs (including *de minimis* AMSs) has been below its allowed level for CTAMS in all of the fourteen years, as shown in Figure 7.4. The sum of all of its support excluding the green box (all AMSs plus support notified under Article 6.2) shows a flat behavior over time oscillating between 3 and 4 percent of the total value of agricultural production in the last ten years. These results indicate that Brazil has ample room for support decisions within its Bound Total AMS commitment and the rules of the Agreement.

Table 7.7 *Projections of Brazil's product-specific support for main commodities, 2008/09–2018/19*

		2008/09	2009/10	2010/11	2011/12	2012/13	2013/14	2014/15	2015/16	2016/17	2017/18	2018/19
		Million US dollars										
Cotton	Output support	275.4	111.4	143.8	114,2	111.0	112.0	91.8	86.2	79.5	78.7	83.3
	AMS/value of production (%)	17.2	6.7	7.3	6.0	5.5	5.5	4.4	4.0	3.6	3.4	3.5
Rice	Output support	203.4	—	85.5	84.0	83.4	87.0	88.6	92.2	98.4	96.6	98.5
	AMS/value of production (%)	5.8	—	2.8	2.8	2.8	2.9	2.9	3.0	3.2	3.1	3.1
Maize	Output support	199.9	131.4	106.7	93.0	88.9	86.9	84.9	84.2	97.3	101.0	—
	AMS/value of production (%)	2.3	1.5	1.1	0.9	0.9	0.8	0.8	0.9	0.9	0.9	—
Wheat	Output support	109.2	62.2	99.5	76.9	68.8	62.4	67.8	63.,8	64.0	68.8	68.9
	AMS/value of production (%)	9.4	7.6	10.5	8.5	7.8	7.3	7.6	7.2	7.2	7.4	7.4

Note: — indicates zero.
Source: Author's calculations from ICONE (2010).

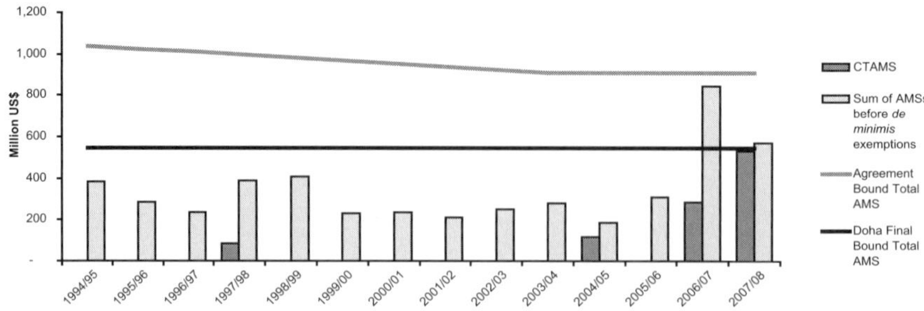

Figure 7.4 Brazil's notifications of product-specific AMS support compared with commitments agreed in the Uruguay Round and proposed in the Doha Round
Sources: Brazil's notifications to WTO and author's estimates.

Under the Doha draft modalities of December 2008, Brazil would face tighter and additional constraints on its domestic support. The rules proposed for developed and developing countries are summarized in Table 2.2 and the new commitments Brazil could take are presented in Table 7.8. Brazil's Base OTDS would be US$13.1 billion calculated as the sum of its existing Final Bound Total AMS (FBTAMS) commitment plus 25 percent of the value of production in a base period 1995–2004. Base OTDS would be reduced by 37 percent to US$8.3 billion over an adjustment period of eight years. Brazil's Bound Total AMS would be reduced by 30 percent to a Doha FBTAMS commitment of US$638.5 million, also over eight years. Brazil would face a new cap on blue box support, but has never notified payments in this category. It would face product-specific caps on AMS support under flexible rules for developing countries (see Appendix B).

Brazil would also be in the group of developing countries that would reduce their *de minimis* percentages from 10 percent to 6.7 percent, implemented over three years. At a value of production of around US$100 billion, this results in a decrease of the value of the summed product-specific *de minimis* thresholds by around US$3 billion and a similar reduction in the non-product-specific *de minimis* threshold. Developing countries that do not have a positive Bound Total AMS under the Agreement are not required to reduce their *de minimis* percentages. The positive Bound Total AMS gives Brazil additional latitude to provide support, compared to countries without a positive commitment under the Agreement. But it leads to a penalty of reduction in Brazil's room to provide support compared to these other countries under the proposed domestic support rules of the Doha Round.

Brazil would not face binding constraints on its past or projected domestic support under the Doha draft modalities. Past

Table 7.8 *OTDS, CTAMS and blue box support limits and the* de minimis *allowance for Brazil under the Doha draft modalities*

	Million US dollars
Final Bound Total AMS	912
Value of production (base period 1995–2004)	48,716
25 percent value of production	12,179
Base OTDS	13,091
Final Bound OTDS (after 37 percent reduction)	8,247
Final Bound Total AMS (after 30 percent reduction)	638
Overall blue box limit (5 percent of base period value of production 1995–2004)	2,436
De minimis (after 33 percent reduction, as a share of annual value of production)	6.7%

Source: Author's calculations based on Doha draft modalities.

non-product-specific AMS support and likely values in the next decade are below the proposed Doha *de minimis* threshold; this level of support is not exceeded even if subsidies notified under Article 6.2 are added to the non-product-specific AMS. Brazil's sum of all product-specific AMS support (before any *de minimis* exclusions from CTAMS) is below the Doha FBTAMS commitment in almost all years. Had the allowed level of *de minimis* been 6.7 percent in the past, product-specific support would have exceeded the thresholds more often than under the Agreement's 10 percent threshold. For cotton, out of the fourteen years (including the shadow notifications), Brazil's support would have exceeded the threshold in six years (1995, 1998–2000, 2007–08). Wheat support also would have exceeded the threshold for seven of the fourteen years (1995–98, 2004–05, and 2008). However, including these AMSs, which are above the proposed Doha threshold, in the CTAMS does not make it exceed the Doha FBTAMS commitment even in the year 2006/07 (the only year this might have occurred because it is the only year for which the sum of all product-specific AMSs exceeds the proposed Doha FBTAMS commitment, as shown in Table 7.5). Likewise, the AMS support for cotton exceeds the product-specific *de minimis* threshold from the Doha modalities in the early years of our projections and the projected support for wheat is above this threshold in all years. But the levels of support for cotton and wheat do not exceed Brazil's Doha FBTAMS in these projections. Thus, as a developing country Brazil is well positioned to seek and accept tighter disciplines on domestic support as proposed in the Doha Round.

As before, one can consider the counterfactual case of Brazil having been treated as a developed country in the Uruguay Round. Had this been the case, had Brazil's Base Total AMS for 1986–88 stayed the same, and were the developed country provisions of the Doha draft modalities applied, then Brazil's Doha FBTAMS commitment would be US$463.4 million and its *de minimis* thresholds 2.5 percent of value of production. Brazil's past and projected product-specific support in excess of the *de minimis* thresholds, when summed across products, would not exceed the FBTAMS commitment under these assumptions, except in years 2007/08 and projected 2008/09. However, the hypothetical non-product-specific AMS for 1998/99 through 2007/08 (including support actually notified under Article 6.2) and also likely future non-product-specific AMS exceed 2.5 percent of the total value of production (see Table 7.6). Including this support in the CTAMS would lead to it being over the hypothetical commitment of Brazil as a developed country in these years.[10]

Summary and conclusions

Brazil has emerged as a major agricultural exporter with potentially large gains from global trade liberalization. It sought a central role in the Doha negotiations and has successfully challenged agricultural support or trade policies of other countries in several WTO dispute settlement cases. In this pivotal position, Brazil has maintained more up-to-date domestic support notifications than many other developing countries and it has undergone a formal non-member external review of its agricultural policies through the OECD.

[10] Had Brazil's Base Total AMS under the Agreement been US$2.5 billion if it is assumed Brazil were treated as a developed country (see earlier footnote), then under the Doha draft modalities its FBTAMS would be correspondingly much higher. Had Brazil been treated as a developed country in the Uruguay Round with a Base Total AMS of US$2.5 billion, and based on the past and shadow notifications, the country would easily have complied with the 20 percent reduction in Bound Total AMS and 5 percent *de minimis* allowances. The same easy compliance is not true for the Doha Round. This is not only because current non-product-specific support is already higher than 2.5 percent of the total value of production and close to the Doha FBTAMS commitment Brazil would have starting from a Base Total AMS for 1986–88 of US$2.5 billion. It is also because this category of support is expected to grow in the future due to larger expenditures on agricultural insurance, debt settlement programs and marketing loans for family farmers.

Brazil's domestic support to agriculture includes agrarian reform policies oriented toward impoverished rural households notified in the green box. These policies have little effect on Brazil's production. Policies directed toward commercial and family farmers focus on output support, credit subsidies and periodic debt payment rescheduling. Ethanol policies are complex in Brazil. It is increasingly relevant to bring biofuel policies under stronger WTO disciplines, but doing so remains a complex issue.

Brazil's output support programs are inherited from past policies of minimum guaranteed prices. The scope of support has been reduced and shifted into two measures: purchases of a limited amount of output (particularly rice) at administered prices and provision of price equalization premiums targeted toward least-developed regions. Although both programs are often referred to in Brazil as income support, AGF/COA programs under which the government procures stocks are notified as MPS, while the equalization premiums are reported as product-specific AMS payments.

The credit programs provide loans at below market interest rates for production, marketing and agricultural investments. Subsidies depend on the rate differentials, with limited-resource family farmers being eligible for particularly low interest. In 1995, 1998, 2002 and 2008, the government renegotiated repayment schedules on debts accumulated by farmers, with additional subsidization resulting from differences between the initial and renegotiated repayment requirements. The 2002 debt rescheduling program applied to a balance of overdue credit of R$29 billion. By August 2007 the estimated debt was nearly R$90 billion.

Unlike many other developing countries, Brazil has a non-zero Bound Total AMS, albeit relatively small. This has given Brazil additional latitude to provide support. However, through 2005/06 a positive CTAMS was only reported for 1997/98 and 2004/05. Brazil, which notifies in US dollars, has reported product-specific *de minimis* support averaging around US$250 million annually, peaking at US$409 million in 1999. Estimated product-specific *de minimis* support increased in 2006/07 and 2007/08. Estimated support in at least one year exceeds the *de minimis* allowance for cotton or wheat, pushing the 2007/08 CTAMS up to US$533 million.

Brazil notifies three types of measures under Article 6.2 development programs: production credit subsidies and debt rescheduling for family farmers and credit subsidies for agricultural investments by commercial and family farmers. The notified subsidies rose from less than US$160 million in 1998/99 to US$764 million in 2005/06 and are estimated to exceed US$1 billion in 2007/08. Through 1997/98, Brazil's non-product-specific *de minimis* support was exclusively comprised of credit subsidies to commercial farmers. Since 1998/99, a calculated cost of debt rescheduling has been included and since 2004/05 credit and marketing subsidies previously notified as product-specific. The notified non-product-specific AMS support rose sharply to an estimated US$1.3 billion in 2005/06. Support through debt rescheduling subsidies notified as non-product-specific *de minimis* AMS is estimated alone to reach US$1.3 billion for 2007/08, and non-product-specific support at US$2 billion.

The debt management programs, although they do not raise concerns about Brazil exceeding its support limits under the Agreement, are capable of influencing farmers' decisions in the medium to long run. They are becoming more sophisticated, with different sets of programs and specific objectives, and their relevance for the domestic support notifications will increase in the future. The successive renegotiations have indicated to farmers that they do not need to be risk averse in taking out credit because debts will be renegotiated at some point. If so, the debt rescheduling programs are leading farmers to high levels of indebtedness. There are no empirical studies assessing this hypothesis, but the release of 2006 agricultural census data will help us to evaluate the consequences of the debt relief policy.

In the process of negotiating the 2008 debt rescheduling, the government decided to be more transparent in releasing data on the level of indebtedness, but lack of transparency remains a problem to be tackled. This lack of transparency is not so much with respect to methodology used for measuring subsidy components, but with respect to making data on rescheduling and debt management programs publicly available.

Taking the reported and calculated notifications into account, Brazil is in a comfortable position in terms of compliance with the Agreement. Its past and projected CTAMS are well below Brazil's commitment and non-product-specific support remains just a few percent of the total value of agricultural production, well within the *de minimis* allowance for developing countries. I conclude that Brazil would be in compliance with the Agreement even if the rules for developed countries were applied, and the subsidies currently notified under development programs were instead included in the non-product-specific AMS calculations and *de minimis* allowances were lowered to 5 percent of the value of production.

Under a possible Doha agreement, Brazil's Final Bound Total AMS commitment would fall to $638 million and *de minimis* allowances would be tightened to 6.7 percent of the value of production. I find that Brazil would not face binding constraints on its past or projected support under the proposed Doha modalities. The projections depend on assumptions about the future path of policy that is more uncertain for Brazil than for major agricultural exporters such as the EU or US. The level of support provided by Brazil, and the instruments of that support, merit careful monitoring. Fortunately, the government of Brazil has recognized the need to be transparent about its policies if it is to be effective in arguing the case for stronger disciplines and tougher commitments in multilateral trade negotiations.

References

BACEN (Banco Central do Brasil; Brazilian Central Bank). Various years. Anuário Estatístico do Crédito Rural. www.bcb.gov.br/?relrural (accessed April 14, 2008, November 11, 2008, and June 4, 2010).

Chaddad, F. R., and M. S. Jank. 2006. The evolution of agricultural policies and agribusiness development in Brazil. *Choices* 21(2): 85–90.

CONAB (Companhia Nacional de Abastecimento; National Food Supply Company). 2008. Aquisição do Governo Federal – AGF. www.conab.gov.br/conabweb/download/comercializacao/arq_link_menu/cartilha_agf_070706.pdf (accessed April 14, 2008).

2008a. Agricultura Familiar. www.conab.gov.br/conabweb/index.php?PAG=47 (accessed April 14, 2008).

2008b. Contrato de Opção de Compra. www.conab.gov.br/conabweb/download/comercializacao/arq_link_menu/cartilhacontratoopcaocompra.pdf (accessed April 14, 2008).

2008c. Contrato de Opção de Venda. www.conab.gov.br/conabweb/download/comercializacao/arq_link_menu/cartilhacontratoopcaovenda.doc (accessed April 14, 2008).

2008d. Prêmio Para Escoamento de Produto – PEP. www.conab.gov.br/conabweb/download/comercializacao/arq_link_menu/cartilha_do_pep_070706.pdf (accessed April 14, 2008).

2008e. Prêmio de Risco Para Aquisição de Produto Agrícola Oriundo de Contrato Privado de Opção De Venda – PROP. www.conab.gov.br/conabweb/download/comercializacao/arq_link_menu/cartilha_do_prop_070706.pdf (accessed April 14, 2008).

2008f. Prêmio Equalizador Pago ao Produtor – PEPRO. www.conab.gov.br/conabweb/download/comercializacao/arq_link_menu/cartilha_pepro_070706.pdf (accessed April 14, 2008).

2008g. Relatório de Gestão 2008. www.conab.gov.br/conabweb/index.php?PAG=54 (accessed April 21, 2010).

Damico, F. S., and A. M. Nassar. 2007. Agricultural expansion and policies in Brazil. In *US Agricultural Policy and the 2007 Farm Bill*, ed. K. Arha,

T. Josling, D. A. Sumner, and B. H. Thomson. Stanford University: Woods Institute for the Environment.

de Gorter, H., and D. R. Just. 2008. "Water" in the US ethanol tax credit and mandate: Implications for rectangular deadweight costs and the corn-oil price relationship. *Applied Economic Policy and Perspectives* 30(3): 397–410.

FAPRI (Food and Agricultural Policy Research Institute). 2010. US and World Agricultural Outlook. Staff Report 10-FSR 1. www.fapri.iastate.edu/outlook/2010/ (accessed June 4, 2010).

ICONE (Instituto de Estudos do Comércio e Negociações Internacionais; Institute for International Trade Negotiations). 2010. Outlook FIESP-ICONE 2010: Projeções do Agronegócio Brasileiro.

MDA (Ministério do Desenvolvimento Agrário; Ministry of Agrarian Development). 2007. Plano de Safra da Agricultura Familiar 2007/2008. www.mda.gov.br/arquivos/Folheto_MDA_PlanoSafra2007_B.pdf (accessed April 14, 2008).

2010. PAA. http://portal.mda.gov.br/portal/saf/programas/paa (accessed April 21, 2010).

MF (Ministério da Fazenda; Ministry of Finance). 2008. Levantamento das Operações de Crédito Rural. Secretaria de Política Economica. www.fazenda.gov.br/spe/publicacoes/Pronaf_Renegociacao_Dividas_tecnica_13032008.pdf (accessed April 14, 2008).

2008a. Levantamento das Operações de Crédito Rural do Pronaf, Procera e Crédito Fundiário. www.fazenda.gov.br/spe/publicacoes/Pronaf_Renegociacao_Dividas13032008.pdf (accessed April 11, 2008).

Nassar, A., M. E. Rodriguez-Alcala, C. Costa, and S. Nogueira. 2009. Agricultural subsidies in the WTO green box: Opportunities and challenges for developing countries. In *Agricultural Subsidies in the WTO Green Box: Ensuring Coherence with Sustainable Development Goals*, ed. R. Meléndez-Ortiz, C. Bellmann, and J. Hepburn. Cambridge University Press.

Nassar, A. M., and D. Ures. 2009. Brazil: Shadow WTO agricultural domestic support notifications. IFPRI Discussion Paper 865.

OECD. 2005. *Review of Agricultural Policies: Brazil.* Paris.

2009. *Agricultural Policies in Emerging Economies: Monitoring and Evaluation.* Paris.

8

India

MUNISAMY GOPINATH

The objective of this chapter is to update the WTO domestic support notifications of India and place them in the context of the Agreement and Doha proposals for further reform. India notified its domestic support to the WTO for 1997/98 in June 2002 and had not submitted any further domestic support notifications as of June 2010. Shadow notifications provide updates on domestic support measures and their components for 1998/99 through 2005/06. Preliminary estimates or forecasts of shadow support are provided for 2006/07 to 2008/09 along with a projection of major support aggregates for 2015/16.

I begin with an overview of agriculture within the Indian economy and key agricultural trade and domestic policies. The section that follows details the domestic support notifications of India with my understanding of how each component is derived. In the following section, I employ this understanding of the methodology from the last notification to sketch the shadow notifications. The information should be interpreted as a best assessment of how India's domestic support might be notified given an understanding of its past notifications. Finally, with a projection for 2015/16, I discuss how the Agreement, or a possible Doha outcome, is likely to impact Indian policies and domestic support measurements. This gives some insights on the future of Indian farm policy.

Agriculture in India

India is a large country from both population and economic viewpoints. The world development indicators of the World Bank rank India as the

Research assistance from P. K. Shinoj, Scientist, National Center for Agricultural Economics and Policy Research (India) is gratefully acknowledged. Thanks are also expressed to P. K. Joshi, Director, National Academy of Agricultural Research Management (India) and Suresh Babu, Senior Research Fellow, IFPRI (Washington, DC) for their support of this project.

second largest country, population wise, and as the tenth largest in terms of gross domestic product (GDP) in 2008. Moreover, India is a rapidly growing economy. As observed in the history of most high-income economies, agriculture's share of India's GDP has declined during the last two decades. However, the decline in agriculture's share of GDP is not matched by that of its employment share. Around the time India's growth spurt began, following a series of major trade and economic reforms in 1991/92, agriculture accounted for 65.3 percent of total employment. By 2005 that share had only fallen to 58.5 percent. Agriculture remains the major source of income for a large share of the Indian population especially in the rural areas.

Since independence in 1947, India's stated agricultural policy objective has been to achieve self-sufficiency in agricultural production (Pursell, Gulati, and Gupta 2009). This goal appears to have been attained for most staples mostly through a policy combination of market price support through border measures and input subsidies. Overall, India is a net agricultural exporter. However, agriculture's importance as a source of India's exports has declined since 1995, as shown in Table 8.1. Except for meat products, none of the major agricultural exports shows a clear upward or downward trend. The sporadic nature of agricultural exports appears coincidental with domestic supply conditions, especially the monsoon rains. Export spikes in good crop years reflect the underlying self-sufficiency objective (Gopinath 2008). Agricultural imports have averaged only 4 percent of total imports since 1995 (Table 8.2). Pulses and vegetable oils account for a majority of agricultural imports, reflecting unmet objectives in the self-sufficiency policy regime.

Agriculture's importance, for both self-sufficiency and employment objectives, has made India less than enthusiastic in its approach to trade reform in the WTO context (Hoda and Gulati 2007). At the time of the Agreement on Agriculture, India completed schedules on market access, domestic support, and export subsidies. However, India claimed exclusion from reduction commitments on two of the three pillars (market access and domestic support) in the period after the Uruguay Round on the basis of the balance-of-payments exemption allowed in the GATT.

In the case of market access, India had maintained a two-tier strategy of protection from imports going into the Uruguay Round (Pursell, Gulati, and Gupta 2009). The first tier involved the licensing of, and quantitative restrictions on, imports of most products including both agricultural and non-agricultural goods. Gulati and Pursell (1993) indicated that nearly 96 percent of tariff lines faced quantitative restrictions in India prior to 1990.

Table 8.1 *India's exports, 1995/96–2006/07*

	Total exports	Agriculture's share	Share of agricultural exports						
			Rice (all)	Wheat	Coffee, tea and spices	Cashew and groundnuts	Marine products	Oil and oil meals	Meat products
	Million US$	%							
1995/96	31,842	19.2	22.3	1.8	17.0	7.2	16.5	15.1	3.4
1996/97	33,498	20.5	13.0	2.9	15.0	6.6	16.4	16.9	3.4
1997/98	35,049	18.9	13.7	0.0	20.2	8.0	18.2	16.3	3.8
1998/99	33,211	18.2	24.7	0.0	22.2	7.0	17.2	10.3	3.5
1999/2000	36,760	15.3	12.9	0.0	20.5	11.6	21.1	11.1	4.4
2000/01	44,147	13.6	10.7	1.5	16.8	8.7	23.3	11.0	6.9
2001/02	43,958	13.5	11.3	4.7	15.3	7.2	21.0	10.3	6.8
2002/03	52,823	12.7	18.0	5.4	13.2	6.9	21.3	6.5	6.4
2003/04	63,886	11.8	12.0	6.9	12.3	6.5	17.6	11.6	7.4
2004/05	83,502	10.1	17.8	3.8	12.6	7.9	17.0	11.2	8.9
2005/06	103,075	9.9	13.8	1.2	12.0	6.9	15.6	12.9	11.0
2006/07	126,246	9.9	12.4	0.1	12.4	5.8	13.9	11.6	7.1
Average	57,331	14.5	15.2	2.4	15.8	7.5	18.3	12.1	6.1

Source: Government of India (Annual budget report, various years).

Table 8.2 *India's imports, 1995/96–2006/07*

	Total imports	Agriculture's share	Share of agricultural imports	
			Pulses	Vegetable oils
	Million US$	%		
1995/96	36,730	3.0	18.6	61.4
1996/97	39,165	3.5	18.3	60.2
1997/98	41,535	4.0	19.2	44.4
1998/99	42,379	6.5	6.1	65.4
1999/2000	49,799	5.3	3.1	70.0
2000/01	50,056	3.4	6.5	77.7
2001/02	51,567	4.5	28.5	58.3
2002/03	61,533	4.4	21.0	67.4
2003/04	78,203	4.4	14.6	74.7
2004/05	111,472	3.2	11.2	70.1
2005/06	149,143	2.2	17.1	62.0
2006/07	190,438	2.1	21.7	53.2
Average	75,168	3.9	15.5	63.7

Source: Government of India (Annual budget report, various years).

In addition to the quantitative restrictions, India maintained high tariffs in the form of three types of import duties: basic customs, auxiliary, and additional tariffs. Hoda and Gulati (2007) noted that the basic customs duty has been as high as 200 percent for some products, while the auxiliary duty ranged between 40 and 50 percent. The list of products with quantitative restrictions significantly overlapped with that of products facing high tariffs, but there were notable exceptions in the latter.[1]

Subject to the balance-of-payments exemption, under the Agreement India bound its tariff rates for agricultural commodities that were not bound in earlier negotiations. The ceiling was set at 100, 150, and 300 percent for commodities, processed products, and edible oils, respectively. For those commodities with bound rates from earlier negotiations, pre-1994 upper bound levels were retained. Interestingly, the latter group

[1] See Pursell, Gulati, and Gupta (2009) for measures of nominal and effective rates of protection in Indian agriculture. Orden *et al.* (2007) provided producer support estimates for 1985–2002.

included some key cereals (rice, maize) and milk products that were bound at zero tariffs because of the continuation of quantitative restrictions. The improvement in foreign exchange reserves in the late 1990s eliminated the balance-of-payments justification for quantitative restrictions forcing India to renegotiate its commitments for rice, maize, sorghum, milk and milk products, and a few other commodities in 1999. The newly negotiated tariffs, in the range of 40–80 percent, included minimum market access in the form of tariff-rate quotas. Hoda and Gulati (2007) reported that the simple average of applied customs duty on agricultural products was 37 percent in 2004, while the bound rates averaged 114.8 percent (Gopinath and Laborde 2008).

India had few export subsidies around the time of the Uruguay Round negotiations. A primary reason for that was the elimination of a cash compensation scheme (CCS) for exports as part of the 1991 trade and economic reforms. Prior to that time, the CCS provided cash incentives to exporters and also allowed for payment of marketing and freight costs. The other major export subsidy program was the income tax exemption of profits from exports. Because the latter did not figure in the export subsidy provisions of the Agreement, India has retained it in the post–Uruguay era. Although the CCS had been eliminated, it provided a justification for renewed export subsidies to wheat and rice in 2002–05, when the Food Corporation of India (FCI) built up large buffer stocks.

With regard to domestic support, the two main instruments are the minimum support prices (MSP) for major agricultural commodities and the input subsidies provided to farmers in general. The former instrument has been used for most crops, including cereals, pulses, oilseeds, and commercial crops (sugarcane, cotton, tobacco, and jute). To ensure markets operate with the MSP as the floor, procurement operations are carried out by public agencies. The FCI is authorized to procure wheat and paddy from farmers, and rice and sugar from millers. The latter is often referred to as a "levy" on millers, who part with a share of their production in return for a free hand in setting prices on the rest of their production. The decision on the level of the MSP is made by the Ministry of Agriculture with recommendations from the Commission on Agricultural Costs and Prices (CACP). Through the MSP, the CACP aims to cover the cost of production of each of the crops, including the imputed value of farm labor, and to provide a reasonable rate of return to farmers (Hoda and Gulati 2007; Pursell, Gulati, and Gupta 2009).

Major inputs supplied at subsidized prices include fertilizer, electricity, irrigation, credit, and seeds (Gulati and Narayanan 2003). As they describe, fertilizer subsidies are needed to maintain a statutory retail price for farmers that is lower than the per-unit domestic cost of production and the import price for nitrogenous and phosphatic fertilizers. In addition to the difference between the statutory retail price and the import price/domestic cost of production, the subsidy also covers the distribution costs of imported fertilizers. For domestic production of fertilizers, a retention price scheme establishes a fixed sales price for each nitrogenous and phosphatic fertilizer manufacturer. The sales price fixed for each manufacturing unit enables farmers to buy fertilizers at the statutory retail price. The government pays for the difference between the cost of production and the fixed sales price and a profit margin for each manufacturing unit. The fertilizer support regime has changed somewhat in recent years, but remains an important source of input subsidies to farmers.

The computation of electricity subsidies is complex because each Indian state has flexibility in choosing its policy for respective electricity boards or departments. As a result, wide regional variation exists in the nature and magnitude of electricity subsidies. The electricity charge on agriculture is either zero or a fraction of the per-unit operating expenses of the electricity boards or departments. Similarly, farmers pay a fraction of the cost of irrigation infrastructure's operating expenses. In both the electricity and irrigation cases, the capital expenditure appears to be a direct allocation from central and state government budgets. Credit subsidies (that is, loan waivers or low interest rates for farmers on short-, intermediate- and long-term loans) also vary by state. Recent policies may have increased the level of this support close to that of fertilizer or electricity subsidies by 2008, as discussed below. Through national seed-testing labs and certification agencies, the Indian government has been providing poor farmers with seeds free of cost. The value of seed subsidies is lower than that of the credit subsidies.

Domestic support notifications, 1995–1997

A summary of the domestic support notifications of India for the three marketing years, 1995/96, 1996/97, and 1997/98, is presented in Table 8.3, along with the shadow notifications for 1998/99 to 2005/06 and the estimates/forecasts for 2006/07 to 2008/09.[2] The Reserve Bank of India's annual

[2] Henceforth in the text of this chapter, the first calendar year is used to denote the entire marketing year for ease of reading: for example 1995 denotes 1995/96.

average exchange rate appears to have been used in converting Indian rupees to US dollars to notify support in the latter currency. Notifying in US dollars has an important implication. By notifying in the US currency, nominal increases in subsidy expenditures and nominal support prices do not show up as increases in notified support to the extent that they are offset (or overcompensated) by nominal rupee depreciation. Conversely, rupee appreciation raises the dollar amount of notified support for a given nominal level in rupees.

For the three notified years (columns 2 through 4 of the tables) total support was negative (-$21.4 billion) in 1995 but rose in the two subsequent years to $6.3 billion in 1997. Positive support under the green box and Article 6.2 development programs were outweighed in the first year by negative elements of product-specific AMS arising from the calculated market price support (MPS). As India did not establish a Bound Total AMS, it has a zero ceiling on CTAMS. The allowable AMS support is therefore limited to the *de minimis* level of 10 percent of a product's value (for each product-specific AMS) and 10 percent of the total value of agricultural production (for non-product-specific AMS). These *de minimis* amounts easily covered any positive elements of AMS support in the three notified years.

The components of each of the major aggregates in Table 8.3 – green box, development programs, and product-specific and non-product-specific AMS (reported as *de minimis*) – are shown in Tables 8.4, 8.5 and 8.6, respectively. The aggregate of green box support increased from $2,196 to $2,873 million between 1995 and 1997. As shown in Table 8.4, the primary item within the green box is the central government's budget expenditure relating to food storage and warehousing (that is, public stockholding for food security) arising out of operations of the FCI and other agencies. On average from 1995 to 1997, such stockholding accounted for 70 percent of the green box support. Other significant components include general services (mostly research) and payments for relief from natural disasters or calamities (including crop insurance). The notifications by India for 1996 and 1997 show support under five of the green box categories articulated in Annex 2 of the Agreement, of which three are different categories of payments (natural disaster relief, investment aids, and environmental payments). Itemized expenditures on green box support are from the budgetary documents of the Government of India's Ministry of Agriculture for various years.

Support under the development program exemption of the Agreement (Article 6.2) witnessed a dramatic increase between 1995 and 1997.

Table 8.3 *Summary of India's domestic support notifications and shadow notifications, 1995–2008*

	Notifications			Shadow notifications		
	1995/96	1996/97	1997/98	1998/99	1999/2000	2000/01
	Million US dollars					
Green box	2,196	2,502	2,873	2,979	3,159	3,670
Development programs	254	4,855	5,172	4,621	5,394	5,515
Blue box	—	—	—	—	—	—
Current Total AMS	—	—	—	—	—	—
Sum of AMS support[a]	–23,847	–1,673	–1,746	–1,936	–2,546	–3,119
Product-specific	–29,619	–2,604	–2,749	–2,925	–3,442	–3,942
Market price support	–29,619	–2,604	–2,749	–2,925	–3,442	–3,942
Other non-exempt measures	—	—	—	—	—	—
Non-product-specific	5,772	930	1,003	989	896	823
Total support	–21,397	5,684	6,299	5,664	6,007	6,066
Value of production	78,765	89,693	90,073	91,971	94,544	89,521
Bound Total AMS	zb	zb	zb	zb	zb	zb

Notes: Small differences in totals are due to rounding. — indicates zero or data not reported or unavailable; zb indicates India has an implied zero binding on CTAMS.

[a] Sums positive and negative values of market price support, unlike the EU (Table 3.1) and Brazil (Table 7.2) in which the negative values are set equal to zero in the now Total *de minimis*.

Sources: WTO notifications and author's calculations.

Table 8.5 shows that support increased from $254 million in 1995 to $5,172 million in 1997. This increase appears to reflect changes in how fertilizer, electricity, and irrigation subsidies are apportioned between Article 6.2 and non-product-specific AMS in the notifications. India's

					Shadow/forecast		
2001/02	2002/03	2003/04	2004/05	2005/06	2006/07	2007/08	2008/09
5,036	5,634	6,996	7,441	7,750	8,011	10,734	12,543
5,169	6,083	6,376	7,138	9,789	10,387	11,040	11,749
—	—	—	—	—	—	—	—
—	—	—	—	—	—	—	—
−4,070	−3,141	−3,033	−2,914	−2,584	−1,002	1,373	1,380
−4,832	−4,080	−3,995	−3,992	−3,700	−2,144	204	185
−4,832	−4,080	−3,995	−3,992	−3,700	−2,144	204	185
—	—	—	—	—	—	—	—
762	939	962	1,078	1,117	1,142	1,169	1,195
6,135	8,575	10,339	11,665	14,956	17,396	23,147	25,673
92,779	87,918	105,121	111,599	125,845	130,776	135,889	141,224
zb	zb	zb	zb	zb	zb	zb	zb

1996 and 1997 Article 6.2 notifications, unlike that for 1995, appear to have included 80 percent of its input-subsidy categories (mainly fertilizer, electricity and irrigation subsidies) under "input subsidies to low-income or resource poor producers" and hence compatible with Article 6.2 (Hoda and Gulati 2007). Consistent with this assessment, the notified input subsidies in the non-product-specific AMS dramatically declined from 1995 to 1996 and 1997 as shown in Table 8.6. The chosen percentage (80) for the allocation of subsidies to resource-poor

Table 8.4 *Composition of India's green box notifications and shadow notifications, 1995–2008*

	Notifications			Shadow notifications		
	1995/96	1996/97	1997/98	1998/99	1999/2000	2000/01
	Million US dollars					
General services	398	239	265	270	389	344
Public stock-holding/food security	1,570	1,709	2,018	2,214	2,243	2,709
Domestic food aid	—	—	—	—	—	—
Decoupled income support	—	—	—	—	—	—
Income insurance	11	—	—	—	—	—
Crop insurance/ disaster relief	125	444	444	378	413	492
Producer retirement	—	—	—	—	—	—
Resource retirement	—	—	—	—	—	—
Investment aids	59	36	76	76	68	70
Drought-prone area program	—	1	—	17	22	42
Environmental programs	33	74	70	40	46	55
Desert development program	—	30	32	19	20	30
Forest conservation/ forestation	—	22	19	18	23	22
Total	2,196	2,502	2,873	2,979	3,159	3,670

Note: — indicates zero, negligible or data not reported or unavailable.
Sources: WTO notifications and author's calculations.

					Shadow/forecast		
2001/02	2002/03	2003/04	2004/05	2005/06	2006/07	2007/08	2008/09
335	363	401	456	531	580	710	632
3,741	4,429	5,543	5,817	5,328	5,434	7,768	9,510
—	—	—	—	—	—	—	—
—	—	—	—	—	—	—	—
—	—	—	—	—	—	—	—
852	708	897	996	1,680	1,782	1,995	2,137
—	—	—	—	—	—	—	—
—	—	—	—	—	—	—	—
47	56	64	67	80	79	95	98
44	52	64	67	80	79	95	98
60	78	100	105	132	136	166	167
32	38	47	48	61	59	66	86
25	35	49	53	64	68	90	72
5,036	5,634	6,996	7,441	7,750	8,011	10,734	12,543

Table 8.5 *Composition of India's development program notifications and shadow notifications, 1995–2008*

	Notifications			Shadow notifications		
	1995/96	1996/97	1997/98	1998/99	1999/2000	2000/01
	Million US dollars					
Investment subsidies to agriculture	105	1,117	1,143	665	1,810	2,224
Input subsidies to low income farmers[a]	149	3,738	4,029	3,956	3,584	3,291
Total	254	4,855	5,172	4,621	5,394	5,515

[a] Shadow notifications include 80 percent of the fertilizer, electricity and irrigation subsidies.

Sources: WTO notifications and author's calculations.

farmers is from a survey by the Government of India published in the 2000 issue of Agricultural Statistics at a Glance. It showed that nearly 80 percent of farm holdings are less than 2 hectares. The other major item in the Article 6.2 notification is investment subsidies generally available to agriculture, which increased from $105 million in 1995 to $1,143 million in 1997.

Table 8.6 shows details of the product-specific AMS. India did not notify any non-exempt direct payments to farmers or other AMS budget outlays in the 1995–1997 period, so MPS is the only element of its product-specific AMS. Applied administered prices are shown for eleven products although minimum support prices (MSP) are also announced for several subcategories of many of these crops. The 1995 MPS appears to be the product of total production of the commodity and the relevant price difference (MSP minus the external reference prices (ERP) from the 1986–88 base period). The MPS amounts summed to -$29,619 million. The reported value is negative because ERP exceeded MSP for all products with the exception of sugar.

There appears to have been at least two changes in AMS methodology in the notifications subsequent to 1995. The first is that product-specific AMSs are reported for only rice (including paddy), wheat, and coarse cereals in

					Shadow/forecast		
2001/02	2002/03	2003/04	2004/05	2005/06	2006/07	2007/08	2008/09
2,119	2,329	2,528	2,826	5,323	5,847	6,424	7,057
3,050	3,754	3,848	4,312	4,467	4,540	4,616	4,692
5,169	6,083	6,376	7,138	9,790	10,387	11,040	11,749

1996 and 1997. Hoda and Gulati (2007) reasoned that this change is caused by government agencies generally not procuring other commodities on a large scale.[3] Furthermore, in the formula for computing MPS, the quantity of product procured by public agencies such as the FCI seems to have replaced total production as the eligible production. Paddy, rice, and wheat are the most commonly procured commodities. In 1996 and 1997 India's notified product-specific AMSs consist almost entirely of only those of rice (possibly including paddy) and wheat. The notified product-specific AMSs sum to -$2,604 and -$2,749 million in 1996 and 1997, respectively.

Hoda and Gulati (2007) detailed a number of concerns on India's calculation of market price support and its interpretation. The ERP may not have best represented India's net trade position during the base years, especially for wheat, coarse cereals, pulses, and cotton.[4] Furthermore the

[3] Procurement of other commodities (e.g., sugar, cotton, jute, pulses) is mostly carried out by the Cotton Corporation of India, the Jute Corporation of India, and the National Agricultural Cooperative Marketing Federation.

[4] During the base period for external reference prices, India was a net importer of rice, wheat, pulses, rapeseed, and sugar, and it was a net exporter of other crops with MSPs. External reference prices should be based on CIF prices at domestic ports for imports versus FOB at these ports for exports.

Table 8.6 *Composition of India's AMS notifications and shadow notifications, 1995–2008*

	Reference[a]	Notifications 1995/96	1996/97	1997/98	Shadow notifications 1998/99	1999/2000	2000/01
Product-specific AMS							
Market Price Support	US *$/metric ton*	*Applied administered price (US $/metric ton)*					
Rice[b]	262.5	168.2	160.6	167.5	156.9	169.6	167.5
Wheat	264.0	113.6	133.8	137.2	130.7	133.9	133.5
Coarse cereals[c]	238.6	89.7	87.3	96.9	92.7	95.8	97.4
Pulses	345.7	231.7	229.6	236.5	224.3	249.8	258.3
Groundnut	514.6	269.1	259.2	263.7	247.2	266.6	267.1
Rapeseed and mustard	513.4	257.1	250.7	253.0	237.7	253.9	262.7
Cotton	1,292.6	343.8	332.4	357.9	342.3	363.5	355.7
Soybean	229.8	191.3	185.9	191.1	178.3	184.6	179.5
Tobacco	912.8	605.4	577.5	592.0	570.5	600.0	591.1
Jute	417.6	146.5	143.7	153.4	154.5	173.1	171.8
Sugarcane	11.6	12.7	12.9	13.0	12.5	12.9	13.0
		Eligible production (million metric tons)					
Rice		81.0	13.0	15.6	11.8	17.3	19.1
Wheat		64.0	8.2	9.3	12.6	14.1	16.3
Coarse cereals[c]		30.4	—	—	—	—	—
		Total production (million metric tons)[d]					
Rice		77.0	81.7	82.5	86.1	89.7	85.0
Wheat		62.1	69.4	66.4	71.3	76.4	69.7
Coarse cereals[c]		29.0	34.1	30.4	31.3	30.3	31.1
		Market Price Support (million US dollars)					
Rice		–7,577	–1,321	–1,480	–1,246	–1,607	–1,815
Wheat		–9,625	–1,281	–1,266	–1,679	–1,835	–2,127
Coarse cereals[c]		–4530	–2	–3	—	—	—
All other commodities[e]		–7,887	—	—	—	—	—
Non-exempt payments		—	—	—	—	—	—
Non-product-specific AMS		5,772	930	1,003	989	896	823
Fertilizer subsidy[f]		1,864	414	516	418	283	388
Credit subsidy		102	—	—	—	—	—
Electricity subsidy[f]		2,437	374	343	492	520	327

					Shadow/forecast		
2001 /02	2002 /03	2003 /04	2004 /05	2005 /06	2006 /07	2007 /08	2008 /09
166.7	170.5	179.5	187.0	193.1	205.4	277.7	290.7
130.0	130.2	137.1	142.4	146.8	187.7	248.5	235.2
101.7	101.2	109.9	114.6	118.6	119.3	149.1	182.9
270.9	268.8	304.7	318.7	334.8	311.4	395.1	435.5
281.0	284.1	304.7	333.9	343.3	335.7	385.2	457.3
272.6	276.9	348.2	378.4	387.4	378.8	447.3	398.5
351.2	350.2	375.4	391.7	397.6	390.9	447.3	544.4
176.1	175.6	192.6	211.4	215.7	212.0	243.5	298.3
587.1	599.2	696.4	734.5	745.4	728.8	820.1	718.6
169.8	175.6	187.2	198.1	205.6	220.8	262.2	272.2
13.0	14.4	15.9	16.6	18.0	17.7	20.2	17.7
21.2	15.8	22.9	24.5	28.0	25.1	26.0	28.1
20.6	19.0	15.8	16.8	14.8	9.2	11.1	18.6
0.3	0.6	0.7	0.8	0.2	0.1	0.2	1.3
93.3	71.8	88.5	83.1	91.8	93.4	96.4	—
72.8	65.8	72.2	68.6	69.4	75.8	78.4	—
33.4	26.1	37.6	33.5	34.1	33.9	40.7	—
–2,031	–1,454	–1,900	–1,851	–1,942	–1,431	395	794
–2,760	–2,543	–2,005	–2,042	–1,734	–702	–172	–535
–41	–82	–90	–99	–24	–12	–18	–73
—	—	—	—	—	—	—	—
—	—	—	—	—	—	—	—
762	939	962	1,078	1,117	1,142	1,169	1,195
261	257	319	444	484	—	—	—
—	—	—	—	—	—	—	—
364	537	482	466	522	—	—	—

Table 8.6 (*cont.*)

	Notifications			Shadow notifications		
Reference[a]	1995 /96	1996 /97	1997 /98	1998 /99	1999 /2000	2000 /01
Irrigation subsidy[f]	1,345	143	145	80	94	108
Subsidy on supply of seeds	24	—	—	—	—	—
	10% of value of production (million US dollars)					
Non-product-specific threshold	7,877	8,969	9,007	9,197	9,454	8,952

Notes: — indicates zero, negligible or data not reported or unavailable.
[a] External reference price, 1986–88.
[b] Applied administered price is procurement price for common paddy. For converting to the equivalent price of rice, a coefficient of 1.5 is used.
[c] Includes bajra, jawar, maize and barley.
[d] Revised production data for 1995/96 differ slightly from earlier notified levels.
[e] Includes pulses, groundnut, rapeseed and mustard, cotton, soybean, tobacco, jute and sugarcane.
[f] Starting in 1996, subsidy applicable to farms with two or more hectares notified to WTO as non-product-specific AMS (20 percent of calculated support); the remainder (80 percent) is reported in development programs.
Sources: WTO notifications and author's calculations.

notified MSPs for wheat, groundnut, pulses, and cotton do not seem to match either the prevailing seasonal prices or the comparable quality in world markets. In addition, Hoda and Gulati (2007) questioned the use of procurements instead of total production in the AMS calculations, where using procurements assumes that MSPs apply to publicly procured quantities only.

India's notified non-product-specific AMS values in Table 8.6 have also changed between 1995 and the subsequent notifications. As described above, in 1995 it appears that the entire subsidy for fertilizer, electricity, irrigation, credit, and seeds, totaling $5,772 million and accounting for 7.5 percent of the total value of agricultural production, is notified as non-product-specific AMS. However, the reported estimates declined to $930 and $1,003 million in 1996 and 1997, respectively. The reason for this decline in notified support appears to have been the change in methodology that allocated about 80 percent of the fertilizer, electricity, and

					Shadow/forecast		
2001 /02	2002 /03	2003 /04	2004 /05	2005 /06	2006 /07	2007 /08	2008 /09
138	144	161	167	111	—	—	—
—	—	—	—	—	—	—	—
9,278	8,792	10,512	11,160	12,585	13,078	13,589	14,122

irrigation subsidies to development programs. The notified non-product-specific AMS accounted for less than 2 percent of the total value of agricultural production in either year, with 85 percent of the total accounted for by fertilizer and electricity subsidies.

For the purpose of notification, India appears to have used an allocation of the total budgetary expenditures on fertilizer subsidies between the industry and farmers that reflects that suggested by Gulati and Narayanan (2003) and their earlier contributions. Their allocation attributed the price difference between domestic and international markets into a part that permitted the domestic production of fertilizers at a price above the world price, which is referred to as a subsidy to the industry, and the subsidy component to farmers. Twenty percent of the farmers' share of subsidies appears to have been reported in non-product-specific AMS as fertilizer subsidies to large farm holdings. The notified electricity subsidy is from the Government of India Planning Commission's Annual Report on the Working of State Electricity Boards and Electricity Departments (various issues). Again, 20 percent of the collective budgetary subvention for agricultural electricity received by states has been identified as the subsidy on electricity for non-product-specific AMS purposes.

With regard to irrigation subsidies, there is less certainty on the methods used in the notifications. Hoda and Gulati (2007) suggested that the notified support is the difference between operating expenditure of the minor irrigation projects and fee receipts from farmers. With the latter being small, the entire operating expenses should translate into notified support. Surprisingly, the notified support is six to seven times that of the operating expenditure of minor irrigation projects. The notified support, however, appears to be about 20 percent of the entire budget for the Government of India's Ministry of Water Resources.

Credit subsidies were not notified for 1996 and 1997, and Hoda and Gulati (2007) suggested that they were likely to have been negligible in those years. Notified seed subsidies, which included the operating expenses of seed testing and certifying labs, have also become a smaller component of input subsidies. The decline in notified seed subsidies also appears to have been related to the apportioning of subsidies between Article 6.2 and non-product-specific AMS.

Shadow notifications, 1998–2008

In order to trace the path of domestic support as it might be notified to the WTO, I undertook the construction of shadow notifications for the period 1998–2005 using data comparable to that in the three actual notifications. I computed measurements for 1997 using my understanding of India's notification methodology before extending them to 2005. All data are expressed in US dollars, using the Reserve Bank of India's annual average exchange rate (Reserve Bank of India, 2007). In the following discussion, any discrepancies are pointed out between the calculations for 1997 and the actual notified 1997 support wherever applicable. The preliminary estimates of shadow notifications for 2006–2008 for green box and product-specific AMS are an extension of the measurements through 2005 based on publicly available data sources at the time of the analysis. For example, product-specific AMS estimates are based on prevailing administered support prices through 2008. Similarly, value of production until 2007 is based on official sources. Forecasts of Article 6.2 support and total non-product-specific support for 2006–08 are primarily made using the average annual growth rates for 1995–2005.

Green box

The estimate of the green box payments for 1997 was \$2,955 million, whereas India's notification was \$2,873, a discrepancy of less than 3 percent of the notified support.[5] The data for computing green box support for shadow notifications came from a variety of sources. Budgetary outlays

[5] For 1996, the discrepancy is only \$20.6 million, which is less than 1 percent of that year's notified green box support. The correspondence between WTO domestic support components and Indian official documents can be obtained from the author on request.

and their revisions are taken from various issues of the annual report Public Finance from the Center for Monitoring Indian Economy (CMIE, various years), which compiles data from the Directorate of Economics and Statistics of the Ministry of Agriculture and the Central Statistical Organisation, Ministry of Statistics and Programme Implementation, Government of India. In most cases, CMIE data was cross-checked with those available at the Ministry of Agriculture (Government of India, Agriculture budget, various dates). For 1997, it appears that the shadow notifications overestimate the support for public stockholding and underestimated the rest. I suspect that revised budgetary expenditures published by the Indian government may be the source of the discrepancy.

Based on these calculations, green box support appears to have increased from $2,979 million in 1998 to $7,750 million in 2005, a 170 percent increase relative to the 1997 level.[6] Green box support as a share of the total value of agricultural production doubled between 1998 (3.2 percent) and 2005 (6.2 percent). The share of public stockholding in green box support continues to be dominant but appears to have declined from 74 to 69 percent between 1998 and 2005 while that of disaster relief subsidies increased from 12 to 19 percent (Table 8.4).

Expenditure on research accounts for the majority of support under general services which nearly doubles from $270 million to $531 million between 1998 and 2005. Marketing and promotion services also show significant growth, but their share of general services has remained well below 5 percent. Public stockholding expenditure in 2005 reported in the green box, mostly due to procurement, storage, and warehousing of rice (including paddy), wheat, and coarse cereals, was about 2.4 times that in 1998. It appears that much of the growth can be attributed to a more than doubling of rice procurement between 1998 and 2005, with wheat procurements also increasing transitionally during 2000–03 (see discussion of product-specific AMS below). The strain on the exchequer was especially evident since 2001. The second largest expenditure in the green box support is the payments for relief from natural calamities. These payments have grown from $352 million to $1,493 million over the period 1998–2005. Expenditure under structural adjustment through investment aids has remained near $70 million, but that of

[6] Given minor differences between the estimates and the official notifications of 1996 and 1997, we might expect discrepancies in the range of 1 to 3 percent in the estimates for 1998–2005 relative to what will eventually be notified.

environmental programs has increased from $40 million to $132 million between 1998 and 2005. Although the growth of environmental program payments is dramatic, its share of the green box support remains below 2 percent.

Development programs

Decoding the methodology of notified development programs remained a key challenge in the analysis. The investment subsidies generally available to agriculture appear to be related to the expenditure of the Ministry of Rural Development, whose budget includes allocations for rural development, land resources, and drinking water supply (Government of India, Ministry of Rural Development, various years). The proportions or components of the rural development budget included in the notification are not clear, but the notified support in 1997 is closest to the sum of the allocations for rural development and land resources. Even so, this budget allocation is only $634 million for 1997, so it significantly underestimates the notified investment development program support level.

Based on the above estimation approach, support under investment subsidies is shown to have increased from $665 million in 1998 to $5,323 million in 2005 (see Table 8.5). This represents an increase from about 1 percent of the total value of agricultural production in 1998 to 4 percent in 2005.[7] These investment subsidies showed moderate growth until 2004 but nearly doubled between 2004 and 2005 coincidental with the launch of a national rural employment guarantee program (named the Mahatma Gandhi National Rural Employment Guarantee Act in 2009).

The reported input subsidies to low-income and resource-poor producers documented under Article 6.2 include 80 percent of the fertilizer, electricity, and irrigation subsidies, as previously described. Among these three major input subsidies, we continue to have more precise information on fertilizer and electricity subsidies than on irrigation. The source of the budgetary fertilizer subsidy for 1998–2005 is in various issues of the Agricultural Statistics at a Glance. Information on the farmers' share of fertilizer subsidy is from the report Central Government Subsidies in India (Government of India, Ministry of Finance, 2004). The data for the electricity subsidy, especially the subvention received by all states,

[7] The value of production from the Government of India, Ministry of Statistics and Programme Implementation, Central Statistical Organisation matched the notified amount in 1996 and 1997 and this data series is utilized for subsequent years.

are from various issues of the Annual Report on the Working of State Electricity Boards and Electricity Departments. The estimated fertilizer and electricity subsidies were identical to those notified by India in 1996 as well as 1997. I compute irrigation subsidies reported under Article 6.2 for 1998–2005 as 80 percent of the budget of the Ministry of Water Resources (Government of India, various years).

The estimates suggest that the sum of these three subsidies declined from $3,956 million in 1998 to $3,050 million in 2001 before increasing to $4,467 million in 2005 (Table 8.5). The total support under Article 6.2, as computed by these methods, increased from 5 percent of the value of production in 1998 to 7.8 percent in 2005. The projection for 2008 is $11.8 billion, of which $7.1 billion is attributable to investment subsidies and the rest to input subsidies.

Product-specific AMS support

With regard to product-specific AMS, the 1997 methodology for market price support appears to be a direct product of the price difference (administered minus external reference prices) and procured quantities taken as the eligible production, as described above. This is consistent with the WTO rules which are ambiguous about what constitutes the eligible volume. The Economic Survey of the Government of India's Ministry of Finance reported stockholding of rice (including paddy), wheat and coarse cereals appears to coincide with the eligible production used in the notification for 1997. To test my methodology against the notification for 1997, administered prices for twenty-three commodities (with more than one price depending on variety/quality for rice, soybean, cotton, tobacco, and copra) were obtained from Agricultural Statistics at a Glance. The price of paddy is multiplied by 1.5 to arrive at the MSP of rice, and the common-grade price was used, as in India's notification for 1997. The estimated 1997 market price support for rice is identical to that notified to WTO. However, reconstruction of the MPS for wheat in absolute value for 1997 was slightly lower than that of the notified value, which may be related to how a bonus to the applied administered price (MSP) was implemented. The data on bonuses are available, but information on the applicable time and quantity is limited. Nevertheless, the gap between the estimates and notified wheat MPS is only -$88 million. Estimated support for coarse cereals for 1997 matched the notified support.

Calculations of the MPS that comprise the shadow product-specific AMS notifications are presented in Table 8.6. Annual MSP and annual eligible production are included in the table. The MSPs are taken from various years of the Agricultural Statistics at a Glance and eligible production from various issues of the Economic Survey. The MSPs are converted into US dollars using the annual average exchange rate. The MSP in Table 8.6 include the bonuses to MSP paid to farmers.

For 1998–2005, rice and wheat MPS values were negative in all years with mixed trends.[8] With little stockholding, coarse cereals drop out of the product-specific MPS computation.[9] Since 1998, the reason for negative product-specific AMS values of commodities has been the higher ERP relative to MSP in all commodities except sugar. Inflation and political forces have led to increases in the applied administered prices even when adjusted from rupees to US dollars. These increases in MSP have resulted in a narrowing of the negative price gap especially in pulses and soybeans but for other crops as well. While the negative difference between MSPs and ERPs has shown a tendency to narrow, the eligible quantities have generally increased during 1998–2005. The opposite effects of these two developments on the calculated MPS result in the mixed trend in the values.

Hoda and Gulati (2007), in presenting a set of alternative MSPs and ERPs, where positive (nominal) price gaps are observed for wheat, coarse cereals, groundnut, and rapeseed, question India's choice of eligible production.[10] The concern on the use of procurements versus total production as eligible production is moot so long as the price gap India would notify remains negative. Through 2005, it looked like it might take another decade or so before inflation and other trend factors brought about a positive wedge between annual MSP as reported in official data sources and ERP established with the WTO. However, with price increases in the range of 10 to 25 percent between 2006 and 2008, and a one-time bonus

[8] Product-specific and non-product-specific AMSs in real and nominal terms until 1999 can be found in Hoda and Gulati (2007).

[9] In 1999, procurement of cotton, mustard, and oilseeds was about 86,000, 250,000 and 60,000 tons, respectively. In 2005, procurement of cotton, mustard, pulses, and oilseeds was about 230,000, 2,000,000, 108,000 and 100,000 tons, respectively. ERP exceeds MSP for these commodities in both years, so computed MPS would be negative but these values are not included in Table 8.6.

[10] Other developing countries, including Brazil, China and the Philippines, also report procured quantities as eligible production. The Dispute Settlement Body (DSB) addressed the issue of eligible production in the case of Korea's beef support, as Brink discusses in Chapter 2. The Korean case dealt with announced and actual procurement quantity but not the issue of total production versus procurement quantities. In the Indian context, an additional issue to deal with is marketable production because many small and poor farmers do not participate in output markets.

paid to farmers, this nominal gap became positive for rice in 2007 and 2008 in my estimation. Hence, positive product-specific AMS for rice is reported in Table 8.6 of $395 million and $794 million, respectively.

Non-product-specific de minimis *AMS support*

Values of the shadow notifications for the three major components of non-product-specific AMS support are also shown in Table 8.6, while forecasts for 2006–2008 are made only for its total value not the components. As noted above, 20 percent of the fertilizer (going to farmers), electricity and irrigation subsidies are reported as non-product-specific AMS, with the other 80 percent classified under the exemption given to development programs for low-income or resource-poor farmers. For the shadow notifications of development programs and non-product-specific AMS fertilizer subsidies, data on the farmers' share of the gross budgetary expenditures reported in the report Central Government Subsidies in India (Government of India, Ministry of Finance 2004) has not been updated since 2002, and so its 1981–2002 average was used for 2003–2005. The fertilizer subsidy has undergone some reforms, where the retention price scheme was applied to nitrogenous manufacturers only for several years. This change is reflected in the budgetary expenditures for fertilizer subsidies in the period until 2002 (Agricultural Statistics at a Glance, various issues). Although the budgetary expenditures on fertilizer subsidies in rupee terms nearly doubled, the depreciation of the Indian rupee ensured its moderate decline, in US dollar terms, until 2003. Concessions for phosphatic manufacturers dramatically increased in subsequent years causing total fertilizer subsidies to increase again in the period 2003–05. With farmers' share averaging nearly 60 percent in 1981–2002, a similar trend is observed in shadow estimates of fertilizer subsidies in non-product-specific AMS.

The electricity subsidy expenditure directed toward agriculture also doubled in rupee terms between 1998 and 2003 and since then it has shown a modest decline. Combined with the rupee depreciation, the shadow notifications of electricity subsidy showed a mixed trend in US dollars, but have generally increased from $492 million to $522 million between 1998 and 2005. The budget of the Ministry of Water Resources doubled between 1998 and 2001. Following modest increases until 2004, the 2005 budget shows a decline in expenditure. As a consequence, the estimates of irrigation subsidies have increased from $80 million in 1998 to $167 million in 2004 (despite the depreciating rupee) before declining

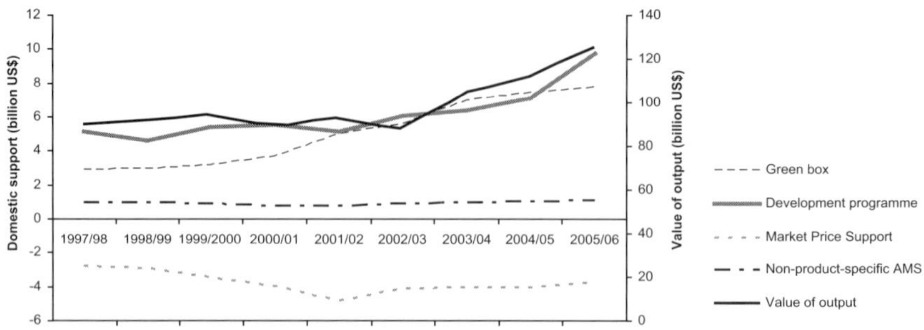

Figure 8.1 Trends in India's domestic support and total value of agricultural output
Sources: India's notifications to WTO and author's calculations.

to $111 million in 2005. The seed subsidies are reported in the Agricultural Statistics at a Glance. However, the Government of India's notification method for seed subsidies is not clear and this relatively small subsidy is not estimated. Overall, the non-product-specific AMS as a percent of the total value of agricultural production averaged about 1 percent per year during 1998–2005.

Domestic support trends

Figure 8.1 summarizes the general trends of various measurements of domestic support and the value of output in Indian agriculture from 1997 through 2005, the final year for which I had relatively complete information. The significant growth of support under green box and development program categories is evident, while non-product-specific AMS remained somewhat constant. The sum of product-specific AMSs has remained negative, but with a mixed trend in the 1997–2005 period. The share of various measurements of domestic support in total value of agricultural output is shown in Figure 8.2. The growth in the value of output in Figure 8.1 as well as the shares of product-specific and non-product-specific AMS in Figure 8.2 demonstrate the substantial flexibilities available to India under both *de minimis* provisions.

Notification alternatives

The *de minimis* thresholds are the *de facto* limits on India's product-specific and non-product-specific support not exempted under the green box, Article 6.2, or the blue box. Several issues arise in terms of alternative notifications for measures in each of the notified categories.

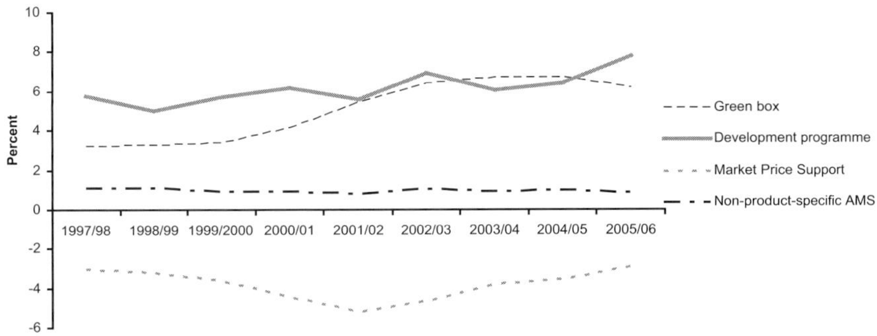

Figure 8.2 India's domestic support as a share of total value of agricultural output
Sources: India's notifications to WTO and author's calculations.

With regard to green box support, India could face questions on the classification of the procurement, storage, and distribution costs of major staples, i.e., rice/paddy, wheat. At present it is not clear how these operations of the FCI and other public agencies are classified for WTO notifications into public stockholding for food security but not domestic food aid. The primary purpose of the FCI and other procurement agencies is to support farmers at or near the farmgate, but they are also responsible, at least partly, for distribution of collected quantities to urban consumers.[11] The challenge lies in separating the expenditure of public agencies procuring food grains and other major crops into those attributable to food security, food aid, and marketing/transport costs of farmers. For the latter, any subsidies not applicable under Article 6.2 would likely find a place in non-product-specific AMS. Alternatively, procurement appears to be limited to a few staples, and hence, this support outside of Article 6.2 may alter the computation of product-specific AMS. Our calculation of stockholding expenditures rises to about $9.5 billion in 2008 and the transfer of part of that support to either product-specific or non-product-specific AMS would begin to cut the slack in the *de minimis* exemptions.

There are several issues on Article 6.2 support notification. The first is the 1996 transfer of the majority of fertilizer, electricity, and irrigation subsidies from non-product-specific AMS to development programs. These subsidies are available to all farmers and they do not specifically target low-income or resource-poor producers. Additionally, the share

[11] It is not clear if the costs of the public distribution system (domestic food aid) are included in the green box support.

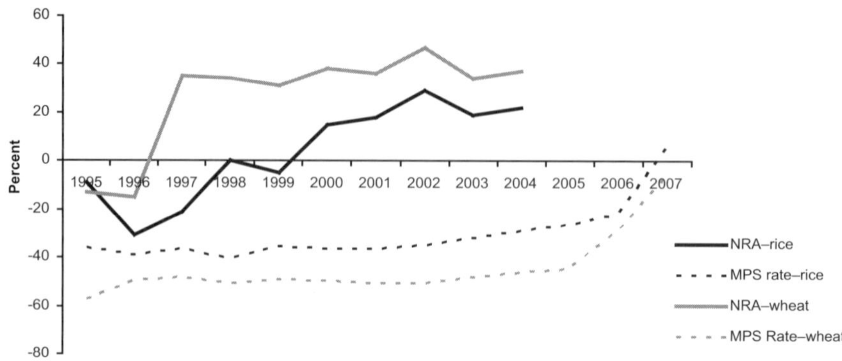

Figure 8.3 India's rates of market price support for rice and wheat in notifications and shadow notifications versus economic measurement

Notes: MPS is market price support; NRA is nominal rate of assistance.

Sources: MPS rates from WTO notifications and author's calculations; NRAs from Pursell, Gulati, and Gupta (2009).

(80 percent) is based on the number of farms with less than 2 hectares in production. However, the share of such small farms in cultivated land is less than 40 percent (Agricultural Statistics at a Glance, 2000). A reallocation based on the latter share would transfer nearly $2 billion into non-product-specific AMS, which, in turn, may increase to about 3 percent of the total value of agricultural production.

With regard to product-specific AMS, India appears to follow the methods outlined in Annex 3 of the Agreement. However, as previously noted, Hoda and Gulati (2007), in addition to questioning India's choice of eligible production, noted reporting errors in notified administered support prices (MSPs) (for example, cotton, pulses, rice, and wheat) and external reference prices (groundnut and sugarcane). Using a shadow exchange rate, Hoda and Gulati (2007) recomputed product-specific AMSs showing a positive gap between MSP and ERP in nominal terms for some products, but the negative gap as seen in Table 8.6 persists in real terms. It is also not clear how the use of nationally announced prices, such as MSPs, match with Annex 3 which requires support to be measured as close to the farmgate as possible.

As in other countries, there is also an issue of the distinction between market price support as notified to the WTO and its assessment on an annual basis in economic terms. This distinction is illustrated in Figure 8.3. It shows the percentage nominal rates of assistance for rice and wheat computed in the World Bank agricultural distortions project (Pursell, Gulati, and Gupta 2009) for 1995–2004. This is compared to the percentage rate of support that enters the notification MPS for these commodities. Clearly, the negative WTO rates based on MSPs less ERPs do not reflect the economic protection that is generally positive after 1998.

In terms of non-product-specific AMS, the separation of fertilizer subsidies into those for industry and for farmers is based on the methodology of Gulati and Narayanan (2003). However, significant issues remain in the computation of electricity, irrigation, credit, and seed subsidies. In the case of electricity and irrigation subsidies, Hoda and Gulati (2007) noted that notified support includes only operating expenses of electricity boards/departments and minor irrigation projects, respectively. The capital expenditures are not counted in the notified support in either of these two cases. Our shadow notification takes into account all types of irrigation projects, but the issue of apportioning input subsidies (budgetary expenditures) between Article 6.2 and non-product-specific AMS remains relevant.

While the above issues of classification and measurement are significant, their incorporation into notifications appears to have limited effects. In the case of product-specific AMS, the effect is not relevant because ERPs remain well above MSPs and the economic measurement of market price support is not the one called for under the WTO rules. Including some of the green box support as product-specific support for rice and wheat does not exhaust India's support latitude under *de minimis* thresholds, but revisions to MSP suggested by Hoda and Gulati (2007) may make it exceed the ERP, so market price support would be positive and also count against the threshold. For non-product-specific AMS, the above alternative definitions and measurements might cut some of the slack in the *de minimis* exemption of India under the Agreement.

Projections and future commitments

Under the Agreement the primary constraint on India's domestic support comes from the *de minimis* thresholds that limit its AMS. In the Doha draft modalities (WTO 2008) developing countries with zero Bound Total AMS are required to compile a Base OTDS, but are exempt from reductions in Base OTDS levels and *de minimis* percentages. India would have a Base OTDS of $25.6 billion. To see whether either the Agreement or possible Doha constraints may impact on India it is necessary to estimate domestic support notifications a few years into the future.

Table 8.7 *Projections of India's domestic support in 2015/16*

	Nominal value[a]	MPS adjusted for inflation[b]
	Million US$	
Green box	22,114	22,114
Public stockholding	16,852	16,852
Crop insurance/Disaster relief	3,681	3,681
Development programs[c]		
Investment subsidies[d]	8,266	8,266
Input subsidies	5,187	5,187
Product-specific AMS (MPS)	6,766	3,664
Non-product-specific AMS	1,654	1,654
10 percent of value of production (*de minimis* threshold)[e]	17,723	17,723
Doha Base OTDS	25,600	25,600

[a] Nominal values based on annual average growth rate in the 1998–2008 period.
[b] Product-specific AMS adjusted to account for an excessive inflation rate of 2 percent per annum.
[c] Total not estimated (see text).
[d] Nominal values based on annual average growth rate in the 2005–08 period.
[e] Product-specific *de minimis* thresholds could be binding for some crops even if product-specific AMS support in total is less than 10 percent of total value of agricultural production.
Source: Author's calculations based on WTO (2008).

Projections of India's domestic support with a projection of the major aggregates for 2015 are shown in Table 8.7. The projection for 2015 is in nominal terms and based generally on the average annual growth rate of support in each category from 1998 through 2008. Given the one-time boost to investment subsidies in 2005 that raised the average growth rate between 1998 and 2008, the 2005–08 growth rate is used to project investment subsidies to 2015, while input subsidies notified under development programs and non-product-specific AMS are projected using the 1998–2008 growth rate. For product-specific AMS Table 8.7 provides two alternative projections for 2015.

In nominal terms, I expect subsidies of about $13.5 billion to be notified under Article 6.2 in 2015, of which input subsidies account for $5.2 billion and the rest ($8.3 billion) fall under investment subsidies. Similar to the discussion in the previous section, some of the Article 6.2 support may be reallocated to non-product-specific AMS. The introduction of a major rural employment guarantee program in 2005 will likely lead to additional support notified under Article 6.2.

Among the notification projections, estimating the level of product-specific AMS is more problematic. If nominal prices were to increase by the average annual growth from 1998–2008 until 2015, we would expect to see positive product-specific AMS in rice and wheat of about $6.8 billion. For other commodities, product-specific AMS will likely be zero, which is consistent with the zero procurement reported in India's past notifications and my shadow notifications.

If the entire volume of production, as opposed to procured quantities, were to be used as eligible production, nominal product-specific AMS may exceed the 10 percent *de minimis* threshold in 2015. The reason for exceeding the *de minimis* threshold is that India produces more than 200 million tons of food grains, which is about four to five times the procured quantities. Moreover, the presumption of zero procurement for other products underlies the assertion of zero market price support and product-specific AMS for those products. Using total production for all commodities may lead to the sum of product-specific AMS exceeding the projected 10 percent of value of production in 2015 (although, of course, the *de minimis* testing is done on each AMS by itself). Fortunately for India, however, the Agreement has provisions for excessive inflation (Article 18.4): members may allow another member to exceed its Bound Total AMS if the excess results from excessive rates of inflation. In real terms, the projected 2015 price gap between MSP and ERP is significantly lower than that in nominal terms if a 2 percent allowance is taken for excessive inflation. The proposed revision to Article 18.4 of the Agreement in the December 2008 Doha draft modalities considers difficulties faced by developing countries in computing AMS as a result of sudden and extraordinary increases in food prices relative to the fixed ERP. In addition, the new terms proposed in Annex B that exempt price support provided to low-income and resource-poor farmers in conjunction with public stockholding from the product-specific AMS calculations could be used to give India additional latitude.

Non-product-specific AMS is likely to remain around 1 percent of the total value of agricultural production if India continues to use the concepts of its 1997 notification. Moving some of the Article 6.2 support back to non-product-specific AMS may increase the latter's share to about 3 percent, well under the proposed Doha limit for India.[12] The share

[12] Hoda and Gulati (2007) calculate non-product-specific support to be nearly 7 percent of the total value of agricultural production, which presumably includes some of the alternative support-definition and measurement issues detailed herein.

may further increase by several percentage points if the proposal by the Government of India in 2008 to provide credit subsidies is fully implemented. The 2008/09 budget allocated about $15.0 billion to absorb the cost of waiving repayment of farm loans. Of that, $12.5 billion is proposed for low-income and resource-poor producers (holdings of less than 2 hectares), while the rest is allocated to help reschedule loan terms to all farmers. It is not certain how the government will apportion credit subsidies over either the past or next five years.

In general, the *de minimis* exemptions are expected to provide substantial flexibility to India in implementing trade-distorting domestic support policies. These exemptions rise with the value of production. By 2015, the sum of product-specific AMS exempted on *de minimis* grounds can be as much as $17.7 billion if all products are included, and an additional $17.7 billion can be exempted as *de minimis* non-product-specific AMS support. Under the Doha draft modalities, India could also face an additional constraint on its OTDS support as well as the *de minimis* limits, but the level of this constraint also still leaves ample room for subsidies in this category compared to the projected levels. Some concerns exist on the application of product-specific AMS limits and whether support may exceed the *de minimis* levels for the key supported commodities. However, it is hard to pin it down because of uncertainty about India's use of procurements versus total production, how applied administered price is reported (as close to the farmgate as possible), and the definition of excessive inflation.

Summary and conclusions

This chapter has broadly outlined India's domestic support policies and an understanding of their classification and measurement for the purposes of WTO notifications. Then, I employed the methods underlying this understanding to prepare shadow notifications of India's domestic support for 1998–2005 and preliminary support estimates/forecasts for 2006–08. Following that, I explored alternative support-definition scenarios and their effects on the shadow notifications. Finally, projections of domestic support for 2015 are provided.

India's notifications began in 1995 with green box support of nearly $2.2 billion, which accounted for 3 percent of the total value of agricultural production. The exemption for development programs was sparsely employed in 1995. Because external reference prices were higher than the administered or minimum support prices, product-specific AMS, computed as market price support using total production in 1995, was negative for most products. Hence, the sum of product-specific AMS was also negative. Non-product-specific AMS, including fertilizer, electricity, irrigation, credit, and seed subsidies, accounted for 7 percent of the total value of agricultural production in 1995.

In subsequent notifications (1996 and 1997), several key changes were observed. The first was the transfer of 80 percent of fertilizer, irrigation, and electricity subsidies from non-product-specific AMS to the development program category (Article 6.2). The justification for this move was that 80 percent of farm holdings have less than 2 hectares of cultivated land. Also, substantial expenditures on rural development, especially investment subsidies, began to be included as development program support. In the case of product-specific AMS, the quantities procured by public agencies replaced total production as eligible production in 1996 and 1997. Because many commodities were not procured by the central government, market price support and product-specific AMS was reported for cereals only. These changes did not much alter the green box support, but development program support grew at the expense of non-product-specific AMS. As a result, the latter fell to 1 percent of the total value of agricultural production.

With this understanding of the 1997 methodology, I prepared a set of shadow notifications for 1998–2005. The shadow notifications show that green box support has grown to nearly $8 billion in 2005, which translates into about 7 percent of the total value of agricultural production. Two major reasons for the growth in the green box support are the public stockholding (food security) expenditures and relief from natural disasters. Both components have witnessed significant growth during 1998–2005. There was less clarity on the source of investment subsidies used in the notification of development program exemptions. However, the shadow estimates of input subsidies to low-income and resource-poor producers show some decline between 1998 and 2001, but they have rebounded since. Such input subsidies amounted to about $4.5 billion or 3.6 percent of the total value of agricultural production in 2005. Product-specific AMS remained negative through 2005 for all products concerned because of the minimum support prices (MSP) below external reference prices. Non-product-specific AMS, with the allocation of 80 percent of fertilizer, electricity, and irrigation subsidies under development programs, accounted on average for about 1 percent of the total value of agricultural production.

Preliminary estimates or forecasts for 2006–08 were made for green box, development programs, and the total non-product-specific AMS values. The last of the three does not exceed the *de minimis* threshold provided for in the Agreement or 2008 Doha draft modalities. For product-specific AMS, the announced MSP for 2007–08 along with one-time bonuses for some commodities are 10 to 25 percent higher than those for 2006. Along with the brief appreciation of the rupee in 2007/08, the gap between ERP and MSP disappeared for some products, e.g., rice. The effects of subsequent rupee depreciation are offset by the 2008 commodity price boom, which has again narrowed the gap between ERP and MSP. For rice, product-specific AMS became positive in 2007 and 2008. If computed with total production figures, market price support for rice would be at least four times as large as that using eligible production.

Alternative support-definition and measurement considerations show a possible increase in product-specific AMS. However, reallocating input subsidies from development programs to non-product-specific AMS would only eliminate some of the slack in the latter's *de minimis* exemption.

Looking at projections for 2015, the total value of Indian agricultural production is expected to be about \$177 billion. So, the *de minimis* exemptions allow up to \$35.4 billion in farm support, about \$17.7 billion each for the sum of the product-specific and the non-product-specific AMS. Under a Doha agreement along 2008 lines, India could also face the constraint of a Base OTDS of \$25.6 billion. Any of these constraints give India ample flexibility in setting and implementing domestic support policies, including trade-distorting support measures. The commodity-price boom since 2006 provides an opportunity for India to possibly shift from trade-distorting domestic and border policies to more decoupled support and investments in sustainable development. Increases in tax revenues and experiences of other large countries in implementing direct payment programs should aid the possible policy transformation in Indian agriculture. However, it is not clear that India policymakers will choose such a path as opposed to continued use of tariff protection and expansion of its support tied to levels of production and prices.

References

Agricultural Statistics at a Glance. Various years. Government of India. Ministry of Agriculture, Directorate of Economics and Statistics http://www.dacnet.nic.in/eands/latest_2006.htm.

CMIE (Center for Monitoring Indian Economy). Various years. Public Finance.

Gopinath, M. 2008. India: Shadow WTO agricultural domestic support notifications. IFPRI Discussion Paper 792.

Gopinath, M., and D. Laborde. 2008. Implications for India. ICTSD/IPC/IFPRI Project on Draft Agricultural Modalities. Paper presented at a seminar in Geneva, March 12.

Government of India. 2004. Central government subsidies in India. Ministry of Finance.

Various years. Agriculture budget. Ministry of Agriculture, Directorate of Economics and Statistics, www.dacnet.nic.in/eands/.

Various years. Annual budget report. Ministry of Commerce and Industry, Directorate General of Commercial Intelligence and Statistics, www.dgsiskol.nic.in/.

Various years. Annual report on the working of state electricity boards/departments. Planning Commission.

Various years. Budget expenditure. Ministry of Rural Development, www.rural.nic.in/.

Various years. Budget expenditure. Ministry of Water Resources, www.mowr.gov.in/.

Various years. Economic Survey. Ministry of Finance.

Gulati, A., and S. Narayanan. 2003. *Subsidy Syndrome in Indian Agriculture.* New Delhi: Oxford University Press.

Gulati, A., and G. Pursell. 1993. Liberalizing Indian agriculture: An agenda for reform. Policy Research Working Paper No. 1172, World Bank.

Hoda, A., and A. Gulati. 2007. *WTO Negotiations on Agriculture and Developing Countries.* Baltimore: Johns Hopkins University Press.

Orden, D., F. Cheng, H. Nguyen, U. Grote, M. Thomas, K. Mullen, and D. Sun. 2007. Agricultural producer support estimates for developing countries. Research Report 152. International Food Policy Research Institute.

Pursell, G., A. Gulati, A., and K. Gupta. 2009. Distortions to agricultural incentives in India. In *Distortions to Agricultural Incentives in Asia*, ed. K. Anderson and W. Martin. Washington, DC: World Bank.

Reserve Bank of India. 2007. Handbook of statistics on the Indian economy, www.rbi.org.in/home.aspx.

WTO. 2008. Revised draft modalities for agriculture. TN/AG/W/4/Rev. 4, 6 December.

9

China

FUZHI CHENG

Chinese agricultural policy has undergone some fundamental changes in the past decade, with major policy shifts in pricing, marketing, trade, investment, and technology. Most notably, China has implemented a series of new policies that directly favor the agricultural sector. These policies include direct payments to farmers, agricultural input subsidies, agricultural tax elimination, protective and minimum prices, dismantling of barriers to private entry into agricultural marketing channels, and increased spending on rural infrastructure, research and development. The policy changes have resulted in higher support for the agricultural sector, which has been documented in various studies. Considering this finding in combination with empirical evidence disclosing disprotection in agriculture in earlier periods, one can conclude that there has been a transition of government policy stance from taxing agriculture to supporting the sector. Recent economic growth has made these subsidy policy changes fiscally feasible.

The agricultural policy changes reflect the Chinese leadership's renewed attention to agricultural problems, concisely described in official documents as the San Nong issue (agriculture, rural areas, and peasants). The policy changes also arrived amidst a sharply widening rural–urban income gap as well as rising social unrest and political tension. In a series of No.1 Documents issued by the Central Committee of the Chinese Communist Party, it is reiterated that increasing farm incomes is at the top of the leadership's agenda. The authorities believe that the provision of various subsidies to farmers will effectively raise their incomes, which would, in turn, pacify the widespread resentment that the economic system has disproportionately benefited people in urban areas. The objective of self-sufficiency in food supply (grains in particular) is also embedded

The author gratefully acknowledges assistance or helpful comments from Lars Brink, Peng Chao, Fred Gale, Will Martin, Dongsheng Sun, Francis Tuan and Shunli Yao.

in the subsidy strategy because farmers are expected to produce more when provided with better economic incentives.

The impacts of China's new subsidy policies are far-reaching both within the country and internationally. The elimination of agricultural taxes and the provision of direct payments to farmers, for example, have been lauded domestically as major achievements in China's agricultural policy reforms – Chinese farmers are for the first time in the country's history being subsidized rather than taxed by the government, a transition that is intended to add significantly to the country's progress in poverty reduction. In the trade arena, however, there is a potential concern that some of the policies may prove contentious, just as agricultural subsidies in developed countries have been under intense scrutiny from the Uruguay Round onward. As China's influence on the world economy continues to increase, the global implications of its domestic policies will receive more attention. Specifically, one can question whether China's policy measures meet the disciplines of the Agreement on Agriculture and whether they will fit within tighter rules that may be negotiated in the future, especially if China continues its current trend of increasing agricultural subsidies.

China provided estimates of domestic support for the period 1996–98 in its accession documents and updated them for 1999–2001 in 2006 and for 2002–04 in 2010. Because of the long lags in its submission of notifications, it is not known to what extent China has been compliant with its WTO commitments in domestic support in more recent years. Ongoing agricultural policy reforms and the delay in reporting suggest the need for an investigation into the consequences of policy changes in terms of China's domestic support commitments as well as a projection of future notifications to examine possible WTO ramifications of continued policy development in China.

This chapter reviews the available domestic support notifications from China and provides a quantitative assessment of shadow notifications in which recent subsidy information is presented and changes in domestic policies and market conditions are discussed. In addition to providing notification calculations, several important controversies about different subsidy definitions and interpretation of the WTO rules are assessed for China. Future subsidies and their WTO compliance are projected and evaluated through 2016.

The chapter is organized as follows. The next section provides a brief overview of China's agricultural sector and recent agricultural policy changes. The third section presents estimates of China's domestic support

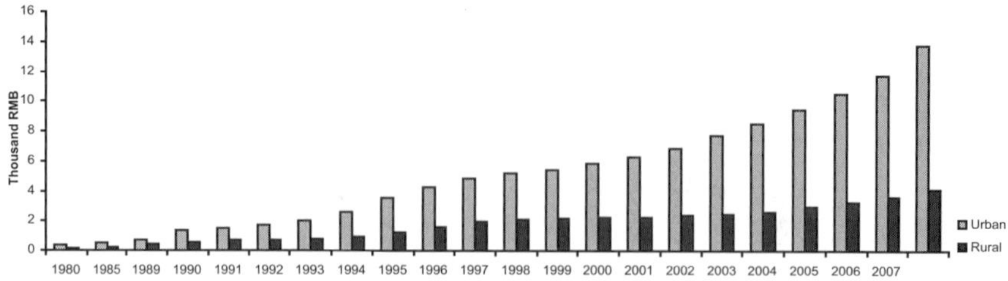

Figure 9.1 Per capita income of China's urban and rural residents
Source: National Bureau of Statistics (NBS), various years.

for the period 1996–2008 and discusses a set of relevant alternative subsidy-definition scenarios and their effects on the calculated levels of support. Projections of domestic support through 2016 are presented and the implications for China of the new Doha constraints that may be negotiated are discussed. The final section provides a summary and conclusions.

Agricultural sector and policy setting

China has a vast agricultural sector encompassing more than half of the population. The sector has witnessed considerable achievements since economic reforms were initiated in 1978. However, despite long-term growth, the agricultural sector has lagged significantly behind its urban counterparts. Incomes in rural areas, after a few years of strong growth in the early years of the reform, have stayed well below those in urban areas (Figure 9.1). The rapidly expanding urban sector and the development of rural off-farm employment in township and village enterprises have alleviated the problem of surplus rural labor to some extent, but restrictions from the household registration (hukou) system and other preferential treatment favoring only urban residents continue to constrain rural labor mobility. Today, a large share of China's idle population remains in rural areas, contributing to a high ratio of labor per unit of land and thus low labor productivity and agricultural returns.

Agricultural production in China remains characterized by a combination of scarce land, abundant labor, limited mechanization and small-scale operations. The sector employs approximately 350 million people, or 45 percent of the total labor force, and the average farm size is less than 0.5 hectares (Fan and Chan-Kang 2005). Income from agriculture is an important component of the Chinese economy, although its contribution

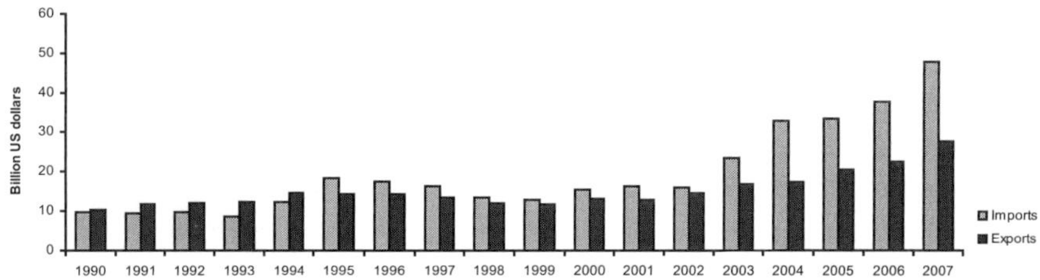

Figure 9.2 China's agricultural imports and exports
Source: FAOSTAT 2009.

to overall GDP has steadily declined. In 2007, agriculture accounted for about 11 percent of GDP, compared to nearly 30 percent in 1980 (NBS 2008). Within the agricultural sector, as defined by China's statistical agency, crop production accounted for 50 percent of total agricultural output, while livestock contributed 33 percent, and fisheries 9 percent in 2007 (NBS 2008). While grain remains the key crop, its growth rate has declined in the past two decades, due primarily to the changing incentive structure that favors production of crops other than grains as well as non-crop products. Recent years have seen a rebound of grain production, while oil crops, fruits and vegetables, meats and fishery products have experienced higher growth rates than others (MOA, various years). The structural change in production has led to a reallocation of resources to products that are more in line with China's comparative advantage in labor-intensive versus land-intensive products. Restructuring also occurred within grain production, with land sown to rice and wheat declining but that sown to maize increasing. This reflects a shift in maize use from food to feed in order to meet increasing consumption demand for livestock products.

China is a major player in world agricultural markets. Although the contribution of agriculture to China's overall trade flows has declined, the values of agricultural imports and exports have steadily increased. In 2007, the total value of China's agricultural trade reached $75.7 billion (imports plus exports), an increase of $46.3 billion from 2001 (Figure 9.2). China has been a net food importer since 1995 with net agricultural imports increasing in recent years due primarily to a dramatic rise in domestic demand for cereals (mainly wheat), oilseeds (mainly soybeans), cotton, and sugar. In the export sector, fruits, vegetables, meats, and fishery products have performed strongly in the past decade.

Adjustments in China's trade policy, including tariff reductions, have significantly changed China's agricultural export and import structure.

Reflecting changes in its production pattern, agricultural trade in China has moved in a direction that is more consistent with its comparative advantage (Huang and Rozelle 2002). Horticultural, animal, and aquatic products accounted for more than 80 percent of agricultural exports in the late 1990s. By grouping trade data according to factor intensity in production, Huang and Rozelle concluded that China's net exports of land-intensive bulk commodities, such as grains, oilseeds, and sugar crops, have fallen, while exports of high value and more labor-intensive commodities have risen.

Agricultural policy

The Chinese economy has long been characterized by discrimination against agriculture arising from government policies, many of which can be dated back to pre-socialist times (Huang *et al.* 2007). The government either taxed agriculture explicitly or set commodity prices below market-determined levels, creating disincentives to agricultural production. Monopoly parastatal marketing firms (e.g., state-owned grain enterprises) fully controlled the distribution of agricultural commodities and, through pan-territorial and pan-seasonal agricultural pricing, served mainly the interests of a select group composed of the urban elite, the industrial sector, and government bureaucrats. By the 1970s, evidence had mounted that government interventions in agriculture had done more harm than good to the economy. Poor economic performance, a stagnating agricultural sector and intensifying political pressure forced the country to accept much-needed agricultural policy reforms within the broader context of economic reforms that started in 1978.

Because of the importance of agriculture in the domestic economy in terms of income generation and employment, agricultural reforms occupied a central place in the initial reform efforts. The agricultural reform measures were generally designed to correct previous biases against agriculture by reducing or eliminating price controls and parastatal marketing (Ke 2007). The expectation was that improving price incentives for farmers and reducing government intervention in the agricultural sector would generate a sizable supply response and promote the rapid emergence of well-functioning markets. The reforms, in general, have been successful, not least because of a government commitment to market liberalization. Agricultural output rose substantially and there was an increase in competition and private trader entry into domestic and foreign agricultural markets. Greater competition and increasingly cost-effective private-sector trading led to lower marketing margins and improved market efficiency. As a result, farmers received a greater share of the rising retail and export prices. Using nominal rate of protection with data since the early 1980s, Huang *et al.* (2009) show that distortions in China's agriculture have been reduced during the reform period; and that by the mid 2000s, the sector was operating in a near-neutral market environment.

Despite greater liberalization, evidence emerged nevertheless that reforms had not succeeded in other areas. In particular, they failed to properly transfer structural and institutional functions previously performed by the state to the private sector (Huang 1998). In some cases, parastatal firms continued to dominate the markets (grain markets in particular), while in others, government withdrawal had left a vacuum in the provision of public goods that could not be filled by the private sector. Deficiencies in research, extension, transportation, storage and communications infrastructure, as well as inadequate legal and other regulatory institutions dealing with contract enforcement, quality control, and property rights, caused high transaction costs that dampened the efficiency gains from better private entry and competition. Operations in agriculture remained informal and small-scale. Moreover, experiences in the 1990s showed that liberalization was associated with sharp price swings for some of the most important commodities, including rice. This high price variability offset gains from increases in producer prices and deteriorated investment incentives for farmers.

Faced with this new set of agricultural problems, the Chinese government has increasingly recognized that further progress in developing the agricultural sector will require not only further liberalization, but also a more concerted effort to go beyond the withdrawal of the public sector from agricultural markets. The government has perceived the need to assume a new, supportive role for agriculture both as a market facilitator and as a producer subsidizer (Kwiecinski and van Tongeren 2007). One aspect of this role is to strengthen public investment in infrastructure, research and extension, and market information, which are deemed necessary for the development of more competitive and efficient markets (Fan and Thorat 2007). A second aspect is to foster stronger government support for agriculture through pricing, marketing, trade, and various transfer mechanisms to secure farm income. Consistent with these new roles, China has in recent years started a new wave of agricultural policy reforms and introduced a series of policy measures that directly favor the agricultural sector.

Trade policies

China's foreign trade policy reforms since 1978 have involved four key steps: lowering trade barriers, depreciating the exchange rate, decentralizing the trading system, and introducing competition into foreign trade so that prices can play a role in determining resource allocation (Martin 2003). China's agricultural trade policies – as part of an agricultural policy stance intended to maintain self-sufficiency in agricultural supply, especially in food grain production – have moved more slowly than in other sectors to remove restrictions and reduce protection. Notwithstanding periodic standstills and reversals, China has progressively liberalized agricultural trade. In its WTO accession protocol, China agreed to phase out state trading, bind 100 percent of its tariff lines, replace quantitative restrictions with a TRQ system, and eliminate export subsidies for all agricultural products.

Applied tariff rates on agricultural products, which are higher than non-agricultural tariff rates, fell from 23.1 percent in 2001 to 15.3 percent in 2005, as compared to the overall average applied rate of 9.7 percent. The tariff structure on agricultural products remained unchanged during 2005–07 (WTO 2008). Tariff dispersion has declined, from a range of 0–121.6 percent in 2001 to 0–65 percent. Tariffs on dairy products dropped from 35.9 percent in 2001 to 12.1 percent in 2005. Tariffs on grain and oilseeds have also fallen substantially since 2001, from 51.9 to 33.9 percent and from 32.0 to 11.1 percent, respectively. Nevertheless, agricultural commodities that have traditionally been highly protected, such as sugar and tobacco, are still subject to higher than average tariffs. Some of the lowest tariffs apply to oilseeds, a sector that was previously highly protected. Lower tariffs apply to subsectors in which China has a comparative advantage (i.e., labor-intensive farm products), such as horticultural and animal products.

Tariff-rate quotas have been gradually increased and out-of-quota tariff rates reduced. In 2006, China eliminated the TRQs on vegetable oils, reducing the number of quota-related agricultural tariff lines to 55. The impacts of changing TRQs on trade flows, however, have been limited because in-quota imports are usually low and most TRQs are unfilled. Imports of grain under TRQs have been especially low. The role of state trading enterprises (STEs) in agricultural trade has diminished even though the government still retains some influence on imports and exports of key commodities. Agricultural imports subject to state trading include wheat, rice, corn, vegetable oil, cotton, sugar, and tobacco.

STEs also control exports of rice, corn, cotton, tobacco, and silk. The TRQ system specifies criteria for allocating import quotas between STEs and private enterprises. Since 2001, the in-quota shares of STEs have decreased substantially for vegetable oils (palm, rapeseed, and soybean), which corresponds to a relaxation of the TRQs on these products. In contrast, the shares of STEs in imports of wheat, rice, corn, cotton, and sugar, have been kept relatively high and fixed. Export quotas are exclusively controlled by the STEs. The continued use of state trading in the import and export of these commodities is deemed strategically important and allows the government to stabilize supply and price in the domestic market.

Toward the end of 2007, China introduced several new agricultural trade policies in response to pressure from high inflation, particularly rising commodity prices. For instance, in early 2008, China's Ministry of Commerce (MOFCOM 2008) announced a temporary quota policy for the export of wheat, corn and rice powder in order to guarantee an adequate domestic supply. In addition, China's Ministry of Finance (MOF) announced in late 2007 that China would eliminate export tax rebates (12 percent) on grains and processed grain products (MOF 2007a), and start levying export taxes on these products in the range of 5–25 percent (MOF 2008a). The tariff for soybeans was temporarily reduced from 3 percent to 1 percent in October 2007 and the reduced rate was effective through the end of September 2008 (MOF 2008b). With the retreat of global commodity prices later in 2008, as well as a series of bumper domestic grain crops that led to swelling stockpiles, China has re-adjusted its trade policies. For instance, the tariff for soybeans was reinstated at 3 percent in October 2008 while temporary taxes on exports of wheat, rice, and soybeans were cancelled in July 2009.

Domestic policies

The post-WTO accession domestic agricultural policy regime in China has been characterized by the relaxation of price and marketing controls, the expansion of government subsidies and investments, and the elimination of agricultural taxes. Following the liberalization of non-strategic agricultural products including fruits, vegetables, livestock, and fish in the 1980s and of materials including cotton, vegetable oil, and sugar in the late 1990s and early 2000s, price and marketing controls were kept only for grains and tobacco. According to China's WTO accession protocol, tobacco was subject to state pricing and grains to government guidance pricing. Government intervention in grain has been gradually minimized.

Prior to 1997, Chinese farmers were required to deliver a fixed amount (quota) of grain at a procurement price (quota price). Farmers could sell surplus output either to the State Administration of Grain (grain bureaus) at a negotiated price or directly to the market; hence there existed a parallel free market price along with the government price. In 1998, the state procurement quota system was dismantled and farmers were allowed to sell any amount voluntarily to the state-owned grain bureaus at a preset protective price. Selling to individuals or private firms was no longer permitted. The protective price scheme was gradually eliminated in the years that followed, but in order to give farmers an incentive to continue growing grains, a minimum price was set, initially for rice in 2004 and then extended to wheat in 2005. Relaxation of grain price controls was accompanied by changing the functions of the grain bureaus, which until the mid 1980s had dominated upstream and downstream distribution of agricultural products. Currently, the grain bureaus are largely decentralized and commercialized, with their roles largely restricted to the provision of information and the maintenance of strategic stocks. Private grain users (e.g., grain processors, feed manufacturers) and traders are generally allowed to enter marketing channels.

China has strengthened its support for agriculture in recent years by subsidizing agricultural inputs, including machinery, fertilizers, pesticides, electricity, fuels, water, and transportation. Charges for such inputs as fuels, water, electricity and transport tend to be lower for farmers, but the level of subsidy is difficult to assess as the cost of provision is different across various users. For instance, to lower prices of fertilizers, manufacturers have been given access to lower priced inputs, such as electricity. In addition, export taxes, temporary exemptions from value-added tax (VAT) and caps on sales prices are occasionally used to curb rises in fertilizer prices. In 2002, the government introduced a subsidy for farmers purchasing improved quality soy seed (through lower prices) that was subsequently extended to include subsidies for purchasing improved seed for production of rice, wheat, corn and soybeans.

China has recently experimented with direct payment policies. Direct payments tied to grain acreage were put in place in 2002 in selected major grain-producing provinces: Anhui, Henan, Hubei, and Jilin (Gale, Lohmar, and Tuan 2005). China introduced its first nationwide direct payments to farmers in 2004. The payment rates vary across provinces, but on average they were RMB10 per mu (1/15 hectare) in 2004 and since then have increased to RMB37 per mu in 2007. The total grain direct payments reached RMB15.1 billion in 2007 according to China's Ministry of Finance. According to Chinese authorities, direct payments to farmers will be continued and strengthened in the coming years (MOF 2007b).

In line with the move to help farmers, China has either eliminated or reduced various taxes on agriculture.[1] The tax on specialty crops (except for tobacco) was the first to be removed, resulting in a RMB9 billion benefit to farmers in 2004. After two years of phasing-out, the government abolished the agricultural and animal husbandry taxes at the beginning of 2006. Taxes were increased on conversions of farmland to non-agricultural uses, but these have limited impacts on farmers. Exemption from various agricultural taxes has effectively reduced the amount farmers would otherwise have to pay and the absolute tax burden on farmers has been alleviated.

Investment in agriculture-related projects is a major instrument for China to achieve rural development targets and is by far the largest component in government budgetary support for agriculture. Projects include spending on production infrastructure, such as improved irrigation facilities, rural hydroelectric plants, pasture enclosures, research, and construction of agricultural high-technology parks. China also boosts farm investment through a system of 35,000 rural credit cooperatives and state-owned commercial and policy banks (e.g., the Agricultural Bank of China and the Agricultural Development Bank of China). These financial institutions have provided preferential loans to rural areas.

Notifications and shadow notifications, 1996–2008

The increase in agricultural subsidies in China in recent years raises the question of whether China has complied with its WTO commitment on domestic support for agriculture. As China was not a WTO member until late 2001, there was technically no need to notify domestic support for 1999–2001, but it did so in January 2006. Notifications for 2002–04, submitted in March 2010, were long overdue as has been the case for many other members.

Table 9.1 provides a summary of China's domestic support from 1996–2008. Data for 1996–2004 are drawn from China's accession

[1] Besides taxes, China also eliminated a myriad of fees levied on farmers to fund road construction, schools, and various other projects and services undertaken by village and township authorities (Gale, Lohmar, and Tuan 2005).

Table 9.1 *Summary of China's domestic support notifications and shadow notifications, 1995–2008*

	Notifications					
	1995	1996	1997	1998	1999	2000
	Million RMB					
Green box	na	112,178	131,254	210,815	184,335	207,899
Development programs	na	na	na	na	na	na
Blue box	na	—	—	—	—	—
Current Total AMS	na	—	—	—	—	—
Sum of AMS support[a]	na	-6,953	4,006	15,500	-95,801	-92,911
Product-specific	na	-34,980	-22,053	-18,622	-96,501	-93,656
Market Price Support	na	-34,980	-22,053	-18,622	-99,355	-97,159
Budget outlays	na	—	—	—	2,854	3,503
Non-product-specific	na	28,027	26,059	34,122	700	745
Total support	na	105,225	135,260	226,315	88,534	114,988
Value of production[b]		1,955,976	2,066,353	2,124,259	2,199,012	2,220,318
Bound Total AMS	na	zb	zb	zb	zb	zb

Notes: Small differences in totals are due to rounding. — indicates zero; na indicates China did not provide information for 1995 upon accession to the WTO in 2001 and is not eligible to use the Article 6.2 exemption; zb indicates China has an implied zero binding on CTAMS.

[a] Sums positive and negative values of market price support similar to India (Table 8.3), but unlike the EU (Table 3.1) and Brazil (Table 7.2) in which negative values are set equal to zero in the row Total *de minimis*.

[b] Based on producer prices (OECD 2009).

Sources: China's notifications to WTO and author's calculations.

and notification documents. These data are supplemented with shadow calculations drawing on more recent data and taking into account changes in policy. My calculations of the support levels utilize the methods laid out in the notifications. I was able to replicate historical support levels with a

				Shadow notifications			
2001	2002	2003	2004	2005	2006	2007	2008
242,331	252,117	257,963	308,493	329,733	359,901	386,473	397,107
na	na	na	na	na	na	na	na
—	—	—	—	—	—	—	—
—	—	—	—	—	—	—	—
-75,328	-38,537	-26,026	6,170	6,358	9,338	13,715	9,776
-76,076	-38,772	-27,309	4,195	—	—	—	—
-77,866	-40,058	-28,750	—	—	—	—	—
1,790	1,286	1,441	4,195	—	—	—	—
748	235	1,283	1,975	6,358	9,338	13,715	9,776
167,003	213,580	231,937	314,663	336,091	369,240	400,189	406,883
2,336,459	2,338,618	2,440,890	3,031,220	3,292,420	3,318,872	4,078,370	4,241,505
zb	zb	zb	zb	zb	zb	zb	zb

reasonable correspondence to the available notifications using national data sources and such international data resources as the OECD PSE analysis and database (2005, 2009) and the World Bank agricultural distortions project (Huang *et al.* 2007).

Based on the support estimates in Table 9.1, China's domestic support for the period through 2008 has been well below the limit agreed at its WTO accession. However, there are a number of interesting features that warrant further examination.

Green box support has increased in China as a result of increased public investment in the agricultural sector. In 2008, total green box support is estimated to have reached RMB397 billion (9.4 percent of the value of agricultural production), which is more than triple the 1996 figure (RMB112 billion, which was 5.7 percent of production value). Within

China's green box, infrastructural services (a major part of general services) and public stockholding for food security purposes are the two largest components through 2003 and in 2004 environmental payments quadruple (Table 9.2). Together these categories account for 85 percent of total green box support in 2004. China's expenditures for domestic food aid have dropped sharply while expenditures on disaster relief have increased. It has made no payments for income insurance programs or structural adjustment assistance (producer and resource retirement and investment aids). China classified the direct payments to grain producers starting in 2004 as decoupled income support and we do likewise in our shadow notifications through 2008, but whether these payments strictly meet the criteria can certainly be questioned. In the future, China will likely use green box subsidies to further strengthen direct payments to farmers, improve infrastructure and research, develop new grain varieties and technologies, address water shortages, and adjust agricultural production structures. However, spending on these programs will also be constrained by availability of funds.

China has a zero Bound Total AMS. Thus China can only provide AMS support to agricultural producers up to the relevant *de minimis* thresholds. In the case of China, this exemption is 8.5 percent of value of production as specified in its WTO accession agreement. Any support in the AMS category over the *de minimis* thresholds would violate China's WTO commitments. However, to date neither the product-specific *de minimis* thresholds nor the non-product-specific *de minimis* threshold have imposed real constraints on domestic support measures in China.

Although China's support level is far from the binding level of the *de minimis* thresholds, setting the threshold percentage was a major hurdle in the final phase of China's WTO membership negotiations. The dispute, in retrospect, was more procedural than substantive. When calculated using the WTO definitions and methodology, the domestic support level has been far below zero for product-specific support as a result of large, negative market price support (MPS) through 2003, zero non-exempt direct payments and limited other budgetary outlays (Table 9.3). Since 1999, China has only notified MPS for wheat, rice and corn and in 2004 it reported that administered prices had been eliminated for wheat and corn when protective prices were repealed. China also asserted in its notification for 2004 that eligible production was zero for all three of these grains. For rice, China argued that there was zero eligible quantity "since the market price was higher than the minimum procurement price, no procurement was actually made." However, procurements of all three grains by the State Administration of Grain continued.[2] The argument seems to stretch the definition of eligible quantity since the rules for calculating MPS do not take market prices into account in computing the relevant price gap when an administered price is announced, and rice procurement by the state grain bureau continued to be reported in its official database. In the shadow notifications, administered prices were included for rice and wheat based on China's policy decisions (the minimum procurement price for wheat is acknowledged to be established in 2005 in China's notification for 2004). I also assumed zero eligible production will be notified based on its notifications for 2002–04 – an assumption considered further in subsequent discussion of alternative measurements of support – and continued strong world prices for grains through 2008.

For non-product-specific support, given China's enormous agricultural sector, there is little chance that this type of support can surpass 8.5 percent of the total value of production. During 1996–2008, non-product-specific support, consisting of input and interest subsidies, never accounted for more than 2 percent of the total value of production. Given a total value of agricultural production cited of RMB4,242 billion for 2008, China could potentially provide up to a maximum of RMB721 billion of product-specific and non-product-specific AMS support combined.[3] Thus there appears to be substantial room for China to increase its AMS support. China may become a heavy user of *de minimis* provisions to shield support from being cut back, but that does not show up in its notifications through 2004 or in the shadow notifications through 2008.

China has given up the right as a developing country to exempt support described in Article 6.2 of the Agreement (certain development programs) from counting towards the Bound Total AMS. In its accession documents, China agreed to include the amounts of such support in the calculation of AMS. This was among the compromises China accepted in return for its WTO membership, which reflect elements of both WTO+ and WTO- provisions (Evenett and Braga 2005).[4]

[2] Procurements of grain during 2000–2004, showing rice procurements in 2004 as 21.4 million metric tons, are available at www.chinagrain.gov.cn/n16/n1062/n1452/n1497/3530265.html.

[3] A series on total value of production China reported to the Committee on Agriculture in 2010 is quite close to the series provided in Table 9.1 through 2007, but gives a value of RMB5,280 billion for 2008. Thus, the above estimates of the *de minimis* thresholds for 2008 are conservative.

[4] WTO+ implies additional obligations that go beyond the ones applying to the incumbent members (WTO+ commitments) and WTO– denotes latitude regarding obligations applying to other WTO members (WTO– rights).

Table 9.2 *Composition of China's green box notifications and shadow notifications, 1995–2008*

	Notifications					
	1995	1996	1997	1998	1999	2000
	Million RMB					
General services	na	66,648	74,542	135,949	109,110	121,230
Public stockholding/ food security	na	28,773	35,335	51,027	47,596	53,799
Domestic food aid	na	2,012	1,875	1,766	2,640	2,360
Decoupled income support	na	—	—	—	—	—
Income insurance/ safety nets	na	—	—	—	—	—
Disaster relief	na	3,791	4,042	5,453	5,023	5,317
Producer retirement	na	—	—	—	—	—
Resource retirement	na	—	—	—	—	—
Investment aids	na	—	—	—	—	—
Environmental payments	na	4,954	5,460	5,620	7,097	12,700
Regional assistance	na	6,000	10,000	11,000	12,869	12,493
Total	na	112,178	131,254	210,815	184,335	207,899

Notes: — indicates zero; na indicates China did not provide information for 1995 upon accession to the WTO in 2001.
Sources: China's notifications to WTO and author's calculations.

Like other members, China can exempt blue box payments from CTAMS. In China's notifications and the shadow notifications, blue box payments are zero because China has not provided such subsidies. However, should future support provided in the current forms approach or even exceed the *de minimis* exemption thresholds for AMSs, China may have to redesign its support programs to remain WTO compliant. One way of doing so without cutting spending is to switch from the more

				Shadow notifications			
2001	2002	2003	2004	2005	2006	2007	2008
145,045	151,418	154,275	165,602	164,510	181,783	197,080	206,838
59,685	53,148	54,526	42,061	53,746	57,650	63,564	63,043
683	401	178	132	93	94	82	82
—	—	—	11,646	13,200	14,200	15,100	15,100
—	—	—	—	—	—	—	—
5,956	5,997	10,920	9,336	12,538	18,204	21,709	18,400
—	—	—	—	—	—	—	—
—	—	—	—	—	—	—	—
—	—	—	—	—	—	—	—
17,475	26,243	21,627	61,624	63,473	65,377	67,338	69,358
13,487	14,910	16,437	18,092	22,173	22,593	21,600	24,286
242,331	252,117	257,963	308,493	329,733	359,901	386,473	397,107

trade/production-distorting AMS support instruments to less distorting blue box payments. However, through 2008 China has not reported any blue box support.

Alternative measurements of support

Direct payments

Controversies arise from different interpretations of subsidy policies and their classification in WTO notifications. Alternative subsidy definitions

Table 9.3 *Composition of China's AMS notifications and shadow notifications, 1995–2008*

		Notifications					
	Reference[a]	1995	1996	1997	1998	1999	2000
Product-specific AMS							
Market Price Support[b,c]	*RMB/metric ton*	*Applied administered price (RMB/metric ton)*					
Wheat	1,698	na	1,480	1,410	1,340	1,254	1,136
Rice	2,659	na	2,161	2,038	1,893	1,152	1,152
Corn	1,199	na	1,120	1,170	1,120	926	936
		Eligible production (thousand metric tons)					
Wheat		na	15,000	46,002	27,956	37,800	35,050
Rice		na	15,750	35,105	25,620	45,100	44,900
Corn		na	12,500	26,922	38,674	53,500	37,250
		Total production (thousand metric tons)					
Wheat		na	110,580	123,276	109,709	113,879	99,637
Rice		na	195,103	200,735	198,713	198,487	187,908
Corn		na	127,470	104,310	132,954	128,084	106,001
		Market Price Support (million RMB)[c]					
Wheat		na	−6,075	−11,223	−6,541	−16,783	−19,698
Rice		na	−17,647	−9,970	−12,011	−67,966	−67,664
Corn		na	−5,767	2,401	6,171	−14,606	−9,797
Other crops[d]		na	−5,491	−3,261	−6,241	—	—
Budget outlays[e]		na	—	—	—	2,854	3,503
Product-specific threshold		*8.5% of value of production (million RMB)*					
Wheat		na	15,227	14,695	12,420	11,685	8,957
Rice[f]		na	26,791	23,666	22,602	19,095	16,528
Corn		na	9,617	7,590	9,213	7,632	7,221
		Million RMB					
Non-product-specific AMS		na	28,027	26,059	34,122	700	745
Input subsidies[g]		na	26,559	24,524	33,242	205	151
Interest subsidies[h]		na	1,468	1,535	880	495	594
		8.5% of value of production (million RMB)					
Non-product-specific threshold		na	166,258	175,640	180,562	186,916	188,727

Notes: — indicates zero; na indicates China did not provide information for 1995 upon accession to the WTO in 2001, it also denotes that administered prices were not notified for wheat or corn in 2004 and it was indicated they would not be notified for corn in subsequent years; ne indicates not estimated.

				Shadow notifications			
2001	2002	2003	2004	2005	2006	2007	2008
1,124	1,240	1,100	na	1,380	1,410	1,410	1,490
1,124	1,080	1,040	1,500	1,500	1,500	1,500	1,590
918	880	860	na	na	na	na	na
38,600	34,850	20,460	—	—	—	—	—
30,600	10,980	7,470	—	—	—	—	—
31,100	21,190	13,040	—	—	—	—	—
93,874	90,290	86,488	91,952	97,445	108,466	109,298	112,460
177,580	174,539	160,656	179,088	180,588	181,718	186,034	191,900
114,094	121,310	115,830	130,287	139,365	151,603		165,910
-22,156	-15,961	-12,235	na	—	—	—	—
-46,971	-17,337	-12,094	—	—	—	—	—
-8,739	-6,760	-4,421	na	na	na	na	na
—	—	—	—	—	—	—	—
1,790	1,286	1,441	4,195	ne	ne	ne	ne
8,380	8,949	8,976	12,037	11,432	13,205	14,110	14,674
16,205	1,779	16,523	25,285	23,842	24,912	26,802	27,874
7,764	11,682	12,346	16,689	12,154	14,131	16,275	16,926
748	235	1,282	1,975	6,358	9,338	13,715	9,776
148	168	1,249	1,576	6,358	9,338	13,715	9,776
600	67	33	399	ne	ne	ne	ne
198,599	198,783	207,476	257,654	279,856	282,104	346,661	360,528

Notes to table 9.3 *(cont.)*

[a] External reference price, average 1996–98.
[b] In calculating the Market Price Support, actual border prices are used as reference prices for 1996–98, and fixed, 1996–98 average border prices are used as reference prices for 1999–2008.
[c] Protective price system as repealed in the 2004 notification with a subsequent minimum procurement price system introduced for rice in 2004 and for wheat in 2005. For 2004, rice eligible quantity was reported as zero explained by "since the market price was higher than the minimum procurement price, no procurement was actually made."
[d] Temporary price support for cotton was provided during 1996–98.
[e] Product-specific support provided through interest subsidies for national cotton stockholdings during 1999–2004. During 2002–04, small subsidies were also notified for rice, wheat, corn and soybeans either for protective price procurement or improved crop strains and seeds. Budgetary outlays are not estimated for later years due to lack of data.
[f] Value of rice production notified apparently incorrectly as only RMB 20,927 million in 2002.
[g] Shadow input subsidy estimates based on notified 2004 level and growth rates from price subsidies for means of production provided to agricultural input manufacturers including fertilizer, pesticide and mulching film firms as reported by OECD.
[h] Interest subsidies were provided to agricultural producers through loans with preferential interest rates (1996–2004). Due to lack of data, interest subsidies are not reported for later years.
Sources: China's notifications to WTO and author's calculations.

could affect the calculated levels of support and make otherwise non-binding commitments become binding. WTO members tend to have incentives either not to notify or to mis-notify trade-distorting support components because a notification of a measure as providing AMS support amounts to admitting that support under the measure is subject to the Bound Total AMS. Typically, members choose a notification scheme that best makes them appear compliant with WTO rules and then wait to see whether their claims are challenged in the Committee on Agriculture or through dispute settlement. Only a small number of disputes have been initiated at the WTO in regard to domestic support (see Chapter 2). While the reporting of domestic support of developed countries attracts most scrutiny, non-notification or mis-notification issues also arise with respect to developing countries.

For China, one issue is whether its direct payments to grain farmers meet WTO green box criteria. Although these payments have been notified in the green box, and therefore exempt from any limits, it is far from clear whether they should be so categorized. According to the Agreement, for a program to be classified as green box support, in addition to the fundamental requirements, a program has to meet specific policy criteria in Annex 2 of the Agreement (see Appendix A). If China's direct payment program does not meet these criteria, the payments must be reported to the WTO as AMS support or as blue box payments.

It appears that direct payments in China would violate a number of the green box provisions for decoupled income support. Various methods have been used to provide these payments to farmers, ranging from fixed subsidies not tied to the current year's production or marketing to those that are tied to market prices or production. Fixed subsidies were based on either historical household deliveries of grain to the government, historical grain production from the household's allocated land based on local tax records, or the actual production or marketing of grain. Thus, the fixed subsidies cannot be completely classified as green box measures as some of them are likely linked to production. In some provinces, price subsidies were used instead of fixed subsidies. Price subsidies paid farmers the difference between a target price set by the government and a market price. This subsidy resembles two product-specific support components reported in the US WTO notification: marketing loan benefits when all outputs are eligible or countercyclical payments when only fixed base acreage and yields are applicable (see Chapter 4).

Using payment rates reported by Gale, Lohmar, and Tuan (2005) for wheat, rice and corn, Table 9.4 shows the payments to farmers for these crops in 2004 and 2005 assuming all production was included. The total for 2004 closely matches the level of decoupled income support notified by China of RMB11.6 billion. An alternative inclusion of these payments in the product's AMS would not bring it above the *de minimis* threshold. However, for wheat the grain payments are large enough to exceed 40 percent of the threshold. Through 2008, the direct grain payments increased by about 14 percent compared to 2005 (Table 9.2) so they remain below the allowed *de minimis* thresholds. If in the future China strengthens its direct payments and the MPS turns positive, both of which may occur, the product-specific *de minimis* threshold could become a binding factor on grain payments if they are classified as non-exempt, product-specific AMS support.

The argument that the direct payments to grain farmers in China are green box measures is even less convincing in light of the WTO panel and Appellate Body rulings in the *United States – Cotton* case. As described by Brink in Chapter 2, Brazil brought a complaint against certain aspects of the cotton policies of the United States. One issue was whether the direct

Table 9.4 *China's direct payments to grain farmers, 2004 and 2005*

	Payment rate	Total grain production	Implied payments[a]	MPS	*De minimis* threshold
	RMB/metric ton	*Thousand metric tons*	*Million RMB*		
2004					
Wheat	48.0	91,952	4,416	—	12,037
Rice	27.3	179,088	4,893	—	25,285
Corn	17.4	130,287	2,265	—	16,689
Total		401,327	11,574	—	54,011
2005					
Wheat	50.5	97,445	4,922	—	11,432
Rice	29.8	180,588	5,383	—	23,842
Corn	20.7	139,365	2,885	—	12,154
Total		417,398	13,190	—	47,428

Notes: — indicates zero.

[a] Assumes payments received for all production.

Source: Author's calculations.

payments notified by the US in the green box were linked to the type of production and thus should be counted in determining the support levels that the US had provided to cotton producers. As the payments were conditional on not planting certain commodities (specifically fruits, vegetables, and wild rice) on the land area upon which payments were based, the panel concluded that the US direct payments did not fully conform to the rules for green box decoupled income support. By the same argument, Chinese grain payments would not satisfy those green box requirements because farmers have to be current grain producers in order to receive the payments.

Even if direct payments in China can be classified as decoupled income support *de jure*, the question of whether they alter farmers' planting decisions and stimulate production *de facto* remains controversial. Figure 9.3 shows the amount of direct payments and grain production in recent years. The two series clearly exhibit some correlation after the direct payment scheme was introduced in 2004. There have been no studies examining the nature of direct payments in China, partly because of the novelty of the policy and partly because of data constraints. However, various studies on payment programs in the US may shed some light on this issue. In general, these studies have presented mixed results, with

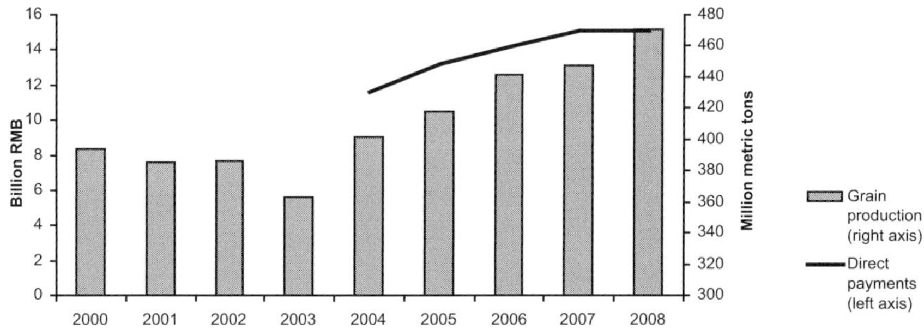

Figure 9.3 China's direct payments to grain farmers and levels of production
Source: Author's calculations from national statistics.

some arguing that the effects of the most decoupled payments are negligible (e.g., Burfisher and Hopkins 2003) and others showing varying degrees of distortion (e.g., Goodwin and Mishra 2006). The mechanisms for production distortion identified in the literature typically include wealth effects that impact attitudes towards risks, decisions on leisure and savings, overcoming credit constraints or other input market imperfections, coverage of short-run production costs, and farmers' expectation about future government decisions on agricultural policy (Abler and Blandford 2005).

Measuring market price support

Several issues arise in relation to notified MPS, as have been discussed for other countries. The notified level of MPS is based on the gap between the annual administered (support) price and the fixed external reference price. The external reference price period for China of 1996–98 differs from that of other WTO members whose base period is 1986–88. China also notifies in its domestic currency. This could potentially pose a problem for China, where inflation rates have followed a cyclical pattern. For example, between the base years 1996–98 and 2002, China experienced mild inflation and even deflation, but since 2003 inflation rates have increased, with price rises reaching 12.3 percent in 2007 for agricultural commodities. Since the external reference prices are fixed in domestic currency terms, and if inflation is not accounted for, the MPS would also follow a cyclical upward trend if administered prices correlate with general domestic prices. This potential problem, however, can be alleviated if WTO members allow China to exceed its commitment as a result of excessive rates of inflation according to Article 18.4 of the Agreement.

The Agreement leaves ambiguity regarding whether the quantity eligible to receive the administered price is total production, the surplus that is sold through markets, or the quantity that is procured by the government under the price support mechanisms. Some members including China (through 2003) have based their eligible production on the quantity procured, whereas other countries have used total production. The logic of using total production in these computations is that the government-designated agency is bound to buy whatever is brought to the market at the pre-announced support price. This was also the requirement made clear in China's protective price policy for grains.[5] However, there is a limit on this because the quantity brought to the market will not be more than the marketable surplus, given that self-consumption accounts for a large share of the output of basic foodstuffs in a country like China. In addition, budget constraints preclude the possibility of unlimited purchases.

The Agreement requires each country to identify products with administered prices, which are those for which MPS needs to be calculated. The administered prices apply in addition to any import barriers or export subsidies that are already in place to keep domestic prices high. For example, China reports administered price support for grains, particularly wheat, rice and corn. However, the grain price support schemes are sometimes inoperative (except for the mandatory procurement portion) as in some years market prices have been well above support prices because of domestic supply and demand conditions and the effects of border measures. In its notification for 2004, China chose to report zero eligible production for rice on this basis, as described above.

Table 9.5 compares estimates of MPS based on different definitions of eligible production and domestic and international prices. Two alternatives are considered through 2008: use of the procured quantities as eligible production and use of total production. For the calculations in Table 9.5 it is also assumed that administered prices are in effect through 2008 for three crops – rice, wheat and corn. Calculations using total production amplify the MPS amount as compared to those using procured quantities. In the notifications, China selected smaller eligible quantities

[5] For example, in the State Council's Decision on Deepening the Reform of the Grain Circulation System, the government required the grain bureaus to purchase all grain that producers wished to sell at the state-set protective price (MOA 2001).

Table 9.5 *China's Market Price Support under different assumptions, 1996–2008*

	Procurements			Total production		
	WTO MPS	Economic MPS	Difference	WTO MPS	Economic MPS	Difference
	Million RMB					
1996	-34,980	-8,979	-26,001	-327,397	-98,855	-228,542
1997	-22,053	-12,829	-9,224	-74,536	-73,292	-1,244
1998	-18,622	-7,809	-10,813	-105,391	-75,142	-30,249
1999	-99,354	-23,646	-75,708	-384,649	-97,514	-287,135
2000	-97,159	-2,410	-94,749	-367,052	-11,283	-355,768
2001	-77,867	2,813	-80,679	-358,529	35,558	-394,087
2002	-64,001	2,817	-66,818	-291,801	26,489	-318,290
2003	-48,137	7,383	-55,520	-218,726	43,045	-261,772
2004	-39,228	5,175	-44,403	-261,219	56,994	-318,213
2005	-50,511	5,168	-55,678	-272,403	21,145	-293,548
2006	-48,046	19,567	-67,613	-271,370	48,310	-319,679
2007	-46,421	3,183	-49,604	-272,059	16,532	-288,591
2008	-37,450	-19,661	-17,789	-240,142	-178,247	-61,896

Source: Author's calculations.

based on procurements in the calculation of the MPS through 2003, which gives it more flexibility in expanding its price support. The effect of different interpretations of eligible production on China's AMSs and on WTO commitment compliance, however, is negligible because the MPS is negative, as is the AMS for all products in both cases and no AMS enters the calculation of CTAMS.[6] But it could become more important whether procured quantities are used as eligible quantities for MPS calculations if administered prices rise and the MPS amounts move to positive territory.

Table 9.5 also shows that the use of annual domestic producer prices and world reference prices (shown in the columns labeled economic MPS)

[6] Using total production instead of the procured amount in the MPS calculation for the base period could have changed a member's Bound Total AMS. However this would not affect China because MPS amounts were negative as were the AMSs, resulting in the zero CTAMS established for the 1996–98 base period.

indicates more protection (or less disprotection). The notified WTO MPS undercounts economic protection compared to this economic measure. This occurs primarily because of the weaker world prices relative to those in the base period (1996–98). The impact of low world reference prices is particularly evident between 2001 and 2007 when the MPS amounts based on actual reference prices became positive whereas those based on fixed base reference price were negative. The economic MPS based on annual prices subsequently turned negative in 2008 following the sharp increase in world commodity prices.

For China, the higher external reference prices for the base period 1996–98 compared to 1986–88 for other members and an undervalued currency for converting world prices into domestic currency terms have meant smaller MPS amounts notified to the WTO than otherwise and thus no difficulty staying below the *de minimis* thresholds. If world commodity prices were to resume their secular decline over time, the implied support from an administered price (along with consumer transfers and border protection) will increase, even though the calculated MPS component of the AMS will not. This may have implications for the effectiveness of China's WTO commitments as a constraint on trade-distorting support.

Appreciation of the Chinese currency has an effect on these calculations. Between 2005 and 2007, the Chinese RMB nominal exchange rate appreciated 12 percent against the US dollar and it remained under pressure to revalue further (Goldstein 2007). An undervaluation of the currency may remain in the range of 20 percent or more (Frankel 2006; Cheng and Orden 2007). Were the appreciation trend to resume, it would make the economic MPS (based on the prevailing exchange rate and world reference prices) diverge further from the notified WTO MPS (using a fixed reference price calculated with the exchange rate and world prices in the base period). The magnitude of the difference will depend on how much the world reference price and the exchange rate change and the degree to which these changes are passed through to domestic and administered prices.

Adjustments in non-product-specific AMS support

Reported input subsidies

China reports only very small non-product-specific support in its notifications for the years after 1998. In contrast, measured input subsidies as reported by OECD have risen sharply in China since 2004. These subsidies are reported to average nearly RMB65 billion during 2004–08, much higher than the notified non-product-specific support shown in Tables 9.1 and 9.3, but still less than 2.5 percent of the total value of agricultural production. Such differences, which arise for other countries as well, are indicative of the issues and judgments – such as what measures to include and how to assess the amounts and distribution of benefits they provide – inherent in assessing subsidy levels.

Notification of government budgetary outlays to state-owned agricultural input manufacturers (such as fertilizer, pesticide or mulching film producers which have received subsidies in China) as non-product-specific support is permitted by the Agreement, although it over-simplifies the calculations.[7] In China, government subsidies to input firms are provided through a combination of direct budgetary payments, VAT rebates (e.g., fertilizer firms are generally given a 50 percent VAT rebate), cash subsidies to firms producing or importing these inputs, and implicit subsidies through lowered transportation and electricity charges. It is thus difficult to assess the total government subsidies (both direct and indirect) that benefit farmers, who usually feel the effects through reduced ex-factory or purchase prices of agricultural inputs.

It is also difficult to determine how much government subsidies actually end up with farmers. Some analysts speculate that in China much of the government subsidies are used to cover losses resulting from inefficient operations; others argue that the subsidies have become part of the profits, even though the profit margin allowed by the government is relatively small. In both cases, however, subsidies may not be fully transferred into lowered input prices that farmers pay. According to the Agreement, subsidy measures directed at agricultural processors "shall be included to the extent that such measures benefit the producers of the basic agricultural products" (Annex 3, paragraph 7). Thus, assuming parallel treatment of input subsidies and agricultural processors, one could argue a downward adjustment of budgetary outlays has to be made to reflect actual subsidies to farmers.

One would expect that the benefits of government input subsidies are distributed between input producers and input consumers (farmers in this case) with the share going to each group depending on supply and demand

[7] Paragraph 13 in Annex 3 of the Agreement stipulates that "Other non-exempt measures, including input subsidies and other measures such as marketing-cost reduction measures: the value of such measures shall be measured using government budgetary outlays..." but it also allows for the use of a price-gap technique (see Appendix A).

elasticities. A rough estimate of subsidies that accrue to farmers can be made by comparing the subsidized prices with the higher, subsidy-free prices. This is consistent with the Agreement provision "where the use of budgetary outlays does not reflect the full extent of the subsidy concerned, the basis for calculating the subsidy shall be the gap between the price of the subsidized good or service and a representative market price for a similar good or service multiplied by the quantity of the good or service" (Annex 3, paragraph 13). In the absence of other distorting factors, the representative market (or subsidy-free) prices would be the relevant world prices, adjusted for transportation and distribution costs. This price-gap method can be applied to estimate subsidies that reduce the end-use price of inputs, omitting from consideration other measures that actually raise the price of inputs to the users. These other measures typically refer to border measures, which, when present, would make subsidy-free prices differ from the comparable world reference prices.

In China, the input manufacturing industry has long been protected from foreign competition (Qiao *et al.* 2003). Imports of agricultural inputs such as fertilizers are subject to TRQs and state trading, which have kept domestic prices high. In some years, domestic agricultural input prices are higher than world reference prices, even after subsidization (and thus the net policy effect is a taxation of consumers of agricultural inputs). In this case, world prices cannot be used as a proper reference price to gauge price gaps as a result of subsidies. Instead, counterfactual simulations are sometimes needed in order to obtain the correct subsidy-free prices. One such counterfactual assessment, based on the Policy Analysis Matrix for Chinese agriculture, indicated that subsidies reduced input prices by between 13 and 30 percent on average between 1996–98 (Fang and Beghin 2000).

Agricultural taxes

Non-product-specific support needs to be further adjusted to take into account various missing components in the notifications, including agricultural taxes and subsidies related to irrigation, electricity and fuel. China's agricultural tax rate on farmers stood as high as an average of 8 percent until recently. Table 9.6 shows the various agricultural taxes from 1990 to 2007. Agricultural taxes burdening farmers have subsequently been eliminated, as discussed above.

Not only were agricultural taxes burdensome but they were levied differently from taxes on other sectors of the economy. For instance, China's urban taxes are generally levied on net profits, which allows adjustments for costs. In contrast, agricultural taxes were based on the amount of cultivated land and number of family members; hence farmers were obliged

Table 9.6 *Agricultural taxes in China, 1990–2005*

	Total	Agricultural/ animal husbandry taxes	Contract tax	Tax on special agricultural products	Tax on use of cultivated land
	Million RMB				
1990	8,786	5,962	118	1,249	1,457
1991	9,065	5,665	189	1,425	1,786
1992	11,917	7,010	361	1,624	2,922
1993	12,574	7,265	621	1,753	2,935
1994	23,149	11,951	1,182	6,369	3,647
1995	27,809	12,812	1,826	9,717	3,454
1996	36,946	18,206	2,520	13,100	3,120
1997	39,748	18,238	3,234	15,027	3,249
1998	39,880	17,867	5,899	12,779	3,335
1999	42,350	16,308	9,596	13,143	3,303
2000	46,531	16,817	13,108	13,074	3,532
2001	48,170	16,432	15,708	12,197	3,833
2002	71,785	32,149	23,907	9,995	5,734
2003	87,177	33,422	35,805	8,960	8,990
2004	90,219	24,200	54,010	—	12,009
2005	93,640	5,941	73,514	—	14,185

Note: — indicates zero.
Source: NBS (2006).

to pay the same amount of taxes both in prosperous and lean years. According to the Agreement, specific agricultural levies or fees paid by producers should be deducted from the AMS (Annex 3, paragraph 4). As contract taxes and taxes on the use of cultivated land do not directly affect farmers, the deduction should at least include agricultural taxes, animal husbandry taxes and taxes on special agricultural products. These taxes added up to RMB42.4 billion in 2003, but dropped sharply to less than RMB6 billion in 2005. China has not deducted agricultural taxes from its notified non-product-specific support and I do not make any adjustments in the shadow notifications.

Non-reported input subsidies

Irrigation subsidies are not included in China's notifications, even though they may constitute a significant component in China's non-product-specific support. In China, irrigation accounts for more than two-thirds of total water use, although its share has been decreasing as a result of rising competition from uses in non-agricultural sectors (Crook and Diao 2000). Major irrigation systems have been built and operated by the Ministry of Water Resources and local Water Resource Bureaus. Typically, irrigation water users are charged only a fraction of the cost of supplying water to them. The charges do not cover operations and maintenance (O&M) costs, and they never cover any of the substantial capital costs incurred in developing water collection and distribution systems. In some areas, charges for water are on a volumetric basis; in others, charges are based on the area irrigated rather than on the amount used. In both cases, however, charges are paid by townships, villages, and irrigation groups, but not by farmers, thus increasing incentives for overuse. For privately financed irrigation (e.g., wells and groundwater delivery systems), energy for water pumping is often subsidized.

A rough estimate of the extent of subsidies for irrigation water can be made from available information. Total annual irrigation costs are the sum of capital investments and O&M costs. Since data on annual depreciation of the capital stock are not available, average annual capital investment is used to approximate annual depreciation. In China, new irrigation land has been created each year during 1996–2007 except for 2003. The average unit cost of supplying irrigation can be assumed to be $5,300 per hectare (1995 prices), an Asian average according to Jones (1995). Annual depreciation, therefore, is approximated by the product of the amount of new irrigation land and the unit cost. Operations and maintenance costs can be roughly estimated as 10 percent of the annual capital investment (Repetto 1986) although these assumptions result in low estimates of depreciation and O&M costs in years when investment declines. Assuming that cost recovery is only 65 percent of operations and maintenance costs, total annual irrigation subsidies in China can be estimated and are presented in Table 9.7. For the period 1996–2007, an estimated average of RMB31 billion is provided to irrigation annually in China. Note that this estimate does not include the opportunity cost of water in alternative uses or the associated environmental externalities.

In China, agricultural users are charged discounted rates for electricity and fuels, relative to other users.[8] Subsidies for agricultural energy uses, however, are not included in the notified support and there are no

[8] Lower electricity prices apply only to agricultural production use not residential use.

Table 9.7 *Estimated subsidies for irrigation in China, 1996–2007*

	Annual increase in irrigated land	Annual capital investment	Annual O&M costs	Total annual costs	Annual irrigation subsidies
	Thousand hectares	*Million RMB*			
1996	1,100	48,481	4,848	53,329	50,177
1997	857	37,657	3,766	41,423	38,976
1998	1,057	46,385	4,638	51,023	48,008
1999	863	37,856	3,786	41,641	39,181
2000	662	29,042	2,904	31,946	30,059
2001	429	18,822	1,882	20,704	19,481
2002	106	4,628	463	5,091	4,790
2003	—	—	—	—	—
2004	464	20,363	2,036	22,399	21,075
2005	551	23,919	2,392	26,311	24,756
2006	721	30,469	3,047	33,516	31,536
2007	768	30,970	3,097	34,067	32,053
Average	677	29,684	2,968	32,652	30,723

Notes: Annual depreciation is estimated by annual capital investment. O&M costs are assumed to be 10 percent of annual investments and cost recovery to be 65 percent of O&M costs. — indicates that estimates for 2003 are not available due to a decrease in irrigated land.
Source: Author's calculations.

budgetary outlay figures available. Similar to other input subsidies discussed above, electricity and fuel subsidies can be measured by the difference between actual prices and reference prices that would prevail in an undistorted market. The reference price can be either the border price for internationally traded energy products (i.e., fuels) or the cost of production for non-traded ones (i.e., electricity). Because of the existence of other distortions that affect the border price as well as the difficulty of obtaining production cost data, a substitute reference price based on the average domestic market energy price is used to make an estimate of the subsidies. This is in accordance with the Agreement, which stipulates that the basis for calculating the subsidy in the absence of budgetary outlays "shall be the gap between the price of the subsidized good or service and a representative market price for a similar good or service multiplied by the quantity of the good or service." However, this price wedge method only captures the market transfers from other energy consumers to agricultural users, or cross-subsidization, which may well underestimate the actual magnitude of the subsidies. Table 9.8 shows electricity subsidies for agricultural uses for 1996–2005.[9]

The inclusion of non-reported subsidies would significantly increase the level of non-product-specific support by China. When only irrigation and electricity subsidies are taken into account, an average of RMB54 billion would be added. However, even if these subsidies were to be reported, the non-product-specific support in the notification would still be much smaller than the *de minimis* thresholds (averaging RMB233 billion for 1996–2008) resulting from China's large value of agricultural production. However, if all non-reported input subsidies were included in the notifications, China would have less room to extend new non-product-specific support to its farmers.

Domestic support projections, 2009–2016

The rapid evolution of China's agricultural support policies has become an important element in international trade policy debates, along with continued discussion of farm policy in developed countries where subsidies are most prominent. Looking ahead, it appears that a reversal of the subsidy-increasing policies in China is unlikely, given the economic progress the country is making. Rather, there are indications that the subsidies will be continued and even strengthened in the coming years. Assuming that China's agricultural policies evolve as expected, one can ask whether its projected support will violate the relevant disciplines on agricultural domestic support contained in the Agreement or the rules and commitments that might be negotiated in the Doha Round.

Table 9.9 shows a projection of domestic support notification through 2016. I continue to assume that direct payments to grain farmers are notified in the green box. I further assume that China will not report any support under the blue box, although it may shift support into this category as a result of higher levels of AMS support, particularly MPS. Subsidies related to irrigation, electricity and fuel from non-product-specific support are excluded because robust estimates are not available; they were not reported in the previous notifications by China, and may not be reported

[9] Fuel subsidies and more recent electricity subsidies are not reported due to data constraints.

Table 9.8 *Estimated agricultural electricity subsidies in China, 1996–2005*

	Agricultural usage	Electricity price			Subsidies
		Average	Agriculture	Difference	
	Billion kWh	*RMB/kWh*			*Million RMB*
1996	168	0.51	0.41	0.10	16,765
1997	198	0.49	0.39	0.10	19,024
1998	204	0.48	0.39	0.09	19,220
1999	217	0.46	0.37	0.09	19,603
2000	242	0.45	0.36	0.09	21,364
2001	261	0.45	0.36	0.09	23,030
2002	299	0.43	0.35	0.08	25,238
2003	343	0.43	0.35	0.08	28,944
2004	393	0.40	0.32	0.08	30,847
2005	438	0.35	0.28	0.07	30,029
Average	276	0.45	0.36	0.09	23,407

Source: Author's calculations.

in the future. Projections of non-product-specific support are based on the subsidies for fertilizer, pesticides and other inputs reported by OECD, which are higher than China's notified support levels as discussed above. The projection of the green box, non-product-specific support, the quantities of production, and the values of production are linear extrapolations from the period 1996–2008. Projected non-product-specific AMS support increases in nominal value but remains well below the *de minimis* threshold.

The remaining analysis shown in Table 9.9 focuses on projected MPS. Two administered price scenarios are considered (high versus moderate administered prices) and the scenarios include up to five supported products. The scenario designs follow recent world commodity market developments. From China's domestic policy deliberations, I base these projections on projections of procured quantities, as procurements were used through 2003 in China's notifications and are discussed above for an alternative notification approach for subsequent years. Clearly, if China continues to notify zero eligible production as it did for 2004, its MPS components of product-specific AMS values will be zero, so no issue of staying below its *de minimis* thresholds would arise on the basis of MPS.

Table 9.9 *Projected levels of China's domestic support, 2009–16*

		2009	2010	2011	2012	2013	2014	2015	2016
		Million RMB							
Green box[a]		383,591	403,370	423,148	442,927	462,706	482,485	502,264	522,043
Non-product-specific AMS support[a]		59,772	64,247	68,722	73,197	77,672	82,147	86,622	91,097
Non-product-specific *de minimis* threshold		324,475	353,214	368,364	383,515	398,665	413,815	428,965	444,115
Product-specific MPS									
	Reference price	*High administered prices (RMB/metric ton)*[b]							
Wheat	1,698	1,788	1,788	1,788	1,788	2,146	2,146	2,146	2,146
Rice	2,659	1,908	1,908	1,908	1,908	2,290	2,290	2,290	2,290
Corn	1,199	1,355	1,355	1,355	1,355	1,626	1,626	1,626	1,626
Cotton	14,584	11,000	11,000	11,000	11,000	13,200	13,200	13,200	13,200
Soybean	2,175	3,500	3,500	3,500	3,500	4,200	4,200	4,200	4,200
		Moderate administered prices (RMB/metric ton)[b]							
Wheat		1,639	1,639	1,639	1,639	1,803	1,803	1,803	1,803
Rice		1,749	1,749	1,749	1,749	1,924	1,924	1,924	1,924
Corn		1,242	1,242	1,242	1,242	1,366	1,366	1,366	1,366
Cotton		10,083	10,083	10,083	10,083	11,092	11,092	11,092	11,092
Soybean		3,208	3,208	3,208	3,208	3,529	3,529	3,529	3,529

	Eligible production (thousand metric tons)[a]							
Wheat	53,225	55,201	57,177	59,153	61,129	63,106	65,082	67,058
Rice	21,349	20,510	19,670	18,831	17,991	17,152	16,313	15,473
Corn	45,089	46,295	47,500	48,705	49,911	51,116	52,321	53,526
Cotton	7,573	7,873	8,174	8,474	8,774	9,075	9,375	9,675
Soybean	17,580	17,850	18,119	18,388	18,658	18,927	19,196	19,466
	Market Price Support with high administered prices (million RMB)							
Wheat	4,790	4,968	5,146	5,324	27,362	28,246	29,131	30,015
Rice	−16,033	−15,403	−14,772	−14,142	−6,646	−6,336	−6,026	−5,716
Corn	7,026	7,214	7,402	7,590	21,302	21,816	22,330	22,845
Cotton	−27,142	−28,218	−29,295	−30,371	−12,144	−12,559	−12,975	−13,391
Soybean	23,297	23,654	24,011	24,368	37,785	38,331	38,876	39,422
	Market Price Support with moderate administered prices (million RMB)							
Wheat	−3,140	−3,257	−3,373	−3,490	6,412	6,620	6,827	7,034
Rice	−19,428	−18,664	−17,900	−17,136	−13,225	−12,608	−11,991	−11,374
Corn	1,936	1,987	2,039	2,091	8,341	8,542	8,744	8,945
Cotton	−34,084	−35,436	−36,787	−38,139	−30,643	−31,692	−32,741	−33,790
Soybean	18,170	18,448	18,726	19,005	25,269	25,634	25,999	26,363
Product-specific *de minimis* thresholds	*8.5% of value of production (million RMB)*							
Wheat	13,207	12,204	12,252	12,300	12,349	12,397	12,445	12,493
Rice	25,086	24,811	25,173	25,534	25,896	26,258	26,620	26,982
Corn	15,233	15,301	15,811	16,321	16,831	17,341	17,851	18,360
Cotton	8,065	8,594	8,971	9,347	9,724	10,100	10,477	10,853
Soybean	3,463	3,862	3,978	4,093	4,209	4,325	4,440	4,556

Table 9.9 (*cont.*)

	2009	2010	2011	2012	2013	2014	2015	2016
Support in excess of *de minimis* thresholds	*High administered prices (million RMB)*							
Wheat	—	—	—	—	27,362	28,246	29,131	30,015
Rice	—	—	—	—	—	—	—	—
Corn	—	—	—	—	21,302	21,816	22,330	22,845
Cotton	—	—	—	—	—	—	—	—
Soybean	23,297	23,654	24,011	24,368	37,785	38,331	38,876	39,422
	Moderate administered prices (million RMB)							
Wheat	—	—	—	—	—	—	—	—
Rice	—	—	—	—	—	—	—	—
Corn	—	—	—	—	—	—	—	—
Cotton	—	—	—	—	—	—	—	—
Soybean	18,170	18,448	18,726	19,005	25,269	25,634	25,999	26,363

Notes: — indicates zero.

[a] See text for discussion of projections.

[b] High administered price scenario assumes an increase of 20 percent for 2009–12 and a further 20 percent for 2013–16. Moderate administered price scenario assumes an increase of 10 percent for 2009–12 and a further 10 percent for 2013–16.

Source: Author's calculations.

Subsequent to the commodity price boom in 2007–08, the international prices of key commodities were forecast to remain above levels from the earlier 2000s consistently through 2016 (USDA 2009). Strong global economic growth, increased oil prices, and strong demand for corn and sugar for ethanol production could lead to upward adjustments in future forecasts: although a steep global economic downturn in 2008–09 dampened commodity prices, they rose sharply again in 2010. Domestic price changes in China will reflect to a large extent the global market situation, although a number of other factors including domestic and trade policies, location and status as exporter or importer, macroeconomic environment and exchange rate fluctuations are also important. Exactly how much of the world price increase passes through to domestic prices and at what point these will trigger a change in administered prices remain largely uncertain. The same uncertainty applies to price forecasts themselves as changes in policies and weather conditions as well as other supply and demand determinants are hard to predict.

Notwithstanding these uncertainties, policy makers in China concluded that the support prices for wheat and rice were too low once world prices rose in 2007 (Xinhua Net 2007), and recommendations to increase these prices were made in various State Council meetings. The minimum prices for wheat and rice which had increased between 2003 and 2005 remained unchanged in 2006 and 2007 but were increased in early 2008 (Table 9.3). Under a high administered-price projection scenario, a further increase of minimum prices by 20 percent is assumed to occur in 2009, remaining in effect through 2012, followed by a second 20 percent increase in 2013, in effect through 2016. Under a moderate price scenario the two price increases are assumed to be 10 percent each.

In addition to price increases, there are also policy discussions on whether the minimum procurement price system should be extended beyond wheat, rice and corn. Given that there has been sporadic or temporary price support to cotton and soybeans, these crops are also included in the product coverage in Table 9.9.

China will comply with its commitments under the Agreement if existing price support programs are continued and there are no dramatic increases in administered prices. This corresponds to the moderate-price, three-commodity (wheat, rice and corn) minimum price support program scenario. However, if domestic administered prices increase at a faster pace, and/or price support extends to cotton and soybeans (and if China utilizes procured quantities as eligible production for these five crops), market price support may make the AMS for soybeans exceed its *de minimis* threshold as early as 2009. Violations of the WTO commitments could occur at a later date (2013) if administered prices for wheat and corn are high. Failure by China to comply with its commitment either in the high prices or extended commodity coverage scenario would result from large MPS amounts; the non-product-specific AMS remains under its *de minimis* threshold despite steady increases.

Under the Doha draft modalities the base level of OTDS for China is equal to 25 percent of the total value of agricultural production in the 1995–2004 base period. China's status as a developing country with a zero Bound Total AMS exempts it from OTDS reductions. For the same reason, China does not have to reduce the *de minimis* percentage. Moreover, as a recently acceded member, China's OTDS commitment will not constrain it from fully using its *de minimis* allowances. China is entitled to make blue box payments of up to 5 percent of the average base-period total value of production while each product-specific cap on blue box support is 10 percent of the overall blue box ceiling. Under these terms, a possible new Doha agreement will have minimal impact on China's latitude to provide trade-distorting support. Most notably, the 8.5 percent *de minimis* thresholds will continue to be the binding factor for both product-specific and non-product-specific AMS support. Because of China's large value of production (an average of RMB2,338 billion during 1996–2004), the limit on OTDS for China is RMB584 billion. This is not a constraint for China even under the highest support scenario (high administered price with five MPS products as shown in Table 9.9). The new blue box implies that China could extend domestic support up to RMB117 billion overall and RMB11.7 billion for a specific product, provided that such support satisfies the blue box criteria set out in the Doha draft modalities. Although China's *de minimis* thresholds on product-specific AMS support under the draft modalities remain the same as under its accession protocol, support to certain key commodities would exceed the limits in the high-price projection scenario (for wheat, corn and soybeans) and moderate-price projection scenarios (for soybean). Even if China simply maintains its administered prices at their 2008 levels, it could exceed its commitment if the price support program were extended to soybeans. However, as evident in its notification for 2004, China is likely to notify zero or small eligible production, and thus negligible MPS, if market prices remain strong through 2016.

Summary and conclusion

This chapter provides an analysis of recent changes in agricultural policies in China and empirical estimates of China's domestic support for agriculture. China joined the WTO in 2001 after intense negotiation over the terms of its accession. China's rapid economic growth has reduced agriculture's share of national income but its mostly very small farms still employ nearly half of the labor force. The urban–rural income gap has widened and by the late 2000s the goal of increasing farm incomes was high on China's policy agenda. Policies had shifted from taxing agriculture to providing subsidies. China liberalized its agricultural trade regime in conjunction with WTO accession and subsequently its net agricultural imports rose substantially.

China's domestic support information provided to the WTO through 2010 covers the period 1996–2004 and its notifications have been submitted after significant delays. Shadow notifications through 2008 were constructed based on the measurements used in the available notifications and publicly accessible data. In general, the results indicate that China's trade-distorting domestic support for the period 1996–2008 has been well below the limits agreed at its WTO accession. However, there are a number of interesting features. A set of relevant alternative subsidy-definition scenarios was discussed and their effects on the calculated levels of support evaluated when applied in the historical period of analysis. A key scenario addressed alternative decisions about the quantities of eligible production for MPS calculations. I also discussed the categories within which to report certain payments, as might arise from domestic reporting decisions or relevant dispute settlement cases at the WTO, and the inclusion of subsidies for irrigation, electricity, and fuel, which are not included in China's notifications.

China's level of green box support has grown as a result of increased public investment in the agricultural sector. In 2008, total green box support is estimated to have reached RMB397 billion, more than double the 1996 figure. General services account for more than half of these expenditures, public stockholding for food security about 20 percent, and expenditures for environmental programs rose sharply in relative importance in 2004. Disaster relief outlays increase although nominal levels were modest. China began to make direct payments to grain farmers in some provinces in 2002 and introduced its first nationwide direct payments program in 2004. The payments for 2004 were notified in the green box as decoupled income support but whether this classification can be defended is questionable because the payments require continued grain production and in some cases are provided as price-related subsidies. The direct payments for wheat amounted to 3.6 percent of the value of production in 2005, while for rice and corn they were less than 2 percent. Payments continued at around the same levels through 2008. If classified as AMS support, these payments would cut into the flexibility China has to provide other support below its product-specific *de minimis* thresholds.

There are several unique aspects of the WTO domestic support rules for China. In its accession negotiations, China waived the right to exempt certain support under development programs from counting towards its zero Bound Total AMS as provided in Article 6.2 of the Agreement. Instead, subsidies of this type are counted as AMS support. They therefore have to be small enough, when added to other AMS support, for each AMS to remain below its *de minimis* threshold. For China, these thresholds are 8.5 percent of the value of production. The base period for MPS fixed external reference prices is the relatively high-price years of 1996–98 instead of the low-price years of 1986–88. China has not reported any blue box support, although it might do so in the future if the need arises.

China's product-specific AMSs are derived almost entirely from MPS. It notified negative MPS through 2003 because its administered prices for wheat, rice and corn were below external reference prices. China asserted that administered prices had been eliminated for wheat and corn when the protective price system was repealed in 2004. It also asserted in its notification for 2004 that eligible production was zero for all three of these grains. In the shadow notifications, I included administered prices for rice and wheat based on China's policy decisions since 2005 but also assumed that zero eligible production will be notified based on its notification for 2004 and continued strong world prices for grains through 2008. Under an alternative assumption that China uses the procured quantities as eligible production, China's notified MPS understates economic market price support, which is estimated to be positive during the years 2001–07, primarily due to relatively weak world commodity prices in those years compared to the 1996–98 base period for China's fixed reference prices.

China's notified non-product-specific AMS support, primarily due to subsidies for fertilizer and pesticides, has averaged less than 1 percent of the value of agricultural production. This type of support increased to nearly 2.5 percent by 2008 according to OECD. Agricultural taxes have not been subtracted from China's notified non-product-specific subsidies, despite WTO rules that allow deduction of such levies and fees. China has not notified subsidies for irrigation, electricity or fuels. Agricultural irrigation accounts for two-thirds of the total water use in China and irrigation charges usually fail to cover operation and maintenance costs. Farmers pay less for electricity than other users. Rough estimates suggest that annual irrigation subsidies have averaged RMB31 billion and electricity subsidies another RMB23 billion. Even with the inclusion of these additional subsidies, China's non-product-specific AMS support would remain below half of its *de minimis* allowances during the 1996–2008 period. Taken together all of these considerations imply China's domestic support has been consistent with its WTO obligations since accession to the WTO in 2001.

The question arises whether China's domestic support for agriculture will increase further with continued economic growth, and if so whether the levels of support will be constrained by its WTO commitments. Green box support is likely to increase but is not constrained. Non-product-specific AMS support likely will also continue to increase, but the large value of China's agricultural production leaves latitude for this expansion. Several assumptions about MPS are considered in projected notifications of product-specific support through 2016. Because China's MPS is calculated in the domestic currency it is susceptible to inflation-driven increases in nominal administered prices. Administered prices are assumed to increase by 10 percent or 20 percent for 2009–12 and again for 2013–16. These increases are inconsequential if eligible production is notified as zero in the future. Under the alternative assumption that projected procured quantities are used as eligible production, China remains within the *de minimis* allowances with the moderate increase, and assuming MPS is provided only for rice, wheat and corn. However, with higher assumed increases in administered prices or the extension of MPS to cotton and soybeans, China would potentially incur MPS above the *de minimis* threshold for soybeans, wheat and cotton by 2016. Thus, the projections indicate that China could exceed its WTO commitment level under certain price support, eligible quantity, and commodity coverage scenarios. Notification of direct payments to grain farmers as product-specific support would exacerbate China's compliance concerns if notified MPS turns positive. Further constraints potentially negotiated in the Doha Round are shown to have only minor impacts, if any, in terms of China's latitude to provide trade-distorting support. Thus, with or without a Doha agreement there is a possibility that China could have to alter its policies in the medium term to avoid its product-specific AMS support exceeding the allowed amounts. The amount of calculated MPS would be crucial in this regard.

References

Abler, D., and D. Blandford. 2005. A review of empirical studies of the acreage and production response to US production flexibility contract payments under the FAIR Act and related payments under supplementary legislation. OECD report AGR/CA/APM(2004)21/Final.

Burfisher, M., and J. Hopkins. 2003. Decoupled payments: Household income transfers in contemporary US agriculture. Agricultural Economic Report No. 822, USDA, Economic Research Service.

Cheng, F., and D. Orden. 2007. Exchange rate misalignment and producer support estimates (PSEs) of China. Paper presented at the Symposium on China's Agricultural Trade: Issues and Prospects, International Agricultural Trade Research Consortium, Beijing, July 8–9.

Crook, F., and X. Diao. 2000. Water pressure in China: Growth strains resources. *Agricultural Outlook* January–February:25–29.

Evenett, S., and C. Braga. 2005. WTO accession: Lessons from experience. Trade Note No. 22, World Bank.

Fan, S., and C. Chan-Kang. 2005. Is small beautiful? Farm size, productivity, and poverty in Asian agriculture. *Agricultural Economics* 32(1):135–146.

Fan, S., and S. Thorat. 2007. Public investment, growth, and poverty reduction: A comparative analysis of India and China. In *The Dragon and the Elephant: Agricultural and Rural Reforms in China and India*, ed. S. Fan and A. Gulati. Baltimore: Johns Hopkins University Press.

Fang, C., and J. Beghin. 2000. Food self-sufficiency, comparative advantage, and agricultural trade: A policy analysis matrix for Chinese agriculture. Working Paper 99-WP 223 (revised October 2000), Iowa State University.

FAOSTAT. 2009. FAO Database. Food and Agriculture Organization of the United Nations. http://faostat.fao.org/default.aspx (accessed November 20, 2009).

Frankel, J. 2006. On the yuan: The choice between adjustment under a fixed exchange rate and adjustment under a flexible rate. *CESifo Economic Studies* 52: 246–275.

Gale, F., B. Lohmar, and F. Tuan. 2005. China's new farm subsidies. Report WRS-05–01, USDA, Economic Research Service.

Goldstein, M. 2007. A (lack of) progress report on China's exchange rate policies. Working Paper 07–5, Peterson Institute for International Economics.

Goodwin, B., and A. Mishra. 2006. Are "decoupled" farm program payments really decoupled? An empirical evaluation. *American Journal of Agricultural Economics* 88(1): 73–89.

Huang, J., and S. Rozelle. 2002. Changes in China's agricultural sector: Trade, market and policy reform. Proceedings of the WCC-101, Washington, DC, April 14–16.

Huang, J., S. Rozelle, W. Martin, and Y. Liu. 2007. Distortions to agricultural incentives in China. Agricultural Distortions Working Paper 29, World Bank.

Huang, J., Y. Liu, W. Martin, and S. Rozelle. 2009. Changes in trade and domestic distortions affecting China's agriculture. *Food Policy* 34(5): 407–416.

Huang, Y. 1998. *Agricultural Reform in China: Getting Institutions Right*. Cambridge University Press.

Jones, W. I. 1995. *The World Bank and Irrigation*. Washington, DC: World Bank.

Ke, B. 2007. Agricultural marketing reforms in China: Striking a balance between sequencing and speed. In *The Dragon and the Elephant: Agricultural and Rural Reforms in China and India*, ed. S. Fan and A. Gulati. Baltimore: Johns Hopkins University Press.

Kwiecinski, A., and F. van Tongeren. 2007. Quantitative evaluation of a decade of agricultural policies in China: 1995–2005. Paper presented at the Symposium on China's Agricultural Trade: Issues and Prospects, International Agricultural Trade Research Consortium, Beijing, July 8–9.

Martin, W. 2003. Implications of reform and WTO accession for China's agricultural policies. In *Agricultural Trade and Policy in China: Issues, Analysis and Implications*, ed. S. Rozelle and D. Sumner. Burlington: Ashgate.

MOA (Ministry of Agriculture). Various years. China Agricultural Yearbook.

2001. State Council's decision on deeping reform of the grain circulation system. http:// cctw.cn/zcfg/nyfg/t20060123_540652.htm, (accessed December 20, 2007).

MOF (Ministry of Finance). 2007a. China to eliminate export tax rebates on grains and processed grain products. www.mof.gov.cn/news/20071218_1500_29938.htm (accessed December 20, 2007).

2007b. Strengthening agricultural subsidies. www.mof.gov.cn/news/20070212_3137_24064.htm (accessed December 20, 2007).

2008a. China to levy export taxes on grains and processed grain products. www.mof.gov.cn/news/20071230_1500_30186.htm (accessed January 2, 2008).

2008b. Temporary import tariffs on soybeans to be effective through September 30, 2008. www.mof.gov.cn/news/20080307_2119_31956.htm (accessed March 6, 2008).

MOFCOM (Ministry of Commerce). 2008. China puts quota on grain powder exports to stabilize domestic prices. http://gpj2.mofcom.gov.cn/aarticle/workaffair/200801/20080105314447.html (accessed January 12, 2008).

NBS (National Bureau of Statistics). Various years. China Statistical Yearbook.

OECD. 2005. *Review of Agricultural Policies – China*. Paris.

2009. PSE Database. www.oecd.org/dataoecd/55/21/38525182.xls (accessed January 2010).

Qiao, F., B. Lohmar, J. Huang, S. Rozelle, and L. Zhang. 2003. Producer benefits from input market and trade liberalization: The case of fertilizer in China. *American Journal of Agricultural Economics* 85(5): 1223–1227.

Repetto, R. 1986. Skimming the water: Rent-seeking and the performance of public irrigation systems. Research Report No. 4, World Resources Institute.

USDA (United States Department of Agriculture). 2009. USDA agricultural projections to 2018. www.usda.gov/oce/commodity/ag_baseline.htm (accessed December 11, 2009).

WTO. 2008. Trade Policy Review – China. WT/TPR/S/161/Rev.1.

Xinhua Net. 2007. China should increase minimum prices for grains. http://news.xinhuanet.com/politics/2007–05/26/content_6156143.htm (accessed January 13, 2008).

10

Philippines

CAESAR B. CORORATON

The Philippine agricultural sector employs over one-third of the labor force and accounts for roughly 14 percent of gross domestic product (GDP). There have been significant shifts in policies affecting this important sector in the Philippines since the mid 1980s. Prior to that time there was a general bias against agriculture effected by a diverse set of policies. These policies included import substitution which favored manufacturing and penalized returns to agricultural investment; export taxes on agricultural commodities and exchange rate overvaluation, which greatly reduced earnings from agriculture; and operations of government corporations, which siphoned off the gains from trade (Intal and Power 1990). However, starting in the 1980s, policy shifted towards protecting agriculture. The system of protection included higher tariffs and nominal protection rates compared to the manufacturing sector, as well as some measures of domestic support (Aldaba 2005, David 2003). The sectoral protection and support was deemed essential for agriculture to be able to provide a stable domestic supply of food at affordable prices. The domestic support came in various forms: roads, market infrastructure, irrigation, post-harvest facilities, and product-specific support that affected markets and behavior of producers. But there are limits to the extent of support the Philippines has provided.

This chapter analyzes government support to agriculture in the Philippines within the framework of the WTO. The next section provides

The author acknowledges assistance and helpful comments received during field work in February 2008 from the following: Marlito Cabuños, WTO and Sanitary and Phytosanitary Specialist, Department of Agriculture (DA); Telma Tolentino, Accountant, DA; Minda Mangabat, Bureau of Agricultural Statistics (BAS); Nora Oliveros, Director, Department of Budget and Management (DBM); Jeremias Paul, Undersecretary, Department of Finance (DOF); Rosario Manasan and Cristina David, Senior Research Fellows, Philippine Institute for Development Studies (PIDS); Janet Cuenca, Supervising Research Specialist, PIDS; and Winnie Gerio, Information Technology Officer, PIDS.

an overview of agriculture and its place in the economy. Trade and domestic support policies are characterized. The sections that follow provide an assessment of how the domestic support policies have been reflected through 2004 in WTO notifications. Shadow notifications through 2008 are calculated and domestic support projected through 2015. Overall, the Philippines has protected agriculture with tariffs but provided relatively low levels of domestic support as notified to the WTO. There are, however, several significant support programs directed particularly toward promoting domestic rice production that the chapter will highlight.

Economic structure and policies

The shift of policy toward protection and support for agriculture has occurred in the context of structural change in the Philippine economy. The share of agriculture in GDP declined from 22 percent in the early 1990s to 14 percent by 2005–07. Over the same period, the shares of industry and manufacturing remained relatively stable at about 30 percent and 20 percent, respectively, while the share of services increased from 45 percent to 54 percent. Although agriculture contributes a declining share of GDP over time, it is still a major sector. If the agriculture-based food-processing sector is included, it contributes 26 percent to GDP.

Palay (rice paddy) is the dominant crop in the Philippines and is favored by government policies. There has been a consequent increase in agricultural land devoted to palay production. Of the available agricultural land, 26.3 percent was planted to palay in 1993 (Table 10.1). The share increased to 35.8 percent in 2008. The share of palay in the total value of agricultural output (including crops, livestock, poultry, and fisheries) increased from 14.3 percent to 18.8 percent. Corn and coconut are also major crops. Corn accounted for 21.3 percent of planted area and 6.1 percent of the total value of agricultural output in 2008, while coconuts covered 27.1 percent of planted area and accounted for 6.4 percent of the total output value. Bananas are a high-value product and livestock, poultry, and fishery are also major agricultural activities.

In terms of foreign trade, the share of agriculture exports has dropped from 40 percent in 1980–84 to 7.2 percent in 2007–08 (Table 10.2). Food exports (the largest component of agricultural exports) followed a similar declining trend. The share of non-agricultural exports surged from 59.7 percent to 92.8 percent over this period largely due to the growth in exports of clothing and garments until the mid 1990s, and then to exports of semi-conductors. The structure of imports indicates a relatively stable

Table 10.1 *Production shares of Philippine agriculture, 1993 and 2008*

	1993		2008	
	Area planted	Value of production	Area planted	Value of production
	%			
Crops		51.6		54.3
Cereals	51.4	20.5	57.1	24.9
Palay[a]	26.3	14.3	35.8	18.8
Corn	25.2	6.2	21.3	6.1
Coconut	24.6	6.6	27.1	6.4
Sugarcane	3.1	3.8	3.2	2.7
Banana	2.6	2.9	3.5	6.0
All other crops	18.3	17.7	9.1	14.3
Livestock and poultry		28.1		27.1
Fisheries		20.3		18.6
Total	100.0	100.0	100.0	100.0

[a] Rice paddy.
Source: DA.

share of agricultural imports, about 10 percent, which are mainly food items.

A notable trend in Table 10.2 is the deterioration in agricultural net trade, particularly in food. From a net exporter in agriculture and its food component of more than $1 billion per year in the first half of the 1980s, the Philippines has experienced a continuous decline in its net trade position. In 2007–08, the annual average agriculture trade deficit was $2.2 billion, of which the bulk was food imports. This occurred despite government's effort to implement food self-sufficiency policies and programs.

The growing trade deficit in agriculture and food results from domestic production lagging behind demand because of declining agricultural productivity and lack of comparative advantage. David (2003) has shown a decreasing trend in revealed comparative advantage in agriculture and agricultural exports, which indicates declining Philippine competitiveness in the international market. As a result, its agricultural export share in the world market has declined sharply. Coxhead and Jayasuriya (2003) have shown declining lowland and upland productivity in the

Table 10.2 *Structure of Philippine foreign trade, 1980–2008*

	1980–84	1985–89	1990–94	1995–99	2000–04	2005–06	2007–08
	Structure of exports (%)						
Agriculture	40.3	28.3	18.5	9.5	6.0	6.6	7.2
Food	34.5	23.9	17.0	8.6	5.5	6.1	6.7
Other	5.8	4.4	1.5	0.9	0.5	0.5	0.6
Non-agriculture	59.7	71.7	81.5	90.5	94.0	93.4	92.8
	Structure of imports (%)						
Agriculture	11.2	12.8	11.0	10.0	8.7	7.5	9.8
Food	9.0	10.1	8.7	8.3	7.5	6.7	9.1
Other	2.2	2.8	2.4	1.7	1.2	0.8	0.7
Non-agriculture	88.8	87.2	89.0	90.0	91.3	92.5	90.2
	Average annual net exports (export – imports, million US dollars)						
Agriculture	1,201	681	57	–1,086	-994	-807	–2,211
Food	1,076	636	291	-719	-765	-638	–2,060
Other	125	45	–234	-367	-228	-169	–151
Non-agriculture	–3,767	–2,217	-6,387	-6,618	32	–4,538	-9,398

Source: WTO.

Philippines. Habito and Briones (2005) have indicated that while the Philippines is at par with other countries in land productivity, the overall productivity in the crop subsector has stagnated. Moreover, while David (2003) noted an improvement in productivity in poultry and livestock, Mundlak, Larson, and Butzer (2004) indicated that on the whole the contribution of total factor productivity in agricultural output growth fell sharply from 36 percent in 1961–80 to 9 percent in 1980–98. This trend is in contrast to the experience of Thailand and Indonesia where substantial total factor productivity improvements occurred over the same period.

Increased imports are a result of increased demand for items with higher income elasticities such as wheat, milk and dairy products, and beef in which the Philippines does not have comparative advantage (David, Intal, and Baliscan 2007). Furthermore, there is high demand because of high growth in population (Dawe, Moya, and Casiwan 2005). Thus, there are also increased imports of basic foods, particularly cereals (mostly rice) imports, despite the increases in domestic production that have occurred. Between 1994 and 2008, the average increase in cereals imports was 4.6 percent per annum.

Trade policies

The import substitution policy that ended in the early 1980s resulted not only in economic inefficiencies but also encouraged and supported rent-seeking activities. Realizing the pitfalls of this development strategy, the government introduced a series of trade reform programs (TRPs) starting in 1981 as components of the structural adjustment programs funded by loans from the World Bank and the International Monetary Fund. TRP1 included tariff reductions, an import-liberalization program, and realignment of indirect taxes. The maximum tariff rates were reduced from 100 to 50 percent and sales taxes on imports and locally produced goods were equalized. The implementation of TRP1 was suspended in the mid 1980s because of a balance of payments crisis, but it was resumed in 1986.

TRP2, which was implemented starting in 1991, realigned the structure of tariff rates over a five-year period by narrowing the divergence of the tariff rates through a series of reductions in the number of commodity lines with high tariffs and an increase in the number of commodity lines with low tariffs. It also included a program to convert quantitative restrictions in agriculture commodities (except rice) into tariff equivalents.

TRP3, which was pursued in 1995, introduced a four-tier tariff schedule consisting of 3 percent for raw materials and capital equipment not available locally, 10 percent for raw materials and capital equipment available from local sources, 20 percent for intermediate goods, and 30 percent for finished goods. Under TRP3, the government implemented a system of tariff quotas for sensitive agricultural products where a relatively low tariff rate was imposed on products up to a minimum import level (in-quota tariff rate) and a higher tariff rate beyond the minimum import level (out-quota tariff rate). The overall goal of TRP3 was to implement a uniform tariff rate of 5 percent by 2005.

The final TRP, which was introduced in 1998, recalibrated the tariff rate schedule to ensure that the tariff regime was aimed at increasing the competitiveness of the local industry and to raise government revenues. Also, the planned uniform tariff rate in TRP3 was suspended under TRP4.

Table 10.3 shows the effects of the TRPs on the average weighted tariff rates. The overall average tariff rate on agriculture (including fisheries and forestry) declined from a peak of 23.8 percent in 1998 to 12.0 percent in 2008. Although tariff rates decreased across commodities, there are differences in the rates of decline especially between agriculture and manufacturing. The annual ratio of agriculture tariffs to manufacturing tariffs varies from 2.5 in 1997 to 4.2 in 1998 and 2005, and was 3.2 in 2008.

David, Intal, and Balisacan (2007) provided estimates, which are updated in Table 10.4, for nominal protection rates (NPRs) for eight major agricultural commodities.[1] These NPRs are equivalent to OECD's rates of market price support measured by the gap between domestic and international prices. In the late 1970s and first half of 1980s the NPR of rice was negative, but adverse effects on producers were counteracted by relatively high world commodity prices, the implementation of the Green Revolution program, and land reform. Rice productivity increased during the Green Revolution because of the expansion of irrigation and the

[1] The estimates of NPRs of David, Intal, and Baliscan (2007) ended in 2004. The series are extended to 2007 or 2008 using data from the World Bank, the International Monetary Fund, and the Philippine Bureau of Agricultural Statistics. In the original estimates of David, Intal, and Baliscan (2007), the NPRs for chicken, pork and beef were derived using Singapore import unit values. To be consistent with the NPRs of the other commodities, the NPRs presented in Table 10.4 for chicken, pork and beef were derived using the world price of these items as reported in the World Bank agricultural distortions database(http://siteresources.worldbank.org/INTTRADERESEARCH/Resources/544824-1146153362267/Philippines_0308rev.pdf). In all cases, to convert world prices to border prices an additional 15 percent was added to the world prices to account for cost, insurance and freight (CIF).

Table 10.3 *Average weighted tariff rates in the Philippines, 1997–2008*

	1997	1998	1999	2000	2001	2002	2003	2004	2005	2006	2007	2008
	%											
Agriculture	20.3	23.8	17.1	15.7	12.2	10.2	8.6	9.2	13.1	12.8	12.8	12.0
Manufacturing	8.0	5.7	5.8	3.9	3.8	3.0	3.2	3.1	3.2	3.3	3.7	3.7
Mining	3.4	3.2	3.1	3.1	3.2	2.9	2.8	2.8	2.9	2.8	2.8	2.8
Overall average	9.1	7.6	6.9	5.0	4.6	3.8	3.7	3.7	4.1	4.1	4.6	4.5
	Ratio											
Agriculture to manufacturing tariff	2.5	4.2	3.0	4.1	3.2	3.3	2.7	3.0	4.2	3.9	3.5	3.2

Notes: Agriculture includes forestry and fisheries. Imports were applied as weights in each sector.
Source: Tariff Commission.

Table 10.4 *Nominal agricultural protection rates in the Philippines, 1980–2008*

				Coconut				
	Rice	Corn	Sugar	Oil	Copra	Beef	Chicken	Pork
	%							
1980–84	–13	25	19	–28	–37	15	100	–28
1985–89	16	67	122	–16	–31	6	56	2
1990–94	26	70	51	–7	–26	31	69	43
1995	64	56	92	–11	–21	3	50	–2
1996	90	30	94	–13	–17	14	37	31
1997	82	96	67	–16	–32	24	39	53
1998	34	95	102	–16	–18	30	25	–2
1999	66	104	182	–5	–11	4	60	23
2000	87	104	85	–17	–33	73	23	53
2001	83	79	81	–21	–33	26	8	37
2002	63	51	133	–13	–18	18	5	76
2003	49	30	153	21	–20	28	–2	49
2004	21	41	119	–10	–23	–1	–5	32
2005	15	53	60	–16	–29	5	0	47
2006	21	51	64	–11	–50	16	22	80
2007	27	48	188	–10	–34	26	27	94
2008	–15	26	143	na	–40	na	na	na

Note: na indicates not available.
Sources: David, Intal, and Balisacan (2007) for 1960 to 2005; IMF primary commodity prices (2008) and DA (2008) for 2006–08.

introduction of new seeds and fertilizer. The government also increased credit facilities to rice farmers. Under the land reform program tenant rice farmers became owner-operators.

A sharp fall in irrigation investments and the stagnation of the yield potential of newer modern varieties in the 1980s slowed down the growth of domestic production of rice. A sharp increase in domestic wholesale prices in 1995 increased the NPR of rice from an average of 16 percent in 1985–89 to an average of 67 percent in 1995–99. It reached a peak of 87 percent in 2000, but there has since been a general decline; in 2005, the NPR of rice dropped to its lowest level of 15 percent, then increased to 27 percent in 2007, before falling to -15 percent in 2008 as world prices surged upward.

There were two reasons behind the declining NPR of rice through 2005: increases in the world price and depreciation of the Philippine currency (PhP, Philippine peso). Table 10.5 shows the exchange rate (PhP/$), the world prices in US dollars and the domestic wholesale prices in pesos that underlie the NPRs shown in Table 10.4. The CIF world price of rice increased from $192 per metric ton in 2000 to $301 per metric ton in 2005 while the exchange rate depreciated from PhP44/$ to PhP55/$. As a result, the border price of rice increased from PhP8,500 per metric ton to PhP16,600. In contrast, the domestic wholesale price of rice increased only from PhP15,900 in 2000 to PhP19,100 per metric ton in 2005. The peso appreciated against the US dollar in 2006–08 but world market prices of rice continued to climb.

The NPR of corn has always been positive and increased in years prior to 2000 when it reached a peak of 104 percent. Similar to rice, there has been a declining trend in the NPR of corn after the peak. The NPR dropped to its lowest value of about 26 percent in 2008. This trend is due to higher world prices of corn and to the depreciation (until 2005) of the Philippine currency. The CIF world price of corn increased from $102 per metric ton in 2000 to $235 in 2008. The domestic wholesale price of corn increased only from PhP9,200 to PhP13,100 per metric ton over the same period.

Sugar has been one of the highly protected crops in the Philippines. However, the NPR has fluctuated especially after 2000. It declined to 81 percent in 2001, but increased to 133 percent in 2002. It dropped to the lowest level of 60 percent in 2005, but surged to 188 percent in 2007. In 2008, the NPR for sugar was 143 percent. The wide swing in the NPR of sugar was due to the erratic movement of the world price of sugar, while the domestic wholesale price of sugar was relatively more stable.

The NPR of coconut (copra and coconut oil) is negative and unfavorable to coconut farmers. Export taxes resulted in revenues for the government and an export ban lowered raw material costs for the coconut oil milling industry through the mid 1980s. Although these measures were eliminated as formal policies in 1986, the continued existence of a government corporation that controls 70–80 percent of the coconut oil milling implies that the government retains its control over domestic prices of copra.

The producers of chicken broilers were highly protected in the first half of the 1980s when the NPR of chicken was 100 percent. Although the NPR of chicken declined over the next ten years, the levels were still above 50 percent. The world price of chicken has not increased significantly except in 2007. It was the depreciation of the peso from 2000 to 2005 that resulted in the drop in the NPR. In 2007, the NPR of chicken was 27 percent. The

Table 10.5 *Exchange rates, world agricultural prices, and Philippine domestic wholesale prices, 1980–2008*

	World price, CIF							
				Coconut				
	Rice	Corn	Sugar	Oil	Copra	Beef	Chicken	Pork
	US$/metric ton							
1980–84	346	147	343	826	541	2,838	907	2,950
1985–89	263	114	202	554	377	2,695	1,096	2,509
1990–94	293	122	267	553	370	2,905	1,290	1,857
1995	334	142	337	670	439	2,193	1,465	1,658
1996	317	191	303	752	489	2,053	1,645	2,442
1997	284	135	288	657	434	2,135	1,610	1,924
1998	287	117	226	658	411	1,985	1,667	1,204
1999	242	104	159	737	462	2,120	1,583	1,172
2000	192	102	205	518	350	2,222	1,504	1,500
2001	171	103	209	366	232	2,449	1,610	1,554
2002	196	114	158	484	306	2,421	1,596	1,196
2003	205	121	176	537	345	2,277	1,675	1,351
2004	256	129	191	760	518	2,889	1,916	1,797
2005	301	113	289	710	476	3,017	1,876	1,724
2006	319	140	375	698	639	2,941	1,749	1,623
2007	352	187	252	1,057	759	2,992	1,978	1,623
2008	722	235	316	na	1,068	na	na	na

Note: na indicates not available.
Sources: David, Intal and Balisacan (2007) for 1960 to 2005; IMF commodity prices (2008) and DA (2008) for 2006–08.

NPRs of both beef and pork became positive in the 1980s and surged to higher levels in the 1990s. While the NPR of beef declined, the NPR of pork remains high.

Until the mid 1980s, the NPRs of agricultural inputs such as fertilizers, agricultural chemicals, and farm machinery were generally higher than the NPRs of agricultural crops except sugar (David, Intal, and Balisacan 2007). This was largely due to the government's industrial promotion policies, which increased domestic prices of manufactured inputs to agriculture. However, after this period and during the trade liberalization, there

Exchange rate	Wholesale price			Coconut				
	Rice	Corn	Sugar	Oil	Copra	Beef	Chicken	Pork
PhP/US$	*Thousand PhP/metric ton*							
17	2.9	1.9	2.9	6.7	3.9	33.5	18.1	21.4
22	6.1	3.8	8.1	9.6	5.4	59.0	34.8	47.4
26	9.4	5.4	10.4	13.5	7.2	99.5	56.8	65.2
26	14.0	7.4	16.6	17.7	10.2	121.3	64.8	73.2
26	15.9	7.7	15.4	19.8	12.3	123.2	62.4	81.0
29	15.2	7.6	14.2	18.7	9.9	129.4	65.2	84.7
41	15.8	8.3	18.6	25.8	15.9	160.7	73.2	103.5
39	15.8	8.5	17.5	31.6	18.4	138.3	77.9	112.0
44	15.9	9.2	16.7	19.1	10.4	169.6	81.6	101.5
51	16.0	9.4	19.3	14.7	7.9	157.5	88.7	108.4
52	16.5	8.9	19.0	21.7	13.0	146.9	86.2	108.8
54	16.5	8.6	24.0	35.3	14.9	157.5	88.5	109.0
56	17.3	10.1	23.4	38.4	22.4	160.4	101.9	132.4
55	19.1	9.5	25.4	33.0	18.7	174.8	103.8	139.3
51	19.5	10.9	31.6	31.8	16.2	175.8	109.9	149.7
46	20.7	11.4	33.5	44.1	23.1	173.6	116.2	145.2
44	27.1	13.1	34.1	na	28.7	na	na	na

was a substantial reduction in the NPRs of agricultural inputs. From 2000 to 2004, the NPRs of agricultural inputs were at a uniform 3 percent.

Agricultural support programs

On the whole, the public funding for agriculture in the Philippines is not substantial, accounting for only about 3 percent of the total government expenditure. The expenditure on agriculture represents about 0.6 percent of GDP and 4 percent of agricultural GDP. There is relative public underspending on agriculture in the Philippines by international comparison (World Bank 2007). In terms of GDP, Philippine spending on agriculture is comparable to the Lao People's Democratic Republic and Vietnam; it is lower than middle-income countries, such as China and Thailand. This modest spending is mainly due to the fiscal constraints in the Philippines and the country's limited public financial capability, as indicated by low tax ratios relative to other middle- and high-income developing countries.

The domestic support for agriculture is provided mainly through the Department of Agriculture (DA) from funds allocated through the General Appropriations Act (GAA). Since 2000, the budget of the DA has been allocated among three major components: The Office of the Secretary (OSEC); other DA attached agencies and corporations, of which the National Food Authority (NFA) is one; and the Agriculture and Fisheries Modernization Program (AFMP). There have been shifts of the DA expenditures on agriculture among these entities. In 2000, OSEC was a major source of the overall expenditure, accounting for 71.3 percent of the total (Table 10.6). However, after the implementation of the AFMP in 2001, a significant portion of the budget for OSEC was reallocated to AFMP. Thus, expenditure in OSEC declined from PhP14.8 billion in 2000 to PhP2.4 billion in 2001. From 2002 to 2005, the budget allocated to OSEC remained within PhP2 to PhP4 billion, whereas the allocation to AFMP was more than PhP10 billion annually.

The Agriculture and Fisheries Modernization Act (AFMA) that authorizes the AFMP was initially approved by the Philippine Congress in 1997 and represented a major shift in agricultural policy. AFMA has five broad objectives: food security; poverty alleviation and social equity; income enhancement and profitability, especially for farmers and fisherfolk; global competitiveness; and sustainability (Republic Act 8435). When President Gloria Macapagal-Arroyo took office in 2001, various AFMP initiatives were launched, including the Golden and Bountiful Harvest (Ginintuang Masaganang Ani, GMA) programs in rice, corn, coconut, sugar, high-value commercial crops, livestock, and fisheries. In 2003, the AFMA was amended by the Philippine Congress to further strengthen the expected impact of the Act. The amendment included exemptions for enterprises engaged in agriculture and fisheries from paying tariffs and import duties on various types of production inputs until 2015. These items include imports of chemicals, seeds, machinery, and equipment.

Table 10.7 shows the breakdown of the expenditure on the AFMP by major commodity groups. The budget allocation process gives a

Table 10.6 *Total Philippine public expenditures on agriculture, 2001–05*

	2000	2001	2002	2003	2004	2005
	Million pesos					
Office of the Secretary (OSEC)	14,783	2,447	3,565	2,818	3,183	2,329
Other DA attached agencies and corporations	5,949	4,636	2,864	12,014	6,527	14,458
Agriculture and Fisheries Modernization Program (AFMP)	—	15,872	13,309	10,064	10,178	13,565
Total	20,732	22,955	19,737	24,897	19,888	30,352
Total as share of	%					
National government expenditure	3.2	3.2	2.5	3.0	2.2	3.2
Gross domestic product (GDP)	0.7	0.6	0.5	0.6	0.5	0.6
GDP of agriculture, fishery and forestry	4.1	4.2	3.6	4.2	3.1	4.1

Note: — indicates zero.
Sources: DBM and NSCB.

disproportionate share to rice production because the government equates the overall concern for food with rice self-sufficiency. From 2001 to 2005, rice received almost 60 percent of the budget. In contrast, government funding for exportable agricultural crops has been quite modest.

Support policies for agriculture are geared towards food self-sufficiency in other ways as well, particularly for rice. The government sets a system of price support to assist rice farmers and imposes a price ceiling to benefit consumers. It procures rice from farmers, exercises monopoly control over rice importation and exportation, and maintains buffer stocks to achieve objectives related to stabilizing supplies and domestic market prices, which include minimizing seasonal price variations within different regions. These interventions are implemented through the NFA.

The NFA's procurement of palay has declined considerably; from more than 10 percent of total production in the early 1980s to only 0.5 percent

Table 10.7 *Distribution of Philippine public agricultural expenditure by commodity group, 2000–05*

	2000	2001	2002	2003	2004	2005
	%					
Rice	39.1	53.8	59.0	53.2	56.6	58.0
Non-rice cereals	11.5	12.6	8.3	7.5	9.6	8.7
Livestock	6.5	8.2	5.7	4.4	5.3	4.2
Fisheries	9.2	12.3	14.0	16.6	13.7	8.5
Other commodities	33.7	13.1	13.0	18.2	14.9	20.6
Total	100.0	100.0	100.0	100.0	100.0	100.0

Source: World Bank (2007).

by 2006, before increasing to 4.2 percent when global food prices spiked upward in 2008. A key reason for the declining trend is the financial difficulty faced by the NFA.[2] In addition to rice, the NFA is also involved in corn, though its influence on this market has recently declined to be almost nil.

Despite its limited procurements of domestic rice, the NFA remains heavily involved in rice importation. From 1998 to 2008, the NFA's rice imports were equal to about 12 percent of rice consumption. Rice prices are politically sensitive in the Philippines and the administered prices (both the support price for farmers and the ceiling price for consumers) play an influential role affecting rice import decisions. In the late 1990s and early 2000s, nominal protection for rice exceeded the bound tariff as the government used quantitative restrictions to limit imports below the level that would have resulted from the tariff alone. In the later years of the 2000s, wholesale rice prices, which tracked just above the administered price ceiling, were less than the world price plus the bound tariff. The applied tariff (an exchange between the NFA and the government itself) was below the maximum bound level or subsidies were used to bring market prices below the world price plus tariff. However, once the administered support price guaranteed to farmers is set, to avoid

[2] There are also claims that some rice farmers are hesitant to sell to the NFA. They fear that their delinquent credit history during the Green Revolution programs of the 1970s might be revived once they transact with the government.

extensive procurements the government cannot reduce tariffs below a level that maintains the market price farmers receive above the administered price. The administered price provides a price floor for all output, even if none is procured.

The fiscal cost of the government's rice stabilization programs is substantial, as reflected in the NFA's financial deficits. Table 10.8 shows the NFA's financial statement, including the annual subsidies from the national government. In 2005, the subsidy was more than PhP13 billion. Despite the subsidies from the national government, the deficits of the NFA (required financing in Table 10.8) have been quite large. From 2000 to 2006, the NFA's cumulative deficit amounted to PhP44.2 billion. In 2005, its deficit of PhP10 billion was almost half the total deficit of all government-owned and controlled corporations both in agriculture and non-agriculture. In 2006, the NFA's deficit deteriorated further to PhP16.4 billion.

The subsidies from the national government to the NFA are expected to continue because of the circumstances in domestic rice markets caused by sharply higher world rice prices in 2008. The subsidies will not be enough to finance the growing deficit of the NFA. The indebtedness of the NFA will therefore continue to increase. Because stability in the rice market has significant political ramifications in the Philippines, the government will be forced to absorb NFA's debt, which will put further pressure on the national government's very tight fiscal circumstances.

The hybrid rice production program

As an additional measure to promote domestic rice production, the government introduced hybrid rice through the Hybrid Rice Commercialization Program (HRCP) in 2001. In the HRCP, domestic hybrid rice seed production is supported and the adoption of these seeds by farmers is encouraged. The program relies heavily on government subsidies. David (2006) conducted a comprehensive evaluation of the HRCP examining the performance of the program, including the budgetary cost, the profitability to farmers, adoption rates, and its viability in the long run. On the program cost, this study estimated that the government provided financial resources of about PhP10 billion between 2001 and 2005.

To provide incentives to hybrid seed producers through the HRCP, the government buys the hybrid seeds at a guaranteed price of PhP2,400 per 20-kilo bag. To encourage farmers to adopt the hybrid seeds and replace their inbred seeds, the government sells these hybrid seeds to farmers at

Table 10.8 *Financial performance of the Philippine National Food Authority, 2000–06*

	2000	2001	2002	2003	2004	2005	2006
	Million pesos						
Total receipts	22,688	14,408	19,472	17,136	25,239	40,591	30,369
Operating receipts	21,523	12,480	19,176	16,886	24,387	40,375	30,101
Sales of goods and services	21,523	12,390	18,256	15,964	19,806	27,204	25,290
Current subsidies	—	90	920	922	4,581	13,171	4,811
Other receipts	1,165	1,928	296	250	852	216	268
Current expenditures	28,474	15,342	23,742	24,765	31,493	46,664	44,041
Operating expenditures	22,768	11,138	19,596	18,810	26,339	40,846	37,625
Other operating expenditures	5,706	4,204	4,146	5,955	5,154	5,818	6,416
Interest payments	1,430	1,718	1,471	1,964	2,748	3,186	3,927
Others	4,276	2,486	2,675	3,991	2,406	2,632	2,489
Internal cash generation	−5,786	−934	−4,270	−7,629	−6,254	−6,073	−13,672
Capital expenditures[a]	−3,888	1,341	3,815	−3,939	−4,418	3,905	2,758
Required financing	1,898	2,275	8,085	3,690	1,836	9,978	16,430
Net domestic financing	1,898	2,578	8,085	3,840	1,853	9,996	16,497
Net domestic bank credits	−89	3,244	8,109	−311	107	5,732	17,328
Net other domestic financing	1,987	−666	−24	4,151	1,746	4,264	−831
Net external financing	—	−303	—	−150	−17	−18	−67

Notes: — indicates zero.

[a] Major component is changes in inventories.

Source: DOF.

half this price during the planting season with the remainder to be paid after harvest. Based on past experience, the rate of non-payment by farmers of the remaining PhP1,200 per bag of seeds is high. In effect the government only recovers half of its seed purchase costs in these cases and it does not recover any of its transaction costs of seed storage and distribution. The government also provides subsidies for other farm inputs to encourage farmers to adopt the hybrid seeds. Farmers are entitled to a PhP500 discount on chemical fertilizers for every bag of hybrid seeds purchased. In addition, some amounts of chemicals such as zinc sulfate, organic fertilizers, foliar fertilizer, and soil conditioners are distributed for free with hybrid seeds obtained by the farmers. David (2006) provides an estimate which amounts to PhP1,000 per bag of additional subsidies to the farmers to encourage them to adopt the hybrid seeds.

Despite the effort and the public financial resources put into the program, the hybrid seed adoption rate of farmers remains low at 5 percent of the total rice area. David concludes that adoption remains low because the yield advantage has not sufficiently compensated farmers for the higher cost of seeds, labor, and other inputs usually required by hybrid varieties.

Notifications of domestic support

The Philippine government had notified the WTO about its domestic support through 2004 as of June 2010. It notifies its levels of domestic support in domestic currency and its submission of January 16, 2009 covered the years 2002, 2003 and 2004. The Philippine domestic support falls into three categories in the notifications: green box expenditures; subsidies under Article 6.2 development programs; and product-specific market price support for rice and corn. Support provided through direct payments has been very small in the green box and non-existent in the blue box and the AMSs. The Philippines has a zero Bound Total AMS. Thus, the effective limits on AMS support for the Philippines are the *de minimis* thresholds, which are 10 percent of the values of production. The Philippines has not notified non-product-specific AMS support in any year.

The domestic support notified through 2004 and shadow estimates of support through 2008 are summarized in Table 10.9 and the components shown in Tables 10.10 to 10.12. In the 1990s, there was substantial variability in the green box expenditures. From PhP3.5 billion in 1995, the green box expenditures increased to PhP15.2 billion in 1997 and then dropped to PhP7.6 billion in 1998. The green box expenditures

Table 10.9 *Summary of Philippine domestic support notifications and shadow notifications, 1995–2008*

	Notifications					
	1995	1996	1997	1998	1999	2000
	Million pesos					
Green box	3,504	7,398	15,179	7,625	9,219	12,960
Development programs	6,264	1,394	2,107	1,932	1,584	3,276
Blue box	—	—	—	—	—	—
Current Total AMS	—	—	—	—	—	—
Total *de minimis*	257	912	766	1,125	3,683	4,368
Product- specific (entirely MPS)	257	912	766	1,125	3,683	4,368
Non-product-specific	—	—	—	—	—	—
Total support	10,025	9,704	18,052	10,683	14,486	20,605
Value of production[a]	342,622	404,535	432,420	416,327	480,899	448,853
Bound Total AMS	zb	zb	zb	zb	zb	zb

Notes: Small differences in totals are due to rounding. — indicates zero; zb indicates the Philippines has an implied zero binding on CTAMS.

[a] Agricultural crops, livestock and poultry.

Sources: Philippine notifications to WTO and author's calculations.

subsequently stabilized at about PhP11 billion to PhP13 billion per year. The largest expenditure in the green box is for general services, primarily infrastructural services and research (Table 10.10). Support of public stockholding has been reported at no more than PhP1.5 billion annually and there are no expenditures notified for domestic food aid, despite the subsidies provided to the NFA. Very small expenditures are reported for crop insurance programs.

There was a relatively large notified expenditure of PhP6.2 billion for Article 6.2 development programs in 1995. The support level again drops sharply the following year and stabilizes at about PhP3 billion per year in the early 2000s. Since 2002, the subsidies have been almost equally divided between support for investment available to agriculture and input

				Shadow notifications			
2001	2002	2003	2004	2005	2006	2007	2008
12,399	13,516	11,045	11,041	14,435	12,201	20,857	22,619
1,336	2,966	2,880	2,866	3,555	3,005	5,137	5,571
—	—	—	—	—	—	—	—
—	—	—	—	—	—	—	—
3,122	2,034	2,011	1,409	554	514	704	8,192
3,122	2,034	2,011	1,409	554	514	704	8,192
—	—	—	—	—	—	—	—
16,857	18,517	15,936	15,316	18,544	15,721	26,698	36,381
476,674	512,648	536,202	633,489	669,614	722,296	793,597	946,847
zb	zb	zb	zb	zb	zb	zb	zb

subsidies available to limited-resource farmers (Table 10.11). Overall, the level of support is quite low, less than 2 percent of the value of agricultural production in all years.

The product-specific AMS support in the Philippines is comprised of market price support for rice and corn only (Table 10.12). The external reference prices from the period 1986–88 are PhP4.56 per kilo for rice and PhP2.26 per kilo for corn. These reference prices are far below the nominal administered prices, which were PhP14 per kilo for rice and PhP 4.5 per kilo for corn by 1995. Eligible production for rice is determined as NFA procurement of rice and palay. Procured palay is converted into a rice-equivalent level using a 65 percent milling recovery rate. Eligible production of corn consists of the grain procurements

Table 10.10 *Composition of Philippine green box notifications and shadow notifications, 1995–2008*

	Notifications					
	1995	1996	1997	1998	1999	2000
	Million pesos					
General services	2,454	6,396	13,290	6,121	7,971	11,581
Research	300	3,386	6,514	1,250	963	1,663
Infrastructure services	1,630	2,167	5,996	3,498	5,396	7,804
Public stockholding	1,000	924	1,500	1,449	1,193	1,242
Domestic food aid	—	—	—	—	—	—
Decoupled income support	—	—	—	—	—	—
Income insurance	—	—	—	—	—	—
Crop insurance/ disaster relief	50	79	390	55	55	138
Producer retirement	—	—	—	—	—	—
Resource retirement	—	—	—	—	—	—
Investment aids	—	—	—	—	—	—
Environmental payments	—	—	—	—	—	—
Regional assistance	—	—	—	—	—	—
Total	3,504	7,398	15,179	7,625	9,219	12,960

Note: — indicates zero.
Sources: Philippine notifications to WTO General Appropriations Act and author's calculations.

by the NFA. The procured quantities have been small compared to production quantities, as shown Table 10.12. As a consequence, the MPS for both commodities are substantially below the 10 percent *de minimis* threshold.[3]

[3] Cororaton (2008) looked closely at the yearly applied administered price for rice in the notifications. He observed that the reported administered price reflects the consumer price ceiling for rice set by the government and not the farmer support price. The latter is more appropriate as the support price for the MPS analysis. Computed using the 65 percent recovery rate, the farmer support price for rice is observed to be relatively higher than the consumer price ceiling for rice. However, the alternative computation of administered price of rice will not alter the conclusion that the MPS is substantially below the *de minimis* limit because NFA procurement of rice is so low.

				Shadow notifications			
2001	2002	2003	2004	2005	2006	2007	2008
11,020	12,456	10,424	10,420	13,516	11,424	19,529	21,178
997	2,526	2,161	2,162	2,783	2,352	4,021	4,361
6,528	8,591	6,698	6,693	8,894	7,517	12,850	13,935
1,242	902	467	467	728	615	1,052	1,141
—	—	—	—	—	—	—	—
—	—	—	—	—	—	—	—
—	—	—	—	—	—	—	—
138	159	154	154	191	161	276	299
—	—	—	—	—	—	—	—
—	—	—	—	—	—	—	—
—	—	—	—	—	—	—	—
—	—	—	—	—	—	—	—
—	—	—	—	—	—	—	—
12,399	13,516	11,045	11,041	14,435	12,201	20,857	22,619

Shadow notifications

In terms of the shadow domestic support notifications calculated for 2005–08, estimating and projecting the MPS for rice and corn is relatively more straightforward than extending the series on the green box and development program support. This is because eligible production in the MPS formula is based on NFA procurement for which data is readily available. Past administered prices are also known. Because procurements are so low, the estimated shadow notifications of MPS for rice and corn shown in Tables 10.12 remain well below the *de minimis* thresholds.

The exercise of extending the green box and the Article 6.2 development program support is not so straightforward because there is no documentation on how the numbers were arrived at, and it is difficult to trace

Table 10.11 *Composition of Philippine development program notifications and shadow notifications, 1995–2008*

	Notifications					
	1995	1996	1997	1998	1999	2000
	Million pesos					
Investment subsidies to agriculture[a]	5,138	909	1,927	1,002	1,203	1,692
Funds for agricultural investment[b]	—	—	—	542	106	49
Input subsidies available to low-income farmers[c]	1,126	485	181	388	276	1,535
Total	6,264	1,394	2,107	1,932	1,584	3,276

Notes: — indicates zero.

[a] Soft loans and grants for agricultural investment. These involve the provision of loans and grants for irrigation and other farm infrastructure support, farm equipment, development, post-harvest facilities, research, training, and extension activities.

[b] Investment credit and grants. Government funds directed to improve rural structure, acquisition of machines, equipment, and post-harvest facilities.

[c] Provision of access to farm inputs. This measure provides low-income resource-poor producers the opportunity to have easier access to good quality inputs such as seeds, planting materials, fertilizers and animal stock in or to improve farm productivity.

Sources: Philippine notifications to WTO, General Appropriations Act and author's calculations.

them back to the main source.[4] Thus a method was devised to project these expenditures. In this method, the overall support level is matched to available aggregate expenditure data similarly to the match observed for recent notified years. It is also assumed that the distribution of support among various measures matches those past years.

In the Philippine notification for 2002–04, it was indicated that the various items in the green box (Table 10.10) were sourced from the General

[4] An interview was conducted with the person in charge of WTO issues in the Department of Agriculture in Manila, but there is no available documentation used to prepare the past WTO notifications.

				Shadow notifications			
2001	2002	2003	2004	2005	2006	2007	2008
—	1,800	1,399	1,374	1,863	1,575	2,692	2,920
145	5	8	1	6	5	8	9
1,190	1,160	1,473	1,491	1,686	1,425	2,437	2,642
1,336	2,966	2,880	2,866	3,555	3,005	5,137	5,571

Appropriations Act, while the three items under development programs (Table 10.11) were based on data from the Philippine Department of Agriculture. I examined the historical values of various support in the green box and found only two measures that corresponded exactly to the values in the GAA. These measures are public stockholding and crop insurance, for which data are available in the GAA for 2005–08. This information was utilized in the shadow notification. However, with no official documentation available as a guide, it is impossible to trace the remaining measures in the green box and development programs to the sources cited in the Philippine notification.

Determining shadow notification support for the rest of the measures in the green box and development programs utilized the data on the AFMP budget that was available through 2008. Table 10.13 shows how the AFMP budget compares with the total support notified for the green box and development programs from 2002–04.

Since data on public stockholding and crop insurance are available, this cost was deducted from the total of green box and development program support. The residuals were compared to the budget of the AFMP. The AFMP budget is 13.7 percent below the residual in 2002, 24.4 percent below in 2003 and 23.4 below in 2004. Since the budget for AFMP is a major support program in agriculture whose data is available, this information was used to compute the shadow notifications. I assumed that between 2005 and 2008, the budget for AFMP was 20 percent below the

Table 10.12 *Composition of Philippine AMS notifications and shadow notifications, 1995–2008*

		Notifications					
	Reference[a]	1995	1996	1997	1998	1999	2000
Product-specific AMS							
Market Price Support	Pesos/kg	*Applied administered price (pesos/kg)*					
Rice[b]	4.56	14.00	14.00	14.00	13.20	14.67	14.62
Corn	2.26	4.50	5.25	6.00	6.00	6.00	6.00
		Eligible production (thousand metric tons)					
Rice[c]		27	93	65	40	364	431
Corn		—	12	40	208	—	8
		Total production (thousand metric tons)					
Rice[c]		6,851	7,334	7,325	5,561	7,661	8,053
Corn		4,129	4,151	4,332	3,823	4,585	4,511
		Market Price Support (million pesos)					
Rice		257	877	617	347	3,683	4,337
Corn		—	35	148	779	—	30
		Million pesos					
Other non-exempt measures		—	—	—	—	—	—
Product-specific thresholds		*10% of value of production (million pesos)*					
Rice[d]		9,633	11,618	11,148	8,775	12,067	12,813
Corn		3,055	3,201	3,306	3,181	3,883	4,150
		Million pesos					
Non-product-specific AMS		—	—	—	—	—	—
		10% of value of production (million pesos)					
Non-product-specific threshold		34,262	40,453	43,242	41,633	48,090	44,885

Note: — indicates zero.

[a] External reference price, average 1986–88.

[b] 2005–08 computed as palay (paddy) support price converted into price of rice using 65 percent milling recovery rate.

[c] Eligible production consists of rice procured plus palay (paddy) procured converted into rice equivalent using a 65 percent milling recovery rate; total production is palay (paddy) converted into rice.

					Shadow notifications			
2001	2002	2003	2004		2005	2006	2007	2008
14.62	15.00	15.00	15.00		15.38	15.38	15.38	22.56
6.00	6.00	6.00	6.00		7.13	8.50	8.50	9.50
310	195	193	135		50	48	65	455
—	—	—	—		3	—	—	—
8,421	8,626	8,775	9,423		9,492	9,962	10,556	10,930
4,525	4,319	4,616	5,413		5,253	6,082	6,737	6,928
3,122	2,034	2,011	1,409		538	514	704	8,192
—	—	—	—		16	—	—	—
—	—	—	—		—	—	—	—
13,465	14,250	14,487	16,302		18,168	19,417	21,809	29,642
4,267	3,848	3,951	5,489		4,980	6,599	7,707	9,757
—	—	—	—	—	—	—	—	—
47,667	51,265	53,620	63,349		66,961	72,230	79,360	94,685

[d] Value of production computed using palay production converted to rice equivalent and valued using wholesale price of rice.

Sources: Philippine notifications to WTO, DA, and author's calculations.

Table 10.13 *Philippine green box and development program support compared with AFMP budgets, 2002–04*

	2002	2003	2004
	Million pesos		
Total of green box and development programs	16,482	13,925	13,907
Less public stockholding and crop insurance	1,061	621	621
Net green box and development programs	15,421	13,304	13,286
Agriculture and Fisheries Modernization Program (AFMP)	13,309	10,064	10,178
Difference	2,112	3,240	3,108
Difference as a percentage (%)	–13.7	–24.4	–23.4

Sources: DBM, General Appropriation Act, various years; Philippine notifications to WTO.

total of the green box and development programs less public stockholding and crop insurance support. Thus, the AFMP budget, augmented by 25 percent, serves as the total. It is distributed to the various remaining items in the green box and development programs using the average historical shares in the notification between 2002 and 2004.

The increases in estimated support for 2007 and 2008 in the shadow notifications are largely due to the surge in the budget for AFMP as the government aggressively pursued the rice program. In 2007, the budget allocation for AFMP increased by 71 percent; from PhP11.5 billion in 2006 to PhP19.6 billion in 2007, and in 2008, by another 19 percent.

Starting in May 2008, the government increased the support price for rice to encourage domestic production in order to minimize the negative impact on the domestic market of the uncertainties in the international rice market. The world price of rice increased from $319 per metric ton in 2006 to $352 in 2007 and to $722 in 2008 (Table 10.5). Because the Philippines imports 12.4 percent (1.7 million metric tons) of its rice requirement annually, the higher international prices had a significant effect on the domestic market. The government increased the support price of palay from PhP10 per kilogram to PhP17 per kilogram. Thus, for the whole of 2008, the average support price was PhP14.67. The PhP22.56 per kilogram price support in 2008 is the corresponding price of rice using the 0.65 recovery rate. The support price of corn was increased from PhP8.5/kg to PhP10/kg for an average support price in 2008 of PhP9.50/kg.

The estimated MPS for rice is higher for 2008 than for 2007 because of higher NFA procurement due to the rice market crisis. However, the NFA's procurement of rice remained low due to its financial difficulties. Thus, despite the widening gap between the average external reference price of PhP4.56/kg and the applied administered price, the MPS for rice in 2008 was still below the 10 percent *de minimis* limit. The 2008 MPS for rice was PhP8.2 billion, while the *de minimis* limit was PhP29.6 billion, so the MPS was below the limit by 72.3 percent. Because there was zero NFA procurement of corn, the MPS for corn was also zero. The *de minimis* limit was PhP9.76 billion.

Alternative calculations of MPS

Consideration of the MPS as notified by the Philippines and alternative methods of calculating its values that might have been adopted highlight a few issues about this support measurement not encountered in previous chapters. Because of the positive gap between the administered price of rice and the fixed external reference price, the Philippines, unlike India or China, has notified positive MPS in all years. When the MPS calculation is expressed in domestic currency, the use of a fixed external reference price may create problems in the calculation for developing countries, where inflation rates are generally higher as compared with developed countries. The price level in the Philippines essentially doubled between the 1986–88 base period and 1994 and had doubled again by 2008. Moreover, increased domestic production with a positive price gap leads to an increased nominal value of MPS if based on total production as the eligible quantity. The Philippines has avoided both of these complications by notifying only procured quantities as eligible production, despite the central role administered prices have played in food policy and decisions about levels of rice imports.

One problematic issue in the Philippines case is that the nominal administered prices are as high relative to the fixed external reference prices for rice and corn. The per-unit rates of market price support implied by the measure notified to the WTO are extreme at nearly 200–300 percent. This rate of WTO MPS price gap is difficult to interpret in economic terms. The wholesale domestic market price of rice, in particular, is usually above the nominal administered price, but the NPR of rice, while reflecting protection, is much lower than the rate of support per unit of output that enters the WTO MPS calculation, as shown in Table 10.4. Rates of MPS notified to the WTO that vastly exceed rates calculated in economic terms have not been common in the previously examined countries. But the core issue is the same: the WTO MPS proves problematic as an indicator of economic support for rice because it does not take the variations in world or domestic prices into account.

In terms of possible commitments of the Philippines under the Agreement, two alternatives to the way rice MPS has been calculated and notified prove interesting to evaluate. First, had the Philippines applied the price gap from its administered price in the base period (PhP6.2 per kilo, average in 1986–88) to total rice production in that period, its level of support would have been PhP5,663 million. This would have exceeded 10 percent of the value of rice production in the base period, which averaged PhP2,141 million. As a result, the Philippines could have determined a positive Base Total AMS in the Uruguay Round and a subsequent Bound Total AMS. Its Final Bound Total AMS would have been PhP4,910 million after the 13.3 percent reduction from base level undertaken by developing countries, assuming it reflected just the rice MPS.

The rice MPS of the Philippines would have reached over PhP65 billion in 1995 if calculated for the total quantity of rice output, as the administered price increased from PhP6.2 per kilo in the base period to PhP14 per kilo and production increased from 3.4 million metric tons to 6.8 million. Its value would have reached PhP98 billion in 2004 and an estimated PhP197 billion in 2008. To remain compliant with the Agreement under this alternative calculation, the Philippines might have requested a number of exceptions to exceed its Bound Total AMS based on excessive inflation, as provided for in Article 18 of the Agreement (see Appendix A). Alternatively, the Philippines would not have been able to raise its administered price by as much as it did. The observed inflation might have been accepted as justification for exceeding the hypothetical Bound Total AMS but the increase in MPS from calculating it based on expanding total production would not justify such an excess.

Alternatively, suppose the Philippines had notified its support levels in US dollars instead of Philippine pesos and had used the total quantity of production as the basis of the calculations. With the notifications in dollars, the rice MPS leads to a Base Total AMS of $278 million. The resulting Final Bound Total AMS would have been $237.6 million. As before, by 1995 the rice AMS under this alternative calculation ($2,515 million) would have exceeded the Bound Total AMS constraint. So again, if total production were used as the eligible quantity in its calculations, the Philippines would have exceeded its nominal constraint in dollars by a large amount or would have had to increase its administered price by much less.

In subsequent years, the trend in notified MPS is different in dollars and in pesos. The administered price in dollars declines after 1995 as the peso depreciates. The MPS based on total production declines to $1,755 million by 2004, although it increases in peso terms. The Philippines would thus have needed continued concurrence to exceed its hypothetical dollar-denominated Final Bound Total AMS also in years after 1995 as a result of excessive inflation between 1986–88 and 1995, in spite of the decline in the dollar-denominated support after 1995. Calculating the notified MPS in dollars would have brought it closer to the declining nominal protection of rice shown in Table 10.4 although still not a very close match with that indicator of economic price support. In particular, from 2007 to 2008 an MPS for rice calculated on the basis of total production in either pesos or dollars would have increased with higher administered prices, while the nominal rate of protection fell as world prices increased.

Projected support and Doha

The projected agricultural domestic support in the Philippines from 2009 to 2015 is presented in Table 10.14. These projections are based on the following assumptions:

a. The geometric growth rate of the overall GAA from 2002 to 2008 was used to extend the series until 2015.
b. The average share of GAA budget for agriculture to the overall GAA from 2002 to 2008 was used to extend the GAA budget for agriculture. The GAA budget of agriculture includes the budgets for the Department of Agriculture, budget support to government corporations in agriculture, and the budget for AFMP.
c. The average share of the budget of AFMP to the GAA for agriculture from 2002 to 2008 was used to extend the budget for AFMP.
d. Similar to the analysis for the shadow notifications, the budget for AFMP was augmented by 25 percent to estimate the notified green box and development program support from 2009 to 2015.
e. The average shares of the green box and development program support in the 2002–04 notifications were used to allocate the total augmented AFMP budget among green box and development program measures.
f. The administered price of palay was assumed to remain at PhP17/kg in 2009, then increase to PhP18/kg in 2011–12, PhP19/kg in 2013–14, and PhP20/kg in 2015. The administered price was converted into the

Table 10.14 *Projected levels of Philippine domestic support, 2009–15*

	Projection						
	2009	2010	2011	2012	2013	2014	2015
Green box	18,115	19,125	20,192	21,318	22,507	23,762	25,088
Development programs	4,462	4,711	4,973	5,251	5,544	5,853	6,179
Blue box	—	—	—	—	—	—	—
Product-specific AMS							
Market Price Support	*Applied administered price (pesos/kg)*						
Rice	26.15	26.15	27.69	27.69	29.23	29.23	30.77
Corn	10.00	10.00	11.00	11.00	12.00	12.00	13.00
	Eligible production (thousand metric tons)						
Rice[a]	585	455	455	390	390	325	325
Corn	—	—	—	—	—	—	—
	Total production (thousand metric tons)						
Rice[a]	11,370	11,828	12,304	12,799	13,314	13,850	14,407
Corn	7,267	7,621	7,993	8,384	8,793	9,222	9,673
	Market Price Support (million pesos)						
Rice	12,630	9,823	10,524	9,021	9,621	8,018	8,518
Corn	—	—	—	—	—	—	—

	Million pesos						
Other non-exempt measures	—	—	—	—	—	—	—
Product-specific thresholds	*10% of value of production (million pesos)*						
Rice[a]	32,246	35,078	38,159	41,510	45,156	49,122	53,436
Corn	10,681	11,109	13,864	14,418	16,245	17,523	18,378
	Million pesos						
Non-product-specific AMS	—	—	—	—	—	—	—
	10% of value of production (million pesos)						
Non-product-specific threshold	97,237	108,822	121,788	136,298	152,537	170,710	191,049

Notes: — indicates zero.

[a] Projections for palay (paddy) converted into rice equivalent using a 65 per cent milling recovery rate.

Sources: DA and author's calculations.

price of rice using the 0.65 recovery ratio. Furthermore, production of palay was assumed to grow by 3.9 percent annually (which is the average production growth between 2000 and 2008). In 2008, rice palay procurement increased to about 4.2 percent of production (455 thousand metric tons) because of market uncertainties. Because instability in the market persisted in 2009, palay procurement was assumed to increase during the year to 5.1 percent of production, which amounted to 585 thousand metric tons. But as the rice market situation stabilizes, procurement gradually declines below 4 percent of production (to 455 thousand metric tons in 2010–2011, 390 thousand metric tons in 2012–13, and 325 thousand metric tons in 2014–2015).

g. The administered price of corn was assumed to remain at PhP10/kg in 2009 and 2010, then increase to PhP11/kg in 2011–12, PhP12/kg in 2013–14, and PhP13/kg in 2015. Corn production was assumed to grow by 4.9 percent annually from 2009 to 2015. However, NFA procurements of corn were assumed to remain zero through 2015.

Under these assumptions, the projected agriculture domestic support from 2009 to 2015 in the green box will increase from PhP18.1 billion in 2009 to PhP25 billion in 2015. Development program support increases from PhP4.5 billion in 2009 to PhP6.2 billion in 2015. The MPS for rice is projected to decline from PhP12.6 billion in 2009 to PhP8.5 billion in 2015. These values are below the *de minimis* threshold, which remains 10 percent of the value of production under either the Agreement or a possible Doha outcome. The notified MPS for corn is zero because there is no NFA procurement. The Base OTDS of the Philippines under a Doha agreement along the lines of the December 2008 draft modalities is PhP117 billion and would not be subject to reduction as a commitment. This commitment leaves ample room for further support beyond observed past levels and projections through the mid 2010s.

Conclusion

The Philippines provides an example of a developing country that has shifted from significant taxation of agriculture to significant protection. Rice, corn, coconut, and bananas are key commodities, with rice alone accounting for more than one-third of the value of crop production. Into the 1980s, when the Agreement was first under discussion, the Philippines was a net agricultural and food exporter, but agriculture was disadvantaged by export taxes, exchange rate overvaluation, high tariffs on manufactured goods, and cumbersome interventions through government corporations. By the 1990s, the Philippines had become a net agricultural and food importer. Relative protection shifted in favor of agriculture, with rice, corn, sugar, and pork becoming highly protected. The rice market remains controlled by the government through the NFA which sets producer-support and consumer-ceiling administered prices, procures from farmers, controls imports and exports, and maintains buffer stocks to stabilize prices in the domestic market.

Overall, government spending on agriculture is about 3 percent of total national government expenditure, a level that is low relative to other middle-income developing countries. There have been major shifts in the government's expenditure pattern in agriculture since 2000, including a reallocation of budget resources to the new Agriculture and Fisheries Modernization Program. There have been substantial subsidies to the NFA. Although the NFA faces ongoing financial stress, it is expected to continue to subsidize rice production and consumption – in particular, holding down the consumer price of rice in the aftermath of the perceived crisis in the domestic market after international rice prices soared in 2008. The Philippine government has invested substantial resources to increase rice productivity through the Hybrid Rice Commercialization Program. Implementation of this program is expected to continue, although adoption rates remain low.

The Philippines has a zero Bound Total AMS commitment and its WTO notifications have shown support under just three categories: the green box, development programs and product-specific *de minimis* AMS for rice and corn. Notifications submitted in January 2009 reported support for 2002–04. Green box expenditures were primarily for infrastructure services while development program support since 2002 has been divided almost equally between investment subsidies and input subsidies. Estimates of shadow notifications for 2004 through 2008 reflect the notified support allocations among these measures and aggregate expenditure levels on agriculture available for those years. These estimates suggest green box support had increased to PhP22.6 billion by 2008, while support under development programs were around PhP5.5 billion, less than 1 percent of the total value of production. Subsequent projections of support through 2015 indicate it will be well within the commitments and obligations of the Philippines under either the Agreement or a potential Doha outcome.

The MPS notifications for the Philippines provide a developing-country case representative of some food importers that intervene in markets for basic food staples. Its administered prices for rice and corn considerably exceed its reference prices. For rice, the administered price has been around PhP15 per kilogram until 2008 compared to the fixed external reference price of PhP4.56 per kilogram. As a consequence, unlike India and China, the Philippines has notified a positive MPS. The price wedge per kilogram is substantial and rose in 2008, but the value of the notified MPS is low because the Philippines used the quantity procured by the NFA as the eligible production. The quantities procured have been small for rice and negligible for corn, so the value of MPS has remained well below the 10 percent product-specific *de minimis* threshold.

For a country with rising administered prices, potential complications arise in compliance with the WTO if total production is used to calculate MPS. Were the Philippines to include its entire production as the eligible quantity in MPS calculations the notified values would greatly exceed the product-specific *de minimis* thresholds or a Bound Total AMS commitment that the Philippines might have established under this alternative calculation. Inflation, increased real administered prices and increased production contribute to raising the calculated values. While the government lacks the fiscal resources to procure such a large quantity, administered prices have been central parameters of food policy in the Philippines. With only tariff barriers the domestic price would settle around the world price plus the applied tariff. But in the Philippines the government intervenes in the rice market by exercising monopoly control of trade as well as setting tariffs. In this circumstance, the administered prices have been important in domestic price determination, providing floor and ceiling levels for domestic prices of all output, even if none is procured. Even so in the absence of any change in the way in which the MPS is calculated, the Philippines will easily remain within its WTO obligations through the mid 2010s.

References

Aldaba, R. 2005. Policy reversals, lobby groups, and economic distortions. Discussion Paper 2005–04. Philippine Institute for Development Studies.

Cororaton, C. B. 2008. The Philippines: Shadow WTO agricultural domestic support notifications. IFPRI Discussion Paper 827.

Coxhead, I. and S. Jayasuriya. 2003. Environment and natural resources. In *The Philippine Economy: Development, Policies and Challenges*, ed. A. M. Balisacan and H. Hill. Quezon City: Ateneo de Manila Press.

David, C. 2003. Agriculture. In *The Philippine Economy: Development, Policies and Challenges*, ed. A. M. Balisacan and H. Hill. Quezon City: Ateneo de Manila Press.

2006. The Philippine Hybrid Rice Program: A case for redesign and scaling down. Research Paper 2006–03. Philippine Institute for Development Studies.

David, C., P. Intal, and A. M. Balisacan. 2007. Distortions to agricultural incentives in the Philippines. Agricultural Distortions Working Paper 28, World Bank.

Dawe, D. C., P. F. Moya, and C. B. Casiwan. 2005. *Why Does the Philippines Import Rice?* Los Baños, Laguna: International Rice Research Institute.

DA (Department of Agriculture). Various Issues. Production Database, Bureau of Agricultural Statistics.

DBM (Department of Budget and Management). Various Issues. General Appropriations Act.

DOF (Department of Finance). Various Issues. Statistics.

Habito, C. and R. Briones. 2005. Philippine agriculture over the years: Performance, policies and pitfalls. Paper presented at the Asian Institute of Management Policy Center conference on policies to strengthen productivity in the Philippines, Makati City, June 27.

Intal, P. S. Jr., and J. H. Power. 1990. Trade, Exchange Rate, and Agricultural Pricing Policy in the Philippines: Comparative Studies on Political Economy of Agricultural Pricing Policy, No. 8485, World Bank.

IMF (International Monetary Fund). 2008. Primary commodity prices. www.imf.org/external/np/res/commod/index.asp.

Mundlak, Y., D. Larson, and R. Butzer. 2004. Agricultural dynamics in Thailand, Indonesia and the Philippines. *Australian Journal of Agricultural and Resource Economics* 48(1): 95–126.

NSCB (National Statistical Coordination Board). Various Issues. National Income Accounts.

Tariff Commission. Various Issues. Tariff and Custom Codes of the Philippines.

World Bank. 2007. Philippines: Agriculture public expenditure review. Technical Working Paper 40493. World Bank Country Office.

WTO. Time Series on International Trade. http://stat.wto.org/StatisticalProgram/WSDBStatProgramSeries.aspx?Language=E.

PART IV

Looking forward: can fair markets be achieved?

11

The difficult task of disciplining domestic support

DAVID ORDEN, DAVID BLANDFORD AND TIM JOSLING

When the WTO was launched at the conclusion of the Uruguay Round negotiations its members committed to a new set of disciplines for agricultural domestic support, market access and export competition. It was recognized at the time that the domestic support disciplines were rather porous. Their architecture was consistent with the modest objectives that WTO members had collectively agreed to reduce distortions in world markets. What was uncertain at that point was just how the agreed-upon disciplines would interact with subsequent domestic agricultural policy decisions. In particular, it was not known to what extent the new rules and commitments would motivate countries to shift their policies in the less trade-distorting direction envisioned by the Agreement on Agriculture.

For domestic support the only fixed numerical commitment under the Agreement was to a nominal ceiling (or zero binding) on the sum of certain trade-distorting amounts of support calculated annually in the Current Total AMS. Countries making ceiling commitments set the ceilings at relatively high levels as a result of using a 1986–88 base period with low world prices and high support. By the time the Agreement was signed prices had increased and support moderated, so it was recognized that these commitments provided substantial flexibility. Green box measures in all countries, and certain types of support through development programs in developing countries, were exempt from any ceiling. The blue box emerged as a late compromise in the negotiations that left exempt from caps or reductions substantial payments linked to supply control programs in the EU and US. Within a product's AMS, market price support was to be measured in a somewhat artificial manner based on the gap between an administered price and a fixed external reference price applied to an (ambiguously-defined) eligible quantity. *De minimis* allowances for product-specific and non-product-specific AMS support were adopted apparently with little consideration of how important these exemptions might turn out to be. Requirements to notify domestic support measures to facilitate verification of compliance with the Agreement also lacked rigorous criteria. Not only were submission deadlines advisory rather than binding, but how various measures should be classified in relation to the agreed rules, and how levels of support should be measured, were subject only to general guidelines.

Under these loose terms, a body of notifications of domestic support began to accumulate. Notifications came fairly steadily in the first few years of the WTO for the eight countries examined in the previous chapters. Yet, for three of these countries, Brazil, the EU and the US that are key players in the often acrimonious international debate over farm policies, the notification delays increased as the Doha negotiations sought to define new disciplines. The timing of the EU and US notifications improved later, but only after it became apparent that the Doha Round was unlikely to be concluded rapidly. This in itself is a perverse pattern. Just at the time that transparency afforded by formal notifications might have been most useful, leading countries chose not to live up to this responsibility. The lack of transparency may be indicative as much of the divisive character of the negotiations as an obstacle to their progress. What is clear from the agreed guidelines is that the notifications should have been provided in a more timely manner. Other key countries, particularly China and India, have lagged even further behind in submitting notifications. The length of some of the delays clearly reflects political decisions not to provide the information, rather than a lack of technical capacity. In deciding whether or not to obscure how they will report their levels of subsidies or shifts in policies, countries reveal their attitude toward the effectiveness of the international rules designed to discipline domestic support.

This chapter builds upon the detailed country experiences evaluated in the book to bring together in the context of the above concerns some conclusions on the usefulness of the disciplines on domestic support provided by the Agreement. The first section summarizes levels of domestic support from 1995 to 2008 from both the notifications submitted by governments to the WTO and the shadow notifications based on official statistics that will in most cases be used in future notifications. Compliance of levels of support with the Agreement and scheduled reductions of commitments is assessed. We are also interested in how well the notifications have tracked changes in farm policies and have contributed to the goal of reducing distortions in world agricultural markets. The interpretation of notified levels of domestic support requires a careful examination of shifts in policy within countries and their economic implications. In some cases variations in notified support reflect real changes in policies, while in others they largely reflect how countries have chosen to categorize and report their policy measures.

We also use the notifications and shadow notifications to examine the evolution of support policies across the countries. Key questions are whether the structure or levels of support have tended to converge toward less trade-distorting forms and whether the Agreement has played a role driving such convergence. Comparisons across countries focus on whether the underlying economic goal of the Agreement has been met, rather than the legal issue of whether individual countries have complied with its terms.

Looking forward, we evaluate the extent to which the proposed 2008 Doha draft modalities would contribute towards stricter limits on agricultural domestic support, drawing on projections of future support notifications made in the preceding chapters. The importance of careful examination of the basis for changes in notified levels of support is reiterated in the context of assessing the consequences of a Doha Round outcome. We then turn to a brief discussion of some issues that remain unresolved in attempting to align the legal framework on domestic support with the goal of reducing distortions in world markets. Meaningful directions for clarification and enhancement of the rules for the long term are outlined, including the strengthening of the notification and monitoring process.

Compliance with WTO commitments

The accumulated database of domestic support notifications has become substantial since the WTO was founded, despite the lack of timeliness in submissions. The addition of shadow notifications where necessary, as described in the previous chapters, makes it possible to evaluate whether the eight countries examined appear to have complied with rules and commitments under the Agreement over a fourteen-year period. The assembling of a consistent time series of information improves policy transparency; countries for which we have supplied missing data could, and eventually will, confirm our unofficial estimates or contribute to an improved database by updating their notifications.

Tables 11.1 and 11.2 present an aggregate picture of domestic support provided by the countries since 1995, its classification into WTO categories, and the extent of compliance with ceiling commitments. The information is consolidated into summary form by deriving averages for the entire period and for its first and second halves, along with showing

Table 11.1 *Summary of domestic support notifications and shadow notifications for four developed countries, 1995–2008*

	EU[a] (billion euros)				US (billion dollars)			
	Averages				Averages			
	All years	First half	Second half	2008/09	All years	First half	Second half	2008
Green box	30.0	20.4	39.6	56.6	61.7	49.9	73.4	99.6
Less food aid and public stockholding	29.6	20.1	39.1	56.1	18.4	15.0	21.8	23.7
Decoupled income support	8.6	0.3	16.8	33.7	5.2	4.5	5.9	6.1
OTDS	56.6	69.1	44.3	28.5	15.2	16.3	14.2	11.2
Blue box	18.1	21.3	14.9	4.7	0.5	1.0	—	—
Current Total AMS	37.4	47.2	27.6	22.1	9.9	11.0	8.9	7.1
of which, MPS	34.5	43.7	25.3	21.4	5.9	5.9	6.0	6.1
Total *de minimis*	1.1	0.6	1.8	1.7	4.8	4.3	5.3	4.2
Product-specific	0.3	0.1	0.6	0.3	0.3	0.1	0.5	0.1
Non-product-specific	0.8	0.5	1.2	1.3	4.5	4.2	4.8	4.1
Total support	86.6	89.5	83.9	85.1	76.9	66.2	87.6	110.8
Less food aid and public stockholding	86.2	89.2	83.4	84.6	33.6	31.3	36.0	34.9
	Assessment of the commitments							
Bound Total AMS	70.7	72.1	69.3	72.2	19.7	20.2	19.1	19.1
CTAMS/Bound Total AMS (%)	52.9	65.4	39.8	31.1	50.4	54.3	46.5	36.9
Total value of production[b]	252.2	226.0	278.4	296.0	226.5	195.4	262.8	335.3
Bound Total AMS/Total value of production (%)	28.0	31.9	24.9	24.4	8.7	10.4	7.3	5.7

	Japan (billion yen)				Norway (billion NOK)			
	Averages				Averages			
	All years	First half	Second half	2008	All years	First half	Second half	2008
Green box	2,380.7	2,781.2	1,980.2	1,887.3	4.8	4.2	5.4	6.9
Less food aid and public stockholding	2,331.0	2,710.2	1,951.8	1,864.5	4.3	3.5	5.1	6.9
Decoupled income support	14.5	-	29.1	102.3	—	—	—	—
OTDS	1,316.0	1,929.5	702.5	632.0	17.1	18.0	16.2	15.0
Blue box	54.2	46.7	61.8	32.4	6.4	7.5	5.3	3.7
Current Total AMS	1,218.7	1,842.6	594.8	510.7	10.6	10.5	10.7	11.1
of which, MPS	1,020.0	1,645.7	394.4	385.3	11.2	10.9	11.5	11.9
Total *de minimis*	43.1	40.3	45.8	88.9	0.1	—	0.1	0.2
Product-specific	18.5	17.4	19.5	15.4	0.0	—	0.1	0.1
Non-product-specific	24.6	22.9	26.3	73.5	0.0	—	0.1	0.1
Total support	3,696.7	4,710.7	2,682.7	2,519.3	21.9	22.2	21.6	21.9
Less food aid and public stockholding	3,647.0	4,639.7	2,654.3	2,496.5	21.4	21.5	21.3	21.9
	Assessment of the commitments							
Bound Total AMS	4,100.2	4,209.4	3,972.9	3,972.9	11.8	12.1	11.4	11.4
CTAMS/Bound Total AMS (%)	29.7	43.8	15.0	12.9	90.1	86.7	94.1	97.6
Total value of production[b]	9,045.5	9,482.3	8,535.9	8,650.9	22.9	22.5	23.3	24.8
Bound Total AMS/Total value of production (%)	45.3	44.4	46.5	45.9	51.5	53.9	48.9	46.0

Notes: — indicates zero.

[a] Reference to the EU15, EU25 and EU27 as presented in Chapter 3. Row "*of which*, MPS" includeds EMS price support.

[b] Determines, in combination with the *de minimis* percentage, the non-product-specific *de minimis* threshold. Product-specific *de minimis* thresholds also apply.

Sources: WTO notifications and authors' calculations.

Table 11.2 *Summary of domestic support notifications and shadow notifications for four developing countries, 1995–2008*

	Brazil (billion US dollars)				India (billion US dollars)			
	Averages				Averages			
	All years	First half	Second half	2007/08	All years	First half	Second half	2008/09
Green box	2.1	2.6	1.6	2.2	6.1	3.4	8.4	12.5
Less food aid and public stockholding	1.4	1.8	1.1	1.5	1.6	0.9	2.2	3.0
Decoupled income support	—	—	—	—	—	—	—	—
Development programs	0.4	0.3	0.6	1.0	7.2	5.1	8.9	11.7
OTDS	1.2	0.7	1.6	2.7	−1.9	−2.5	−1.4	1.4
Blue box	—	—	—	—	—	—	—	—
Current Total AMS	0.1	—	0.1	0.5	—	—	—	—
Total *de minimis*[a]	1.1	0.7	1.5	2.1	−1.9	−2.5	−1.4	1.4
Product-specific	0.3	0.3	0.2	0.1	−2.9	−3.4	−2.5	0.2
Non-product-specific	0.8	0.4	1.3	2.1	1.0	0.9	1.1	1.2
Total support	3.7	3.6	3.8	5.9	11.4	6.0	16.0	25.7
Less food aid and public stockholding	3.0	2.8	3.3	5.2	6.9	3.5	9.7	16.2
	Assessment of the commitments							
Bound Total AMS	1.0	1.0	0.9	0.9	zb	zb	zb	zb
CTAMS/Bound Total AMS (%)	7.9	1.2	14.6	54.8	zb	zb	zb	zb

Total value of production[a]	55.3	50.1	60.5	99.4	106.7	91.4	119.8	141.2
Bound Total AMS/Total value of production (%)	1.7	2.0	1.5	0.9	zb	zb	zb	zb

	China (billion RMB)				Philippines (billion pesos)			
				Averages	Averages			
	All years	First half	Second half	2008	All years	First half	Second half	2008
Green box	260.1	181.5	327.4	397.1	12.4	9.8	15.1	22.6
Less food aid and public stockholding	208.0	133.5	271.8	334.0	11.4	8.5	14.3	21.5
Decoupled income support	5.3	—	9.9	15.1	—	—	—	—
Development programs	na	na	na	na	3.1	2.6	3.7	5.6
OTDS	–20.8	–41.9	–2.7	9.8	2.1	2.0	2.2	8.2
Blue box	—	—	—	—	—	—	—	—
Current Total AMS	—	—	—	—	—	—	—	—
Total *de minimis*[a]	–20.8	–41.9	–2.7	—	2.1	2.0	2.2	8.2
Product-specific	–31.1	–57.0	–8.8	—	2.1	2.0	2.2	8.2
Non-product-specific	10.2	15.1	6.1	9.8	—	—	—	—
Total support	239.2	139.6	324.6	406.9	17.7	14.3	21.0	36.4
Less food aid and public stockholding	187.1	91.6	269.0	343.8	16.7	13.1	20.2	35.2

Table 11.2 (*cont.*)

	China (billion RMB)				Philippines (billion pesos)			
	Averages				Averages			
	All years	First half	Second half	2008	All years	First half	Second half	2008
	Assessment of the commitments							
Bound Total AMS	zb	zb	zb	zb	zb	zb	zb	zb
CTAMS/Bound Total AMS (%)	zb	zb	zb	zb	zb	zb	zb	zb
Total value of production[b]	2,741.9	2,150.4	3,248.8	4,241.5	558.4	428.9	687.8	946.9
Bound Total AMS/Total value of production (%)	zb	zb	zb	zb	zb	zb	zb	zb

Notes: — indicates zero; na indicates that China is not eligible to exempt the development program category of support from AMS; zb indicates a zero Bound Total AMS.

[a] For India and China this is the sum of AMS support including negative values of MPS (see Tables 8.3 and 9.1).

[b] Determines, in combination with the *de minimis* percentage, the projected non-product-specific *de minimis* threshold. Product-specific *de minimis* thresholds also apply.

Sources: WTO notifications and authors' calculations.

estimated 2008 values. The break points are somewhat arbitrary, but the latter three columns provide an indication of trends in domestic support when compared to the overall averages. Notified levels of support are presented in the currency in which the notifications are made.

From the data it is evident that neither developed nor developing countries have had difficulty meeting the domestic support obligations specified in the Agreement. Among the developed countries, Norway stands out as having regularly notified annual CTAMS close to its Bound Total AMS commitment. As described by Gaasland, Garcia and Vårdal in Chapter 6, notifying support close to the commitment arises for two reasons: administered prices for main crop and livestock products serve as an anchor for Norway's border measures and consequently its domestic market prices; and the MPS calculations use total domestic production as the eligible production. Norway's MPS has exceeded its CTAMS, since the latter includes a negative component due to estimated costs imposed on livestock farmers through high prices for feed. With a strong relationship between administered and market prices, the MPS notified by Norway comes closer to reflecting the economic protection provided to farmers than in other countries. With its CTAMS deriving almost entirely from MPS, Norway occasionally employs slight changes in the notified administered prices to keep MPS low enough to avoid any violations of its commitment.

The notified MPS shows differing relationships to the CTAMS and commitment levels among the remaining countries. The United States, like Norway, has notified a stable MPS, but this accounts for a much smaller share of the US support commitment and in the early years a smaller share of its CTAMS. For the EU and Japan, the MPS in the 1986–88 base period (and related EMS price support used primarily by the EU for fruits and vegetables) was the predominant component determining their commitment levels. Since the Agreement was implemented, EU notifications reflect a systematic direction of policy reform that has shifted support from MPS to exempt direct payments, and consequently the notified CTAMS has fallen steadily over time. The EU payments initially were notified as exempt on blue box grounds. As the reforms unfolded, EU payments were further decoupled from production bases or levels of production and have been notified almost entirely in the green box as decoupled income support.

The change in the domestic support regime in the EU has been associated with a decline in economic market price support to farmers, although to a lesser extent in 1995–2008 than the reduction in the notified MPS, as discussed by Josling and Swinbank in Chapter 3. The situation in Japan is even more stark, as described by Godo and Takahashi in Chapter 5. Elimination of the administered price for rice in 1998 resulted in a reduction in the notified MPS from 70 percent of Japan's commitment to just 20 percent, with essentially no change in economic market price support for rice in that year and only a modest decline in subsequent years. While the EU has implemented relatively few measures providing non-exempt AMS support payments, Japan's AMS non-exempt direct payments have accounted for about one-third of the notified CTAMS since its rice MPS was eliminated. Non-exempt payments have been the cornerstone of domestic support for the US. Linked to market prices, these payments have made the CTAMS of the US uniquely variable on an annual basis compared to other countries. The period averages in Table 11.1 include several years when the notified CTAMS exceeded 85 percent of the US ceiling commitment. In contrast, as the EU shifted from a notified MPS unaffected by world price fluctuations to fixed direct payments it avoided introducing variability into its notified support.

Brazil is the only developing country included in our analysis that has a non-zero (though small) Bound Total AMS. It is also the only developing country among the four analyzed that regularly notifies support other than MPS within the AMS category (in Brazil's case, primarily credit subsidies and debt rescheduling, as discussed by Nassar in Chapter 7). The AMS for one or more products (cotton or wheat) has exceeded the *de minimis* threshold in a few years in Brazil, but the resulting CTAMS has always been well below Brazil's commitment.

Among the other developing countries, the MPS for China and India has been negative because administered prices have been below fixed external reference prices for key food staples (rice and wheat). The MPS does not accurately reflect the economic market price support provided in either country because of the way that the price gap is defined in the Agreement and the choice made by these countries to report eligible quantities on the basis of government grain procurements or other limiting criteria, rather than total or marketed production. Farmers growing rice or wheat in China or India have been disprotected (implicitly taxed) in certain years since 1995, but mostly they have received positive economic price support, as described by Gopinath and Cheng in Chapters 8 and 9, respectively.

An exaggerated positive difference between the rate of price support implied by the notified MPS and economic market price support is apparent for the Philippines. In this case, rice is protected by border measures, with domestic prices up to twice world price levels, as Cororaton describes in Chapter 10. The applied administered price in the MPS calculations was three times the fixed external reference price by 2008. Yet, the Philippines notified a rice MPS below the *de minimis* AMS threshold because it counted only small procured amounts as the eligible quantity of production. The policy debate in the Philippines shows that administered prices are an anchor for border policies that determine market prices, similar to the situation in Norway. Calculating the MPS based on procured quantities understates the policy importance of the administered price of rice in the Philippines, while the use of the nominal administered prices relative to a fixed nominal reference price overstates the actual rate of economic protection.

Under the Agreement, a product-specific AMS need only be included in CTAMS if it exceeds the applicable *de minimis* threshold. Countries can make use of this provision to report relatively modest levels of support for identified products. The four developed countries have made relatively little use of product-specific *de minimis* exemptions. A negative MPS has been reported by the EU when administered prices have fallen below its external reference prices (notably for durum wheat, oats, and occasionally beef). In those cases, when the calculated AMS support has been negative the product-specific AMS has been notified as zero.

The non-product-specific AMS can be excluded from CTAMS as *de minimis* if it falls below the threshold percentage of the total value of agricultural production. Some countries choose to include support that is concentrated on a limited number of products in the non-product-specific AMS. Among the eight countries, the US stands out as having made substantial use of the non-product-specific *de minimis* AMS exemption. This has allowed price-dependent payments made in years of relatively low world prices for certain crops (primarily corn, soybeans, wheat, rice, and cotton) to be excluded from the CTAMS. This non-product-specific AMS support actually reflects an element of reform in US policy, with payments less tied to the production of specific products or to supply control requirements than for the blue box measures they replaced. Yet, the classification of these price-linked payments as non-product-specific AMS has been controversial, as discussed by Brink in Chapter 2 and Blandford and Orden in Chapter 4.

The *de minimis* thresholds on AMS support are constraints for China, India and the Philippines under the Agreement because they do not have a Bound Total AMS identified in their schedules of commitments. These countries have notified various types of non-product-specific AMS support below *de minimis* thresholds. India and the Philippines, and also Brazil, have notified similar or identical measures under exemptions for development programs. Such notifications, particularly by Brazil and India, have been subject to both domestic and international scrutiny because they include input subsidies, which are key forms of support in these countries.

The exemption for development programs allows developing countries to address rural poverty by assisting farmers in ways that affect production and trade. In principle, this reduces the effectiveness of WTO rules to direct countries away from trade-distorting forms of support. In practice, the effect of the exemption has not been consequential, at least through 2008. Even if support under development programs were to be included in the AMS, such support has been low enough that the *de minimis* thresholds of Brazil, India and the Philippines would not have been binding. The *de minimis* threshold level of support has only been approached by the sum of the non-product-specific support notified in the two categories (*de minimis* and development programs) for India, in part because in its few notifications India reported subsidies for electricity and irrigation that other countries are less conscientious about including in their notifications. As incomes continue to increase in large developing countries such as China or India, domestic support seems to be growing and MPS may turn positive. For those countries eligible for the development program exemption (China is not eligible, under the terms of its accession to the WTO), this exemption could prove important for future compliance with support limitations in the Agreement. Questions of whether MPS should be computed using government procurements or total production, or whether direct payment programs qualify for the green box or blue box or belong in AMS, could also prove important in determining the scope these countries have for providing support while remaining within WTO commitments.

To summarize, each country has found room within the exemptions and *de minimis* exclusions provided by the Agreement to allocate domestic support among the allowed categories in order to claim it has remained in compliance with the rules and well under its commitment. Alternative assessments of the categorization of measures or measurement of support levels alter the compliance picture in some cases, as earlier chapters have shown. Challenges to notifications can be raised in the WTO Committee on Agriculture and a few have reached the level of the formal dispute settlement process. But overall there has been only limited capacity to demonstrate noncompliance given the porous disciplines that the Agreement enshrines.

Trends in support among countries

The WTO notifications are designed first and foremost to provide transparency in monitoring compliance with legal obligations under the Agreement. But these legal obligations draw their purpose from an underlying economic motivation. Interest in compliance with the Agreement therefore is tied to the objective of correcting and preventing distortions in world agricultural markets. So the broader question is how well the notifications reflect policy reform decisions over time and what they convey about trends in forms and levels of support among countries. Some of these insights can be deduced from notified nominal support levels and from assessments of compliance by individual countries with the Agreement. But the nominal data and unilateral compliance assessments fail to bring out some of the comparative information conveyed by the notifications.

Two key questions in this regard concern the motivation for policy reform under the Agreement and whether it has played a role in promoting policy convergence among countries. Insight into these questions can be obtained from assessment of the composition of domestic support and its level as a percentage of the total value of agricultural production (Table 11.3 and Table 11.4). Within each country, this normalization facilitates comparisons of types and levels of support across years relative to the size of its agricultural sector. Japan stands out (see Table 11.1) in this regard as the only country for which the notified nominal total value of agricultural production against which support levels are evaluated has declined over time.

In terms of the convergence question, the notifications of domestic support expressed as a percentage of the total value of agricultural production provide useful information for drawing comparisons. For these comparisons a caveat is in order because of the manner in which the notifications are prepared and reviewed. Each country exercises substantial discretion in the measures it notifies to the WTO and in the measurement of levels of support. The WTO notifications are not specifically designed to provide a systematic comparison across members, unlike the support estimates provided by the OECD's PSEs for a smaller group of countries. Although some scrutiny of the notifications occurs through the WTO Committee on Agriculture and through dispute settlement, no systematic

Table 11.3 *Summary of domestic support as percent of total value of agricultural production for four developed countries, 1995–2008*

	EU[a]				US			
	Averages(%)				Averages (%)			
	All years	First half	Second half	2008/09	All years	First half	Second half	2008
Green box	11.9	9.0	14.2	19.1	27.2	25.5	27.9	29.7
Less food aid and public stockholding	11.7	8.9	14.0	19.0	8.1	7.7	8.3	7.1
Decoupled income support	3.4	0.2	6.1	11.4	2.3	2.3	2.3	1.8
OTDS	22.4	30.6	15.9	9.5	6.7	8.3	5.4	3.3
Blue box	7.2	9.4	5.4	1.6	0.2	0.5	—	—
Current Total AMS	14.8	20.9	9.9	7.5	4.4	5.6	3.4	2.1
of which, MPS	13.7	19.3	9.1	7.2	2.6	3.0	2.3	1.8
Total *de minimis*	0.4	0.3	0.6	0.5	2.1	2.2	2.0	1.2
Product-specific	0.1	0.1	0.2	0.1	0.1	0.1	0.2	—
Non-product-specific	0.3	0.2	0.4	0.4	2.0	2.1	1.8	1.2
Total support	34.3	39.6	30.1	28.7	33.9	33.9	33.3	33.0
Less food aid and public stockholding	34.2	39.5	29.9	28.6	14.9	16.0	13.7	10.4

	Japan				Norway			
	Averages (%)				Averages (%)			
	All years	First half	Second half	2008	All years	First half	Second half	2008
Green box	26.3	29.3	23.2	21.8	21.0	18.7	23.2	27.8
Less food aid and public stockholding	25.8	28.6	22.9	21.6	19.6	15.5	21.9	27.8
Decoupled income support	0.2	—	0.3	1.2	—	—	—	—
OTDS	14.5	20.3	8.2	7.3	74.7	80.0	69.5	60.4
Blue box	0.6	0.5	0.7	0.4	28.0	33.2	22.9	14.9
Current Total AMS	13.5	19.4	7.0	5.9	46.4	46.7	46.0	44.9
of which, MPS	11.3	17.4	4.6	4.5	48.8	48.4	49.1	48.0
Total *de minimis*	0.5	0.4	0.5	1.0	0.3	—	0.6	0.6
Product-specific	0.2	0.2	0.2	0.2	0.1	—	0.3	0.2
Non-product-specific	0.3	0.2	0.3	0.8	0.2	—	0.3	0.4
Total support	40.9	49.7	31.4	29.1	95.7	98.7	92.7	88.3
Less food aid and public stockholding	40.3	48.9	31.1	28.9	93.4	95.5	91.4	88.3

Note: — indicates zero.

[a] Refers to the EU15, EU25 and EU27 as presented in Chapter 3. Row "*of which*, MPS" includes EMS price support.

Sources: WTO notifications and authors' calculations.

Table 11.4 *Summary of domestic support as percent of total value of agricultural production for four developing countries, 1995–2008*

	Brazil				India			
	Averages (%)				Averages (%)			
	All years	First half	Second half	2007/08	All years	First half	Second half	2008/09
Green box	3.8	5.1	2.7	2.2	5.7	3.7	7.1	8.9
Less food aid and public stockholding	2.6	3.6	1.8	1.6	1.5	1.0	1.8	2.1
Decoupled income support	—	—	—	—	—	—	—	—
Development programs	0.8	0.6	1.0	1.0	6.7	5.6	7.5	8.3
OTDS	2.1	1.4	2.7	2.7	−1.8	−2.8	−1.2	1.0
Blue box	—	—	—	—	—	—	—	—
Current Total AMS	0.1	—	0.2	0.5	zb	zb	zb	zb
Total *de minimis*[a]	2.0	1.4	2.5	2.2	−1.8	−2.8	−1.2	1.0
Product-specific	0.5	0.6	0.4	0.1	−2.7	−3.7	−2.1	0.1
Non-product-specific	1.5	0.8	2.1	2.1	0.9	1.0	0.9	0.8
Total support	6.7	7.1	6.4	5.9	10.6	6.5	13.3	18.2
Less food aid and public stockholding	5.5	5.6	5.4	5.3	6.4	3.9	8.1	11.4

	China				Philippines			
	Averages (%)				Averages (%)			
	All years	First half	Second half	2008	All years	First half	Second half	2008
Green box	9.5	8.4	10.1	9.4	2.2	2.3	2.2	2.3
Less food aid and public stockholding	7.6	6.2	8.4	7.9	2.0	2.0	2.1	2.2
Decoupled income support	0.2	—	0.3	0.4	—	—	—	—
Development programs	na	na	na	na	0.6	0.6	0.5	0.6
OTDS	−0.8	−1.9	−0.1	0.2	0.4	0.5	0.3	0.8
Blue box	—	—	–	—	—	—	—	—
Current Total AMS	zb	zb	zb	zb	zb	zb	zb	zb
Total *de minimis*[a]	−0.8	−1.9	−0.1	—	0.4	0.5	0.3	0.8
Product-specific	−1.1	−2.6	−0.3	—	0.4	0.5	0.3	0.8
Non-product-specific	0.4	0.7	0.2	0.2	—	—	—	—
Total support	8.7	6.5	10.0	9.6	3.2	3.3	3.1	3.7
Less food aid and public stockholding	6.8	4.3	8.3	8.1	3.0	3.1	2.9	3.6

Notes: — indicates zero; na indicates that China is not eligible to exempt the development program category of support from AMS; zb indicates a zero Bound Total AMS.

[a] For India and China, this is the sum of AMS support including negative values of MPS (see Tables 8.3 and 9.1).

Sources: WTO notifications and authors' calculations.

corroboration is undertaken to ensure comparability of the notified support. Thus some caution is appropriate in making cross-country comparisons of levels of support in the notifications, especially at an aggregate level involving summations across multiple measures in various categories, as opposed to comparing support from a specific measure reported by more than one country.

Green box support has increased in nominal value and as a percentage of the total value of production in six of the countries, with the exceptions being Brazil and Japan. The composition of the green box, its level as a percentage of total production value, and the explanation for growth in support differ markedly among countries. Green box support was near or exceeded 20 percent of production value in the EU, Japan, Norway and the US by 2008, but was less than 10 percent in Brazil, China, India, and the Philippines. Green box support is high but declining in Japan particularly because of the inclusion of substantial infrastructure investments. These also make up a large component of China's green box notifications, but such investments are not included to the same extent in the notifications of other countries. Norway's high green box support relative to the total value of production includes a unique program of farm-operator vacation payments that Gaasland, Garcia and Vårdal argue is a labor input subsidy and should not qualify for inclusion.

The green box in India and in the US includes large expenditures directed toward food consumers. Without domestic food aid programs, whose subsidies can be applied to purchases of domestic or foreign produced groceries, US green box support averages about 8 percent of the total value of agricultural production, compared to 27 percent if domestic food aid is included. Without public stockholding for food security, India's green box support is about 1.5 percent of the total value of production, compared to 6 percent with stockholding. For the EU, almost the entire growth of green box support comes from the policy shift to payments notified as decoupled income support to agricultural producers. These payments rose to more than 11 percent of the total value of agricultural production in 2008. The US shifted to direct payments notified as decoupled income support a decade earlier than the EU but annual US payments have remained less than 3 percent of the total value of production. China's payments to grain producers notified as decoupled income support since 2004 are less than 1 percent of total agricultural production value.

The extent to which both the EU and US have abandoned blue box payments is noticeable; notified blue box subsidies have almost disappeared. The blue box was created in the final stages of the Uruguay Round negotiations mainly to provide a haven for some of the support provided by the EU and US that was argued to be less trade-distorting than non-exempt direct payments in the AMS. While levels of blue box support remain unconstrained by the Agreement, the use of this category was subsequently overtaken in both cases by policy decisions that involved movement away from supply control measures. Norway has continued its use of blue box measures and notifies significant blue box payments, but even in Norway's case the value and relative importance of these payments has declined. Japan continues to enact policies to divert land from rice production into other crops but has notified only limited blue box payments associated with these measures.

India has reported a relatively high level of support under the development program exemption. In its notifications for 1996/97 and 1997/98, 80 percent of the reported subsidies for fertilizer, electricity, and irrigation were included in the development program category based on the share of small farms in the total number of farms, as described by Gopinath. Brazil and the Philippines have notified smaller amounts of support under the development program exemption. The level of China's non-product-specific AMS notified as *de minimis* is much lower as a percentage of the value of production than the sum of India's non-product-specific support under development programs plus *de minimis* AMS, as already noted. China has not notified subsidies for irrigation or electricity, a potentially important omission that Cheng examines.

A broad measurement of support is provided by the concept of the OTDS (overall trade-distorting support: the sum of CTAMS, *de minimis* AMS support and blue box payments) as discussed in the Doha Round. This measurement has declined slightly in nominal value in Norway and the US, and more dramatically in the EU and Japan, over the period 1995–2008. The decline in the EU reflects changes in policy, with the significant qualification that the MPS notified to the WTO is not an accurate measure of the economic value of market price support. For Japan, there is little correspondence between its low notified MPS, and hence the OTDS, and its continued border protection of rice. This results in a major disconnect between the illusion of policy reform through a reduction in notified MPS and the reality that domestic rice prices in Japan have remained substantially above world levels because of high tariffs and Japan's diversion of land from rice production. Even with a reduced MPS, both the OTDS and the total of all support (including also that in the green box) is higher in the EU and Japan than in the US as a percentage of the total value of agricultural production when domestic food aid is excluded. The OTDS and the total of all support are particularly high as percentages of the value of production for Norway.

The developing countries have notified less support than the developed countries but the level has been increasing in all four cases, except for the total of all support for Brazil as a percent of value of production because of its declining green box support. When domestic food aid and public stockholding for food security programs are excluded from the green box notifications, the estimated total of all support for China and India relative to the total value of agricultural production in 2008 is of a similar order of magnitude to that for the US. Of course, there are many more farms in China and India producing that agricultural output and receiving low levels of support per farm, though per farm support is not disciplined in the WTO.

When all notified support is combined, the nominal level among developed countries has risen in the US, been stable in Norway, declined slightly in the EU, and declined sharply in Japan between 1995 and 2008. Total support has declined in the four developed countries as a percentage of the total value of agricultural production, whereas it has increased in China, India and the Philippines. With a porous international Agreement on Agriculture, domestic support policies remain heterogeneous across the countries in our analysis.

Doha's enhanced disciplines on domestic support

In the Doha Round countries have been negotiating over new rules and commitments to achieve further reductions in agricultural support and protection. The potential disciplines for domestic support incorporated in the draft modalities of December 2008 reflect progress toward that objective. They could have the effect of reducing the disparity among countries in the level of domestic support provided, though the rules will still reflect the continued accommodation of differences in the measures and levels of support that have been discussed in this book. Though some disagreement persists on how much additional discipline should be introduced and how quickly, detailed and intense negotiations lie behind the proposed rules, initial commitments and phased-in commitment reductions reflected in the draft modalities.

The potential Doha commitments are shown side-by-side for the eight countries in Table 11.5. The top portion of the table shows commitments in the currency used by each country for its notifications, while the lower portion provides a basis for comparison by expressing commitments in

Table 11.5 *Doha limits on OTDS, CTAMS, and overall blue box in currency of notification and Doha* de minimis *percentages*

	EU27	US	Japan	Norway	Brazil	India	China	Philippines
	Billion euro	*Billion US$*	*Billion Yen*	*Billion NOK*	*Billion US$*	*Billion US$*	*Billion RMB*	*Billion pesos*
Basis for calculations								
Pre-Doha Final Bound Total AMS (FBTAMS) (%)	72.2	19.1	3,972.9	11.4	0.9	—	—	—
Value of production (1995–2000)	259.3	195.9	9,849.6	22.6				
Value of production (1995–2004)					48.7	102.5	2,337.6	468.8
10 percent of value of production (1995–2000)	25.9	19.6	985.0	2.3				
20 percent of value of production (1995–2004)					9.7	20.5	467.5	93.8
5 percent of value of production (1995–2000 or 1995–2004)	12.9	9.8	492.5	1.1	2.4	5.1	116.9	23.4
Notified blue box (if greater than 5 percent of value of production)[a]	20.8			7.5				
Base OTDS (sum of selected components above)	118.9	48.5	5,450.3	21.2	13.1	25.6	584.4	117.2

Table 11.5 (*cont.*)

	EU27	US	Japan	Norway	Brazil	India	China	Philippines
Full reduction percentage from Base OTDS (%)	80	70	75	55	37	—	—	—
Final Bound OTDS after any reduction	23.8	14.5	1,362.6	9.5	8.3	25.6	584.4	117.2
Full reduction percentage from pre-Doha FBTAMS (%)	70	60	70	53	30			
Final Bound Total AMS after reduction	21.7	7.6	1,191.9	5.4	0.6	—	—	—
Overall blue box limit (2.5 per-cent or 5 percent of value of production)[b]	6.5	4.9	246.2	3.6	2.4	5.1	116.9	23.4
De minimis percentage after any reduction (%)	2.5	2.5	2.5	2.5	6.7	10.0	8.5	10.0
	Commitments in US dollars[c]							
Final Bound OTDS	33.1	14.5	14.6	1.5	8.3	25.6	85.5	2.5
Final Bound Total AMS	30.1	7.6	12.7	0.9	0.6	—	—	—
Overall blue box	9.0	4.9	2.6	0.6	2.4	5.1	17.1	0.5

	Commitment as a share of base-period value of production (%)							
Final Bound OTDS	9.2	7.4	13.8	42.1	17.0	25.0	25.0	25.0
Final Bound Total AMS	8.4	3.9	12.1	24.0	1.3	—	—	—
Overall blue box	2.5	2.5	2.5	15.7	5.0	5.0	5.0	5.0

Notes: — indicates zero. Value of production in base periods is average of those reported in WTO (2010), which includes certain qualifications attaching to the data.

[a] Tests for paragraph 1(c) condition, picks up blue box payments when above 5 percent of value of production (See Table 2.2 and Appendix B).

[b] Norway is treated as a special case under paragraph 39.

[c] Country data were converted from currency of notifications to US dollars using IMF average yearly exchange rates for 2009.

Source: Based on WTO (2008) and prepared for this chapter by Lars Brink with country chapter authors.

US dollars (using 2009 average exchange rates) and as percentages of the base-period total agricultural production value for each country.

Among the developed countries, Final Bound Total AMS levels are brought down by 70 percent in the EU and Japan and by somewhat smaller percentages for the US (60 percent) and Norway (53 percent). These significant reductions would not only cut allowable nominal levels of CTAMS but also would rebalance the relative magnitude of commitments among countries, measured on a dollar basis or as a percentage of the value of production. The ratio of FBTAMS of the EU compared to that of the US measured in US dollars at 2009 exchange rates falls from 5.2 under the Agreement to 4.0 under the Doha proposals as the EU27 limit drops from 72.2 billion euro to 21.7 billion euro and that of the US from $19.1 billion to $7.6 billion. Japan and Norway retain higher FBTAMS commitments than the EU or US as a percentage of the 1995–2000 base-period value of production; the support limit is brought closer to the EU or US levels than in the past using this criterion for Japan but less so for Norway.[1] The *de minimis* thresholds are reduced uniformly for the developed countries from 5 percent of the future annual nominal value of production to 2.5 percent. The overall blue box would be limited to 2.5 percent of the 1995–2000 value of production, instead of being unconstrained (Norway's constraint would be calculated differently). Product-specific caps would apply to AMS support and to blue box payments – these additional commitments are discussed in the previous chapters but are not shown in Table 11.5.

The Doha commitments would create a Base OTDS for developed countries that includes the FBTAMS under the Agreement plus 10 percent of the total value of production for the period 1995–2000. The Base OTDS also includes either an additional 5 percent of the 1995–2000 production value or the average of notified blue box payments in that period if it is higher (as is the case for the EU and Norway). The Doha OTDS commitments would cap the sum of CTAMS, *de minimis* AMS support and blue box payments for the first time. Substantial reductions from the base would be phased in as Bound OTDS commitments for the developed countries over five years. The percentage reductions are largest for the EU, followed by Japan, the US and Norway.

[1] The projected total value of production is subject to uncertainty, but using the projections of the preceding chapters leads to similar findings about relative levels of support that would be allowed under the proposed Doha commitments.

For the EU and Japan, the Final Bound OTDS exceeds the Final Bound Total AMS by only small amounts (2.1 billion euro and 170 billion yen, respectively) under the proposed Doha modalities. As a result, *de minimis* and blue box support would be tightly constrained unless the CTAMS were held well below its commitment level. Conversely, for Norway and the US the formulas negotiated into the 2008 Doha draft modalities leave a substantial gap between the two commitments. This gives the Norway and the US more room to provide blue box or *de minimis* AMS support even with CTAMS near its limit. The OTDS limit for the US is closer to the OTDS limit for the EU than the FBTAMS of the US is to that of the EU. The same is true for the US relative to Japan. Norway retains higher commitments as a percentage of its value of production.

The commitments for Brazil have a similar pattern as those of the developed countries under the Doha draft modalities but the reductions reflect the more lenient treatment for developing countries. Brazil's Base OTDS is calculated using a more recent period (through 2004) and higher percentages of the base-period value of production (totaling 25 percent). Its small FBTAMS is reduced by 30 percent (to $0.6 billion), its *de minimis* thresholds by one-third (to 6.7 percent of value of production), its OTDS by 37 percent, and its overall blue box limit is set at 5 percent of the 1995–2004 total value of agricultural production.

The Doha implications for the commitments of the other three developing countries differ. China, India and the Philippines remain constrained by their obligation under the Agreement to provide no more than *de minimis* levels of AMS support. Their Base OTDS is calculated using the longer 1995–2004 period and the higher percentage of total value of production. Overall blue box support also would be capped at 5 percent of base-period production value for these developing countries.

For China, India and the Philippines no reductions from Base OTDS or in *de minimis* thresholds are required by the Doha draft modalities and product-specific AMS caps are determined quite loosely. As a consequence, their allowable OTDS will be double or more those of the EU, US or Japan as a percentage of base-period value of production. On a dollar basis, the OTDS support that could be provided by China and India would be $85.5 billion and $25.6 billion, respectively. These are much higher nominal values than for Japan or the US and, in the case of China, more than double the limit for the EU. The design of the Doha modalities thus shifts the balance of future support commitments compared to the historical support patterns among these six countries. These results re-illustrate the point made more broadly by Brink for developed and developing countries in Chapter 2.

Within their overall scope for allowable support, the three developing countries face the additional constraint of maintaining a zero CTAMS. This imposes significant limits on how their OTDS can be provided: in particular, it constrains product-specific AMS support to be less than future *de minimis* thresholds. These limits on product-specific support are much less than the support developed countries have provided in the past to certain products. However, as the value of production grows in nominal value, the *de minimis* thresholds also grow while the relatively tighter product-specific AMS limits the Doha draft modalities would impose on developed countries stay constant. Past *de minimis* thresholds are therefore not reliable guides for the future patterns of allowable product-specific AMS support across countries. Brazil retains two-thirds of its modest FBTAMS, amounting to 1.3 percent of the 1995–2004 total value of production. Because it has a non-zero FBTAMS Brazil takes reduction commitments from its Base OTDS, in contrast to the other developing countries. Consequently Brazil's latitude for OTDS is 17 percent of base period total value of production, compared to the 25 percent for other developing countries.

How binding are the potential Doha constraints?

One perspective on the degree to which the draft Doha disciplines would exert a tighter constraint on domestic support comes from analyzing how the support notified in the past would have related to the new rules and commitments. As summarized in our introduction and discussed in more depth in the country chapters, this question was particularly relevant during the early years of the negotiations (2001–05) when the broad outlines of possible commitments were being hammered out and world market prices were generally expected to remain relatively low. Japan has been well positioned to accept tighter domestic support disciplines after it stopped notifying rice MPS in 1998. The EU has positioned itself since the MacSharry reforms of 1992 and the Fischler reforms of 2003 to accommodate tighter domestic support commitments, through its shift from MPS to blue box and subsequently to green box payments. It would have had to move in this direction much faster if the Doha commitments had been in effect in the past. For Norway and the US, the proposed Doha commitments would also have compelled changes in policies pursued through 2005 in order to achieve compliance. Higher market prices during 2006–2008 subsequently brought US support to nominal levels within the limits set in the Doha proposals, but Norway's policies would still have required modifications to comply with the proposed commitments. For the developing countries we have examined in this analysis, the levels of support provided in the past have been in compliance with the proposed commitments under a Doha agreement.

More germane to the future are projected levels of support compared to the proposed commitments. Estimates from the previous chapters are summarized in Table 11.6. For the developing countries, anticipated support remains well below the relatively loose commitments of the Doha draft modalities. China and India might face some nominal constraints on MPS provided to staple crops – a somewhat artificial constraint as we have argued and one that may be alleviated by the Doha provision to allow price support associated with public stockholding in developing countries to be exempted in the green box, as discussed by both Brink and Gopinath. It is anticipated that India will continue to provide substantial exempt support under development programs. Brazil and the Philippines remain far below allowed support levels in all dimensions. Thus, these developing countries have substantial flexibility with respect to trade-distorting domestic support under the Doha proposals.

For the developed countries that have provided most of the domestic support historically, the Doha commitments would be a somewhat more substantive constraint on future policies. The EU's projected decoupled income support in the green box remains high but this is not subject to WTO nominal constraint. The EU's CTAMS and OTDS would have been projected to be near or above its Doha commitments by the year 2015/16, without a decline of EMS first notified for 2007/08. Past reforms would be locked in were the Doha agreement in place. Likewise, the support for the US is projected to be 30–35 percent below the Doha FBTAMS and Final Bound OTDS commitments. This is the result of some additional flexibility the US achieved in 2008 by reducing its dairy MPS through modest re-definitional policy changes with little economic effect. Even so, given the price-dependent character of past US support, the Doha constraints could require future policy modifications in periods of declining prices. In particular, new countercyclical support such as that provided through the ACRE revenue-guarantee program introduced in 2008 could be constrained.

For Japan, the Doha ceilings would preclude levels of AMS and blue box support that Godo and Takahashi argue were planned by the government

Table 11.6 *Projected levels of support (mid 2010s) and Doha constraints (2008 draft modalities fully implemented) for eight countries*

	EU27		US		Japan		Norway	
	Projection[a]	Ceiling	Projection[a]	Ceiling	Projection[a]	Ceiling	Projection[a]	Ceiling
	Billion euros		*Billion dollars*		*Billion yen*		*Billion NOK*	
Green box	56.7		117.5		1,526		6.9	
OTDS	17.2	23.8	10.2	14.5	1,558	1,362	15.3	9.5
Blue box	4.7	6.5	—	4.9	560	246	3.7	3.6
Current Total AMS[b]	10.9	21.7	5.0	7.6	909	1,192	11.4	5.4
of which, MPS	10.3		5.0		334		11.9	
Total *de minimis*	1.6		4.9		89		0.2	
Product-specific[c]	0.3	7.5	0.1	7.3	15	209	0.1	0.6
Non-product-specific	1.3	7.5	4.8	7.3	73	209	0.1	0.6
Total support	73.9		127.7		3,084		22.2	
Total value of production[d]	299.7 [e]		265.2		8,378 [e]		24.1 [e]	
	Brazil		India		China		Philippines	
	Projection	Ceiling	Projection	Ceiling	Projection	Ceiling	Projection	Ceiling
	Billion US dollars		*Billion US dollars*		*Billion RMB*		*Billion pesos*	
Green box	2.3 [e]		22.1		522.0		25.1	
Development programs	0.7 [e]		13.5		—	—	6.2	
OTDS	2.0	8.3	8.4	25.6	183.4	584.4	8.5	117.2
Blue box	—	2.4	—	5.1	—	116.9	—	23.4
Current Total AMS[b]	—	0.6	—	—	—	—	—	—

Total *de minimis*	2.0		8.4		183.4		8.5	
Product-specific[c]	0.3	5.3	6.8	17.7	92.3[f]	444.1	8.5	191.0
Non-product-specific	1.7[e]	5.3	1.7	17.7	91.1	444.1	—	191.0
Total support	5.0[e]		44.0		705.4		39.8	
Total value of production[d]	78.7[e]		177.2		5,224.9		1,910.0	

Notes: — indicates zero and a blank means that no entry is applicable.

[a] Projected support levels assuming no adjustment to accommodate possible Doha ceilings (see Chapters 3–6).

[b] Cannot exceed ceiling on CTAMS (i.e., Doha Final Bound Total AMS) or, if no FBTAMS exists in the country's Schedule, cannot exceed zero.

[c] The AMS for any product (sum of MPS and EMS, non-exempt direct payments and other non-exempt support) is subject to the product's *de minimis* threshold (for the countries with a FBTAMS commitment) or limit (for those with a zero ceiling on CTAMS). These thresholds or limits are not shown individually: see chapters for details.

[d] Determines, in combination with the Doha *de minimis* percentage, the projected non-product-specific *de minimis* threshold and the sum of all product-specific *de minimis* thresholds as entered in the ceiling column (the sum of the values of production for all products is the total value of production).

[e] Average value during 2006–08 as no projection is made in the country chapters.

[f] Projected AMSs for wheat, corn and soybeans exceed *de minimis* thresholds under certain assumptions as the result of a large market price support component (see Chapter 9).

Source: Authors' calculations.

holding power in 2009 – the levels of support involved are not precluded under the Agreement, but would exceed Japan's overall blue box and OTDS Doha commitments. Likewise, a Doha agreement would require significant policy changes for Norway, as assessed by Gaasland, Garcia and Vårdal. Although domestic support measures could be introduced that would maintain most of Norway's production under the Doha disciplines, this would require a shift from MPS to direct payments and changes in Norway's policies that have been subject to little reform since 1995.

Taking these projections into account, we conclude that a Doha agreement built on the December 2008 draft modalities would achieve real progress on the path toward substantial progressive reductions in agricultural support envisioned in the preamble of the 1994 Agreement on Agriculture. A Doha agreement with tightened and extended commitments would impose some meaningful constraints, especially for developed countries that have provided high levels of support in the past. The Doha disciplines would clearly alter the tone of policy discussions about compliance by countries as the tighter limits loomed larger in national deliberations. The EU reform path would be locked in by its commitments, although room would remain for some increases compared to recently notified trade-distorting support. The disciplines would be particularly germane for the US if nominal agricultural prices move sharply downward or resume a downward trend. Japan would be constrained in pursuing measures that have entered its domestic policy debate and Norway would have to undertake a reconfiguration of its support programs. These would all be steps in the direction of a progressive reduction in trade-distorting support.

Strengthening international disciplines beyond Doha

The disciplines on domestic policies embedded in the Agreement and monitored through the notifications are designed to limit the support that countries provide under certain measures to their agricultural sectors. A new agreement in line with the Doha Round proposals would do so to a greater extent. The main rationale for the disciplines has always been that they are necessary to reduce production and trade distortions resulting from domestic support.

While the constraints rarely have proved binding, the policies of developed countries have shown a degree of convergence in the past twenty years, anchored by the Agreement but also related to national developments and changes in the nature of their agricultural industries. Developing countries have, in general, taken a somewhat different path in their agricultural policies; again not heavily constrained by WTO rules but consistent both with the limits the Agreement imposes and the flexibility it affords.

In the nine years of unsuccessful Doha negotiations through 2010, one persistent question has been whether and how to take further steps to tighten the disciplines on domestic support so as to draw a stronger link between WTO agreements and national policy decisions. The Doha draft modalities would establish rules and support ceilings that are more complicated than those of the Agreement and more heterogeneous across countries. These characteristics were necessary to satisfy competing aims and to achieve even a tentative blueprint for a new agricultural agreement. There are risks inherent in locking such diversity into the architecture of the international disciplines, yet even this compromise has not yet been enough to forge a consensus and bring the negotiations to closure.

The purpose of strengthening the Agreement through the Doha Round and beyond is to achieve the long-term objective of limiting protection and the distortions national policies create in world agricultural markets. It implies further movement towards policy convergence that would include five main dimensions: moderate tariffs and related impediments to imports; elimination of explicit and implicit export subsidies; limited scope for trade-distorting domestic support; the provision of support for public goods and other agreed purposes under well-defined green box criteria; and the transparent monitoring of international commitments.

If this is to happen, greater attention will need to be directed to the appropriate end point of policy convergence, the path for achieving this, and how consensus on the need for convergence can be secured. One can no longer view domestic support for agriculture as merely a developed country aberration that needs to be eliminated. Multilateral and comprehensive disciplines on domestic support are in a real sense the embodiment of an agricultural policy for the global economy. The parameters of such a policy still need to be determined.

The analysis of what has already been achieved under the Agreement and what might be achieved under proposed Doha disciplines on domestic support lays some of the groundwork for a strategic exploration of the longer term policy issues. We close with some observations that have emerged from our analysis that are germane to the ultimate aim of achieving greater policy cohesion around domestic support, recognizing that this will involve a very long period of deliberations and policy evolution. Some of the ideas we propose and the related recommendations have been aired in the Doha negotiations. However, countries have not yet been prepared collectively to adopt the expanded disciplines and obligations that are implied.

Greater international transparency

The role of the notifications as a device for monitoring policies and verifying compliance has been hampered by delays in submissions to the WTO. Shadow notifications and projections of likely future notifications along the lines we have presented add transparency to the monitoring process, but cannot substitute for formal submissions.

The Doha draft modalities would strengthen the notification obligations of countries and subject implementation of commitments to enhanced monitoring and review. For domestic support, an annual notification would be required. A complementary approach that could further improve the timeliness and content of reporting for certain members would be to link the WTO domestic support notifications to the mechanism of the annual policy review process of OECD. The OECD's regular publication of PSEs was initiated in 1987 during the Uruguay Round negotiations with the aim of improving transparency about agricultural policy measures, including domestic support and border measures, and the support they provide. An enormous investment has been made in the OECD's reporting and evaluation system. It makes sense to benefit from this investment in strengthening transparency in the WTO.

Linking the preparation of WTO notifications for some countries to OECD's annual monitoring process would not require the OECD and governments notifying the WTO to use exactly the same categories or even measurements of support, nor a completely common process for generating their reports. But instituting this linkage could ensure annual submissions on a regular basis by a large group of countries. The adoption of such linked reporting could also result in adherence to more uniform guidelines for notifications across countries. Transparency would not be improved for all WTO members under this mechanism (unless the country coverage under the OECD's system were expanded), but it would include most of the main importers and exporters engaged in agricultural trade, including emerging-market, non-OECD members such as Brazil and China that participate in OECD agricultural policy reviews. A mechanism of this type would demonstrate an increased level of commitment by leading countries to the integrity of WTO monitoring through timely notifications, which could only have beneficial effects on the credibility of commitments and the process of verifying compliance. The notifications would be subject to more prompt review through the Committee on Agriculture, to possible challenges by other WTO members, and to public scrutiny.

A more dramatic step for addressing late notifications would be to introduce disincentives for delayed submissions. Putting teeth into the agreement's notification requirement would have to recognize normal lags inherent in their preparation. Some delay is inevitable due to the nature of the information required – it takes time to collect and organize the detailed data underlying calculations in the notifications some of which may not be available until well after the particular period for which support was provided. The responsibility that governments bear under WTO processes, including those through dispute settlement, means that care is taken in the preparation of notifications.

Countries also want to take advantage of rules for exempting support under certain measures from their commitments. This could be automatically disallowed for a given year if notification was not made within a specified period of time, such as a year or eighteen months after the end of the period to be notified. If applied uniformly, both developed and developing countries would have a strong incentive to provide timely notifications under this stipulation in order to take advantage of the substantive distinctions that WTO rules make among different categories of support. Even *de minimis* allowances could be disallowed after the grace period. This would make almost mandatory the timely notification of domestic support by developed and developing countries and signal greater seriousness about the commitments. The processes for finding a country to be in violation of its obligations through WTO dispute settlement (see Chapter 1) would not change by adding a provision that late notification precludes exempting from commitment certain support that otherwise would be eligible for exemption, but the range of circumstances that could give rise to a violation would expand.

Accurate and meaningful measurements of support

We have emphasized the importance of accurate and meaningful notifications of domestic support not only as a legal requirement but also to achieve the economic objectives that underlie the Agreement. A troubling characteristic, as we have shown, is that countries often calculate key measurements of domestic support in different ways. Countries exercise substantial discretion in the types of policies they report, their placement in categories, and methods for calculating support levels. In part this arises from different agricultural circumstances across countries and consequent differences in policies. But it also results from the use of approaches that best appear to show that a country is complying with its WTO commitments.

A more coordinated process for the preparation of notifications, such as the proposal to link this to the OECD's annual monitoring and evaluation exercise, could reduce the heterogeneity apparent in the notifications for many countries. A more widespread understanding of what types of policies fit the criteria of the green box could lead to less divergence among countries in the measures that have been included or excluded from this category. Input subsidies could also be reported more uniformly among countries.

A critical issue in disparity that we have highlighted concerns the discretion that countries have in measuring market price support, in addition to inherent technical limitations of the WTO measurement. As we have shown, reductions in notified MPS often run ahead of real changes in the economic value of price support that countries provide. This precludes the notified MPS from being an accurate and meaningful measurement of support – and hence of the extent of trade distortion. In turn, this undermines the meaningful measurement of AMS and thus the usefulness of the ceiling commitments as indicators of restraint on levels of certain trade-distorting support.

Ambiguity in measurement of the MPS is going to be difficult to resolve. The initial decision to combine measures providing MPS and certain non-exempt direct payments and other non-exempt support into the AMS category has a rationale based on the potential economic effects of these measures. MPS is potentially the most distorting policy, since effective price support influences both production and consumption decisions, while the principal effect of direct payments is on production incentives. Thus, implicit in the Agreement is that it is desirable in terms of reducing and preventing distortions in world agricultural markets to substitute AMS (i.e., non-exempt) direct payments for MPS or to introduce new exempt payments that would qualify for the blue or green boxes in lieu of MPS. However, our analysis has shown that countries often reduce notified MPS without corresponding effects on price-linked market distortions.

Some progress can be made by adopting clearer rules for what constitutes an applied administered price and the eligible quantity of production. One might argue further along this line that the domestic support disciplines should be applied to the economic measurement of price support, as calculated by the OECD and as used in economic studies. But a difficulty arises from the separation of domestic support measures from market access and export competition measures for purposes of imposing disciplines under three distinct pillars in the WTO.

As we have emphasized, MPS through administered prices, market access as determined by tariffs and other import policies, and export competition as affected by taxes and subsidies have intertwined effects on domestic markets. Outcomes of policies considered under any one pillar are affected by the conditions defined by the other pillars. Adopting an economic measurement of market price support for commitments under the domestic support disciplines would introduce variation in the notified support that agricultural policymakers cannot control, due to fluctuations in world prices and exchange rates. Moreover, it would subsume under the domestic support discipline the effects of tariffs and other border policies, including levels of TRQs, export subsidies, and the effects of non-tariff measures, that are the domain of other WTO commitments and agreements. Such a breadth of commitment was rejected early in the Uruguay Round negotiations and is unlikely ever to be ceded to the domestic support disciplines alone.

Given the severe limitations of the MPS it could be dropped from inclusion in AMS support in the future and commitments adjusted downward accordingly. We reject this alternative because of the important policy role of administered prices in some cases and the desirability of disciplining their use.

A better alternative would be to take steps within the domestic support disciplines to ensure that the latitude allowed by the MPS provisions does not undermine commitments to limit other forms of AMS and OTDS support. A distinction could be drawn between MPS and non-exempt direct payments and other support within the AMS. With this distinction, countries with Final Bound Total AMS or Final Bound OTDS commitments attributed to MPS in the relevant base period would retain the option of using MPS to a corresponding level as long as they are in compliance with other domestic support rules and commitments. The non-exempt direct payments and other budgeted outlays reported in AMS would also be bound by these other commitments, less the support attributable to MPS. Without this distinction, eliminating MPS opens up an equivalent amount within CTAMS for substitute non-exempt measures. Those countries we have examined that have reduced MPS the most (the EU and Japan) have not substituted non-exempt payments for the MPS. But our analysis suggests that other countries, such as the US, if they were to face a tight FBTAMS constraint, might use reductions in MPS that do not reduce economic price support to make room for expanded non-exempt direct payments. Making a distinction between MPS and other non-exempt support within AMS could avoid such substitutions.

Green box disciplines

The legal provisions of the Agreement and its proposed Doha Round extension divide domestic support measures at a fundamental level into two types: those that have at most minimal trade-distorting effects in the green box category and all others that are included in OTDS categories (unless exempted in development programs as an aspect of special and differential treatment for developing countries). Many of the green box measures have desirable social objectives and many have less of an effect than other support on a country's competitors, while most of the trade-distorting measures stimulate production and drive down world prices to the detriment of non-subsidized producers. The WTO rules are designed to maintain the separation between these types of policies, and to guard against the possibility that trade-distorting measures slip into the green box for which expenditures are not capped.

Strengthened WTO rules and OTDS commitments would encourage shifts to green box measures. This will require greater scrutiny to assure consistency of notified measures and their implementation with specific green box criteria, in order to achieve the public benefits that green box programs are designed to encourage while discouraging new forms of subsidies that distort production and trade. The need for enhanced scrutiny of green box measures receives considerable attention in a collection of policy and analytical papers edited by Meléndez-Ortiz, Bellmann, and Hepburn (2009). Their overall policy orientation, as we would also argue, is that green box policies appropriately disciplined and administered provide the foundation for permanent agricultural support policy.

Meléndez-Ortiz, Bellmann, and Hepburn trace the Uruguay Round negotiations that determined the green box rules and examine how to make them most effective. They focus on those measures that legitimately meet the agreed non-distorting criteria and the enforcement needed to preclude the inclusion of distortionary measures. The green box policies notified since the Agreement came into effect are described for numerous countries and their social implications, such as effects on the distribution of income among large and small farms, are evaluated. The environmental impacts of green box policies are examined, as well as the use of green box policies to enhance rural income and promote poverty reduction in developing countries.

Our analysis has highlighted a number of cases where further disciplines on green box measures are warranted in order to exclude measures that have more than minimal effects on production or trade. We focus here on one of these issues: the subcategory in the green box of decoupled income support payments to farmers. We believe that greater discipline on these payments will be necessary if a consensus on long-term policy for agricultural support is to be achieved.

The reasoning underlying the inclusion of measures that meet the decoupled income support criteria in the green box is that in principle these payments neither depend on nor affect current prices or production. There has been an economic presumption to this effect, in part based on a longstanding literature suggesting that quota rents from supply control programs are captured in the price of quotas or land (Orden, Paarlberg, and Roe 1999). The decision on the level of decoupled income transfers to agricultural producers is therefore left as a sovereign issue. There has been some convergent policy movement towards payments notified in this category among China, the EU, and the US. But large differences remain among these three countries in the levels of the payments, and there is a clear division between the few countries that make such payments and all others that do not. In the EU and US, decoupled income support has been subject to substantial internal public debate, indicative of sovereign policy choices being made and contested and consistent with their discretion under the Agreement.

The problem that arises given these differences in levels of decoupled income support is whether payments, especially at high levels, have more than a minimal trade-distorting or production effect, and thus should be constrained. A number of mechanisms through which decoupled income support might stimulate production have been identified (Elbehri and Sarris 2009; Abler and Blandford 2005). Among these mechanisms are a wealth effect, making producers less risk averse; easing of credit constraints, so additional purchased inputs are utilized; impacts on labor allocation decisions, such that more labor is devoted to farm production; coverage of fixed costs, so that the number of farms or levels of profit-maximizing output are increased; and anticipation of future rebasing of payment eligibility criteria, that rewards the expansion of current production.

With the increased adoption of payments notified as decoupled income support, greater attention has been directed towards assessing their effects. Various analytical techniques have been utilized, but the time series of data on these payments are short. Analysis has focused not only on those payments notified as decoupled income support in the green box but also on measures such as the US countercyclical and similar payments provided since 1998 that are price-linked but not dependent on current production levels.

Some of the analysis shows the quite limited effects of these measures on output (Goodwin and Mishra 2005, 2006). However, several recent studies have questioned this conclusion. De Gorter, Just, and Kropp (2008) present theoretical arguments that fixed and countercyclical payments can have a substantial impact by deterring exit and affecting choice of output levels. They show substantial effects on dairy output due to US Milk Income Loss Contract payments. Kirwan (2009) concludes that less of the value of US fixed direct and countercyclical payments is passed through to landowners than earlier studies have implied. He finds that 75 percent of the value of payments is retained by operators of rented land, with only 25 percent reflected in rental rates. Kirwan does not address the effects of the payments on production, but their retention by farm operators could enhance production along several of the lines mentioned above. Femenia, Gohin, and Carpentier (2010) demonstrate that earlier studies underestimated the wealth effects of income support. Gardner, Hardie, and Parks (2010) use advanced statistical techniques to evaluate the effects of US support programs since 1987 – a point in time at which those programs became increasingly separated from production decisions and include (since 1996) the US direct payments notified as decoupled income support. Gardner, Hardie, and Parks find that US support has induced 45 to 90 million more acres into agricultural production than would otherwise have been the case.

In light of this newly emerging evidence and the remaining uncertainty about the extent to which decoupled income support affects production, we conclude that some nominal limits will be required on this type of support. As long as a reasonable case can be made that alleged decoupled income support has production effects, a consensus will not form around policy convergence where a few countries that can afford to make unlimited payments of this type.

Ensuring fair markets for food consumers

The final issue we raise places domestic support disciplines in the context of the broader forces that will influence agriculture in the coming decade.

The existing rules of the Agreement for domestic support and those being negotiated in the Doha Round are targeted primarily toward disciplining policy measures and support that stimulate production and depress world prices to the detriment of agricultural producers in other countries. This has been a concern of non-subsidizing exporters, who see their competitive position in world markets eroded, and of food-importing countries, who blame low world prices for undermining farmers' incomes and long-term investments in their agricultural sectors.

The emergence during the late 2000s of a period of relatively high agricultural prices does not eliminate the need for traditional disciplines on price-depressing domestic support. We have shown evidence to this effect in evaluating such measures as continued price support interventions by Norway, the new ACRE revenue-guarantee program enacted by the US in 2008, and the increased subsidies middle-income countries provide to agriculture as their economies grow. But production-stimulating policies are the not the only ones that create economic distortions in world markets. Measures that restrict supply or augment demand beyond market-driven levels are also potentially trade distorting. Such measures have become more prevalent, have contributed to the relatively high agricultural prices since 2007, and could come to dominate policy interventions affecting agriculture in the future.

Supply-restricting and demand-augmenting policies come under scrutiny when higher world food prices create difficulties for low-income food importers and poverty rises in these countries. Karapinar and Häberli (2010) examine these concerns about the dramatic price increases in 2008 in an historical perspective and offer assessments of the extent to which these can be addressed in the WTO.

In the framework of WTO domestic support notifications, one set of supply-control measures are those notified in the blue box, for which subsidy payments but not the level of supply restraint is reported. Use of these measures is waning, as we have described.

Some other supply-restricting policies are notified in the green box, particularly conservation programs that have the effect of reducing planted crop acreage. Green box rules limit payments for environmental measures to revenue forgone or additional costs entailed in their adoption. This has not been a sufficient constraint to preclude subsidy payments large enough to draw land out of production. More discipline on these payments may be necessary if a convergence consensus is to emerge on future agricultural policies, especially if prices remain relatively high for staple grains and oilseeds.

Moreover, the green box environmental support rules are inadequate to address two of the most policy-laden challenges facing agriculture: the rising demand for farm-based biofuels and the other, still undetermined, mitigation opportunities and adaptation strategies that may arise from global climate change. These challenges will place significant new demands on agricultural markets – for example, as rising fossil fuel prices create incentives to produce biofuels or as increased trade is needed to moderate greater climatically induced variability in agricultural production. The demands on agriculture as a source of biofuels and for other responses to climate change will also be driven to a large extent by policy decisions that involve mandates or incentives for certain uses of land and other agricultural resources.

We have noted that the demand-augmenting effects of biofuel subsidies and mandates in Brazil, the EU and the US already have had significant impacts on production and prices. Yet, such policy measures remain largely outside existing or proposed WTO disciplines. Certainly, the most important of these measures have not been notified under the Agreement as agricultural domestic support.

The domestic support rules could be strengthened to address the problems that arise from policies that reduce production, limit exports or increase demand for non-food uses of agricultural products to the detriment of consumers. Doing so is complicated, as we have discussed in chapters on Brazil and the US, and it seems unlikely that countries will attempt to negotiate disciplines on measures that increase the demand for agricultural products, even though such measures have an impact on world prices and hence on poor consumers. A case can be made for a cohesive approach to a multilateral food security initiative that would include disciplines on certain measures of this kind of domestic support.

The need for greater transparency in the area of biofuel subsidies has been emphasized in a study by Josling, Blandford, and Earley (2010). Such transparency has not been forthcoming from the system of notification to the WTO under either the Agreement on Agriculture or the Agreement on Subsidies and Countervailing Measures. In both cases, basic notification information is scant and the information needed to estimate the trade impact of the subsidies has been lacking. Under the Agreement on Agriculture, governments in their notifications to the WTO seem content to ignore support to ethanol through biofuel mandates or tax concessions, even though an argument can be made that at least part of this should be reported as domestic support in favor of agricultural producers. Nor have governments been persuaded to report biofuel subsidies in enough detail to allow analysis of their effects under the ASCM. These measures will require more discipline for convergent domestic support policies to evolve.

The challenge ahead

This book has spelled out in depth the international rules and commitments, subsequent policy decisions, and notification and monitoring of those policies that have led to the current juncture in disciplining agricultural domestic support. Domestic support disciplines are a key part of the Agreement on Agriculture and new disciplines on domestic support will have to be part of any successful further negotiations on a new agricultural agreement. It may or may not prove possible for a consensus to emerge in the near-term on an architecture of strengthened multilateral rules and commitments. Meanwhile, countries continue to utilize many unilateral domestic support measures with adverse effects. Notification of those domestic support measures has been slow and inconsistent. The result has been to devalue the process of reporting and the integrity of the international disciplines, even if explicit violations have been rare. Should there be a Doha Round agreement, its credibility will hinge on more timely and consistent monitoring as many more countries will find themselves closer to agreed limits.

Longer term, the challenges we have identified are indicative of both the importance of disciplining agricultural domestic support and the difficulty of doing so. Many complex issues in terms of goals, rules, commitments, implementation, and monitoring will have to be tackled in any attempt to bring greater cohesion to a global regime for agricultural policies. The experiences of countries under the Agreement provide a tangible starting point for such an attempt, illuminate potential pitfalls to be avoided, and offer lessons to guide the negotiations and future policy developments. There is a need to make agricultural domestic support policies more consistent and beneficial in a world economy in which future production technologies and the food supply are uncertain and in which the efficient functioning of agricultural markets and trade is increasingly needed to contribute to an effective, robust and sustainable global food system.

References

Abler, D., and D. Blandford. 2005. A review of empirical studies on the acreage and/or production response to US production flexibility contract payments under the FAIR Act and related payments under supplementary legislation. OECD report AGR/CA/APM(2004)21/Final.

de Gorter, H., D. R. Just, and J. D. Kropp. 2008. Cross-subsidization due to infra-marginal support in agriculture: A general theory and empirical evidence. *American Journal of Agricultural Economics* 90(1): 42–54.

Elbehri, A., and A. Sarris. 2009. *Non-distorting Farm Support to Enhance Global Food Production*. Rome: FAO.

Femenia, F., A. Gohin, and A. Carpentier. 2010. The decoupling of farm programs: Revisiting the wealth effect. *American Journal of Agricultural Economics* 92(3): 836–848.

Gardner, B., I. Hardie, and P. J. Parks. 2010. United States farm commodity programs and land use. *American Journal of Agricultural Economics* 92(3): 803–820.

Goodwin, B. K., and A. K. Mishra. 2005. Another look at decoupling: Additional evidence of the production effects of direct payments. *American Journal of Agricultural Economics* 87(5): 1200–1210.

2006. Are "decoupled" farm program payments really decoupled? *American Journal of Agricultural Economics* 88(1): 73–89.

Josling, T., D. Blandford, and J. Earley. 2010. Biofuel and biomass subsidies in the US, EU and Brazil: Towards a transparent system of notification. IPC Position Paper. International Food and Agricultural Trade Policy Council.

Karapinar, B., and C. Häberli (ed.) 2010. *The End of Cheap Food and the WTO*. Cambridge University Press.

Kirwan, B. E. 2009. The incidence of US agricultural subsidies on farmland rental rates. *Journal of Political Economy* 117(1): 138–164.

Meléndez-Ortiz, R., C. Bellmann, and J. Hepburn (ed.) 2009. *Agricultural Subsidies in the WTO Green Box: Ensuring Coherence with Sustainable Development Goals*. Cambridge University Press.

Orden, D., R. Paarlberg, and T. Roe. 1999. *Policy Reform in American Agriculture: Analysis and Prognosis*. University of Chicago Press.

WTO. 2008. Revised draft modalities for agriculture. TN/AG/W/4/Rev.4, 6 December.

2010. Total value of agricultural production: Note by the Secretariat. TN/AG/S/21/Rev.4, 23 February.

Appendix A

Domestic support provisions of the Agreement on Agriculture

Editors' note: Appendix A provides the key provisions of the Agreement on Agriculture relevant to the domestic support disciplines. The full text of the Agreement and others are published in *The Results of the Uruguay Round of Multilateral Trade Negotiations – The Legal Texts* (WTO 1995) and are available on the WTO website. We exercise some judgment for brevity of the appendix. The preamble and other generally relevant articles are included for context while only the titles are given for articles related to market access and export competition, and a few others only indirectly related to domestic support.

Members

Having decided to establish a basis for initiating a process of reform of trade in agriculture in line with the objectives of the negotiations as set out in the Punta del Este Declaration;

Recalling that their long-term objective as agreed at the Mid-Term Review of the Uruguay Round "is to establish a fair and market-oriented agricultural trading system and that a reform process should be initiated through the negotiation of commitments on support and protection and through the establishment of strengthened and more operationally effective GATT rules and disciplines";

Recalling further that "the above-mentioned long-term objective is to provide for substantial progressive reductions in agricultural support and protection sustained over an agreed period of time, resulting in correcting and preventing restrictions and distortions in world agricultural markets";

Committed to achieving specific binding commitments in each of the following areas: market access; domestic support; export competition; and to reaching an agreement on sanitary and phytosanitary issues;

Having agreed that in implementing their commitments on market access, developed country Members would take fully into account the particular needs and conditions of developing country Members by providing for a greater improvement of opportunities and terms of access for agricultural products of particular interest to these Members, including the fullest liberalization of trade in tropical agricultural products as agreed at the Mid-Term Review, and for products of particular importance to the diversification of production from the growing of illicit narcotic crops;

Noting that commitments under the reform programme should be made in an equitable way among all Members, having regard to non-trade concerns, including food security and the need to protect the environment; having regard to the agreement that special and differential treatment for developing countries is an integral element of the negotiations, and taking into account the possible negative effects of the implementation of the reform programme on least-developed and net food-importing developing countries;

Hereby *agree* as follows:

PART I

Article 1

Definition of Terms

In this Agreement, unless the context otherwise requires:

(a) "Aggregate Measurement of Support" and "AMS" mean the annual level of support, expressed in monetary terms, provided for an agricultural product in favour of the producers of the basic agricultural product or non-product-specific support provided in favour of agricultural producers in general, other than support provided under programmes that qualify as exempt from reduction under Annex 2 to this Agreement, which is:
   (i) with respect to support provided during the base period, specified in the relevant tables of supporting material incorporated by reference in Part IV of a Member's Schedule; and
   (ii) with respect to support provided during any year of the implementation period and thereafter, calculated in accordance with the provisions of Annex 3 of this Agreement and taking into account the constituent data and methodology used in the tables of supporting material incorporated by reference in Part IV of the Member's Schedule;

(b) "basic agricultural product" in relation to domestic support commitments is defined as the product as close as practicable to the point of first sale as specified in a Member's Schedule and in the related supporting material;

(c) "budgetary outlays" or "outlays" includes revenue foregone;

(d) "Equivalent Measurement of Support" means the annual level of support, expressed in monetary terms, provided to producers of a basic agricultural product through the application of one or more measures, the calculation of which in accordance with the AMS methodology is impracticable, other than support provided under programmes that qualify as exempt from reduction under Annex 2 to this Agreement, and which is:

(i) with respect to support provided during the base period, specified in the relevant tables of supporting material incorporated by reference in Part IV of a Member's Schedule; and

(ii) with respect to support provided during any year of the implementation period and thereafter, calculated in accordance with the provisions of Annex 4 of this Agreement and taking into account the constituent data and methodology used in the tables of supporting material incorporated by reference in Part IV of the Member's Schedule;

(e) "export subsidies" refers to subsidies contingent upon export performance, including the export subsidies listed in Article 9 of this Agreement;

(f) "implementation period" means the six-year period commencing in the year 1995, except that, for the purposes of Article 13, it means the nine-year period commencing in 1995;

(g) "market access concessions" includes all market access commitments undertaken pursuant to this Agreement;

(h) "Total Aggregate Measurement of Support" and "Total AMS" mean the sum of all domestic support provided in favour of agricultural producers, calculated as the sum of all aggregate measurements of support for basic agricultural products, all non-product-specific aggregate measurements of support and all equivalent measurements of support for agricultural products, and which is:

(i) with respect to support provided during the base period (i.e., the "Base Total AMS") and the maximum support permitted to be provided during any year of the implementation period or thereafter (i.e., the "Annual and Final Bound Commitment Levels"), as specified in Part IV of a Member's Schedule; and

(ii) with respect to the level of support actually provided during any year of the implementation period and thereafter (i.e., the "Current Total AMS"), calculated in accordance with the provisions of this Agreement, including Article 6, and with the constituent data and methodology used in the tables of supporting material incorporated by reference in Part IV of the Member's Schedule;

(i) "year" in paragraph (f) above and in relation to the specific commitments of a Member refers to the calendar, financial or marketing year specified in the Schedule relating to that Member.

Article 2

Product Coverage

This Agreement applies to the products listed in Annex 1 to this Agreement, hereinafter referred to as agricultural products.

PART II

Article 3

Incorporation of Concessions and Commitments

1. The domestic support and export subsidy commitments in Part IV of each Member's Schedule constitute commitments limiting subsidization and are hereby made an integral part of GATT 1994.
2. Subject to the provisions of Article 6, a Member shall not provide support in favour of domestic producers in excess of the commitment levels specified in Section I of Part IV of its Schedule.
3. Subject to the provisions of paragraphs 2(b) and 4 of Article 9, a Member shall not provide export subsidies listed in paragraph 1 of Article 9 in respect of the agricultural products or groups of products specified in Section II of Part IV of its Schedule in excess of the budgetary outlay and quantity commitment levels specified therein and shall not provide such subsidies in respect of any agricultural product not specified in that Section of its Schedule.

PART III

Article 4

Market Access (not reproduced)

Article 5

Special Safeguard Provisions (not reproduced)

PART IV

Article 6

Domestic Support Commitments

1. The domestic support reduction commitments of each Member contained in Part IV of its Schedule shall apply to all of its domestic support measures in favour of agricultural producers with the exception of domestic measures which are not subject to reduction in terms of the criteria set out in this

Article and in Annex 2 to this Agreement. The commitments are expressed in terms of Total Aggregate Measurement of Support and "Annual and Final Bound Commitment Levels".

2. In accordance with the Mid-Term Review Agreement that government measures of assistance, whether direct or indirect, to encourage agricultural and rural development are an integral part of the development programmes of developing countries, investment subsidies which are generally available to agriculture in developing country Members and agricultural input subsidies generally available to low-income or resource-poor producers in developing country Members shall be exempt from domestic support reduction commitments that would otherwise be applicable to such measures, as shall domestic support to producers in developing country Members to encourage diversification from growing illicit narcotic crops. Domestic support meeting the criteria of this paragraph shall not be required to be included in a Member's calculation of its Current Total AMS.
3. A Member shall be considered to be in compliance with its domestic support reduction commitments in any year in which its domestic support in favour of agricultural producers expressed in terms of Current Total AMS does not exceed the corresponding annual or final bound commitment level specified in Part IV of the Member's Schedule.
4. (a) A Member shall not be required to include in the calculation of its Current Total AMS and shall not be required to reduce:
   (i) product-specific domestic support which would otherwise be required to be included in a Member's calculation of its Current AMS where such support does not exceed 5 per cent of that Member's total value of production of a basic agricultural product during the relevant year; and
   (ii) non-product-specific domestic support which would otherwise be required to be included in a Member's calculation of its Current AMS where such support does not exceed 5 per cent of the value of that Member's total agricultural production.

   (b) For developing country Members, the *de minimis* percentage under this paragraph shall be 10 per cent.
5. (a) Direct payments under production-limiting programmes shall not be subject to the commitment to reduce domestic support if:
   (i) such payments are based on fixed area and yields; or
   (ii) such payments are made on 85 per cent or less of the base level of production; or
   (iii) livestock payments are made on a fixed number of head.

   (b) The exemption from the reduction commitment for direct payments meeting the above criteria shall be reflected by the exclusion of the value of those direct payments in a Member's calculation of its Current Total AMS.

Article 7

General Disciplines on Domestic Support

1. Each Member shall ensure that any domestic support measures in favour of agricultural producers which are not subject to reduction commitments because they qualify under the criteria set out in Annex 2 to this Agreement are maintained in conformity therewith.

2. (a) Any domestic support measure in favour of agricultural producers, including any modification to such measure, and any measure that is subsequently introduced that cannot be shown to satisfy the criteria in Annex 2 to this Agreement or to be exempt from reduction by reason of any other provision of this Agreement shall be included in the Member's calculation of its Current Total AMS.

(b) Where no Total AMS commitment exists in Part IV of a Member's Schedule, the Member shall not provide support to agricultural producers in excess of the relevant *de minimis* level set out in paragraph 4 of Article 6.

PART V

Article 8

Export Competition Commitments (not reproduced)

Article 9

Export Subsidy Commitments (not reproduced)

Article 10

Prevention of Circumvention of Export Subsidy Commitments (not reproduced)

Article 11

Incorporated Products (not reproduced)

PART VI

Article 12

Disciplines on Export Prohibitions and Restrictions (not reproduced)

PART VII

Article 13

Due Restraint

During the implementation period, notwithstanding the provisions of GATT 1994 and the Agreement on Subsidies and Countervailing Measures (referred to in this Article as the "Subsidies Agreement"):

(a) domestic support measures that conform fully to the provisions of Annex 2 to this Agreement shall be:

  (i) non-actionable subsidies for purposes of countervailing duties[4];

  (ii) exempt from actions based on Article XVI of GATT 1994 and Part III of the Subsidies Agreement; and

  (iii) exempt from actions based on non-violation nullification or impairment of the benefits of tariff concessions accruing to another Member under Article II of GATT 1994, in the sense of paragraph 1(b) of Article XXIII of GATT 1994;

(b) domestic support measures that conform fully to the provisions of Article 6 of this Agreement including direct payments that conform to the requirements of paragraph 5 thereof, as reflected in each Member's Schedule, as well as domestic support within *de minimis* levels and in conformity with paragraph 2 of Article 6, shall be:

  (i) exempt from the imposition of countervailing duties unless a determination of injury or threat thereof is made in accordance with Article VI of GATT 1994 and Part V of the Subsidies Agreement, and due restraint shall be shown in initiating any countervailing duty investigations;

  (ii) exempt from actions based on paragraph 1 of Article XVI of GATT 1994 or Articles 5 and 6 of the Subsidies Agreement, provided that such measures do not grant support to a specific commodity in excess of that decided during the 1992 marketing year; and

[4] "Countervailing duties" where referred to in this Article are those covered by Article VI of GATT 1994 and Part V of the Agreement on Subsidies and Countervailing Measures.

(iii) exempt from actions based on non-violation nullification or impairment of the benefits of tariff concessions accruing to another Member under Article II of GATT 1994, in the sense of paragraph 1(b) of Article XXIII of GATT 1994, provided that such measures do not grant support to a specific commodity in excess of that decided during the 1992 marketing year;

(c) export subsidies that conform fully to the provisions of Part V of this Agreement, as reflected in each Member's Schedule, shall be:

(i) subject to countervailing duties only upon a determination of injury or threat thereof based on volume, effect on prices, or consequent impact in accordance with Article VI of GATT 1994 and Part V of the Subsidies Agreement, and due restraint shall be shown in initiating any countervailing duty investigations; and

(ii) exempt from actions based on Article XVI of GATT 1994 or Articles 3, 5 and 6 of the Subsidies Agreement.

PART VIII

Article 14

Sanitary and Phytosanitary Measures (not reproduced)

PART IX

Article 15

Special and Differential Treatment

1. In keeping with the recognition that differential and more favourable treatment for developing country Members is an integral part of the negotiation, special and differential treatment in respect of commitments shall be provided as set out in the relevant provisions of this Agreement and embodied in the Schedules of concessions and commitments.

2. Developing country Members shall have the flexibility to implement reduction commitments over a period of up to 10 years. Least-developed country Members shall not be required to undertake reduction commitments.

PART X

Article 16

Least-Developed and Net Food-Importing Developing Countries

1. Developed country Members shall take such action as is provided for within the framework of the Decision on Measures Concerning the Possible Negative Effects of the Reform Programme on Least-Developed and Net Food-Importing Developing Countries.
2. The Committee on Agriculture shall monitor, as appropriate, the follow-up to this Decision.

PART XI

Article 17

Committee on Agriculture

A Committee on Agriculture is hereby established.

Article 18

Review of the Implementation of Commitments

1. Progress in the implementation of commitments negotiated under the Uruguay Round reform programme shall be reviewed by the Committee on Agriculture.
2. The review process shall be undertaken on the basis of notifications submitted by Members in relation to such matters and at such intervals as shall be determined, as well as on the basis of such documentation as the Secretariat may be requested to prepare in order to facilitate the review process.
3. In addition to the notifications to be submitted under paragraph 2, any new domestic support measure, or modification of an existing measure, for which exemption from reduction is claimed shall be notified promptly. This notification shall contain details of the new or modified measure and its conformity with the agreed criteria as set out either in Article 6 or in Annex 2.
4. In the review process Members shall give due consideration to the influence of excessive rates of inflation on the ability of any Member to abide by its domestic support commitments.

5. Members agree to consult annually in the Committee on Agriculture with respect to their participation in the normal growth of world trade in agricultural products within the framework of the commitments on export subsidies under this Agreement.
6. The review process shall provide an opportunity for Members to raise any matter relevant to the implementation of commitments under the reform programme as set out in this Agreement.
7. Any Member may bring to the attention of the Committee on Agriculture any measure which it considers ought to have been notified by another Member.

Article 19

Consultation and Dispute Settlement

The provisions of Articles XXII and XXIII of GATT 1994, as elaborated and applied by the Dispute Settlement Understanding, shall apply to consultations and the settlement of disputes under this Agreement.

PART XII

Article 20

Continuation of the Reform Process

Recognizing that the long-term objective of substantial progressive reductions in support and protection resulting in fundamental reform is an ongoing process, Members agree that negotiations for continuing the process will be initiated one year before the end of the implementation period, taking into account:

(a) the experience to that date from implementing the reduction commitments;
(b) the effects of the reduction commitments on world trade in agriculture;
(c) non-trade concerns, special and differential treatment to developing country Members, and the objective to establish a fair and market-oriented agricultural trading system, and the other objectives and concerns mentioned in the preamble to this Agreement; and
(d) what further commitments are necessary to achieve the above mentioned long-term objectives.

PART XIII

Article 21

Final Provisions (not reproduced)

ANNEX 1

PRODUCT COVERAGE (not reproduced)

ANNEX 2

DOMESTIC SUPPORT: THE BASIS FOR EXEMPTION FROM THE REDUCTION COMMITMENTS

1. Domestic support measures for which exemption from the reduction commitments is claimed shall meet the fundamental requirement that they have no, or at most minimal, trade-distorting effects or effects on production. Accordingly, all measures for which exemption is claimed shall conform to the following basic criteria:
   (a) the support in question shall be provided through a publicly-funded government programme (including government revenue foregone) not involving transfers from consumers; and,
   (b) the support in question shall not have the effect of providing price support to producers; plus policy-specific criteria and conditions as set out below.

Government Service Programmes

2. General services
   Policies in this category involve expenditures (or revenue foregone) in relation to programmes which provide services or benefits to agriculture or the rural community. They shall not involve direct payments to producers or processors. Such programmes, which include but are not restricted to the following list, shall meet the general criteria in paragraph 1 above and policy-specific conditions where set out below:
   (a) research, including general research, research in connection with environmental programmes, and research programmes relating to particular products;
   (b) pest and disease control, including general and product-specific pest and disease control measures, such as early-warning systems, quarantine and eradication;

(c) training services, including both general and specialist training facilities;
(d) extension and advisory services, including the provision of means to facilitate the transfer of information and the results of research to producers and consumers;
(e) inspection services, including general inspection services and the inspection of particular products for health, safety, grading or standardization purposes;
(f) marketing and promotion services, including market information, advice and promotion relating to particular products but excluding expenditure for unspecified purposes that could be used by sellers to reduce their selling price or confer a direct economic benefit to purchasers; and
(g) infrastructural services, including: electricity reticulation, roads and other means of transport, market and port facilities, water supply facilities, dams and drainage schemes, and infrastructural works associated with environmental programmes. In all cases the expenditure shall be directed to the provision or construction of capital works only, and shall exclude the subsidized provision of on-farm facilities other than for the reticulation of generally available public utilities. It shall not include subsidies to inputs or operating costs, or preferential user charges.

3. Public stockholding for food security purposes[5]
Expenditures (or revenue foregone) in relation to the accumulation and holding of stocks of products which form an integral part of a food security programme identified in national legislation. This may include government aid to private storage of products as part of such a programme. The volume and accumulation of such stocks shall correspond to predetermined targets related solely to food security. The process of stock accumulation and disposal shall be financially transparent. Food purchases by the government shall be made at current market prices and sales from food security stocks shall be made at no less than the current domestic market price for the product and quality in question.
4. Domestic food aid[6]

[5] For the purposes of paragraph 3 of this Annex, governmental stockholding programmes for food security purposes in developing countries whose operation is transparent and conducted in accordance with officially published objective criteria or guidelines shall be considered to be in conformity with the provisions of this paragraph, including programmes under which stocks of foodstuffs for food security purposes are acquired and released at administered prices, provided that the difference between the acquisition price and the external reference price is accounted for in the AMS.

[5&6 [sic]] For the purposes of paragraphs 3 and 4 of this Annex, the provision of foodstuffs at subsidized prices with the objective of meeting food requirements of urban and rural

Expenditures (or revenue foregone) in relation to the provision of domestic food aid to sections of the population in need. Eligibility to receive the food aid shall be subject to clearly defined criteria related to nutritional objectives. Such aid shall be in the form of direct provision of food to those concerned or the provision of means to allow eligible recipients to buy food either at market or at subsidized prices. Food purchases by the government shall be made at current market prices and the financing and administration of the aid shall be transparent.

5. Direct payments to producers
Support provided through direct payments (or revenue foregone, including payments in kind) to producers for which exemption from reduction commitments is claimed shall meet the basic criteria set out in paragraph 1 above, plus specific criteria applying to individual types of direct payment as set out in paragraphs 6 through 13 below. Where exemption from reduction is claimed for any existing or new type of direct payment other than those specified in paragraphs 6 through 13, it shall conform to criteria (b) through (e) in paragraph 6, in addition to the general criteria set out in paragraph 1.

6. Decoupled income support
   (a) Eligibility for such payments shall be determined by clearly-defined criteria such as income, status as a producer or landowner, factor use or production level in a defined and fixed base period.
   (b) The amount of such payments in any given year shall not be related to, or based on, the type or volume of production (including livestock units) undertaken by the producer in any year after the base period.
   (c) The amount of such payments in any given year shall not be related to, or based on, the prices, domestic or international, applying to any production undertaken in any year after the base period.
   (d) The amount of such payments in any given year shall not be related to, or based on, the factors of production employed in any year after the base period.
   (e) No production shall be required in order to receive such payments.

7. Government financial participation in income insurance and income safety-net programmes
   (a) Eligibility for such payments shall be determined by an income loss, taking into account only income derived from agriculture, which exceeds 30 per cent of average gross income or the equivalent in net income terms (excluding any payments from the same or similar schemes) in the preceding three-year period or a three-year average

poor in developing countries on a regular basis at reasonable prices shall be considered to be in conformity with the provisions of this paragraph.

based on the preceding five-year period, excluding the highest and the lowest entry. Any producer meeting this condition shall be eligible to receive the payments.

(b) The amount of such payments shall compensate for less than 70 per cent of the producer's income loss in the year the producer becomes eligible to receive this assistance.

(c) The amount of any such payments shall relate solely to income; it shall not relate to the type or volume of production (including livestock units) undertaken by the producer; or to the prices, domestic or international, applying to such production; or to the factors of production employed.

(d) Where a producer receives in the same year payments under this paragraph and under paragraph 8 (relief from natural disasters), the total of such payments shall be less than 100 per cent of the producer's total loss.

8. Payments (made either directly or by way of government financial participation in crop insurance schemes) for relief from natural disasters

(a) Eligibility for such payments shall arise only following a formal recognition by government authorities that a natural or like disaster (including disease outbreaks, pest infestations, nuclear accidents, and war on the territory of the Member concerned) has occurred or is occurring; and shall be determined by a production loss which exceeds 30 per cent of the average of production in the preceding three-year period or a three-year average based on the preceding five-year period, excluding the highest and the lowest entry.

(b) Payments made following a disaster shall be applied only in respect of losses of income, livestock (including payments in connection with the veterinary treatment of animals), land or other production factors due to the natural disaster in question.

(c) Payments shall compensate for not more than the total cost of replacing such losses and shall not require or specify the type or quantity of future production.

(d) Payments made during a disaster shall not exceed the level required to prevent or alleviate further loss as defined in criterion (b) above.

(e) Where a producer receives in the same year payments under this paragraph and under paragraph 7 (income insurance and income safety-net programmes), the total of such payments shall be less than 100 per cent of the producer's total loss.

9. Structural adjustment assistance provided through producer retirement programmes

(a) Eligibility for such payments shall be determined by reference to clearly defined criteria in programmes designed to facilitate the retirement of persons engaged in marketable agricultural production, or their movement to non-agricultural activities.

(b) Payments shall be conditional upon the total and permanent retirement of the recipients from marketable agricultural production.

10. Structural adjustment assistance provided through resource retirement programmes

(a) Eligibility for such payments shall be determined by reference to clearly defined criteria in programmes designed to remove land or other resources, including livestock, from marketable agricultural production.

(b) Payments shall be conditional upon the retirement of land from marketable agricultural production for a minimum of three years, and in the case of livestock on its slaughter or definitive permanent disposal.

(c) Payments shall not require or specify any alternative use for such land or other resources which involves the production of marketable agricultural products.

(d) Payments shall not be related to either the type or quantity of production or to the prices, domestic or international, applying to production undertaken using the land or other resources remaining in production.

11. Structural adjustment assistance provided through investment aids

(a) Eligibility for such payments shall be determined by reference to clearly defined criteria in government programmes designed to assist the financial or physical restructuring of a producer's operations in response to objectively demonstrated structural disadvantages. Eligibility for such programmes may also be based on a clearly defined government programme for the re-privatization of agricultural land.

(b) The amount of such payments in any given year shall not be related to, or based on, the type or volume of production (including livestock units) undertaken by the producer in any year after the base period other than as provided for under criterion (e) below.

(c) The amount of such payments in any given year shall not be related to, or based on, the prices, domestic or international, applying to any production undertaken in any year after the base period.

(d) The payments shall be given only for the period of time necessary for the realization of the investment in respect of which they are provided.

(e) The payments shall not mandate or in any way designate the agricultural products to be produced by the recipients except to require them not to produce a particular product.

(f) The payments shall be limited to the amount required to compensate for the structural disadvantage.

12. Payments under environmental programmes
    (a) Eligibility for such payments shall be determined as part of a clearly defined government environmental or conservation programme and be dependent on the fulfilment of specific conditions under the government programme, including conditions related to production methods or inputs.
    (b) The amount of payment shall be limited to the extra costs or loss of income involved in complying with the government programme.
13. Payments under regional assistance programmes
    (a) Eligibility for such payments shall be limited to producers in disadvantaged regions. Each such region must be a clearly designated contiguous geographical area with a definable economic and administrative identity, considered as disadvantaged on the basis of neutral and objective criteria clearly spelt out in law or regulation and indicating that the region's difficulties arise out of more than temporary circumstances.
    (b) The amount of such payments in any given year shall not be related to, or based on, the type or volume of production (including livestock units) undertaken by the producer in any year after the base period other than to reduce that production.
    (c) The amount of such payments in any given year shall not be related to, or based on, the prices, domestic or international, applying to any production undertaken in any year after the base period.
    (d) Payments shall be available only to producers in eligible regions, but generally available to all producers within such regions.
    (e) Where related to production factors, payments shall be made at a degressive rate above a threshold level of the factor concerned.
    (f) The payments shall be limited to the extra costs or loss of income involved in undertaking agricultural production in the prescribed area.

ANNEX 3

DOMESTIC SUPPORT: CALCULATION OF AGGREGATE MEASUREMENT OF SUPPORT

1. Subject to the provisions of Article 6, an Aggregate Measurement of Support (AMS) shall be calculated on a product-specific basis for each basic agricultural product receiving market price support, non-exempt direct payments, or any other subsidy not exempted from the reduction commitment ("other non-exempt policies"). Support which is non-product-specific shall be totalled into one non-product-specific AMS in total monetary terms.

2. Subsidies under paragraph 1 shall include both budgetary outlays and revenue foregone by governments or their agents.
3. Support at both the national and sub-national level shall be included.
4. Specific agricultural levies or fees paid by producers shall be deducted from the AMS.
5. The AMS calculated as outlined below for the base period shall constitute the base level for the implementation of the reduction commitment on domestic support.
6. For each basic agricultural product, a specific AMS shall be established, expressed in total monetary value terms.
7. The AMS shall be calculated as close as practicable to the point of first sale of the basic agricultural product concerned. Measures directed at agricultural processors shall be included to the extent that such measures benefit the producers of the basic agricultural products.
8. Market price support: market price support shall be calculated using the gap between a fixed external reference price and the applied administered price multiplied by the quantity of production eligible to receive the applied administered price. Budgetary payments made to maintain this gap, such as buying-in or storage costs, shall not be included in the AMS.
9. The fixed external reference price shall be based on the years 1986 to 1988 and shall generally be the average f.o.b. unit value for the basic agricultural product concerned in a net exporting country and the average c.i.f. unit value for the basic agricultural product concerned in a net importing country in the base period. The fixed reference price may be adjusted for quality differences as necessary.
10. Non-exempt direct payments: non-exempt direct payments which are dependent on a price gap shall be calculated either using the gap between the fixed reference price and the applied administered price multiplied by the quantity of production eligible to receive the administered price, or using budgetary outlays.
11. The fixed reference price shall be based on the years 1986 to 1988 and shall generally be the actual price used for determining payment rates.
12. Non-exempt direct payments which are based on factors other than price shall be measured using budgetary outlays.
13. Other non-exempt measures, including input subsidies and other measures such as marketing-cost reduction measures: the value of such measures shall be measured using government budgetary outlays or, where the use of budgetary outlays does not reflect the full extent of the subsidy concerned, the basis for calculating the subsidy shall be the gap between the price of the subsidized good or service and a representative market price for a similar good or service multiplied by the quantity of the good or service.

ANNEX 4

DOMESTIC SUPPORT: CALCULATION OF EQUIVALENT MEASUREMENT OF SUPPORT

1. Subject to the provisions of Article 6, equivalent measurements of support shall be calculated in respect of all basic agricultural products where market price support as defined in Annex 3 exists but for which calculation of this component of the AMS is not practicable. For such products the base level for implementation of the domestic support reduction commitments shall consist of a market price support component expressed in terms of equivalent measurements of support under paragraph 2 below, as well as any non-exempt direct payments and other non-exempt support, which shall be evaluated as provided for under paragraph 3 below. Support at both national and sub-national level shall be included.
2. The equivalent measurements of support provided for in paragraph 1 shall be calculated on a product-specific basis for all basic agricultural products as close as practicable to the point of first sale receiving market price support and for which the calculation of the market price support component of the AMS is not practicable. For those basic agricultural products, equivalent measurements of market price support shall be made using the applied administered price and the quantity of production eligible to receive that price or, where this is not practicable, on budgetary outlays used to maintain the producer price.
3. Where basic agricultural products falling under paragraph 1 are the subject of non-exempt direct payments or any other product-specific subsidy not exempted from the reduction commitment, the basis for equivalent measurements of support concerning these measures shall be calculations as for the corresponding AMS components (specified in paragraphs 10 through 13 of Annex 3).
4. Equivalent measurements of support shall be calculated on the amount of subsidy as close as practicable to the point of first sale of the basic agricultural product concerned. Measures directed at agricultural processors shall be included to the extent that such measures benefit the producers of the basic agricultural products. Specific agricultural levies or fees paid by producers shall reduce the equivalent measurements of support by a corresponding amount.

ANNEX 5

SPECIAL TREATMENT WITH RESPECT TO PARAGRAPH 2 OF ARTICLE 4 (not reproduced)

Appendix B

Domestic support provisions of the Doha draft modalities

Editors' note: Appendix B provides the key provisions of the Doha draft modalities as revised in December 2008 relevant to the domestic support disciplines. The full text and others under negotiation in the Doha Round are available on the WTO website. We exercise some judgment for brevity of the appendix. The introductory comments of the chairman related to the entire draft modalities for agriculture are included for context. Then only Section I, Annex A and Annex B related specifically to domestic support are reproduced, along with the subsections of Annex M (Monitoring and Surveillance) related to domestic support notifications and review.

World Trade Organization
TN/AG/W/4/Rev.4, 6 December 2008
Committee on Agriculture Special Session

I think we have made progress since July, and the attached text, together with the separate papers, are an attempt to capture that.

Within the text itself there are a number of square brackets that have been deleted. It is clear that on a number of those, there cannot be said to be formal agreement. But, in earlier versions of the drafts where there were no square brackets, there was not always formal agreement either. Everything is conditional in the deepest sense in any case. But the changes made at this time now represent a best estimate of where there is additional good reason to believe there would prove to be consensus if everything was to come together as a modalities package.

Negotiations and discussions that took place during the July meetings have been a strong input in arriving at that estimate, particularly as regards square brackets dropped in the section on domestic support and in certain parts of market access. But in these and in other areas, negotiations and discussion subsequent to July have also generated or confirmed that sense. Indeed a considerable part of the time devoted to consultations over the last few weeks has been in checking whether things that might have hypothetically worked in July would still work now.

By and large that has been the case, and some other issues have come somewhat closer also since even in July. But, clearly, there is still not formal agreement on any or all of this. Indeed, there is still certain divergence where even the device of square brackets has been dropped, and I have felt it was both instructive and fair to highlight within the text itself a few points where there is still very real divergence (sensitive products being a principal example) or where there is, to say the least, somewhat more heat detectable than on some others (tariff simplification being an example).

Of course, that conditionality remains, as always, paramount. Certain things are manifestly not yet agreed. And, depending on where we end up on these matters, other areas that seem relatively "stable" may well be revisited. That is an undeniable reality in any negotiation. It has been made pretty clear to me in consultations generally, and on a subject like Special Products in particular where Members concerned would, I suspect, be able to go with what is in the text at a pinch. But whether or not that actually happens will be contingent on overall balance – including not just other parts of the agriculture text but elsewhere in the negotiations. And that balance can be decisively affected by where elements that are still not settled end up. The same can be (and has been) said for any issue you choose: domestic support; export competition; etc. But it is still more responsible in the present circumstances, I believe, to describe the glass as (albeit conditionally) half-full rather than half-empty. We are, after all, trying to get to an agreement rather than to find additional reasons why we cannot.

There are other areas where progress has been made since July, but it has not made it to the point where there is a basis to incorporate fully defined wording within the four corners of the text at the moment.

This has been the case with certain elements regarding Sensitive Products, tariff quota creation, non-Sensitive Products with tariffs higher than 100 per cent, tropical and diversification products, preference erosion and the SSM.

While Members have at last been prepared to step (albeit tentatively) outside their comfort zones, they have not been prepared to get as far as a real convergence. As always, one cannot invent consensus where it does not exist. Indeed it is utterly counter-productive to do so because, lacking any real basis in the negotiation, it simply provokes a counter-reaction that sends us back to square one.

But it would have been selling short the progress made to simply have nothing new on the table on these matters. So what has been done in such cases is to provide certain working hypotheses which, if the political will to conclude is genuinely there, could become a platform to get us to closure. I have taken some liberties here as it is, but, hopefully, not to the point of pure invention.

Some of those forms of words are being seen for the first time, albeit that they have not emerged in a vacuum: they are there because they reflect, hopefully, emerging elements of convergence. But even in these areas there is an inevitable unevenness because some things are, unavoidably, somewhat better developed than others.

On Sensitive Products, the text is, on the surface, more clear than in July. That said, the fact remains that there appear to be effectively only two developed Members among the importers that are actually prepared to live with 4 per cent of Sensitive Products despite a seeming view that "4 per cent" was what was a source of quasi-consensus in July. I see no alternative, therefore, but to put that in the text unambiguously. But the reality is that others are not in agreement with that. There is no sign at this point of agreement to bridge that on the table. The best I have been able to do is to outline in a separate document some possibilities of how to "fix" this (if any fix other than applying 4 per cent without limitation will ever fly). But even these ideas are speculative to some extent because no one has a common view on what uniform "payment" would work for going beyond 4 per cent.

On non-Sensitive Products above 100 per cent, battle-lines remain drawn. The text is accordingly still square-bracketed, albeit with a few minor changes. I do sense that, under the surface, progress is being made but, nothing that is as yet textually in the frame. I have also made a suggestion in the attached working paper, for what it is worth, as another angle of approach.

Because tariff quota creation is such a sensitive issue, the text retains the two options. But consultations indicate that a strictly limited and transparent way out could be found. Because, however, transparency is demanded by one side but the other side says it cannot be done, the matter remains moot. But with good will there is at least an emerging structure for getting to closure.

On tropical and diversification products and preference erosion, the text remains the same. I had wanted to record in a separate paper the considerable progress that had been made in July. As of yesterday I had drafted that on the basis that if everything fell into place – and bananas was key to that – there was a deal there for the taking. And it would have been useful for everyone to see how close we were to that. But I was advised yesterday that, on bananas certain material changes had occurred which, in the view of at least one set of Members, vitiated any assumptions about what might even be hypothetically possible. I cannot ignore such a strongly held view so, yet again, all we get for the time being is the 10 July text.

It is a pity, in my view, but I cannot intrude on bilateral negotiations of this intensity. All I would add is that the parties have been working on their bilateral lists as well. Clearly everything else is contingent on satisfaction being found here also. But there are Members that are uncomfortable about not knowing what would appear in importing Members' lists based on the percentages canvassed below. The parties to discussions have developed, I believe, understandings on these matters among themselves to which I, among others, am not privy. If this remains a difficulty among Members I can only continue to urge those involved to consult in good faith with those concerned as soon as possible with a view to alleviating concerns about transparency.

On the SSM, we have made some progress. It is uneven; it is fragile; it has never been consolidated into a single structure. All previous informal efforts have failed. So, this is the first time this particular structure has seen the light of day. It is not, therefore, ready for inclusion in the text *per se* because it is utterly untested. But hopefully it can at least help materially in getting us to that. There appear to remain still subsequent issues to deal with as yet unresolved.

Then there is cotton. Here we have, since July, at least re-established a good dialogue and a sense of trust that had been seriously eroded by events at the end of July. We have also got a robust and common view on the numbers that need to be crunched to get a final decision. That said the fact remains that, textually, I regret that I can only report that neither I nor, as far as I can tell, anyone else involved in the consultations are any wiser today on what the deal will be than we were in July.

I. DOMESTIC SUPPORT

A. Overall reduction of trade-distorting domestic support: A Tiered Formula

Base level

1. The base level for reductions in Overall Trade-Distorting Domestic Support (hereafter "Base OTDS") shall be the sum of:
   (a) the Final Bound Total AMS specified in Part IV of a Member's Schedule; plus
   (b) for developed country Members, 10 per cent of the average total value of agricultural production in the 1995–2000 base period (this being composed of 5 per cent of the average total value of production for product-specific and non-product-specific AMS respectively); plus
   (c) the higher of average Blue Box payments as notified to the Committee on Agriculture, or 5 per cent of the average total value of agricultural production, in the 1995–2000 base period.
2. For developing country Members, item (b) of paragraph 1 above shall be 20 per cent of the average total value of agricultural production in the 1995–2000 or 1995–2004 period as may be selected by the Member concerned. For developing country Members, the base period for the purposes of item (c) of paragraph 1 above shall be 1995–2000 or 1995–2004 as may be selected by the Member concerned.

Tiered reduction formula

3. The Base OTDS shall be reduced in accordance with the following tiered formula:

(a) where the Base OTDS is greater than $60 billion, or the equivalent in the monetary terms in which the binding is expressed, the reduction shall be 80 per cent;
(b) where the Base OTDS is greater than $10 billion and less than or equal to $60 billion, or the equivalents in the monetary terms in which the binding is expressed, the reduction shall be 70 per cent;
(c) where the Base OTDS is less than or equal to $10 billion, or the equivalent in the monetary terms in which the binding is expressed, the rate of reduction shall be 55 per cent.

4. Developed country Members with high relative levels of Base OTDS in the second tier (i.e., at least 40 per cent of the average total value of agricultural production in the 1995–2000 period) shall undertake an additional effort. The additional reduction to be undertaken shall be equal to one-half of the difference between the reduction rates specified in paragraphs 3(a) and 3(b) above.

Implementation period and staging

5. For developed country Members, the reductions shall be implemented in six steps over five years.
   (a) For Members in the first two tiers specified in paragraphs 3(a) and 3(b) above, the Base OTDS shall be reduced by one-third on the first day of implementation. The remaining reductions shall be implemented annually in five equal steps.
   (b) For Members in the third tier specified in paragraph 3(c) above, the Base OTDS shall be reduced by 25 per cent on the first day of implementation. The remaining reductions shall be implemented annually in five equal steps.

Special and differential treatment

6. Developing country Members with no Final Bound Total AMS commitments shall not be required to undertake reduction commitments in their Base OTDS.
7. For developing country Members with Final Bound Total AMS commitments, the applicable reduction in the Base OTDS shall be two-thirds of the relevant rate specified in paragraph 3(c) above. However, net food-importing developing countries (hereafter "NFIDCs") listed in document G/AG/5/Rev.8 shall not be required to undertake reduction commitments in their Base OTDS.
8. For those developing country Members, the reductions shall be implemented in nine steps over eight years. The Base OTDS shall be reduced by 20 per cent on the first day of implementation. The remaining reductions shall be implemented annually in eight equal steps.

Recently-Acceded Members

9. Saudi Arabia, the Former Yugoslav Republic of Macedonia, Viet Nam and Ukraine, as very recently-acceded Members (hereafter "RAMs") shall not be required to undertake reduction commitments in their Base OTDS. Small low-income RAMs with economies in transition[1] shall not be required to undertake reduction commitments in their Base OTDS. Reduction commitments for other RAMs with Final Bound Total AMS commitments shall be two-thirds of the relevant rate specified in paragraph 3(c) above and shall be implemented in accordance with the provisions in paragraph 8 above.

Other commitments

10. All Members, other than NFIDCs which undertake not to use their entitlement to the Blue Box, and least-developed country Members,[2] shall schedule their Base, Annual and Final Bound OTDS entitlements, as provided above, in monetary terms, in Part IV of their Schedules. Developing country Members that are not required to undertake *reduction commitments* under any of the provisions of these modalities shall only be required to schedule their Base OTDS.
11. For those Members that, under these modalities are subject to *reduction commitments* in their Base OTDS, such commitments shall apply as a minimum overall commitment. Throughout the implementation period and thereafter, each Member shall ensure that the sum of the applied levels of trade-distorting support under each OTDS component does not exceed the Annual and Final Bound OTDS levels specified in Part IV of its Schedule.
12. The Agreement on Agriculture shall be amended in order to provide for these OTDS modalities including amendments to existing Articles, where necessary, to ensure consistency with the above provisions. The data on value of production shall, for all Members undertaking OTDS reduction commitments, be annexed to these modalities. This Scheduled OTDS shall be understood not to have the effect of constraining the access of RAMs to their *de minimis* entitlements under the terms of their accession to the WTO.

[1] This shall be applicable to Albania, Armenia, Georgia, Kyrgyz Republic, Moldova and Mongolia.

[2] Cameroon, Congo (Brazzaville), Ghana, Nigeria and Swaziland shall have access also to this provision.

B. *Final Bound Total AMS: A Tiered Formula*

Tiered reduction formula

13. The Final Bound Total AMS shall be reduced in accordance with the following tiered formula:
    (a) where the Final Bound Total AMS is greater than US$40 billion, or the equivalent in the monetary terms in which the binding is expressed, the reduction shall be 70 per cent;
    (b) where the Final Bound Total AMS is greater than US$15 billion and less than or equal to US$40 billion, or the equivalents in the monetary terms in which the binding is expressed, the reduction shall be 60 per cent;
    (c) where the Final Bound Total AMS is less than or equal to US$15 billion, or the equivalent in the monetary terms in which the binding is expressed, the rate of reduction shall be 45 per cent.
14. Developed country Members with high relative levels of Final Bound Total AMS (i.e., at least 40 per cent of the average total value of agricultural production during the 1995–2000 period) shall undertake an additional effort in the form of a higher cut than would otherwise be applicable for the relevant tier. Where the Member concerned is in the second tier, the additional reduction to be undertaken shall be equal to the difference between the reduction rates specified in paragraphs 13(a) and 13(b) above. Where the Member concerned is in the bottom tier, the additional reduction to be undertaken shall be one-half of the difference between the reduction rates specified in paragraphs 13(b) and 13(c) above.

Implementation period and staging

15. For developed country Members, reductions in Final Bound Total AMS shall be implemented in six steps over five years. For developed country Members in the top two tiers specified in paragraphs 13(a) and 13(b) above, this shall be implemented by means of a 25 per cent reduction on the first day of implementation, followed by reductions in equal annual instalments over five years. For other developed country Members, the reductions shall be implemented in six equal annual instalments over five years, commencing on the first day of implementation.

Special and differential treatment

16. The reduction in Final Bound Total AMS applicable to developing country Members shall be two-thirds of the reduction applicable for developed country Members under paragraph 13(c) above. The reductions in Final

Bound Total AMS shall be implemented in nine equal annual instalments over eight years, commencing on the first day of implementation. However, developing country Members with Final Bound Total AMS levels at or below US$ 100 million shall not be required to undertake reductions.

17. NFIDCs listed in document G/AG/5/Rev.8 shall not be required to undertake reduction commitments in their Final Bound Total AMS.
18. The provisions of Article 6.2 of the Agreement on Agriculture shall remain unchanged.

Recently-Acceded Members

19. Saudi Arabia, the Former Yugoslav Republic of Macedonia, Viet Nam and Ukraine, as very recently-acceded Members shall not be required to undertake reduction commitments in their Final Bound Total AMS. Small low-income RAMs with economies in transition shall not be required to undertake reduction commitments in their Final Bound Total AMS.[3] In the case of such Members, investment subsidies which are generally available to agriculture, agricultural input subsidies and interest subsidies to reduce the costs of financing, as well as grants to cover debt repayment, may be excluded from the calculation of the Current Total AMS.[4] The reductions in Final Bound Total AMS for other RAMs with such commitments shall be two-thirds of the rate specified in paragraph 13(c) above and shall be implemented in accordance with paragraph 16 above.

Other

20. Article 18.4 of the Agreement on Agriculture shall continue to apply in order to respond to the situations referred to in that provision. Due consideration shall also be given in the event that a developing country Member faces difficulties in its AMS calculation as a result of extraordinary and sudden increases in food prices relative to the fixed external reference price.

[3] This shall be applicable to Moldova which is the only such Member with a Final Bound Total AMS.

[4] This shall be applicable to Albania, Armenia, Georgia, Kyrgyz Republic, Moldova and Mongolia.

C. *Product-Specific AMS Limits*

General

21. Product-specific[5] AMS limits shall be set out in terms of monetary value commitments in Part IV of the Schedule of the Member concerned in accordance with terms and conditions specified in the paragraphs below.
22. The product-specific AMS limits specified in the Schedules of all developed country Members other than the United States shall be the average of the product-specific AMS during the Uruguay Round implementation period (1995–2000) as notified to the Committee on Agriculture. These shall be tabulated by individual product for each Member in an Annex to these modalities.
23. For the United States only, the product-specific AMS limits specified in their Schedule shall be the resultant of applying proportionately the average product-specific AMS in the 1995–2004 period to the average product-specific total AMS support for the Uruguay Round implementation period (1995–2000) as notified to the Committee on Agriculture. These shall be tabulated by individual product in the Annex to these modalities referred to in the paragraph above.
24. Where a Member has, after the base period specified in paragraphs 22 and 23 above, introduced product-specific AMS support above the *de minimis* level provided for under Article 6.4 of the Uruguay Round Agreement on Agriculture, and it did not have product-specific AMS support above the *de minimis* level during the base period, the product-specific AMS limit specified in the Schedule may be the average amount of such product-specific AMS support for the two most recent years prior to the date of adoption of these modalities, for which notifications to the Committee on Agriculture have been made.
25. In cases where the product-specific AMS support for each year during the base period specified in paragraphs 22 and 23 above was below the *de minimis* level provided for under Article 6.4 of the Uruguay Round Agreement on Agriculture and the Member concerned is not in the situation covered by paragraph 24 above, the product-specific AMS limit specified in the Schedule for the product concerned may be that *de minimis* level, expressed in monetary terms. The application of the provisions in this paragraph and paragraphs 21 to 24 shall not require a Member's product specific AMS limit to be lower than the base period *de minimis* level, expressed in monetary terms as set out in this paragraph.

[5] "Product-specific" commitments have the same meaning as they are used in the Uruguay Round Agreement on Agriculture.

26. The scheduled product-specific AMS limits shall be implemented in full on the first day of the implementation period. Where the average notified product-specific AMS in the two most recent years for which notifications are available was higher, the limits shall be implemented in three equal annual instalments, with the starting point for implementation being the lower of the average of those two years or 130 per cent of the scheduled limits.

Special and differential treatment

27. Developing country Members shall establish their product-specific AMS limits by choosing one of the following methods, and scheduling all their product-specific AMS commitments in accordance with the method chosen:
    (a) the average product-specific AMS during the base period 1995–2000 or 1995–2004 as may be selected by the Member concerned, as notified to the Committee on Agriculture; or
    (b) two times the Member's product-specific *de minimis* level provided for under Article 6.4 of the Uruguay Round Agreement on Agriculture during the base periods referred to in subparagraph (a) above; or
    (c) 20 per cent of the Annual Bound Total AMS in the relevant year during the Doha Round implementation period.
28. Where a developing country Member chooses paragraph 27(a) above as its method for the establishment of product-specific AMS limits that Member shall also have access to the provisions of paragraphs 24 and 25 above.
29. Article 6.3 of the Agreement on Agriculture shall be amended to reflect these modalities.

D. *De minimis*

Reductions

30. The *de minimis* levels referred to in Article 6.4(a) of the Uruguay Round Agreement on Agriculture for developed country Members (i.e., 5 per cent of a Member's total value of production of a basic agricultural product in the case of product-specific *de minimis* and 5 per cent of the value of a Member's total agricultural production in the case of non-product-specific *de minimis*) shall be reduced by no less than 50 per cent effective on the first day of the implementation period. Furthermore, where, in any year of the implementation period, a lower level of *de minimis* support than that resulting from application of that minimum percentage reduction would still be required to ensure that the Annual or Final Bound OTDS commitment for that year is not exceeded, a Member shall undertake such an additional reduction in what would otherwise be its *de minimis* entitlement.

Special and differential treatment

31. For developing country Members with Final Bound Total AMS commitments, the *de minimis* levels referred to in Article 6.4(b) of the Uruguay Round Agreement on Agriculture (i.e., 10 per cent of a Member's total value of production of a basic agricultural product in the case of product-specific *de minimis* and 10 per cent of the value of a Member's total agricultural production in the case of non-product-specific *de minimis*) to which they have access under their existing WTO obligations shall be reduced by at least two-thirds of the reduction rate specified in paragraph 30 above. The timeframe for implementation shall be three years from the first day of implementation. Furthermore, where, in any year of the implementation period, a lower level of *de minimis* support than that resulting from application of that minimum percentage reduction would still be required to ensure that the Annual Bound or Final OTDS commitment for that year is not exceeded, a Member shall undertake such an additional reduction in what would otherwise be their *de minimis* entitlement.
32. Developing country Members with no Final Bound Total AMS commitments; or with such AMS commitments, but that either allocate almost all that support for subsistence and resource-poor producers, or that are NFIDCs listed in document G/AG/5/Rev.8; shall continue to have the same access as under their existing WTO obligations to the limits provided for product-specific and non-product-specific *de minimis* in the current Article 6.4(b) of the Uruguay Round Agreement on Agriculture.

Recently-Acceded Members

33. Saudi Arabia, the Former Yugoslav Republic of Macedonia, Viet Nam and Ukraine, as very recently-acceded Members shall not be required to undertake reduction commitments in *de minimis*. Small low-income RAMs with economies in transition[6] shall not be required to undertake reduction commitments in *de minimis*. Other RAMs with Final Bound Total AMS commitments and which have existing *de minimis* levels of 5 per cent shall reduce such levels by at least one-third of the reduction rate specified in paragraph 30 above and the timeframe for implementation shall be five years longer.

Other

34. The provisions of Article 6.4 of the Uruguay Round Agreement on Agriculture shall be amended accordingly to conform to these modalities.

[6] This shall be applicable to Albania, Armenia, Georgia, Kyrgyz Republic, Moldova and Mongolia.

E. Blue Box

Basic criteria

35. The value of the following domestic support, provided that it is consistent also with the limits as provided for in the paragraphs below, shall be excluded from a Member's calculation of its Current Total AMS but shall count for purposes of that Member's Blue Box commitments and OTDS:
   (a) Direct payments under production-limiting programmes if:
      (i) such payments are based on fixed and unchanging areas and yields; or
      (ii) such payments are made on 85 per cent or less of a fixed and unchanging base level of production; or
      (iii) livestock payments are made on a fixed and unchanging number of head.

   Or

   (b) Direct payments that do not require production if:
      (i) such payments are based on fixed and unchanging bases and yields; or
      (ii) livestock payments are made on a fixed and unchanging number of head; and
      (iii) such payments are made on 85 per cent or less of a fixed and unchanging base level of production.
36. Each Member shall specify in its Schedule which of these categories – (a) or (b) – it has selected for the purposes of establishing all its Blue Box commitments in this Round. Any exception to this universal application would be with the agreement of all Members prior to finalization of Schedules. In no circumstances could both domestic support categories be made available for any particular product or products.
37. Any Member that is in a position to move its domestic support from AMS to Blue pursuant to paragraph 43 below, or introduce product-specific Blue Box support pursuant to paragraphs 47 and 50 below subsequent to the conclusion of this negotiation shall have the option to do so on the basis of either criterion above but, once selected and scheduled, this shall be binding.

Additional criteria

(a) Overall Blue Box limit

38. The maximum value of support that can, under the above criteria of "Blue Box", be provided under Article 6.5 shall not exceed 2.5 per cent of the average total value of agricultural production in the 1995–2000 base period on the basis of notifications to the Committee on Agriculture where they exist. This limit shall be expressed in monetary terms in Part

IV of Members' Schedules and shall apply from the first day of the implementation period.

39. In cases where a Member has, consistent with the terms of Article 6.5(a) of the Uruguay Round Agreement on Agriculture, placed in the Blue Box an exceptionally large percentage of its trade-distorting support – defined as 40 per cent – during the 1995–2000 base period, the limit for that Member shall, instead, be established by application of a percentage reduction in that average base period amount. That percentage reduction shall equal the percentage reduction that the Member concerned is to make in its Final Bound Total AMS. This Blue Box limit shall be expressed in monetary terms and bound in Part IV of that Member's Schedule. An implementation period of no more than two years may be provided for any such Member in the event that immediate implementation is unduly burdensome.

(b) Product-specific limits

40. For all Members other than the United States, the limit to the value of support that may be provided to specific products as Blue Box entitlements shall be the average value of support provided to those products at an individual product level, consistent with Article 6.5(a) of the Uruguay Round Agreement on Agriculture, during the 1995–2000 period and with notifications to the Committee on Agriculture. These product-specific limits shall be expressed in monetary terms at an individual product level, annexed in that format to these modalities, bound in Part IV of the Schedule of the Member concerned, and shall apply from the first day of the implementation period.

41. In any case where Article 6.5(a) consistent Blue Box support was not provided for the entirety of the 1995–2000 period, the Member concerned shall use the average value of support for the years notified within that period, provided that there are at least three consecutive notified years within that period.

42. For the United States, the limits to the value of support that may be provided to specific products under paragraph 35(b) above shall be [(110) (120)] percent of the average product-specific amounts that would result from applying proportionately the legislated maximum permissible expenditure under the 2002 Farm Bill for specific products at an individual product level to the overall Blue Box limit of 2.5 per cent of the average total value of agricultural production during the 1995–2000 period. These product-specific limits shall be expressed in monetary terms at an individual product level, annexed in that format to these modalities and shall be bound in Part IV of that Member's Schedule.

43. Blue Box entitlements for specific products may nevertheless exceed the limits determined under paragraphs 40–42 above but only where there

is a corresponding and irreversible one-for-one reduction in the product-specific AMS limits for the products concerned (except for cotton, where that rate would be two-for-one).

44. Where this arises in the context of this particular negotiation, full documentation must be provided in support of this "transfer" to ensure that the starting point is verifiably, on the one hand, the product-specific AMS limit that would have been otherwise inscribed in the Schedule through application of the methodology provided above and, on the other, the Blue Box entitlement otherwise inscribed pursuant to application of the methodology set out above.
45. Where this arises as a result of continuation of the reform process after scheduling and during the implementation period, there must be an exact reciprocal reduction in the scheduled product-specific AMS limit for, as the case may be, a new, or an increase in the scheduled, product-specific Blue Box limit.
46. In both such situations, the overall Blue Box limit cannot in any case be exceeded.
47. Notwithstanding the above, where, for a particular product, there is no product-specific entitlement to a Blue Box limit under the provisions above, and no Current AMS support in the base period for that particular product, a product-specific Blue Box limit may still be scheduled but only where the total support for any such products concerned does not exceed 5 per cent of the overall Blue Box limit; there is a maximum for any single product of 2.5 per cent of the overall Blue Box limit; and the overall Blue Box limit is still respected. This is available to developed country Members with direct payments of the kind that meet the terms of paragraph 35(a) above, and is a once-only provision for commitment in this Round of negotiations. The monetary value and the products concerned shall be inscribed in a Member's Schedule.

Special and differential treatment

48. For developing country Members, the maximum permitted value of support referred to in paragraph 38 above shall be 5 per cent of the average total value of agricultural production in the 1995–2000 or the 1995–2004 base period as may be selected by the Member concerned. That limit shall be expressed in monetary terms and bound in Part IV in developing country Members' Schedules. However, in cases where there is a movement from AMS to Blue subsequent to the conclusion of this negotiation, the developing country Member concerned shall have the option of selecting as its base period the most recent five-year period for which data are at that time available. An NFIDC which chooses not to avail itself of its Blue Box entitlement and thereby is not obliged to Schedule its OTDS under paragraph 10 above, shall so indicate by marking "nil" in the appropriate section of Part IV of its Schedule.

49. Where a product accounted both for more than 25 per cent of the average total value of agricultural production and 80 per cent of the average Annual Bound Total AMS during the base period, a developing country Member that chooses to switch its support from AMS to Blue for that product, on a one-for-one and irreversible basis, shall be entitled to do so even if this would otherwise lead to exceeding the overall Blue Box limit provided for in the paragraph above.
50. Where, for a particular product, a developing country Member has no product-specific entitlement to a Blue Box limit for that product under the above provisions, and no Current AMS support in the base period for it, a product-specific Blue Box limit may still be scheduled but only where the total support for the totality of any such products concerned does not exceed 30 per cent of the overall Blue Box limit; there is a maximum for any single product of 10 per cent of the overall Blue Box limit; and the overall Blue Box limit is still respected. For least-developed country Members and for NFIDCs these limits shall be 75 per cent and 25 per cent respectively.

Recently-Acceded Members

51. For RAMs, the maximum value of support referred to in paragraph 38 above shall be 5 per cent of the average total value of agricultural production in the 1995–2000 base period or the 1995–2004 base period as may be selected by the Member concerned. However, in cases where there is a movement from AMS to Blue subsequent to the conclusion of this negotiation, the Member concerned shall have the option of selecting as its base period the most recent five-year period for which data are at that time available.

Other

52. Article 6.5 of the Agreement on Agriculture shall be amended to reflect the above modalities accordingly.

F. Green Box

53. Annex 2 of the Agreement on Agriculture shall be amended as set out in Annex B of this document.

G. Cotton: Domestic Support

Reductions in support for cotton

54. The development aspects of cotton shall be addressed as provided for in paragraph 12 of the Hong Kong Ministerial Declaration. AMS support for cotton shall be reduced according to the following formula:

$$Rc = Rg + \frac{(100 - Rg) \times 100}{3 \times Rg}$$

Rc = Specific reduction applicable to cotton as a percentage
Rg = General reduction in AMS as a percentage

55. This shall be applied to the base value of support calculated as the arithmetic average of the amounts notified by Members for cotton in supporting tables DS:4 from 1995 to 2000. The Blue Box limit applicable to cotton shall amount to one third of the product-specific limit that would otherwise have been the resultant from the methodology generally applicable above.

Implementation

56. The reductions for trade-distorting domestic support on cotton shall be implemented over a period which is onethird of the implementation period.

Special and differential treatment

57. Developing country Members with relevant AMS and Blue Box commitments for cotton otherwise applicable under the relevant provisions of this Agreement, including paragraph 27 above, shall provide a rate of reduction for cotton that is two-thirds of that which would be applicable under paragraph 54 above.
58. Developing country Members shall implement their reduction commitments for cotton over a longer time period than for developed country Members.

ANNEX A

UNITED STATES – PRODUCT SPECIFIC BLUE BOX LIMITS

US Product-Specific Blue Box Limits As Notified by the United States

1. For the United States, the average total value of agricultural production during the 1995–2000 period is equal to $194,139.3 million.

Year	Total value of agricultural production (million dollars)	2.5% of the value of agricultural production
1995	190,109.7	4,752.7
1996	205,701.3	5,142.5
1997	203,883.7	5,097.1
1998	190,886.0	4,772.2
1999	184,734.6	4,618.4

2000	189,520.3	4,738.0
Average	194,139.3	4,853.5

2. Under the 2002 Farm Bill, countercyclical payments for each eligible commodity are equal to the countercyclical payment rate times 85 per cent of base acres times the countercyclical payment program yield. The countercyclical payment rate is determined as the difference between the target price for that commodity, minus the direct payment rate for that commodity, minus the higher of the season average price or the legislated national loan rate for that commodity. The countercyclical payment rate is highest when the market price is below the loan rate and is equal to the target price minus the direct payment rate minus the loan rate.
3. The legislated maximum permissible expenditures for each of the years 2002–07 are given in appendix Table 1. The figures show slight variation from year to year and reflect the fact that the 2002 Farm Bill legislated different loan rates and target prices over the period. In addition, eligible production shows slight variation due to land entering and exiting from the Conservation Reserve Program over the period. The proportionate level for each commodity is determined by dividing the average maximum payment for the 2002–07 crop years by the total average maximum payments for all commodities.
4. Product-specific limits for Blue Box expenditures are calculated by multiplying 2.5 per cent of the value of agricultural production times the proportionate level of payment under the 2002 Farm Bill times 110 and 120 per cent.

Crop	Average maximum payment 2002–07 crop years	Payment as share of total payment
Corn	3,224.2	44.2%
Grain sorghum	147.4	2.0%
Barley	46.7	0.6%
Oats	8.7	0.1%
Wheat	1,421.5	19.5%
Soybeans	550.3	7.5%
Upland cotton	1,376.5	18.9%
Rice	323.1	4.4%
Peanuts	200.9	2.8%
Total	7,299.2	100.0%

Product-Specific Blue Box Caps

Crop	110%	120%
Corn	2,359.8	2,574.3
Grain sorghum	106.8	116.5
Barley	32.0	34.9
Oats	5.3	5.8
Wheat	1,041.1	1,135.7
Soybeans	400.4	436.8
Upland cotton	1,009.0	1,100.8
Rice	234.9	256.3
Peanuts	149.5	163.1

Table A1 *Maximum countercyclical payments under 2002 Farm Bill*

		A	B	C	D = A-B-C	E	F = 0.85*E	G	H = D*F*G	
	Unit	Target price	Direct payment rate	Loan rate	Maximum payment rate	Crop base	Payment acres	Payment yield	Payment	Share of total
		Dollars per unit				*Million acres*		*Unit per acre*	*Million dollars*	%
2002										
Corn	Bushel	2.60	0.28	1.98	0.34	87.86	74.68	114.3	2,902.3	42.6%
Sorghum	Bushel	2.54	0.35	1.98	0.21	12.10	10.29	58.0	125.3	1.8%
Barley	Bushel	2.21	0.24	1.88	0.09	8.80	7.48	48.7	32.8	0.5%
Oats	Bushel	1.40	0.024	1.35	0.03	3.10	2.64	49.8	3.4	0.1%
Wheat	Bushel	3.86	0.52	2.80	0.54	76.20	64.77	36.1	1,262.6	18.5%
Soybeans	Bushel	5.80	0.44	5.00	0.36	53.50	45.48	34.1	558.3	8.2%
Upland cotton	Pound	0.72	0.0667	0.52	0.1373	18.86	16.03	639.0	1,406.3	20.6%
Rice	cwt	10.50	2.35	6.50	1.65	4.51	3.83	51.24	324.2	4.8%
Peanuts	Pound	0.2475	0.018	0.1775	0.05	1.53	1.30	2,989	202.7	3.0%
Total									6,817.7	100.0%
2003										
Corn	Bushel	2.60	0.28	1.98	0.34	87.83	74.66	114.4	2,903.8	42.8%
Sorghum	Bushel	2.54	0.35	1.98	0.21	12.10	10.29	58.1	125.5	1.9%
Barley	Bushel	2.21	0.24	1.88	0.09	8.80	7.48	48.7	32.8	0.5%

Table A1 (*cont.*)

		A	B	C	D = A-B-C	E	F = 0.85*E	G	H = D*F*G	
	Unit	Target price	Direct payment rate	Loan rate	Maximum payment rate	Crop base	Payment acres	Payment yield	Payment	Share of total
		Dollars per unit				*Million acres*		*Unit per acre*	*Million dollars*	%
Oats	Bushel	1.40	0.024	1.35	0.03	3.10	2.64	50.0	3.4	0.1%
Wheat	Bushel	3.86	0.52	2.80	0.54	76.20	64.77	36.1	1,262.6	18.6%
Soybeans	Bushel	5.80	0.44	5.00	0.36	53.50	45.48	34.1	558.3	8.2%
Upland cotton	Pound	0.72	0.0667	0.52	0.1373	18.42	15.66	639.0	1,374.0	20.3%
Rice	cwt	10.50	2.35	6.50	1.650	4.49	3.81	51.2	322.2	4.8%
Peanuts	Pound	0.2475	0.018	0.1775	0.052	1.52	1.29	2,989	200.3	3.0%
Total									6,782.8	100.0%
2004										
Corn	Bushel	2.63	0.28	1.95	0.400	87.64	74.49	114.2	3,402.9	44.7%
Sorghum	Bushel	2.57	0.35	1.95	0.270	12.00	10.20	58.1	160.0	2.1%
Barley	Bushel	2.24	0.24	1.85	0.150	8.70	7.40	48.7	54.0	0.7%
Oats	Bushel	1.44	0.024	1.33	0.086	3.10	2.64	49.8	11.3	0.1%
Wheat	Bushel	3.92	0.52	2.75	0.650	76.00	64.60	36.1	1,515.8	19.9%
Soybeans	Bushel	5.80	0.44	5.00	0.360	52.90	44.97	34.1	552.0	7.3%
Upland cotton	Pound	0.72	0.0667	0.52	0.1373	18.72	15.91	636	1,389.4	18.3%

Rice	cwt	10.50	2.35	6.50	1.650	4.51	3.84	51.24	324.3	4.3%
Peanuts	Pound	0.2475	0.018	0.1775	0.052	1.52	1.29	2,990	200.7	2.6%
Total									7,610.4	100.0%
2005										
Corn	Bushel	2.63	0.28	1.95	0.400	87.15	74.08	114.3	3,386.8	44.8%
Sorghum	Bushel	2.57	0.35	1.95	0.270	11.90	10.12	58.1	158.7	2.1%
Barley	Bushel	2.24	0.24	1.85	0.150	8.70	7.40	48.7	54.0	0.7%
Oats	Bushel	1.44	0.024	1.33	0.086	3.10	2.64	49.8	11.3	0.1%
Wheat	Bushel	3.92	0.52	2.75	0.650	75.40	64.09	36.1	1,503.9	19.9%
Soybeans	Bushel	5.80	0.44	5.00	0.360	52.50	44.63	34.1	547.8	7.3%
Upland cotton	Pound	0.72	0.0667	0.52	0.1373	18.47	15.70	634	1,366.9	18.1%
Rice	cwt	10.50	2.35	6.50	1.650	4.49	3.82	51.26	322.9	4.3%
Peanuts	Pound	0.2475	0.018	0.1775	0.052	1.52	1.29	2,990	201.0	2.7%
Total									7,553.4	100.0%
2006										
Corn	Bushel	2.63	0.28	1.95	0.400	86.76	73.75	114.4	3,374.6	44.9%
Sorghum	Bushel	2.57	0.35	1.95	0.270	11.80	10.03	58.2	157.6	2.1%
Barley	Bushel	2.24	0.24	1.85	0.150	8.60	7.31	48.6	53.3	0.7%
Oats	Bushel	1.44	0.024	1.33	0.086	3.10	2.64	49.9	11.3	0.2%
Wheat	Bushel	3.92	0.52	2.75	0.650	74.80	63.58	36.1	1,491.9	19.9%
Soybeans	Bushel	5.80	0.44	5.00	0.360	52.01	44.21	34.1	542.7	7.2%

Table A1 (*cont.*)

		A	B	C	D = A-B-C	E	F = 0.85*E	G	H = D*F*G	
	Unit	Target price	Direct payment rate	Loan rate	Maximum payment rate	Crop base	Payment acres	Payment yield	Payment	Share of total
		Dollars per unit				*Million acres*		*Unit per acre*	*Million dollars*	%
Upland cotton	Pound	0.72	0.0667	0.52	0.1373	18.40	15.64	634	1,361.3	18.1%
Rice	cwt	10.50	2.35	6.50	1.650	4.48	3.81	51.28	322.4	4.3%
Peanuts	Pound	0.2475	0.018	0.1775	0.052	1.51	1.29	2,993	200.3	2.7%
Total									7,515.4	100.0%
2007										
Corn	Bushel	2.63	0.28	1.95	0.400	86.76	73.75	114.4	3,374.6	44.9%
Sorghum	Bushel	2.57	0.35	1.95	0.270	11.80	10.03	58.2	157.6	2.1%
Barley	Bushel	2.24	0.24	1.85	0.150	8.60	7.31	48.6	53.3	0.7%
Oats	Bushel	1.44	0.024	1.33	0.086	3.10	2.64	49.8	11.3	0.2%
Wheat	Bushel	3.92	0.52	2.75	0.650	74.80	63.58	36.1	1,491.9	19.9%
Soybeans	Bushel	5.80	0.44	5.00	0.360	52.01	44.21	34.1	542.7	7.2%
Upland cotton	Pound	0.72	0.0667	0.52	0.1373	18.40	15.64	634	1,361.3	18.1%
Rice	cwt	10.50	2.35	6.50	1.650	4.48	3.81	51.28	322.4	4.3%
Peanuts	Pound	0.2475	0.018	0.1775	0.052	1.51	1.29	2,993	200.3	2.7%
Total									7,515.4	100.0%

Average, 2002–07			
Corn	Bushel	3,224.2	44.2%
Sorghum	Bushel	147.4	2.0%
Barley	Bushel	46.7	0.6%
Oats	Bushel	8.7	0.1%
Wheat	Bushel	1,421.5	19.5%
Soybeans	Bushel	550.3	7.5%
Upland cotton	Pound	1,376.5	18.9%
Rice	cwt	323.1	4.4%
Peanuts	Pound	200.9	2.8%
Total		7,299.2	100.0%

ANNEX B

ANNEX 2 OF THE AGREEMENT ON AGRICULTURE SHALL BE AMENDED AS FOLLOWS:

Government Service Programmes

General services (paragraph 2)

Add the following subparagraph (h) to the existing paragraph 2:

(h) **policies and services related to farmer settlement, land reform programmes, rural development and rural livelihood security in developing country Members, such as provision of infrastructural services, land rehabilitation, soil conservation and resource management, drought management and flood control, rural employment programmes, nutritional food security, issuance of property titles and settlement programmes, to promote rural development and poverty alleviation**.

Public stockholding for food security purposes

Modify the existing footnote 5 as follows:

> For the purposes of paragraph 3 of this Annex, governmental stockholding programmes for food security purposes in developing countries whose operation is transparent and conducted in accordance with officially published objective criteria or guidelines shall be considered to be in conformity with the provisions of this paragraph, including programmes under which stocks of foodstuffs for food security purposes are acquired and released at administered prices, provided that the difference between the acquisition price and the external reference price is accounted for in the AMS. **However, acquisition of stocks of foodstuffs by developing country Members with the objective of supporting low-income or resource-poor producers shall not be required to be accounted for in the AMS**.

Modify the existing footnote 5 and 6 as follows:

> For the purposes of paragraphs 3 and 4 of this Annex, **the acquisition of foodstuffs at subsidised prices when procured generally from low-income or resource-poor producers in developing countries with the objective of fighting hunger and rural poverty, as well as** the provision of foodstuffs at subsidised prices with the objective of meeting food requirements of urban and rural poor in developing countries on a regular basis at reasonable prices

shall be considered to be in conformity with the provisions of this paragraph. This is understood to mean, *inter alia*, that where such programmes referred to in this footnote and paragraph 4 above, including those in relation to lowering prices to more reasonable levels, involve also the arrangements referred to in footnote 5 to paragraph 4, there is no requirement for the difference between the acquisition price and the external reference price to be accounted for in the AMS.

Decoupled income support (paragraph 6)

Modify the existing subparagraph (a) as follows:

(a) Eligibility for such payments shall be determined by clearly-defined criteria such as income, status as a producer or landowner, factor use or production level in a defined, fixed **and unchanging historical** base period **which shall be notified to the Committee on Agriculture. Transfer of entitlements to existing decoupled income support between producers or landowners shall not be precluded. An exceptional update is not precluded, provided that producer expectations and production decisions are unaffected, in particular due to (a) ensuring that any updated base period is not only a significant number of years in the past[1] but is also determined and promulgated by the administering authority in such a way that the updated base concerned could not have been reasonably anticipated by producers such that their production decisions could be materially altered, (b) that such updating is not made in conjunction with, or otherwise amounts *de facto* to, a decision to increase the uniform unitary rate per crop[2] and (c) that this updating shall not, in itself or otherwise by reason of its introduction, have the effect, directly or indirectly, of circumventing the obligations regarding domestic support measures and price support to producers pursuant to paragraph 1.**

Members which have not previously made use of this type of payment and thus have not notified and which cannot establish a historical base period because of a lack of data shall not be precluded from

[1] Where a Member has, at the time of entry into force of this Agreement, more than one type of direct payments within the same system of decoupled income support, it shall be possible to decide, within a period of no more than five years from the date of entry into force of this Agreement, to move from one to another type of direct payments for all or part of the territory of that Member, including the use of a changed base period. This decision shall be taken once and for all for each part of the territory of the Member concerned. Where a Member intends to exercise this possibility, it shall notify its decision to the Committee on Agriculture within 180 days of the entry into force of this Agreement.

[2] This shall mean the rate used to calculate the support per recipient on the basis of criteria such as area or yields.

establishing an appropriate base period which, provided that it is not based on any future factor use or production, need not be based on a pre-existing determinate historical record, but which shall be fixed and unchanging and shall be notified[3]. This is without prejudice to the possibility for Members to establish appropriate base periods for substantially different decoupled income support in accordance with the conditions laid down in this paragraph.

Payments (made either directly or by way of government financial participation in crop insurance schemes) for relief from natural disasters (paragraph 8)

Modify the existing subparagraphs (a), (b) and (d) as follows:

(a) Eligibility for such payments shall arise:

(i) **In the case of direct payments related to disasters** only following a formal recognition by government authorities that a natural or like disaster (including disease outbreaks, pest infestations, nuclear accidents, and war on the territory of the Member concerned) has occurred or is occurring; and shall be determined by a production loss[8[sic]] which exceeds 30 per cent of the average of production in the preceding **five**-year period or a three-year average based on the preceding five-year period, excluding the highest and the lowest entry. **In the case of developing country Members, payments for relief from natural disasters may be provided to producers when the production loss is less than 30 per cent of the average of production in the preceding five-year period or a three-year average based on the preceding five-year period.**

(ii) **In the case of government financial participation in crop or production insurance schemes, eligibility for such payments shall be determined by a production loss which exceeds 30 per cent of the average production in a period demonstrated to be actuarially appropriate. In the case of a developing country Member's government's financial participation in crop or production insurance schemes, eligibility for payments may be provided to producers when the production loss is less than 30 per cent of the average of production in the preceding five-year period or a three-year average based on the preceding five-year period.**

(iii) **In the case of the destruction of animals or crops to control or prevent pests, diseases, disease-carrying organisms or**

[3] Developing country Members may not have the capacity to fully assess the impact of innovation in their agricultural policies. Accordingly, the base period of a time-limited experimental or pilot programme may not be taken as the fixed and unchanging base period for the purposes of this paragraph.

disease-causing organisms named in national legislation or international standards, the production loss may be less than 30 per cent of the average of production referred to in paragraph 8(a)(i) or 8(a)(ii), as applicable.

(b) Payments made **under this paragraph** shall be applied only in respect of losses of income, **crops**, livestock (including pay ments in connection with the veterinary treatment of animals), land or other production factors due to the natural disaster **or destruction of animals or crops** in question.

(d) Payments made **under this paragraph** shall not exceed the level required to prevent or alleviate further loss as defined in criterion (b) above.

8[sic] Developing country Members may determine the production loss of the affected sector(s) or region(s) on an aggregate basis.

Structural adjustment assistance provided through investment aids (paragraph 11)

Modify the existing subparagraph (b) as follows:

(b) The amount of such payments in any given year shall not be related to, or based on, the type or volume of production (including livestock units) undertaken by the producer in any year after the base period other than as provided for under criterion (e) below. **The base period shall be a defined, fixed and unchanging historical base period which shall be notified to the Committee on Agriculture. Transfer of entitlements to existing decoupled income support between producers or landowners shall not be precluded.**

An exceptional update is not precluded, provided that producer expectations and production decisions are unaffected, in particular due to (a) ensuring that any updated base period is not only a significant number of years in the past[4] **but is also determined and promulgated by the administering authority in such a way that the updated base concerned could not have been reasonably anticipated by producers such that their production decisions could be materially altered, (b) that such updating is not made in conjunction with, or otherwise amounts *de facto* to,**

4 Where a Member has, at the time of entry into force of this Agreement, more than one type of direct payments within the same system of decoupled income support, it shall be possible to decide, within a period of no more than five years from the date of entry into force of this Agreement, to move from one to another type of direct payments for all or part of the territory of that Member, including the use of a changed base period. This decision shall be taken once and for all for each part of the territory of the Member concerned. Where a Member intends to exercise this possibility, it shall notify its decision to the Committee on Agriculture within 180 days of the entry into force of this Agreement.

a decision to increase the uniform unitary rate per crop[5] and (c) that this updating shall not, in itself or otherwise by reason of its introduction, have the effect, directly or indirectly, of circumventing the obligations regarding domestic support measures and price support to producers pursuant to paragraph 1.

Members which have not previously made use of this type of payment and thus have not notified and which cannot establish a historical base period because of a lack of data shall not be precluded from establishing an appropriate base period which, provided that it is not based on any future factor use or production, need not be based on a pre-existing determinate historical record, but which shall be fixed and unchanging and shall be notified[6]. This is without prejudice to the possibility for Members to establish appropriate base periods for substantially different decoupled income support in accordance with the conditions laid down in this paragraph.

Payments under regional assistance programmes (paragraph 13)

Modify the existing subparagraphs (a), (b) and (f) as follows:

(a) Eligibility for such payments shall be limited to producers in disadvantaged regions. Each such region must be a clearly designated contiguous geographical area with a definable economic and administrative identity, considered as disadvantaged on the basis of neutral and objective criteria clearly spelt out in law or regulation and indicating that the region's difficulties arise out of more than temporary circumstances. **Developing country Members shall be exempted from the condition that a disadvantaged region must be a contiguous geographical area.**

(b) The amount of such payments in any given year shall not be related to, or based on, the type or volume of production (including livestock units) undertaken by the producer in any year after the base period other than to reduce that production. **The base period shall be a defined, fixed and unchanging historical base period which shall be notified to the Committee on Agriculture. Transfer of entitlements to existing decoupled income support between producers or landowners shall not be precluded.**

An exceptional update is not precluded, provided that producer expectations and production decisions are unaffected, in particular

[5] This shall mean the rate used to calculate the support per recipient on the basis of criteria such as area or yields.

[6] Developing country Members may not have the capacity to fully assess the impact of innovation in their agricultural policies. Accordingly, the base period of a time-limited experimental or pilot programme may not be taken as the fixed and unchanging base period for the purposes of this paragraph.

due to (a) ensuring that any updated base period is not only a significant number of years in the past[7] but is also determined and promulgated by the administering authority in such a way that the updated base concerned could not have been reasonably anticipated by producers such that their production decisions could be materially altered, (b) that such updating is not made in conjunction with, or otherwise amounts *de facto* to, a decision to increase the uniform unitary rate per crop[8] and (c) that this updating shall not, in itself or otherwise by reason of its introduction, have the effect, directly or indirectly, of circumventing the obligations regarding domestic support measures and price support to producers pursuant to paragraph 1.

Members which have not previously made use of this type of payment and thus have not notified and which cannot establish a historical base period because of a lack of data shall not be precluded from establishing an appropriate base period which, provided that it is not based on any future factor use or production, need not be based on a pre-existing determinate historical record, but which shall be fixed and unchanging and shall be notified[9]. This is without prejudice to the possibility for Members to establish appropriate base periods for substantially different decoupled income support in accordance with the conditions laid down in this paragraph.

(f) The payments shall be limited to the extra costs or loss of income involved in undertaking agricultural production (**including livestock production**) in the prescribed area.

ANNEX M

MONITORING AND SURVEILLANCE

1. The existing Article 18 of the Agreement on Agriculture will be replaced by the text below. Enhanced monitoring also requires that, as a

[7] Where a Member has, at the time of entry into force of this Agreement, more than one type of direct payments within the same system of decoupled income support, it shall be possible to decide, within a period of no more than five years from the date of entry into force of this Agreement, to move from one to another type of direct payments for all or part of the territory of that Member, including the use of a changed base period. This decision shall be taken once and for all for each part of the territory of the Member concerned. Where a Member intends to exercise this possibility, it shall notify its decision to the Committee on Agriculture within 180 days of the entry into force of this Agreement.

[8] This shall mean the rate used to calculate the support per recipient on the basis of criteria such as area or yields.

[9] Developing country Members may not have the capacity to fully assess the impact of innovation in their agricultural policies. Accordingly, the base period of a time-limited

matter of urgency, the Committee's Working Procedures (G/AG/1) and the Notification Requirements and Formats (G/AG/2) be amended to reflect the new commitments that result from the current negotiations which require amendments to existing notification formats, additional notification obligations and an enhanced role for the Committee in reviewing and monitoring implementation of commitments and disciplines under the Agreement on Agriculture.

2. In addition to the provisions set out below, the revision of G/AG/2 shall require that a Member that provides support which it claims is consistent with Annex 2 of the Agreement, shall include in the initial notification required under 4(b)(ii) of the possible Article 18 a summary of the measure, including, where appropriate, base periods and yields, the sources where full details may be found, the expected budgetary outlay under each programme and such other information as the Committee on Agriculture may decide. Any revision to a measure claimed to be consistent with Annex 2 of the Agreement shall also be so notified before the revision takes effect.
3. In revising the Working Procedures of the Committee on Agriculture and Members' Notification Requirements and Formats, Members shall provide for an enhanced surveillance role for the Committee so as to improve transparency and the contribution of obligations established under these modalities to the long-term objective of establishing a fair and market-oriented agricultural trading system.

Possible new Article 18 to Replace the Current Article 18 of the Agreement on Agriculture

Review of the Implementation of Commitments

Objectives

1. The Committee on Agriculture shall review and monitor the implementation of Members' obligations established under this Agreement. The Committee on Agriculture shall provide effective surveillance of compliance with obligations through ensuring transparency and give an opportunity to Members to assess the contribution of these obligations to the long-term objective of establishing a fair and market-oriented agricultural trading system.

experimental or pilot programme may not be taken as the fixed and unchanging base period for the purposes of this paragraph.

Institutional aspects

2. The Committee on Agriculture shall meet as necessary, but not less than four times per year, for the purposes established in this Article and to afford Members the opportunity of consulting on any matter relating to the provisions of this Agreement. The Committee shall carry out such responsibilities as assigned to it under this Agreement or by Members. The Committee shall establish subsidiary bodies, as appropriate, which shall carry out such responsibilities as may be assigned to them by the Committee in accordance with the relevant provisions of this Agreement. The Committee shall establish Working Procedures and Notification Requirements and Formats to reflect Members' obligations as set out in this Agreement and Members' Schedules and taking into account the requirements established in this Article. With respect to the Notification Requirements and Formats, there shall be special and differential treatment for developing country Members with respect to the deadlines to be met.

The review process

3. The review process shall be primarily undertaken on the basis of notifications submitted by Members in relation to their specific binding commitments and the disciplines applicable to them and in relation to other matters which may be agreed, using the Notification Requirements and Formats to be established under paragraph 2.
4. The basis for the review process shall be supplemented by such documentation as the Secretariat may be requested by the Committee to prepare in order to facilitate the review process, including the advance circulation of Members' questions. Should a Member be unable to submit a final notification by the appropriate deadline set out in the Notification Requirements and Formats, that Member should submit a provisional notification pending the provision of the final notification. Where appropriate, a Member shall include in its notifications the sources for the domestic provisions that regulate the measure.
   (a) In relation to market access, (not reproduced)
   (b) In relation to domestic support commitments:
      (i) Members shall provide an annual notification of domestic support measures, to allow Members to assess compliance with their Scheduled commitments concerning Overall Trade-distorting Domestic Support, Bound Total Aggregate Measurement of Support, product-specific AMS limits, *de minimis* levels and limits to support under Article 6.5. The annual notifications shall also include information on support which is claimed to be consistent

with Article 6.2, Article 6.5 and Annex 2. The notifications shall include: information on support measures; the details of the calculation of support for each measure; the monetary value of such support; and, where appropriate, the value of production by product; the total value of agricultural production; and sources for the information and data included in the notification.

(ii) A Member providing support which it claims to be consistent with Article 6.5, Article 6.2 or Annex 2 shall provide a comprehensive one-off notification setting out the programmes under each provision, the source for the domestic legislation under which support is provided and a summary description of the measure. A Member introducing or amending a programme which it claims to be consistent with Article 6.5, Article 6.2 or Annex 2 shall provide a notification for each new or modified measure.

(c) In relation to export competition, (not reproduced)

(d) In relation to export prohibitions and restrictions, (not reproduced)

(e) Members shall also submit additional notifications on these and other matters within the scope of the provisions of this Agreement, including commitments undertaken with respect to cotton, and other matters relevant to the Agreement on Agriculture as may be agreed by the Committee on Agriculture.

(f) Annual notification shall be submitted according to the periods set out in the Notification Requirements and Formats established under paragraph 2. Notifications of new measures or modifications of existing ones shall be submitted immediately after they have been decided and, in any case, before their entry into force.

5. In the review process Members shall give due consideration to the influence of excessive rates of inflation on the ability of any Member to abide by its domestic support commitments.
6. In the review process, any Member may bring to the attention of the Committee on Agriculture any measure which it considers ought to have been notified by another Member, including by means of a counter notification.
7. The review process shall provide an opportunity for Members to raise any matter relevant to the implementation of commitments under the reform programme as set out in this Agreement.

The surveillance process

8. The Committee, and any working bodies established under its Working Procedures, shall provide an effective forum for Members to monitor compliance with commitments and disciplines under the Agreement on

Agriculture and to undertake surveillance of progress towards the long-term objective of establishing a fair and market-oriented agricultural trading system. In the discharge of its surveillance functions, and based on factual reports from the Secretariat as requested by the Committee, the Committee and its working bodies shall review the implementation of commitments and obligations at such intervals and in relation to such matters to be agreed, including:

(a) The follow-up to the Decision on Measures Concerning the Possible Negative Effects of the Reform Programme on Least-Developed and Net Food-Importing Developing Countries;
(b) Special review of implementation of special and differential treatment provisions of this Agreement and related development concerns;
(c) The implementation of cotton-related commitments;
(d) Conformity with notification obligations;
(e) As requested by Members, factual background papers based on information provided by Members in notifications, including annual summaries of notifications of support claimed to be in compliance with Annex 2 of the Agreement on Agriculture, notifications relating to Food Aid and export prohibitions and restrictions. For support claimed to be in compliance with Annex 2 of the Agreement on Agriculture, Members shall notify the base period and all other criteria relevant to programmes under the provisions. Notifications under paragraph 6(a) shall include regular and periodic updates on how the programmes concerned achieve the stated objectives.

Special and Differential Treatment

9. The Secretariat of the WTO shall give priority, within the limits of its resources, to requests for technical co-operation from developing country Members, including advice and assistance in meeting notification obligations, with the objective of enhancing their participation in the Committee's work. Members should also give consideration to the provision of technical assistance to developing country Members to assist meeting the provisions of this Article and complementary obligations.

Appraisal

10. Members shall review the effectiveness of monitoring and surveillance mechanisms, with the objective of making further improvements, following a period of three years from the entry into force of this Agreement.

INDEX

Page numbers with t are tables; fig are figures; n are notes. Page numbers in italics are text from the Agreement on Agriculture and Doha draft modalities.